ALBA

Alba, c. 1567, by Willem Key, Collection of the Dukes of Alba,
Liria Palace, Madrid.

ALBA

A Biography of
Fernando Alvarez de Toledo,
Third Duke of Alba
1507-1582

WILLIAM S. MALTBY

UNIVERSITY OF CALIFORNIA PRESS
BERKELEY   LOS ANGELES   LONDON

University of California Press
Berkeley and Los Angeles, California

University of California Press, Ltd.
London, England

© 1983 by
The Regents of the University of California

Library of Congress Cataloging in Publication Data

Maltby, William S., 1940–
  Alba: a biography of Fernando Alvarez de Toledo,
third duke of Alba, 1507–1582.

  Includes index.
  1. Alba, Fernando Alvarez de Toledo, duque de,
  1507–1582. 2. Statesmen—Spain—Biography. 3. Spain—
  Nobility—Biography. I. Title.
DP181.A6M34 1983   946'.04'0924 [B]   82-8537
ISBN 0-520-04694-3   AACR2

Printed in the United States of America

1 2 3 4 5 6 7 8 9

Contents

Maps

Illustrations

(following p. 206)

Alba de Tormes today.
Alba, c. 1550, artist unknown.
Alba in 1557, by Antonis Mor.
Don Fadrique de Toledo, artist unknown.
Garcilaso de la Vega.
Doña Ana de Mendoza y de la Cerda, Princess of Eboli.
Charles V in 1548, by Titian.
Philip II in 1554, by Titian.
William of Orange in 1555, by Antonis Mor.
Margaret of Parma, by Antonis Mor.
Anton Perenot, Bishop of Arras (later Cardinal Granvelle) in 1549, by Antonis Mor.
Don Hernando de Toledo (Alba's illegitimate son), by Antonis Mor.
The Statue at Antwerp.

Preface

In the paintings, engravings, and tapestries that mark the great events of sixteenth-century Europe one figure appears with noticeable regularity. It is that of a tall, lean man dressed in somber black. His pose is erect and motionless, his features sharp and aquiline over a long, forked beard. Sometimes he wears a soft high-crowned hat that emphasizes his height and attracts the eye, but visually this distraction is rarely needed. The artists normally place him at or near the center of their focus either as one of the principal actors or as a contrast to the often frenzied activity going on around him. The overall impression is one of great dignity and grim certainty of purpose.

The figure is that of Fernando Alvarez de Toledo, third Duke of Alba, one of the most powerful and controversial figures of his day. Soldier by preference, courtier, diplomat, and political manipulator by necessity, he was involved in virtually every political question of the mid-sixteenth century and is best known for his six tragic years as governor of the Netherlands under Philip II. His historical importance is established, but it was his character that fascinated and repelled contemporaries and caught the imagination of later ages through the writings of Schiller and John Lothrop Motley. A strange mixture of rigid fanaticism, political sophistication, and blunt common sense, he was one of those rare individuals whose personality can be shown to have influenced events, yet he has not found a modern biographer.

In 1643 at Milan, the Conde de la Roca published a modest collection of materials about Alba. Twenty-six years later Antonio Ossorio produced a two-volume Latin biography based on family papers and what appears to have been a rich oral tradition. Translated into Spanish in 1945, it remains the only full-length treatment of Alba's life drawn from primary sources. Fortunately it is a good one, but it does not fully satisfy the demands of the modern reader. Ossorio was related to the house of Alba and his work is openly partisan. He was also addicted to such tiresome historical conceits of his day as the invention of imaginary dialogues, but his greatest weakness is that he is least informative on those points that most intrigue us. His treatment of the years in the Netherlands is cursory and his description of the Italian and Portuguese campaigns is little better. He seems to have had no access to official papers or to a variety of other sources that are now available, and his knowledge of events outside Spain was limited. Still, his use of the sources he had was intelligent and his treatment of Alba's life in Spain is the basis of nearly everything written since.

With the exception of a two-volume compilation based on Ossorio and published by Rustant in 1752, and a more original description of his campaigns by Martín Arrue in 1880, most of the subsequent biographies are brief and modern. Some appear to have been part of Franco's attempt to revive the virtues of the *siglo de oro*, and only one, Berrueta's *El Gran Duque de Alba*, contains new material. Most recently, Walther Kirchner has published *Alba, Spaniens eisener Herzog* (1963), a summary of existing knowledge based, like its predecessors, on Ossorio and a number of secondary sources.

The only relief from this derivative tradition was provided by the late Duke of Berwick y Alba. An avid student of history, he found time in the midst of an active public career to supervise the collection and publication of his ancestor's correspondence. The *Epistolario* was a massive undertaking and some items were inevitably omitted, but it remains the best source for those who would confront the *Gran Duque* without intermediaries. He also published a *Discurso* when he was elected to the Real Academia de Historia in 1919, and delivered a lecture at Oxford in 1947 on "The Duke of Alba as a Public Servant." His article on Alba's wife appeared in the same year. All were drawn from materials in his private archive, parts of which were destroyed by fire in 1936.

These works, old and new, are uniformly sympathetic to their subject, but few are widely known outside Spain, where Alba is generally regarded as a hero. The rest of the world sees him in a different light. It was this contradiction that first attracted my interest. In the course of my earlier work on the Black Legend, Alba emerged as one of its greatest villains, a man whose name was used to quiet unruly children for generations after his death and whose deeds, real and imagined, are still capable of raising the hackles of otherwise staid historians. It amazed me that in three centuries no one had attempted a fresh analysis of such a controversial and extraordinary career.

After more than a decade of hard labor I am no longer amazed. Alba is not an easy man to capture on paper. Reticent and complex, he left a mass of information on his activities but relatively little about himself. Given the nature of his responsibilities this is hardly surprising, but it consigns the biographer to a purgatory in which he is overwhelmed by data while at the same time hopelessly uninformed. The one exception to this dismal state of affairs lies in the area of Alba's social and economic relationships. The incendiaries who attacked the Alba archives in 1936 may have been *rojos* but they had no consideration for those who would seek the economic roots of history. They somehow managed to destroy virtually all the papers on Alba's household and estates while leaving the political documents intact.

As a result, the themes of this work are largely traditional. It hopes, as biographies have always done, to display the interaction of personality with events, and it assumes that this is still a legitimate historical activity. At the same time it tries to avoid the murkier depths of psychohistory, for if the sources on Alba are sometimes revealing they are not so intimate as to permit a clinical diagnosis. Finally, no attempt has been made to provide moral judgments. Readers who object to this omission are invited to supply their own.

Acknowledgments

In the course of writing this book its author has accumulated more personal debts than he will ever be able to pay. The research itself was made possible by generous grants from the National Endowment for the Humanities, the American Philosophical Society, and the University of Missouri–St. Louis. Librarians and archivists in five countries were generous with their time and advice, as were literally scores of my friends and colleagues. Without their counsel and often saintly patience the work would have been impossible, but they are too numerous to mention individually. I am especially grateful to Geoffrey Parker of St. Andrews University and David Lagomarsino of Dartmouth, who were repaid for their invaluable help by having to read the manuscript, and to the late Professor S. T. Bindoff, whose painstaking examination of the text was a last act of kindness and generosity. Finally, I should like to thank Patricia Minute for transforming my crabbed handwriting into a legible typescript. Her contribution was in itself a feat of scholarship.

A Note on Spelling, Currency, and Spanish Terminology

Any work dealing with Alba or the Netherlands is troubled to an inordinate degree by problems of orthography. Even the spelling of the protagonist's name is a matter of arbitrary judgment. English, Dutch, and German readers generally know him as Alva, but the modern Spanish spelling with a *b* is now current in scholarship. The pronunciation is in any case the same; the latter form has been adopted here partly out of servility to the present fashion and partly because it corresponds to the name of the estate from which the title derives. The duke himself often used the *v* for his name and the *b* for his estate.

Other names present similar difficulties. Monarchs and other figures well known to English-speaking readers have been given the established English form of their names where such a form exists, e.g., Philip II, William of Orange, Henry II of France. Otherwise I have used the spellings and titles favored by the subjects themselves. Similar standards have been applied to place-names. Where there is a common English name for a city (Florence, Rome, Brussels), I have used it, but this method creates problems in the Netherlands, where most towns have both a Flemish and a French name. In those cases I have chosen the name preferred by the present inhabitants unless it would be totally unfamiliar to most English-speaking readers: thus Brugge is Bruges, Ieper is Ypres, and Leuven is Louvain, though Mechelen remains Mechelen and not Malines. The Netherlands in this book refers to all the provinces in northwestern Europe that were inherited by Philip II.

In sixteenth-century Spain the smallest unit of account was the *maravedí*. A ducat, the unit of account normally used for large governmental transactions, equaled 375 *marevedís*. The *real* was a silver coin of 34 *maravedís;* the *escudo* was a gold coin, 22 carats fine, at first equivalent to 350 *maravedís* but raised to 400 in 1566. The *escudo* was also used by the Spanish army as a unit of account. The florin referred to in this book is the Netherlands florin of 20 pattards, equivalent to approximately half a ducat. Ten Netherlands florins equaled one pound sterling, which was at this time also a money of account.

Every effort has been made to avoid gratuitous use of Spanish terms. Those that appear in the text are defined herewith.

alcalde	A magistrate. There were several types; the ones most frequently referred to in this text are *alcaldes* of the court.
alférez	An officer equivalent to company lieutenant.
asiento	A contract with a banker for a short-term loan.
audiencia	A high court with some administrative and executive functions found in certain parts of Spain and her dependencies.
ayuda de costa	A grant to compensate a subject for expenses incurred in the royal service.
cámara	Chamber or cabinet; often a formally constituted advisory body.
cédula	A royal decree issued by a council over the king's signature.
consulta	A written recommendation from a council to the king.
contador	An accountant. His office was known as a *contaduría;* the Contaduría Mayor de Cuentas was the chief accounting and auditing office of the Spanish government.
encamisado	A night raid, usually on an enemy camp, so called because the troops usually wore their shirts (*camisas*) outside their corselets or jerkins as a means of identification in the dark.
entretenimiento	A permanent monthly salary paid to a soldier from the military treasury. It is to be distinguished from the *ventaja*, a wage-supplement paid to soldiers who had distinguished themselves through valor or long service.

étape	A halting-place where food and equipment were collected to provision an army on the march.
maestro de campo	The commander of a *tercio* (q.v.).
mayorazgo	A royal grant vesting the right of succession in the firstborn son. Castilian law normally mandated an equal division of inherited property.
merced	A payment made by the Crown as a reward to a favored subject—literally, a favor.
nao	A ship. In this period the term usually referred to a transport or cargo vessel.
oidor	A judge on an *audiencia* or chancellery.
tercio	The basic infantry unit of the Spanish army after 1534. Nominally composed of 12 companies and approximately 3,000 men, in practice it rarely reached this level of strength. In the early days there were two pikemen for every arquebusier, but Alba changed this to equal proportions of pike and shot during his campaigns in the Netherlands.
veedor	An inspector whose primary task was to review army musters, accounts, pay warrants, and contracts.

I

THE TRADITION

The town of Piedrahita lies in the shadow of the Sierra de Gredos not far from the headwaters of the Rio Tormes. Its houses, at least the older ones, are low structures of gray stone with post-and-lintel doorways that recall the monuments of the Bronze Age. Dominated by a squat, fortress-like church, they seem to press down upon the earth with almost unbearable weight. This is the province of Avila, but the sunlit spaces of the Meseta are far away. Instead there is an overwhelming impression of remoteness, of rugged imperturbability, and of an antiquity that pre-dates the Flood. Here, on October 29, 1507, Doña Beatríz de Pimentel, the wife of Don García Alvarez de Toledo, gave birth to a son whom they named Fernando in honor of Ferdinand the Catholic, King of Aragon and Regent of Castile.[1]

The choice of names was not fortuitous. Don García was the eldest son of Fadrique, second Duke of Alba de Tormes, and Fadrique was first cousin to the king. He was also one of the few Castilian nobles who supported Ferdinand when Philip the Handsome arrived to claim the throne for his wife, Ferdinand's daughter Juana la Loca. The naming of the child was not intended to curry favor but to honor an old friend and master who was, in 1507, not much past the nadir of his career.

Genealogy is the curse of biography. First chapters all too often read like Genesis, and it is easy to forget that, given a sufficient number of generations, everyone is descended from everyone else.

1

Still, for the infant Fernando, genealogy was destiny in more ways than one. His ancestors bequeathed to him a robust constitution and an exalted place in society, and they determined his values and allegiances to a degree that is now almost unthinkable. In part, this was due to the social structure of sixteenth-century Castile. Kinship ties are traditionally strong in Mediterranean societies, especially among the upper classes, and the Castilian nobility of the later Middle Ages was no exception to this rule. If anything, the disorders of the fifteenth century had strengthened family loyalties by forcing the great clans to fall back on their own resources. When institutions break down and the bonds of social trust dissolve, the family reasserts itself as a last refuge for the individual, and the ties of dependency thus formed may take more than a single generation to break. The great Castilian families, including the Alvarez de Toledo, emerged from the reign of Enrique IV as self-conscious political entities with elaborate clientage systems and the unspoken belief that they could only prosper at each other's expense. This did not preclude a sense of class interest, but within that broader framework a factionalism based on kinship and clientage was inevitable. Fernando inherited a host of friends, enemies, and obligations along with his genes.

He also inherited a family tradition. Most families have such a thing, in the broadest sense, whether they are aware of it or not. At the very least it consists of certain characteristic patterns of thought and behavior handed down more or less unconsciously over a number of generations. In aristocratic families, pride of caste and a more certain acquaintance with the exploits of their forebears often conspire to turn these patterns into a consciously articulated system of values, which is then drummed into their children's heads from an early age and powerfully reinforced by whatever sanctions the family can bring to bear. Among the dukes of Alba this tradition was unusually strong and they were exceptionally ruthless in using it to mold the characters of their offspring.[2]

The origins of this tradition, like those of the family itself, were old, but perhaps not as old as its devotees thought. The Alvarez de Toledo traced their ancestry with some certainty to the Reconquista and with considerably less to the Paleologus emperors of Constantinople.[3] Like the rest of the Castilian nobility, they became historically prominent only after the death of Pedro the Cruel in 1369.[4] Pedro, whose "cruelty" sprang largely from his efforts to subdue an anarchic nobility, was assassinated by his illegitimate half-brother, Enrique II of Trastámara. As a bastard and an acknowledged murderer, the new king was on shaky ground and relied upon the creation of an equally new nobility to prop up his regime. Nearly all the old grandee families thus owe their position to some ancestor who was wise enough to support Enrique II, and among those supporters was one Fernán Alvarez de Toledo, who died fighting for his master at the siege of Lisbon.[5]

His sons, Gutierre, Bishop of Palencia, and García, Lord of Oropesa and Valdecorneja, backed Juan II in his struggles with the infantes of Aragon. In 1429, Gutierre was given the rich estate of Alba de Tormes as a reward. During the 1430s, a period of confusion exceptional even for Castile, the family was one of the few to support the king's favorite, Alvaro de Luna. Don Alvaro worked against the interests of the nobility and was ultimately brought to the scaffold by their opposition, but Juan II never forgot those who had supported him in his hour of need. Gutierre was promoted to the diocese of Seville and ultimately became Archbishop of Toledo, while Don García's son Fernando was created first Count of Alba de Tormes.[6]

The next reign, that of Enrique IV, was to see an even more spectacular increase in the family's fortunes. The architect of this splendor, García, second Count of Alba de Tormes, seems to have been an extraordinary character whose greed and cunning were as celebrated as his military talents. Few men have ever used the follies of a king to better advantage.

Enrique the Impotent was a pathetic monarch. Lacking both character and judgment, he turned the government over to lowborn favorites and quickly ran afoul of the nobles, who throughout the reign behaved with unprecedented license. In all fairness, they had little choice. As Suárez-Fernández has pointed out, they were not "birds of prey" but men who held a perfectly respectable theory as to the nature of good government.[7] By any measure, Enrique failed to provide this. When there is no royal justice, subjects must provide it for themselves. A situation quickly developed in which the great nobles had to be on constant guard against the depredations both of the favorites and of each other. Private armies flourished, and the result was a wholesale land-grab which has been condemned by historians who should know better. In the midst of anarchy, it is not enough to protect the integrity of one's own holdings. Each increase in the resources of a neighbor represents a threat because it enables him to raise more troops and bribe more judges. Survival therefore depends upon expanding rents and manpower at a rate equal to that of the most rapacious of one's fellows, and no one knew this better than Don García de Toledo.

The count's basic tactic was to remain loyal to the king while letting it be known that he was open to offers from the other side. He would collect his rewards in advance and then be unaccountably absent on the day of reckoning. The wonder is that it worked so well for so long. Though the king granted him extensive lands and a half-share of the rents from the fair at Medina del Campo,[8] he left the relief of that city to the Constable of Castile, arriving only after the fight was over.[9] When the count failed to appear at the epic battle of Olmedo, it was discovered that he had accepted two towns from the king's enemies in return for his 1,500 lances. A royalist to the end, he solved his consequent moral dilemma by staying home. The street urchins cried, "Who gives more for the Count of Alba who is sold on every street corner?"[10] but he had gained a valuable foothold in the valley of the Tagus.

His basic plan seems to have been to control both slopes of the Sierra de Gredos, and northern Extremadura as far as the Portuguese border. His inheritance of the ancestral señorío of Valdecorneja gave him the north slope from El Barco de Avila to Navarredonda de la Sierra. The condado of Alba, together with its sister condado of Salvatierra, gave him the entire valley of the Tormes almost to the gates of Salamanca. He might have gone further, but his attempts to seize the great city itself were foiled by the vigilance of its inhabitants.[11]

In Extremadura, his father had left him the sizable estate of Granadilla, which took in the upper valley of the Alagón between Las Hurdes and the Béjar-Plasencia road. The remainder of the region fell into his hands when the commanders of the Order of Alcántara rebelled against its Master, Gómez de Cáceres. Gómez, in a panic, sent his brother, the Count of Coria, to Don García for help. García, the uncle of the count's wife, agreed—but only on condition that he be given Coria in advance. He failed in successive attempts to relieve Alcántara, Valencia, and Badajoz, but kept his prize anyway, thus rounding off one corner of his estates in exemplary fashion.[12]

Only in the Vera and the valley of the Tagus did he ultimately fail. In addition to Montalban and Puente del Arzobispo, which were part of his price for avoiding Olmedo, he had seized many of the lands of his cousins, the Toledo counts of Oropesa. This extensive and fertile region had been part of the original patrimony of Fernán Alvarez but had passed to a collateral branch of the family with the acquisition of Alba de Tormes. A firm believer in primogeniture,

García meant to have these lands back, but this time he went too far. The other nobles were apprehensive, and in 1472, as part of the general settlement after Toros de Guisando he was persuaded to surrender all his gains south of the Sierra. It was a statesmanlike decision which, if the chronicler is right, prevented a civil war,[13] but it was not without compensations. The king gratefully elevated him to ducal rank and confirmed his dubious title to Coria.

García died in 1488, but not before he had redeemed himself in the eyes of posterity by his steadfast support of Ferdinand and Isabella. One of the architects of their succession, he fought valiantly in the war against Portugal and played a major role in the great victory won in the lands between Toro and Zamora on March 1, 1476. For many years afterward, this day was commemorated at Alba de Tormes with parades and bullfights.[14] It also brought him another estate: San Felices de los Gallegos, which lies along the Portuguese border some 37 km north of Ciudad Rodrigo.

Not surprisingly, it was this later Don García, the loyalist soldier and statesman, who was remembered by his family in the development of their tradition. His son Fadrique, second Duke of Alba and grandfather of Fernando, seems wholly to have forgotten the days of aristocratic freebooting and modeled himself according to the requirements of a new age. His career was in many ways a distinguished one.

The buffoon Francesillo de Zúñiga described Fadrique as "long in spirit and short in the greaves, more round than a two-ducat piece,"[15] but he was a formidable soldier. His special aptitude was for what might today be called counter-insurgency warfare, and he had ample opportunity to exercise it in the long and bitter struggle for Granada. He shared in every phase of that campaign and demonstrated not only military expertise but cunning, ferocity, and immense personal courage.[16] In 1503 he relieved the French siege of Salsas and in 1514 he annexed Navarre for Ferdinand. He accompanied Charles V on his return to Flanders in 1520 and served briefly as a member of the emperor's council in 1526. At the heart of his character lay an almost Victorian rectitude and an obsessive sense of personal loyalty to the king. This was partly rooted in his exalted concept of a noble's duty, but it was also an expression of personal friendship. This is hard to understand except as an attraction of opposites, for Ferdinand was not a lovable man. His cold, serpentine mind and fondness for sexual immorality could hardly have recommended him to the rigid Fadrique, yet it was Fadrique who stood by

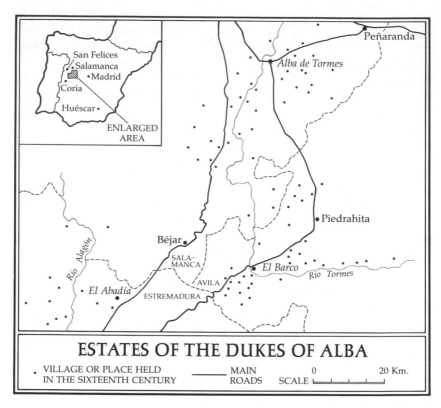

ESTATES OF THE DUKES OF ALBA

. VILLAGE OR PLACE HELD
  IN THE SIXTEENTH CENTURY

—— MAIN
   ROADS

0   20 Km.
SCALE

Map 1.

him when the rest of the nobles turned to Philip of Habsburg, and in the end it was Fadrique who "closed his dead eyes."[17] Perhaps because of his altruism, he added little to the Alba patrimony other than the tiny duchy of Huéscar in what had been the kingdom of Granada.

At the birth of Fernando, then, the estates he could one day expect to inherit comprised a substantial piece of western Castile. Perhaps the richest was Alba de Tormes itself, a substantial town with a castle whose huge circular keep towers over the wheatlands of the Meseta. Together with neighboring Salvatierra, it was economically and socially part of old Castile, as was the smaller, more isolated property of San Felices.

Further south the character of the land changes. The wheatlands give way to thin pasturage dotted with cork oaks and outcroppings of slate. At Piedrahita the chief crops are those of the Sierra—chestnuts and flax. The road of the Mesta passes through the heart of this region, and the great transhumant flocks had been, in earlier times, a major source of difficulty for the inhabitants.

Granadilla and Coria, on the other hand, are part of the sparse world of Extremadura. It is warmer there, and drier. The villages are widely separated from each other by immense tracts of scrub oak, and the population, at least in the sixteenth century, scraped a meager living from stockraising and incidental farming.

The new duchy of Huéscar was a different matter. Consisting almost entirely of the town itself and the surrounding *vega*, it was inhabited largely by Moriscos who had deeply resented its passing to Don Fadrique. Remote, inaccessible, and administered by corrupt stewards who knew that a ducal visit was unlikely, it produced more trouble than rents.

Overall, these properties, though vast, were not intrinsically rich. As with most Spanish estates, little was owned or exploited directly, and the bulk of its income was derived from a bewildering variety of rents, fees, and obligations, not all of which were easily collected. In 1533 the Italian humanist Marineo Sículo estimated that it produced 50,000 ducats per annum, a tidy sum but one exceeded by at least five other noble houses.[18] There is no way to express the equivalent of this in modern currencies, but at the time that Marineo Sículo was writing, a laborer could survive on 20 ducats a year.[19]

It was, in other words, enough to enable the dukes of Alba to cut a figure in the world, but it was under a heavy burden of obligations imposed by family tradition. The main components of that tradition should already be evident from this summary of the family's history. Briefly stated, they are like those of any other noble house: filial piety, military glory, and service to the Crown. What makes them different was the peculiar intensity with which they were distilled in the character of Don Fadrique and passed on to his sons and grandsons. While other clans were withdrawing from active political life and retiring to live off the riches that Ferdinand and Isabella had been wise enough to confirm, Fadrique simply refused to take the hint. He raised his sons to be professional soldiers and encouraged them to believe that they had a moral obligation not only to fight for but to advise the Crown.

The reasons for this tendency to swim against the current were undoubtedly complex. Aside from his reading of the family tradition, Fadrique may unconsciously have reacted against the self-seeking high-handedness of his father, who even in his most loyal moments could not resist snapping up some unprotected piece of property.[20] He must also have been influenced by his close relationship with Ferdinand. It was the policy of the Catholic kings to keep the grandees at one remove from the levers of power while permitting them to line their pockets almost at will, but Fadrique, as the king's personal friend, did not see why this should apply to him. He seems actually to have been puzzled by his relative exclusion from power by Charles V, though his propensity for speaking the unspeakable made him difficult company. In 1527 alone, he criticized the emperor for the sack of Rome[21] and suggested that his son, the future Philip II, be named Ferdinand in honor of the man who had left no stone unturned to prevent Charles's succession.[22] It is little wonder that the jester Don Francesillo said that Fadrique had died in 1518![23]

On a more conscious level Fadrique justified himself by maintaining an ideal of kingship in which the nobility played an essential part. No throwback to the Middle Ages, it appears to have been related in some way to Castiglione's ideal of the Courtier. Fadrique, as we shall see, was much influenced by Italianate ideas, and it is no accident that he retained Boscán, the eventual translater of Castiglione, as a kind of tutor to young Fernando.

The other major component of the tradition, at least as it concerns Fernando, was a crusading mentality that developed with time into a passionate hatred of the infidel. Such attitudes, deeply ingrained in Spanish life, were unduly concentrated in Fadrique by virtue of his experiences in the struggle for Granada. It had been a war to the death between hereditary enemies of differing faiths, and, as such, was a nasty business replete with atrocities on both sides. In those circumstances it was easy to see the enemies of Christendom in highly personal terms, and Fadrique did so. Inevitably, he transmitted these feelings to his sons and by so doing laid the foundation for a tragedy that would reinforce them to the point of obsession.

Fadrique had five sons: García, the eldest, Pedro, who was to earn distinction as Marqués of Villafranca and Viceroy of Naples (1532–1553), Diego, who became prior of the Order of St. John of Jerusalem, Juan, the cardinal, and Fernando, Comendador de Alcántara.[24] García, in particular, was a promising and graceful youth already celebrated as an embodiment of the knightly ideal. He married Doña Beatríz de Pimentel, daughter of the opulent Count of Benavente, and by 1510 the couple had produced four children: Catalina, Maria, Fernando, and Bernardino. Fadrique had seen to it that García had been reared in the stern traditions of his house, so that when the chance came to serve on a campaign in Africa he welcomed the opportunity.

The Spanish coasts had long been plagued by Muslim pirates operating out of North African ports. Their frequent raids on towns and shipping were a futile source of complaint and would remain so for two centuries, while Spanish kings responded only with sporadic and uncoordinated attacks on individual bases. In 1509 such a raid had resulted in the taking of Bougie by Pedro Navarro, who then went on to attack Tripoli. The king gave the *tenencia* (governorship of the town) to Don García, who had not participated in the original campaign. A fleet was assembled at Málaga but, owing to an outbreak of plague at their destination, García and his men remained idling in port for three months. By this time Tripoli had fallen and Don García was becoming restive at the prospect of garrison duty in a plague-ridden Moorish outpost. He and Navarro decided to abandon the original plan, join forces, and attempt to seize the island of Djerba.

The importance of this objective was unquestioned. Located strategically between Tripoli and Tunis, it was the center of date production for the entire coast and an ideal base for further adventures in Africa. Unfortunately, when they arrived there on August 28, 1510, their fleet was short of water and supplies and their troops in poor condition. The heat was intense: it dehydrated the men and bore like a solid weight upon their heavy armor, distorting judgment and slowing the process of disembarkation. All was quiet, but no one seemed to find this threatening or ominous.

The landing proceeded without incident, but as the scarcity of water was becoming desperate, García offered to lead a party to a well located somewhere among the endless plantations of date palms. He found it, but the discovery proved fatal. Imbued with the wisdom of the desert, the Moors had elected to guard the water rather than the shore, and their entire force was lying in ambush among the trees. Though García and his men fought savagely, they were overwhelmed, and the Moors, following their advantage, then turned and drove the rest of the Christians into the sea.[25]

Four thousand men died at Djerba. The tragedy was mourned in popular songs,[26] but for most of Spain it was to be a seven days' wonder buried in the pages of obscure chroniclers. At Alba de Tormes, it was a wound that never healed. Fadrique's first reaction was to ask how his son had comported himself. When told of the heaps of Moors slain by his son he exclaimed, *"O buen hijo!"*[27] but pride inevitably took second place to other emotions. There seem to have been no oaths of the sort imposed upon Hannibal by his father, but there is little doubt that Fadrique, with slow and deadly purpose, began to mold the three-year-old Fernando into an edged weapon against the enemies of Christendom. All the warlike and crusading traditions of the house, all the military knowledge of this formidable grandfather were brought to bear, with terrifying intensity, upon the child.[28] They met with little resistance. From an appallingly early age the child showed an intelligent fascination with the arts of war that was the talk of contemporaries. He is said to have spent happy hours drilling his playmates in the courtyard of Alba de Tormes[29] and at age thirteen to have known the *De re militari* of Vegetius by heart.[30]

Of the rest of Fernando's childhood we know little. After the fashion of the time, he and his family moved back and forth between their residences at Alba, at Piedrahita, and at Coria. His grandfather devoted much time and effort to him in a rather tutorial way, and Fernando seems to have been fond of his younger brother, Bernardino. His relationship with his mother and sisters is a blank page. A retrospective psychoanalysis based on his early years is therefore impossible, as no one thought the record of his childhood worth preserving, but it might be possible to hazard some guesses based upon his adult character.

In a time and place noted for its somber manners, Don Fernando grew to be among the most reserved and formal of them all. Though he was often charming and even humorous, it is difficult to recall a single instance of real playfulness in seventy-five years of life, and his wit held a glimpse of inner darkness that could be remarkably disquieting. Loyal to a fault, he sincerely mourned the death of kinsmen, soldiers, and even an occasional enemy, but his relations with the living were at best distant. In all his vast correspondence, his expressions of affection are so few and so curiously twisted that one wonders if they are really there at all and not just a projection of the reader's imagination. Young Fernando may have had a warm, sunlit, and affectionate childhood, but the end result argues strongly against it. On the other hand, his boundless self-confidence and careful education are evidence that he was not deprived of personal support or of the amenities of civilized existence.

His education was indeed remarkable. Don Fadrique was determined that his grandson should be a soldier, but he was wise enough to know that were he ever to exercise real influence, he would have to be something more. Here Fadrique's flirtation with the Renaissance bore real fruit. Not only did he attempt to educate the child in something like the humanist manner but to create a court of his own in which to nurture him. This was necessary because he could send him neither to the king nor to any other noble house for instruction. Ferdinand was peripatetic and a dubious example in any case. The nobles either fell short of Fadrique's standards or they were not on friendly terms with him.

Fortunately, there was something of a tradition on which to build. When not meditating pillage and treachery, the first Duke had written *canciones* which were later set to music by the Flemish composer Wrede.[31] Fadrique had collected a small but distinguished library[32] and had tried to alleviate the medieval gloom of his surroundings by extensive redecoration in the Italian manner. In short, the historical tendency to picture the dukes of Alba as throwbacks to the Dark Ages is uninformed. They may never have achieved the intellectual distinction of certain Mendozas but they shared fully in the enthusiasms of their age.

The choice of tutors for young Fernando is a case in point. It was customary among the wealthier nobles to provide both a tutor who dealt with academic subjects and an *ayo*, who was generally a young man of good family and knightly attainments. The function of the *ayo* was to provide companionship and informal teaching in the arts of war, athletics, deportment, and civilized conversation. This was in line with the Renaissance notion that education should mold the character as well as the intellect. For the role of tutor Fadrique originally picked the distinguished humanist Juan Luis Vives but, owing to an obscure intrigue, he had to settle for an immensely fat Dominican named Severo.

This unlikely turn of events occurred in 1521, when the duke and his entourage, including Fernando, made a brief journey to the Netherlands after attending the coronation of the new emperor. While there, he apparently decided to make the young man more cosmopolitan by replacing his first preceptor, Bernardo Gentile, a Benedictine monk from Messina,[33] with one of the great figures of the learned world. According to Vives, who complained about it in a letter to Erasmus, he sent Severo to Vives to offer him the job. Whether through accident or, as Vives believed, by design, the message was never delivered, and Fadrique, receiving no reply, gave the post to Severo instead.[34]

Though he was no Vives, the choice of Severo may not have been a bad one. A native of Piacenza in Lombardy, he was a dedicated teacher and an enthusiastic Latinist.[35] From him Fernando learned not only the classics but a healthy suspicion of Erasmian humanism. It is refreshing to note that as a grown man he knew enough to ridicule the Latin of his Flemish counselors[36] while at the same time writing more than three thousand letters without the Latin tags so beloved of his contemporaries. Much of this was probably due to Severo's Italian and Dominican background. As J. A. Fernández-Santamaria has recently pointed out, the Italians were able to maintain their love of the classics without wholly rejecting the rigorous analytical methods of the Middle Ages.[37] The curriculum Severo followed is not known, but in later years when Fernando supported a university intellectual it was invariably someone like Juan Ginés de Sepúlveda or Benito Arias Montano, who combined humanist learning with a genuine respect for Aristotle and the precepts of natural law. It is also a tribute to the tutor's character that his pupil seems to have liked and respected him. At any rate, Severo seems to have been kept on at Alba de Tormes until his death.[38]

By contrast, Fernando's *ayo* was anything but obscure. Juan Boscán was born, probably around 1500, into a patrician family of Barcelona. He imbibed humanism from Marineo Sículo and had become something of a model for the ideal courtier even before his meeting with Castiglione.[39] He came to Alba in 1520, at an annual salary of 107 ducats, and was to remain with Fernando until his death at Roussillon in 1542.[40] It was during these years that he translated *The Courtier* into Spanish and wrote nearly all the works for which he is famous.

Boscán must have been greatly aided by Fadrique's efforts to maintain a congenial literary atmosphere in this "court of virtue." Figures such as the chronicler Alonso de Palencia were frequent guests, often for long periods, and Garcilaso de la Vega was virtually a permanent resident. This great poet was in fact the inseparable companion of both Fernando and Boscán until his death, during the tragic Provence campaign of 1536. His days at Alba de Tormes are described affectionately, if allegorically, in his *First Eclogue*.

So much for literature and good manners. The practical side of Fernando's education was undertaken by Fadrique himself, with even more substantial results. The boy, who accompanied Fadrique everywhere, developed a thorough familiarity with every village on his estate and a love for country ways that never left him. From early childhood he was carried along as his grandfather's companion on military campaigns, a practice he would later follow with his own infant sons. At the age of six he witnessed the seizure of Navarre and apparently loved every minute of it,[41] but such high points are to some extent illusory in evaluating his experience. He was a child of the camps as much as of the court, and he learned early that military life is far more than battles and heroics. Before he was well into his teens he had learned to manage estates, armies, and, above all, himself, for he had discovered what it means to be always in the public eye and to be beloved by grizzled veterans and raw recruits alike, who first saw him as a mascot and then learned to trust him with their lives.

It would be easy to romanticize this picture of the fat old general and his toddler grandson, but the temptation should be avoided. The lessons taught by Don Fadrique were not pretty. If the child learned self-discipline, he also learned a spartan indifference that could be called bloody-minded. If he absorbed grand strategy, he also grew increasingly expert at the devious tactics of small war and discovered the manifold uses of cruelty. From the modern point of view, deliberate immersion of a child in such horrors is nearly unthinkable, but Fadrique did not stop there. He continued to indoctrinate him in the legend of his dead father. We are told that at the time of Don García's death the three-year-old Fernando was "dolorously" affected and conceived a great hatred for the Moors.[42] By this it can be assumed that every effort was made to dramatize the event and impress it on the child's mind, with God knows what effect. We also know that in 1522, when García's body was finally returned by the Moors, Fadrique turned the occasion into a spectacle that was remembered for years. The body was literally paraded through the entire estate amid extraordinary lamentations and was finally interred at San Leonardo after a magnificent funeral with a Solemn High Mass.[43]

The product of all this training and indoctrination was a rather formidable youth. Fernando was tall and lean like his mother's side of the family,[44] with a sallow complexion and prominent nose. Though "full of fire and bile," as Ossorio has it,[45] he kept himself under iron control and seems to have been generally free of vice. He dressed well but not ostentatiously, drank little, and set a modest table. His chief interests were horses, of which he kept a fine stable,[46] and war. Of the latter he seemed unable to get enough. At the age of sixteen he left home without Fadrique's consent and went to join the Constable of Castile at the siege of Fuenterrabía. The Constable managed with some difficulty to keep him out of harm's way, but his courage, leadership, and popularity with the men led to his being appointed governor of the castle after its fall. The appointment was temporary and may have been intended only to indulge the grandson of an old friend, but it was nevertheless significant.[47]

Fernando's activities were well publicized and he began to develop the sort of reputation that had characterized his late father. The difference was that Fernando, even at sixteen, would have been unlikely to march into enemy territory without prior attempts at reconnaissance. This is not to say that he was incapable of youthful folly, but given the available opportunities, his escapades were few and their consequences minor.

We know of only two incidents in which he behaved as other young men of his class regularly behaved. One was a duel, fought by night on the bridge of San Pablo at Burgos when he was seventeen. Though usually a model of courtesy, he had already developed the quick temper and filed tongue that were to characterize him in later life, and on this occasion it nearly caused him serious trouble. He was, or so the story goes, the rival of another young man for the favors of an unnamed lady. One evening, in the lady's presence the other fellow bragged at great length about his prowess with the arquebus, a weapon still thought to be plebeian. After a while, Fernando could stand no more; holding a handkerchief to his nose, he said: "What a stink of powder there is in this place!" To his rival's chagrin, the lady thought this bit of repartee hilarious. A challenge was issued forthwith. That night Fernando came with sword and dagger to the appointed place. Unfortunately, his enemy had forgotten his dagger, so with a grandiloquent gesture Fernando cast his own into the river below. They crossed swords, somehow honor was satisfied without injury, and the two were reconciled on the spot. An attempt to keep the affair secret failed when they accidentally went home wearing each other's cloaks.[48] All in all, it was an episode worthy of a true *señorito*, and its memory must have caused a twinge of embarrassment after the Great Duke had put away childish things. To his own eternal shame, Garcilaso incorporated several lines on this business into his *Second Eclogue*.

The second incident, of an entirely different sort, resulted in the birth of his illegitimate son Hernando. One warm afternoon in the summer of 1527 Fernando was traveling on horseback from El Barco de Avila to Piedrahita along the old road of the Mesta. A sudden thunderstorm forced him to take refuge in the mill of Saltillo, and there he encountered the miller's beautiful daughter. According to the tale that later became Lope de Vega's *Mas mal hay en la Aldehuela del que sueña*, he thought no more about the matter until he visited the region many years later. A bullfight was held in his honor, and one youth distinguished himself above the others. When asked his name, the boy is said to have replied, "Hernando, son of the miller-girl of Saltillo and of . . . Your Excellency." The duke, for he had by then come into his title, immediately acknowledged him as his son, took him into his own household, and had him educated as a gentleman.[49]

It is in many ways a pretty story, but one that has no doubt been enhanced by the dramatist's art. We know only that the child was born, that he was acknowledged, and that he received a superior education. Maria, the mother, may have remained silent about her child's illustrious parentage, but if so she was a subject more worthy of Calderón than of Lope de Vega. Moreover, if Hernando had been raised as a mere village lad until his mid-teens, it is unlikely that he would have developed as he did. More than any of Don Fernando's legitimate children he was his father's son. Soldier, statesman, scholar, and trusted advisor to the king, he was a man of great learning and sophistication, and it is difficult to believe that these qualities were not cultivated in him from a relatively early age.[50]

As far as the historical record goes, this was the only episode of sexual indiscretion in Fernando's life. Diego Hurtado de Mendoza alludes to what may or may not have been another, but the passage is subject to different interpretations and was in any case written in a humorous vein. At one point in his life the great author and historian took great pleasure in teasing the *Gran Duque*, and in 1551 wrote all the way from Siena to tell him: "You must see to it that your history is corrected by this wicked secretary unless you want him to publish how badly you behaved in the alley of Toledo, where I have an example of my manliness that now shines splendidly in these republics."[51] The events in question occurred in 1525; it may be, as Mendoza's most recent biographer suggests, that this refers to an amorous intrigue,[52] but it could as easily mean a street brawl or other such adolescent scrape. Rather more serious is a letter from one Magdalena Ruiz, written in 1568 when Alba was in the Netherlands, in which she calls him "my love" and looks forward to kissing his flushed cheeks.[53] This might refer to an affair, or it could be a court lady's way of teasing a notorious prude. No other letters of the kind have survived.

The issue is not an important one, and the only reason for dealing with it is that this apparent restraint was highly unusual. Many men of his age and class were either avowed lechers or the continual victims of scurrilous innuendo, yet Fernando was neither. If he sowed wild oats, he did so with great circumspection. After his marriage he was a model of fidelity, and after the age of forty he probably remained celibate for long periods.

Part of the reason for this was undoubtedly religious. One character trait not entirely accounted for by a description of his upbringing was a truly exceptional piety. A conventional attachment to the Catholic faith coupled with rank bigotry might be expected, but his deep personal religiosity is another matter. It is impossible to trace its origin or even its later development. Only his confessors, men of the caliber of Alonso de Contreras and Luis de Granada, knew his innermost feelings, for he rarely went beyond the conventional in his letters, yet there can be little doubt that he was, or became, one of those men for whom religion served as the mainspring of action.[54] He could be devious, self-interested, and appallingly cruel. He was perfectly capable of suing an archbishop or making war on a pope, but his fervent attachment to the Faith was never questioned, nor was he accused of hypocrisy even by the worst of his enemies. Faith was to him not only a cause but a way of life and a yardstick by which he measured every act.

It is equally possible to see his chastity through modern eyes, and to ask if it was not perhaps symptomatic of a larger difficulty in forming intimate relationships. He certainly had few friends, and most of these were blood relatives who served as his accomplices in political and financial matters. He was also, for a Spaniard, much given to solitude, often preferring to eat in private at a time when such behavior was still quite rare. If this view is accepted—and whatever its merits, it is wholly alien to the thinking of his own time—it can be made to account for a number of personality traits that emerged in the course of his career. The habitual air of melancholy and the barely controlled violence that are reflected in his portraits and in the accounts of his contemporaries, the rare but terrible outbursts of rage, might all be seen in Freudian terms as the consequence of sexual frustration.

It is, however, almost impossible to transpose the psychological insights of the twentieth century into a time and place so radically different from our own. The king, after all, took his meals in solitary splendor. Might not Alba have followed suit in order to maintain the symbolism of rank? Could a man in his position have friends, much less confidants? And those portraits . . . like all such works by great masters, are they not ambivalent documents?[55] There is melancholy there, and something unsettling about the eyes, but there is slyness, too, and a sense that though this is clearly a serious man, he may not have been as simple and straightforward as his reputation suggests. It is said that when he remodeled his house at El Abadía he installed a pavilion lined with mirrors and fitted with a powerful sprinkler system to drench his guests as they preened before their glassy images.[56] It was a practical joke typical of the age, but it should remind us not to penetrate too far into the maze of psycho-history without benefit of more adequate sources.

It is impossible to consider such questions without reference to his fifty-three years of marriage. Unfortunately, our information on this score is as sketchy and ambiguous as on every other aspect of his personal life. The wedding took place at Alba de Tormes on April 27, 1529, as part of a tripartite agreement between the house of Alba and that of Alba de Liste. Don Diego Enríquez de Guzmán, third Count of Alba de Liste, had been married to Doña Leonora de Toledo, the daughter of Fadrique and thus Fernando's aunt. They had, among other children, a daughter named Maria and a son, Enrique, who was to inherit the estate. When Doña Leonora died, leaving the count a widower, her brother Diego, Prior of San Juan, organized a match that would tie Fernando to Maria, the count to Fernando's sister Catalina, and Enrique to Fernando's younger sister Maria. It was typical of the nearly incestuous arrangements that characterized the Spanish upper classes, and the negotiations must have been worthy of an international treaty. Fernando was to receive a dowry of nearly 55,000 ducats from his uncle, Don Diego. The count and his son were to receive nothing, and Diego agreed to secure the necessary dispensations; among other impediments, Fernando and Maria were first cousins. As a wedding gift, Fernando gave his bride 7,000 ducats' worth of arras.[57]

It seems, on the whole, to have been a good marriage, though whether it would be regarded as such by modern standards is difficult to say. Maria Enríquez was perhaps a few years younger than her husband. Her education appears to have been conventional, with a heavy emphasis on domestic and religious, as opposed to literary, concerns. Her knowledge of the classics was imperfect and her penmanship indifferent, but she could manage a great estate, control scores of unruly servants, and engage, when necessary, in politics at both the highest and the lowest levels of court. She was, in fact, a formidable woman even by the exacting standards of her class.[58]

That she should have been in many ways the feminine counterpart of her husband is not surprising. Consanguinity and a common share of the family tradition ensured that there would be community of values and interests. Like Fernando, she was deeply religious and an enemy of vice, though perhaps a bit more ostentatious than he in her personal tastes. In later years she would become a patron and confidante of Santa Teresa de Avila, an avid reformer of nunneries, and a leading guardian of morals at the royal court.[59] These qualities, with her administrative ability, account for her several major appointments to the households of various queens.

In person she was usually gracious, but dignified and extremely watchful of her prerogatives. As she grew older her disposition, like that of her husband, did not improve, and there seem to have been few who cared to confront her directly. She developed the habit of addressing everyone in the familiar, which did little to increase her popularity. One story, the source of which remains obscure and which cannot be properly translated into English, was retold by the late Duke of Berwick and Alba, and provides a good example of her relations with lesser mortals.

Upon receiving an old captain who had served under her husband, she said: "Hace tiempo que deseaba conocerte. Eres rico?"

The captain, somewhat annoyed by the use of the familiar verb form, did not answer, and the duchess, insisting, added:

"No me acuerdo tu nombre. Como te llamas?"

The soldier, adopting a childlike falsetto and making the reverent bow of a page, responded: "Alfonsito, Señora."[60]

The other side of her character is more attractive. Her generosity went beyond conventional charities; she incorporated into her household a number of people, especially widows, who might otherwise have found themselves in difficult straits.[61] Her loving acceptance of Don Hernando, who was raised virtually as her own son, caused much favorable comment,[62] and her prickly temper does not seem to have intruded on her relations with her husband. In fact, their marriage was at the very least a highly successful partnership in which two rather similar people worked steadily for the same ends in an atmosphere of mutual respect and concern.

There may even have been a romantic component, at least at the beginning. In his *Second Eclogue*, Garcilaso shows Albanio pining for his love, by whom he clearly means Maria Enríquez. There is also the legend that Fernando made a long and arduous ride from Hungary to Alba de Tormes in 1533 just to visit his bride. Though the celebrated journey was actually made from Barcelona, it was rightly seen as a sign of great passion.[63] A round trip of 1,200 km on horseback in little more than two weeks is no laughing matter.

Why not, then, declare it a happy marriage, or even a delightful one, and pass on to other matters? The problem is threefold. First of all, it is easy to counterfeit a good marriage if there are sound political and economic reasons for doing so, and if the couple does not have to spend much time together. Second, it is obvious that sixteenth-century nobles entered into marriage with ideas and expectations very different from those usual today. Finally, the evidence concerning Fernando's marriage is in some respects conflicting. Garcilaso's poetic reverie is thoroughly conventional. It might mean much or nothing. The ride from Barcelona may have been a symptom of grand passion or it may simply have happened because Fernando, now Duke of Alba, had been away on campaign for more than a year and was expected to remain at the emperor's side for an indefinite time to come. Whatever a nobleman's other duties may have been, his primary concern was always to provide for the continuity of his house, and the child-bearing years, especially in the sixteenth century, could be pitifully brief. Like many others, Alba was continually begging leave to "tend to his estate," which was little more than a euphemism for conceiving children. For a couple in their mid-twenties with only one child (a boy, García, had been born in 1530), to go two or three years without trying to conceive another would have been irresponsible.

Then there is the question of his letters, or the lack of them. In all his vast correspondence there are scarcely any addressed to her in his own hand. He was away for many years on a variety of missions, but though she fretted about his health and sent him presents of fresh fruit and other delicacies it was his secretary who kept her informed of his doings. In most cases Fernando did not even bother to sign these letters. As he occasionally said to others that he wished she were present, this, too, may mean nothing, but to modern eyes it is certainly odd.

In the end it is perhaps best to ignore these quibbles. The relationship is closed to historians in all but its most superficial aspects, but that it appeared close and mutually supportive to contemporaries is beyond doubt. Even at the end of his life, reports that she was ill could send him into a frenzy,[64] and there is every reason to suppose that they gave each other far more than the social support expected by the mores of the day.

She also bore him four children, three of whom lived to reach maturity. The eldest, García, died in 1548, aged eighteen. Of the others, Beatríz (b. 1534), Fadrique (b. 1537), and Diego (b. 1542), only Fadrique was to become a figure of historical note, and even his meager eminence was dearly bought. His life was a tragedy, unwittingly engineered by an ambitious father whom he survived by only three years, and his problems will form a dismal accompaniment to the later chapters of this book. Beatríz married the Marqués de Astorga. Little is known about Diego save that he married Brianda de Beaumont, Countess of Lerín, that he kept out of sight as much as possible, and that he died in 1583. His son Antonio became the fifth Duke of Alba.[65]

Surprisingly little is known of the way in which these legitimate children were reared and educated. That military values predominated may be inferred from the fact that five-year-old García was dragged off to the siege of Tunis because his father feared he was being softened by feminine influences at home.[66] Beyond that, little effort seems to have been expended on the acquisition of formal learning, and none of them approached their father in erudition, poise, or linguistic accomplishment.

This is probably due to yet another aspect of Fernando's character that is difficult to explain on the basis of existing evidence. He was, paradoxically, an educated anti-intellectual and cosmopolitan xenophobe. His indifference to the Erasmian subspecies of humanism was a legacy of Severo, but Erasmianism was by no means the only or even the most popular school of thought in early sixteenth-century Spain. The fact is that though he enjoyed the conversation of a few learned men and even, on occasion, subsidized their activities,[67] he was largely indifferent to speculation. Though he knew Latin, French, Italian, and enough German to complain that his use of that language was imprecise,[68] his own vigorous style was free of foreign influences and often colloquial or even rustic in its turns of phrase. He neither liked nor trusted foreigners,[69] and the "Castilianism" in his demeanor sometimes approached caricature.

All of this has led to his being pictured as a sort of early Castilian nationalist,[70] but this may be going too far. It is more likely that his imagination was simply captured by the world of the camps rather than by that of books, for even a cursory reading of his letters shows that he thought of himself as a soldier and modeled his behavior accordingly. It is true that in more disingenuous moments he became the "simple" soldier, bluff and uncomprehending of subtleties that might stand in his way, but this pose was no more than a deliberate highlighting of traits that ran deep and true. He loved the drama, activity, and relative simplicity of the soldier's world. An authoritarian to his fingertips, he disliked argument, and his religious faith, which ran very much to ironclad certainties, left him little about which to argue. He preferred the company of men like himself, and if his soldiers loved him it was not merely because he brought them victories and was careful of their lives but because he shared with them both outlook and language.

As with most people, his image of himself was to some extent delusional. He was, in fact, a masterful and none-too-scrupulous debater,[71] adept at intrigue, and even in war more likely to rely on cunning than on brute force, but he was not especially proud of this side of his character and was apparently unaware that these traits were an important component of his success. He raised his children not in accordance with what was but with what he thought ought to be. It is a wonder they did not turn out worse.

Information on other aspects of their home life is equally sketchy, particularly in the early years. The period from 1529 to 1531 is virtually a blank. What they did, where they lived, the size and composition of their household: all are unknown. Fernando's career had not yet really begun, and it is as though he were simply marking time.

All of this changed abruptly in September, 1531. His grandfather, Don Fadrique, died of the tertian fevers after twenty days in bed, "during which time he never arose or soiled himself," or at least so we are told by an admiring Alonso Enríquez de Guzmán.[72] At one stroke Fernando became Duke of Alba and Huéscar, Marqués of Coria and Count of Salvatierra. Like his father before him, Fadrique had entailed everything in *mayorazgos*, thus evading the division of property otherwise demanded by Spanish law, and along with the titles went the income from at least three thousand square miles of territory. As it happened, the new duke would need every *maravedí* of it.

First there was the household. A full run of household expenses is unavailable, as nearly all of the family's economic documents were destroyed in 1936 when their palace in Madrid fell victim to incendiaries; we have only the testimony of the eighteenth duke's *Discurso*, which he presented to the Real Academia de Historia in 1919, and a handful of incomplete documents dating from the 1550s and 1560s.[73] It is not much, but it is enough to provide an indication of what was involved. During the middle years of his life the duke's household contained 69 men and 21 women, whose salaries amounted to more than 9,600 ducats per year. Among them were his *mayordomo* Juan Moreno, a treasurer, a secretary, and no fewer than twelve pages. In addition, he retained six physicians and surgeons plus two pharmacists and a veritable army of chaplains, dentists, embroiderers, cooks, bakers, kneaders, tailors, coachmen, heralds, and a Negro errand-boy. The duchess also maintained a staff, including a famous chef, her private silversmith, and her fool Juan Martín de Villatoro. They were nearly forty in all, and their salaries came to another 4,000 ducats annually, not including the maintenance of her eighteen slaves.[74] Food and drink for this multitude was listed in a separate account.

Exorbitant as these costs may seem, they were imposed not by vanity but by necessity; had the duke been seriously interested in hunting or music they would have been far higher.[75] As in any other institution, the structure of his household was determined by its function and its physical circumstances. Geographic isolation demanded that it be largely self-sufficient and capable of providing hospitality for wellborn travelers and their retinues. As a regional economic and administrative center it offered a number of services to the community as a whole, as well as temporary accommodations to those who came and went on the business of the estate.

It was also the nucleus of a much wider circle of retainers, clients, and hangers-on who were expensive but essential to the maintenance of the family's influence. Like other powerful clans, the house of Alba stood atop a pyramid of clientage relationships whose internal workings remain somewhat obscure. Historians have long been aware that these structures existed, particularly in the Mediterranean world, but have found them exceedingly difficult to analyze. That they were of immense importance to the daily life of all but the most destitute seems evident, but their very nature has inhibited an understanding of how they functioned. They were, above all, personal relationships based on a sense of mutual obligation and therefore on understandings that were rarely if ever recorded in formal documents. Unlike feudalism, with which it has sometimes been confused, clientage had no standing in law but was firmly buttressed by practical necessity and, presumably, by strong social pressures as well. At the very least, it was sanctioned by the high priority given to loyalty by medieval value systems and by immemorial custom. The *patronus* and his clients had been a commonly remarked feature of life in antiquity.

In its simplest form, the relationship was one in which the powerful undertook to protect the weak in return for goodwill and services. These services might be economic, political, or even personal; their exact nature and the limits beyond which the bond might be broken may have depended as much on the personalities involved as on customary sanctions. It is tempting to say that the strength of clientage lay in the relative weakness of more formal institutions, but its persistence into the modern period makes this arguable at best. Suffice it to say that in sixteenth-century Castile, jobs, economic security, and safe passage through the courts of law were often dependent on the favor of the great.[76]

In the case of the Dukes of Alba, these clientage relationships were exceedingly numerous and varied, though lack of documentation makes it impossible to provide an accurate measure of their extent. A few examples should indicate something of their nature. One is provided by Garcilaso de la Vega, who served as Fernando's companion and attempted to immortalize his house in verse. In return, Fernando paid his expenses, intervened on his behalf when he was out of favor with the emperor, and supported his widow after his death.

An even more interesting case is that of Alonso Enríquez de Guzmán. A distant and impecunious relative of Maria Enríquez, Don Alonso was introduced to the old duke, Don Fadrique, at Cologne in 1521. Fadrique commended him to the emperor and got him a place in the royal household together with the promise of a knighthood in the Order of Santiago, which he received seven years later.[77] In 1524, Fadrique secured his acquittal on charges of rape and murder arising out of an obscure embroilment on the island of Ibiza.[78] In return the house of Alba gained a fervent apologist and perhaps something more, for Don Alonso was a popular man to whom all doors were open. At the very least he was a fertile source of information on happenings at court and in the households of the other nobles.

Along with the duchy, Fernando inherited Don Alonso, who arrived at Alba de Tormes only eight days after Fadrique's death, with the evident purpose of cementing his relationship with the new *patrón*. He was received with extraordinary courtesy owing, as he put it, to "past services and acquaintances." Fernando placed him in his own chamber with his bed at the foot of his own and treated him with "much love, goodwill, and honor." Four days later Don Alonso fell ill, and after twenty days' recuperation and many presents, was sent on his way with a new mule and 100,000 *maravedís*.[79]

This sort of generosity was both typical and expected. If done graciously, it enabled one man to serve another without shame and with the certainty that his efforts would be rewarded. It was, in fact, the cement of the clientage relationship, and the new Duke of Alba, in spite of his forbidding personality, was a master of this gentle art of ingratiation and reward.

It is difficult to map the precise extent of Fernando's patronage, but it was undeniably great. Beginning with kinsmen, servants, and retainers inherited from his grandfather, it gradually expanded to include soldiers, churchmen, and bureaucrats until in the end all sorts of people from viceroys to humble villagers looked to him for support. They were, of course, prepared to offer valuable favors in return. Their goodwill was essential if a man were ambitious; even if he were not, their dependency imposed a tremendous moral burden that could not lightly be set aside. To ignore them and drift into a life of private pleasures was unthinkable—to do so would have been to deny the essence of noble status as it was then conceived. But the maintenance of a clientage system was no easy matter. The duke's correspondence included the innumerable letters of recommendation, requests for employment, demands for reward, and general hand-holding that were part of the job, while the case of Alonso Enríquez de Guzmán, sufficiently multiplied, suggests that it required not only infinite patience but a long purse.

The problem was that clientage was essentially a one-way street. Once embarked upon a career as *patrón* there could be no turning back. In order to provide for his friends, a noble had to increase his influence at court, which was the primary source of patronage. This in turn led to acquisition of still more friends and retainers, all of whom had to be supported as well. Alba really was ambitious, but had he been merely conscientious his career might not have developed in a radically different way. A powerful family tradition impelled him toward a career of service; so, too, did his social position and the needs of his dependents. When, in the year after Don Fadrique's death, the emperor issued a call for volunteers to drive the Turk from the gates of Vienna, Alba was among the first to offer his services. This enthusiastic response was grounded in chivalry and hatred of the infidel, but also in something very like necessity: only through proximity to the emperor could he advance the interests of his house, and at the age of twenty-five he had little to justify that proximity except a name and a sword.

II

THE MAKING
OF A SOLDIER

To the Christians of the sixteenth century the Turks were a recurring nightmare that never quite vanished with the break of dawn. The Turkish empire was a shadowy enigma, but Ottoman ferocity, military sophistication, and ruthless expansionism were well known and rightly feared. During the 1520s they had begun a series of campaigns in the Danube valley under the personal leadership of Suleiman the Magnificent. At Mohács, in 1526, they had destroyed the kingdom of Hungary and by 1529 they had reached the outskirts of Vienna. Their armies, like their fleets, were larger than any the Europeans could muster against them, and their reserves of wealth and manpower seemed inexhaustible.

The primary responsibility for stemming this onslaught lay with the emperor Charles V. He was, in name at least, the secular head of Christendom and the only Western prince whose resources and multiple centers of power were in any way analogous to those of the sultan. More important, by invading Austria, Suleiman had for the first time laid infidel hands on the possessions of the family of the Habsburgs. Thus when the new Duke of Alba embarked upon the first of his adult campaigns, it must have seemed the perfect overture to a great career: a crusade for the protection of all Christians fought on a distant battlefield against the most formidable of opponents. Instead, it turned out to be both militarily and personally inconclusive.

Alba, with Garcilaso and a substantial retinue, left in late January,

1532, to join the emperor at Brussels. Almost from the start their travels were dogged by hindrance and misdirection. The party had gone no further than Tolosa when, on February 3, they were halted by authority of the empress, who had, improbably enough, put out a general order for Garcilaso's arrest. It appears that on August 14 of the preceding year he had witnessed the betrothal of his nephew to Isabel de la Cueva, daughter of the Duke of Albuquerque. As the nephew was of inferior rank and the son of a disgraced *comunero*, Albuquerque had been horrified and asked the emperor to block the match. Charles complied, but as there was some doubt as to what had happened, Garcilaso was needed for questioning.

At first Garcilaso refused to discuss the matter, and Alba, unaware that he would one day find himself in a situation reminiscent of Albuquerque's, backed him with such vigor that the empress came to suspect him as the author of the plot. Finally, the poet confessed under threat of imprisonment and was duly banished from further attendance at court. Alba responded with a letter of protest, saying that he would not go to Flanders without Garcilaso. The empress, understandably, refused to reconsider; Alba, with the high-handedness that was to become characteristic of him in later life, simply ignored her. He marched off to Flanders with an apprehensive Garcilaso firmly in tow.[1]

The incident, though absurd, is instructive not only because similar disputes over unsanctioned marriages were to cloud Alba's later career but because it reveals so much of the man's temper and his attitude toward royal authority. Neither then nor at any other time was there a question as to his loyalty, but it is evident that he intended to dictate the terms of his service. Only a young man whose self-confidence bordered on megalomania would have chosen to make his debut at court by openly flouting an imperial decree. It is unlikely that he was in any sense the author of his friend's intrigue, but once the poet was involved the ducal sense of obligation asserted itself. He protested the royal orders, threatened to withhold his own services, and when all else failed did what he pleased. It was to be a pattern for the future.

All of this took time, and there was a further delay in Paris, where Alba fell ill of an undisclosed ailment. By the time he reached Brussels, Charles had already left. It was late March before they caught up with him at the Diet of Regensburg. There, Alba was greeted warmly, Garcilaso was imprisoned on an island in the Danube,[2] and everyone settled down to four months of negotiation with the German princes. It was not that they were opposed to a united effort against the Turks. On the contrary, even the Protestants were enthusiastic, but the crisis in the East was from their point of view an unparalleled opportunity to extract new concessions from Charles. It is a tribute to the emperor's patience and to the reality of the Ottoman threat that anything whatever was accomplished, but it was August before an army could be gathered.

In the meantime the Turks were experiencing a delay of their own. Against all reason or expectation, the minor fortress of Güns near the border of Hungary and Styria withstood the full might of the Turkish army from August 7 to the twenty-eighth,[3] leaving Suleiman with a difficult choice. He knew that even now Charles and his commanders were maturing their plans in the castle of Linz. The Christian army, though smaller than his own, was a good one, and it was doubtful that he could both defeat it and breach the defenses of Vienna before the onset of winter. As the Turks, like Napoleon's Grande Armée, lived largely by foraging, a winter on the upper Danube was unthinkable. He decided to retreat. On September 13 at Fernitz in Styria, a contingent of Germans did grave damage to the Turkish rearguard, but beyond that and the usual skirmishing, little blood was shed. The Turks had withdrawn for another year, but there had been no decision. For Alba, still a month short of his twenty-fifth birthday, it must have been a terrible anticlimax.

The experience was more valuable than it appeared. Alba had made the acquaintance of the leading commanders of the day and had been included in their councils. His eagerness to learn from them created a favorable impression, as did his surprisingly extensive knowledge of war.[4] Moreover, he apparently sided with those who wanted to pursue the enemy into Hungary.[5] Charles had no great interest in a final settlement in Hungary, and cooler heads prevailed,[6] but the young duke's zeal might someday be put to good use. For all his insolence in the matter of Garcilaso he would henceforth be accepted as one of the emperor's inner circle.

The last desultory skirmish of the campaign took place on September 23. Almost immediately, Charles, accompanied by his court and the small force of Spanish, Italian, and German professionals that made up the core of his army, headed into Italy by way of Carinthia and Friuli. Alba, who in the campaign itself had commanded no more than a squadron of Croatian light horse, was now given the entire rearguard,[7] but it was a sign of favor rather than a recognition of his military gifts. The imperial retinue was in no danger of attack.

Charles's mission was in fact pacific. Though himself only seven years older than Alba, he carried upon his shoulders an immense burden of which the Turks were only a part. His vast polyglot empire, though subject to internal strains and constant harassment from without, was threatening to its neighbors and oppressive to many of its subjects. The Turks had been driven off, but everyone knew they would be back. The French, though apparently quiescent after their humiliation at Pavia, were gathering strength for another war while intriguing against Charles in every capital from London to Constantinople. Perhaps worst of all, German Protestantism showed signs of developing into a unified political movement. The formation of the Schmalkaldic League in 1531 and the ambitious demands of the Lutheran princes at Regensburg were omens that could not be ignored. It was entirely possible that Charles might one day have to face all his adversaries at once.

The apparent solution to many of these difficulties lay with Pope Clement VII. Charles believed that a council of the Church was needed to heal the schism begun by Luther, and it was obvious that only a pope could call it into being. The best hope of forestalling the French lay in a general pacification of Italy: the breakdown of the alliance system created in 1454 by the Peace of Lodi had brought them across the Alps in the first place, and the ongoing struggles of the city states provided them with endless excuses for returning. Here too the pope was the key. As ruler of the Papal States he was a territorial prince in his own right; and as a Medici his attitude would determine that of Florence.

The journey into Italy was therefore an attempt to resolve the impending crisis through negotiation, for Charles knew that Clement's position on both these issues was at best equivocal. The pope was extremely reluctant to call a council, for councils had traditionally interfered with papal prerogatives, and he was even less enthusiastic about the emperor's plan for an Italian alliance. Little more than five years had passed since he had cowered helplessly in the Castel' de Sant' Angelo while imperial troops ravaged the Eternal City. The Sack of Rome had been a mistake for which Charles was not strictly accountable, but Clement might be forgiven for thinking that Charles rather than Francis I was the principal menace to the Holy See. An Italian alliance dominated by the emperor would create alarm in Paris and might even cost him the friendship of the one monarch who could protect him against Habsburg domination. Above all, it would jeopardize the greatest dynastic coup of his career, the forthcoming marriage of his niece Catherine de' Medici to the king's son, the Duke of Orleans.

The resulting discussions and their aftermath must have been a liberal education for the young Duke of Alba. After being sumptuously entertained at Mantua by Ferrante Gonzaga, the imperial court went on to Bologna, where Clement awaited them.[8] The negotiations lasted from December, 1532, through February, 1533. In the end Charles had what he wanted: an Italian alliance and papal consent to a council, though Clement still refused to call it without the agreement of the French. In fact, the pope had no intention of abiding by any of this. His assent was due solely to the fact that Charles was present with armed men and there seemed to be no way of denying him his wish. Charles sailed off to Spain bearing his scraps of paper, and Francis soon made it known that he was not interested in a council and that preparations were underway for another invasion of Italy. Catherine's wedding was duly held in October at Marseilles with Clement in attendance, and it was on this joyous and spectacular occasion that the pope wrote to Charles, blandly informing him that the Most Christian King of France, the beloved ally of the Holy See, had recently concluded a treaty of alliance with the Grand Turk.[9]

No one could tell what might eventually come of such an agreement, but Charles needed no reminder that his business with the infidel remained unfinished. He was in Spain now, wandering from place to place or hearing the ritual complaints of the Cortes of Aragon at Monzón. His Spanish subjects were—as always—concerned about the Muslim peril in the western Mediterranean, and the dispatches from Italy also brought pleas for action. The Turks had turned their energies to the sea and were raiding in the Adriatic, carrying off thousands of Christians to slavery in the East. The danger was increased by the fact that they controlled not one but two great fleets, their main squadron generally located east of Messina and another under their tributary, Kheirredin Barbarossa, at Algiers.

Barbarossa, born a Christian, was now old but by no means retired. A pirate by trade, he had developed political ambitions and with Turkish support had gained control of a number of towns and garrisons along the North African coast. His seizure of Algiers in 1529 had been a major strategic blow, and his raids along the Neapolitan and Valencian coasts were added insults. Finally, in August, 1534, he deposed the Bey of Tunis, Muley Hassan, thereby completing his domination of the littoral from Morocco to Djerba. A response was clearly needed, and a plan for the recapture of Tunis began to form in the emperor's mind.

Preparations were begun in the fall of 1534, though the obstacles were formidable and varied. Even in Spain, there was a party, headed by the Archbishop of Toledo, that regarded adventures in Africa as little better than moonstruck folly. In the rest of Europe the situation remained extremely threatening, though as yet neither the French nor the Protestants had done anything concrete. Tedious and delicate negotiations were needed to prevent a Franco-Protestant alliance or a French descent into Italy, but in the end a great fleet of 100 galleys and three times as many transports left Sardinia on June 10, 1535. Alba, whom the emperor had visited at Alba de Tormes in 1534,[10] commanded the men-at-arms.

Militarily it was not an important post, as the day of armored knights had long since passed and their value in amphibious operations was especially questionable, but it was at least a mark of honor befitting his rank. True to the customs of his house, he brought along not only his brother Bernardino but his five-year-old son García.[11]

Tunis lies on the western edge of a circular harbor whose narrow entrance was commanded by a fortified town known to the Spaniards as La Goleta. They besieged this fortress, their first objective, shortly after the armada arrived on June 15. Heavy cavalry contributes little to such operations. Alba spent the first fortnight of the campaign on the sidelines, concerning himself with such matters as the reception of Charles' ally, Muley Hassan, on June 29.[12] On July 4 he finally saw action, but it was limited, accidental, and inconclusive. He had gone off with his squadron at dawn to find forage for the horses and was prowling about near the ruins of Carthage when he was set upon by a force of some 500 Moorish horse. Though he was outnumbered by more than two to one, this was not to be a reprise of his father's catastrophe at Djerba. Unlike Don García, the duke had marked his position and secured a line of retreat. After a sharp and thoroughly satisfactory skirmish he was able to retire in good order, reaching the camp at 9:00 A.M. Unhappily, this well-fought but limited engagement kept him out of the major event of the day. The Moors in La Goleta, seeing the dust from his skirmish, concluded that a substantial part of the besieging forces were involved and launched a sally of their own. They were driven back with heavy losses, but as the attack had come just when Alba and his men were removing their armor, they were wholly unable to participate in the rout.[13]

Another ten days of relative inactivity followed. Then on the morning of the fourteenth, Goleta fell to a massive frontal assault. It is probable that Alba participated, but the exact nature of his activities on that day is unknown. Ossorio loyally claims that Alba's cavalry spread death and terror among the Moors,[14] but no one else mentions him aside from Santa Cruz, who notes only that he heard Mass with Charles before the attack.[15]

To a man with Alba's professional orientation this must have been difficult to bear, but the rest of the campaign was an improvement. To some of the courtiers the collapse of La Goleta raised hopes of an early departure, and they argued against an attempt on Tunis itself. Incredibly, Charles wavered, but in the end, under the prodding of Alba and the Infante of Portugal, he came to his senses.[16] On July 20, they marched toward Tunis along the northern rim of the bay.

At first it appeared that the doubters had been right after all, for the march lay through a blasted, waterless region of sand and scrub, and it required seven hours to cover the five miles between La Goleta and the first cluster of water-holes. Horses died in the blazing heat, and men harnessed themselves to the cannon only to discover, when they reached the precious water, that a reception had been prepared for them by Barbarossa. The wells lay between the bay on the imperial left and a large olive grove on the right; the Moors had placed several thousand arquebusiers and twelve cannon squarely in the center by the water, and large numbers of cavalry lay on either flank. Sandoval estimates the total force at nearly 30,000 men,[17] but this is almost certainly an exaggeration.

Weary and almost literally perishing of thirst, the Christians drew themselves into a rough order of battle. The emperor, his personal guard, and the artillery occupied the center, the Italian infantry of the vanguard kept to the shore on the left, and the olive grove was covered by the Spanish veterans. Alba, who on the march had led a pitiful rearguard composed of his 200 men-at-arms and a gaggle of raw Spanish recruits, found himself guarding the baggage. His state of mind and that of his knights, half-broiled as they were in their heavy armor, can be imagined.

Barbarossa opened by turning part of his artillery on the Italians. They fell into some confusion but rallied as Charles bombarded the Moorish center. With his remaining cannon Barbarossa retaliated in kind. Charles had his horse shot under him, but the main Moorish assault failed and was followed by an imperial counterattack that ultimately cleared the enemy from the wells. In the meantime, Alba, forgotten and fuming in the rear, had his chance. In an attempt at encirclement, Barbarossa had dispatched a body of cavalry through the olive groves. They emerged on the flank of Alba's position just as Charles began his counterattack. It was a dangerous moment, for they were very numerous, but Alba wheeled and charged home, breaking their attack and driving them back into the groves whence they had come.[18] On a man-to-man basis the light Moorish cavalry were no match for the Europeans, but it was nonetheless an important contribution deftly carried out in the face of superior numbers. Perhaps more to the point, by refusing to allow pursuit Alba demonstrated that he was not a harebrained adventurer but a soldier who used his head. Long after Barbarossa had slunk back within the walls of Tunis, this would be remembered.

Described in capsule form, the battle appears more orderly than it actually was. To the participants it was little more than a general melee for which the Christians, at least, had been woefully unprepared. Their success probably came as a surprise, but if so, it was followed by a miracle. On that very night, the thousands of slaves penned within the city rebelled and Barbarossa, who was no fanatic, fled to Algiers.

Charles wasted little time in the enjoyment of his prize. Within a month he was on his way to Sicily. There, at Trapaní on August 26, Alba's brother Bernardino died of a veneral disease.[19] The two had been close, but if the duke commented on his loss no word of it has been preserved.

The landing at Trapaní marked the beginning of a triumphal march across Sicily and up the Italian boot which consumed most of the autumn. At Monreale and Palermo, at Messina and in every town along the route to Naples, the emperor was greeted as the new Scipio Africanus.[20] The festivals were marvels of Renaissance ingenuity, but again, Alba's personal reactions have not been preserved. We know only that he was ever at the emperor's side, and that while he presumably grieved for his brother he had at least one cause for profound satisfaction. Packed carefully in his baggage lay the arms of his father, lost so many years ago at Djerba and now gloriously recovered from the armory at Tunis.[21] This was a triumph and Charles knew it, for he had presented them to the duke with great ceremony, but though Alba took visible pleasure in his prize it did little to blunt his ardor. His account with the infidel was a long one and would never really be settled.

The winter of 1535/36 was spent at Naples attending to high politics, and the spring at Rome conferring with the pope. The emperor's purpose in all this had not changed significantly since 1533. He still wanted a council and he still hoped for an Italy united against the French, but this time he felt that his chances for success were greatly improved. In October, 1534, to the undisguised relief of nearly everyone, Clement VII had passed to whatever reward awaits a vacillating pope. His successor Paul III was anything but indecisive. Though an inspired nepotist and in many other ways a throwback to more relaxed times, Alessandro Farnese had no illusions about the need for reform. At his first consistory he had commented on the necessity for a council, and in the months thereafter had packed the College of Cardinals not only with youthful relatives but with distinguished reform-minded churchmen from every state in Europe.

Charles was convinced that he had at last found an ally, but in this he was only partially correct. As the discussions at Rome were to show, Paul wanted a council but only on his own terms, and he had no intention whatever of discarding papal neutrality in the matter of the French. This last was particularly annoying, as the French had seized Turin just as Charles arrived in Rome and it was only a matter of time before they would try to make good their claims against Milan. Still, genuine neutrality was better than open French partisanship, and in the next few years Paul would make valuable efforts on behalf of peace.

Alba no doubt found these months far more productive and less frustrating than did his master. His activities are not known in detail, as he rarely wrote out of mere friendship, and there are always great gaps in his correspondence whenever he was at court, but we know that he had constant access to the emperor and that, in the words of the Count of Nieva, "the Duke of Alba enters continually into council and the emperor treats him very well."[22] In practical terms, he was developing a close working relationship with Charles that was to last until the latter's death, and a personal devotion that transcended even the grave. How far this was reciprocated is open to doubt, as Charles was too suspicious to indulge in favoritism, but it was increasingly evident that Alba's company pleased him and that, at least within certain well-defined limits, the emperor was beginning to listen to the advice of his duke.

This is hardly surprising. In age the two men were only seven years apart, and they shared a degree of piety and seriousness of purpose that led to natural agreement on most issues. Both of them were also reserved, formal men and were therefore comfortable with one another. If Charles lacked the controlled ferocity that was so much a part of Alba's character, he had the good sense to know that the trait could be put to use. Their relationship seemed free of tension or resentment on either side. They were not friends—this would have been inconceivable, given their common vision of a hierarchic universe and of the emperor's role within it—but they would share much in the years to come, and the cornerstone of their association was laid at this early date.

The second effect of this sojourn in Italy was of an entirely different sort. Without conscious purpose but with unerring political instinct, the duke began to weave a mesh of connections that would one day make him a substantial if shadowy figure in Italian politics. His entrée into this labyrinthine world came in part from his association with the emperor. In the end, however, the position of his uncle, Don Pedro de Toledo, Viceroy of Naples, was more important. Stocky, choleric, and supremely competent, Don Pedro had already become a force to reckon with in the Peninsula. Both he and his son, Don García, were to remain firm allies of the ranking member of their house. The relationship developed further significance when Don Pedro's daughter married Cosimo II, Duke of Florence, and another uncle, Juan, became Cardinal Archbishop of Santiago. By mid-century there would be Toledos at work in Naples, Florence, and the Vatican, and Alba, for all his steadfast Castilianism, would be the head of an "Italian" clan comparable in influence to the Farneses or Gonzagas. None of this was foreordained in 1536, but the more astute Italians, ever alert to new tremblings on the edges of their tenuous web, took careful note of the young Spaniard as he made his way among courts, embassies, and the palaces of cardinals.

Politics, however, soon gave way to war. Something had to be done about the French, and Charles, having gained what he could from the pope, took counsel with his military advisors. Three courses of action were open to him: he could ignore the invasion of Piedmont; he could try to drive the French out and secure the Alpine passes; or he could use the incident as an excuse to carry the war into France. The first choice was unacceptable on several grounds. The Italians, predictably, leaned toward the second, while the Spaniards favored the third. The emperor, flushed with his victory at Tunis, was inclined to the Spanish view, but his final decision proved catastrophic. Among the Spaniards, de Leyva counseled an attack on Marseilles, a city which, though heavily fortified, was the key to French seapower in the Mediterranean. He was seconded by Andrea Doria, the great Genoese admiral, who had obvious reasons for wishing to cripple his city's rival. Alba argued that this would be madness. The French army was weakened by its recent exertions and would have time to rebuild if the imperial forces were tied down to the siege of a fortified city. Instead, he advocated an attack on Lyons, which was rich and poorly defended. Francis would have to answer the pleas of his subjects and could thus be drawn into a decisive battle that would presumably leave open the road to Paris.[23] Charles decided in favor of his senior commander. He believed that an invasion of Provence could be supported by his fleet and that his commander in the north, Henry of Nassau-Dillenburg, could create a worthwhile diversion along the Flemish frontier. He was wrong on both counts.

From the beginning the campaign suffered from confusion and mutual resentment, in no small part due to Charles himself. During the long dry march from Italy to Marseilles he persisted in changing the commands of the various units and then effectively dividing them. The vanguard, for example, was placed first under Gonzaga, then under Alba, and then under the Mosén de Sistán.[24] In the meantime Alba, presumably the captain-general of the men-at-arms, had to contend with a subordinate who was his equal in rank—his cousin, the immensely wealthy Count of Benavente, commander of the Imperial Guard.[25] At the top, Antonio de Leyva was himself constrained by the presence of the emperor, who had now embarked in earnest on his long career as a field commander. Rancor was inevitable, and long before the imperial forces reached Marseilles internal communications had largely broken down.

The Provence of 1536 was a very bad place for this to happen. Few today would find a journey through Nice, Antibes, and Cannes onerous, but it was then a poor, barren country that offered a North African level of sustenance to inhabitants and invaders alike. The French under the wily Constable, Anne de Montmorency, made matters worse by adopting a scorched-earth policy that did little to improve either logistics or the disposition of the local peasantry. In fact, their campaign was an early example of effective guerrilla warfare. With skill, ferocity, and imagination, the natives harassed lines of communication and cut off stragglers while retaining close contact with the regular army. At first this caused only moderate concern, as Charles intended to support his army from the sea, but it soon became evident that the coordination required for such an effort was wholly beyond him. Neither his organization nor the available technology was equal to the task. Alba's one surviving letter from the campaign speaks volumes: he does not know where Doria is, there are no ships around, and the French have just seized a boat carrying 136 sacks of precious flour.[26]

Whatever glory attached itself to this wretched effort was credited to Alba. After much delay the emperor established his camp at Aix and ordered a general reconnaissance. One glance convinced him that, as Alba had predicted, Marseilles was impregnable, and he decided to retreat. Unfortunately, even this would be impossible until someone made contact with Doria. Having seen the road back, Charles knew that fresh supplies were needed and that the sick and wounded would have to be carried off by ship if they were to survive. By all reports the Genoese fleet lay off the mouth of the Huveaune, where it was screened from the city by the heights of Notre Dame de la Garde. To reach it the invalids, the baggage, and their military escort would have to descend by the valley of Aygalades and make a partial circuit of Marseilles by way of Le Canet, Plombières, and the valley of Jarret.[27] During much of the journey they would be within range of the walls. A large, experienced force was obviously necessary, and Alba, still "muy sentido" over being superseded by the Mosén de Sistán,[28] was appointed to command it. The reasons for this decision are unknown.

On August 31 Alba marched toward Marseilles at the head of the *tercios* of Sicily and Lombardy, the German mercenaries, and a troop of 600 light horse under Sancho de Leyva. They camped that night within half a league of the city, and on the following morning made their way toward the shore, with the main body of the troops screening the baggage against possible attack. Predictably, a large force of horse and foot issued forth, covered by heavy fire from the walls, but Alba drove them off and rendezvoused that evening with Doria's galleys, which were, for once, precisely where they were supposed to be.[29]

The unloading of supplies began immediately. With his already habitual caution, Alba sent Don Sancho and the light horse off on a series of patrols throughout the neighborhood. Toward late afternoon they encountered about five hundred French cavalry and a detachment of arquebusiers lurking in the vicinity of the camp to observe the operation and pick off stragglers. Alba's internal lines of communication must have been both unobtrusive and effective, for he was able to hold de Leyva back until he could arm his men secretly in their quarters and form them into squadrons for an attack in force. The French were driven back to the walls with heavy losses.

A number of prisoners were taken, but the duke ordered their release and provided an escort to carry the wounded safely back to the city. He had no intention of being burdened with hostages. All that night a detachment of Spaniards prowled about the walls trading insults with the French and preventing them from making an *encamisado*, a night raid on the camp.[30]

The next day's operations were decidedly more ticklish. To cover the embarkation of the wounded, Alba drew up his force in full battle array and sent the redoubtable de Leyva to create a diversion near the city. Once again the French came out and were treated to an afternoon of skirmishing while the main operation continued without hindrance. By September 4, the wounded and the surplus baggage had been completely evacuated, the fresh supplies landed, and Doria was able to spend a day at Aix in consultation with the emperor. Imperial losses were negligible.

As a second fleet of galleys was expected at Rens, Alba then withdrew about a league further along the coast, but not before providing the French with another object lesson in the rules of small war. To cover his withdrawal he placed a detachment of Spaniards in a house outside the city and sent Don Sancho to lay an ambush along the road between the city and the house. He then marched off as ostentatiously as he could, and the French, frustrated and howling for vengeance, poured out to claim the sacrificial victims. The trap was sprung, and only a few of them regained the safety of the town.[31]

Unfortunately, the weather began to deteriorate, and as of the seventh the galleys had not yet arrived. When they did get there they could not get out again, and Alba was forced to spend his time in ingenious but indecisive minor actions to protect their anchorage. In the meantime the ranking commander, Antonio de Leyva, died at Aix. The chronicler Sandoval spitefully notes that he had urged the invasion because his astrologer had told him that he would die in France and be buried at St. Denis. He had his wish. He died in France and was buried at San Dionysio in Milan.[32] It must have been a relief for Alba to get back to imperial headquarters when the seas moderated on September 11.

This otherwise modest sequence of events has been described in detail for two reasons: it was Alba's first independent field command, and it was a textbook example of how such operations should be conducted. In it he fully demonstrated his mastery of one aspect of the art of war and established his style as a commander. Cunning, attention to detail, and economy of means were to become his hallmarks, and in these last moments of a failed campaign he demonstrated them all. It was a remarkably mature performance for a soldier of twenty-eight, and with the emperor, at least, his reputation was made.

There was nothing, though, that could mitigate the final nightmare of the retreat. According to the *Mémoires* of the du Bellays, the man-made desolation and savage resistance of the peasants created "so horrible and piteous a spectacle that it made miserable even the most obstinate and intransigent of enemies, and those who witnessed the desolation could not conceive it to be less than that described by Josephus in the destruction of Jerusalem."[33]

It also cost the life of Garcilaso de la Vega. The poet's death was as pedestrian as it was meaningless. At Le Muy a number of peasants, resolved to make a stand, barricaded themselves in a tower. Garcilaso was given the task of dislodging them, and the peasants, rightly taking him for the enemy leader, dropped a rock on his head. He was carried to Nice where he died, and his body was deposited there in the monastery of the Dominican Friars.[34]

For Alba the myths, like the companions of his childhood, were falling one by one. After Provence there would be no more heroic speeches in council, no more urging of headlong advances. He had learned the importance of logistics and had seen at first hand the dangers of campaigning amid a hostile peasantry. His view of war was becoming long-headed, and if his solutions to these problems were rarely original they would prove to be very thorough.

Alba was now firmly entrenched in the emperor's confidence, but the next several years offered few opportunities to test his military skill. He used the time to extend the maturity earned in war to the fields of diplomacy and statecraft. The campaign in Provence had weakened both sides, and for the next eighteen months Charles and Francis were involved, warily and through intermediaries, in efforts to find a successful formula for peace. The year 1537 was therefore passed in Spain. Alba tended to his duties, marital and otherwise, and left his estates only to accompany Charles on such occasions as the celebration of Easter at Valladolid.[35] On July 10 his mother, Doña Beatríz, died.[36] On November 21 his second son, Fadrique, was born. It was not until the spring of 1538 that the duke emerged once more from rustic seclusion to resume his travels.

The occasion was a great peace conference involving the pope, the emperor, and the king of France. The year after the invasion of Provence had seen a grim but indecisive campaign on the borders of

Flanders and a French demonstration in Piedmont that was countered by an imperial movement into Languedoc. Negotiations, though lengthy, ultimately reached a stalemate. The breakthrough came in February, 1538, when Charles concluded an alliance with Venice, the pope, and his brother Ferdinand. Though its ostensible purpose was to thwart the Turk, the French were thoroughly alarmed; when the pope called for a general meeting at Nice they at last agreed to serious discussions.[37]

As usual, Charles hoped for a settlement that would leave him free to deal with the Turks and Protestants, but the conference at Nice was to prove neither conclusive nor especially pleasant. Charles and his entourage, Alba included, arrived at Savona on May 9 and proceeded to Nice, where the emperor was reunited with his sister Eleanora, the wife of Francis I. Conditions were less than regal. The beds were so miserable that the ladies preferred to sit up all night, and dinner the next day was little better. There was wine and even ice-water, but the heat was so great that Charles had to commit the supreme impropriety of removing his hat at table, and throughout the meal Alba stood behind him with gloves to ward off the insects.[38]

The diplomatic results were proportionate to the elegance of the setting. At no time did Francis and Charles meet face to face; they went separately to the pope, who served as an intermediary. In the end they agreed to a ten-year truce, without resolving the problem of Milan or any other basic issue. As if to disguise the failure, Francis invited Charles to meet with him at the castle of Aigues Mortes, but so suspect were his intentions that Charles and several of his councillors hesitated to accept. It was Alba who tipped the balance. He argued that a refusal would appear hostile and irresponsible in the eyes of the world, whereas, if he accepted, Francis would dare nothing for fear of being labeled an irredeemable scoundrel.[39] Fortunately, this view prevailed, and in mid-July the two monarchs met first on Charles's galley and then at Aigues Mortes itself. Nothing of substance was discussed, but there were several good-humored exchanges among Charles, Francis, and Alba, whose company the French king apparently enjoyed.[40]

The emperor had no illusions about this. Brandi is probably correct in saying that the talks had finally convinced him that a lasting peace with France was impossible,[41] but they had bought time, and it was this above all that he needed to pursue an illusion of far greater scope and magnificence. Specifically, he meant to settle accounts with the Turks once and for all. This was to be no mere *razzia* on Algiers, as the Spanish would have preferred, but a crusade in high medieval fashion. Constantinople was even mentioned as its goal.[42] The sheer lunacy of this scheme was eventually to dawn upon him, but not before he had provoked a major confrontation, in which Alba played an important part, with the Castilian nobility.

Charles was not so far gone in quixotic fantasies as to forget that even a holy war had to be financed, and the Cortes of Castile was convened shortly after his return from Aigues Mortes. For reasons that will become abundantly obvious, it was the last cortes in which the nobility participated.

The emperor's purpose was to gain approval for a *sisa* (excise tax) that would fall most heavily on the nobles. Convoked by *cédula* on September 6, 1538, the company assembled in Toledo in late October. Present were seventy-four nobles, twenty-four prelates, and the *procuradores* or representatives of the seventeen royal towns that still possessed voting rights. The mood of the nobles was evident from the start. On November 2 they gathered and voted that their proceedings be kept secret, that a committee of twelve—including Alba—be appointed to look into the matter, and that Don Luis de la Cerda, the member of the empress's household who had convened them, be excluded on the grounds that neither he nor his father held land in Castile.

Three weeks of deliberation revealed that the committee was deeply divided and unable to issue a report. Accordingly, an attempt was made to raise the prior issue of whether to vote by simple or by two-thirds majority. When the former view prevailed, Alba, together with fifteen of his friends and relatives, walked out, saying that "he was not of that opinion."

The issue was painfully simple. A majority of the nobles, headed by the Constable of Castile, were not about to end their traditional immunity from taxation. A minority, headed by Alba and composed largely of his relatives and a number of men who had followed Charles in his travels, hoped for a compromise. One of them, the Count of Ureña, remained after the walk-out and tried to postpone consideration on the theory that not everyone was present. This too was overruled, and in the end they decided to consider the majority a quorum and a simple majority of those present as sufficient for action. Once a decision was made it would be presented to the emperor as unanimous.[43]

Alba was thus placed in an uncomfortable position. During the next several weeks he was subjected to great pressure and to bitter accusations that he was a traitor to his class. It was the first time that his loyalty to the Crown had been put to the test, but it was to be by no means the last. The unhappy fact was that at least two elements of his personal ideology were hopelessly irreconcilable. His Castilianism and pride of caste would always be at war with his allegiance to an international and theoretically absolute monarchy, and if he generally came down on the side of the latter the decision was rarely made without great personal cost. Much of his testiness in dealing with his masters was a result of this inner struggle.

An example was soon forthcoming. As always, the Cortes proceeded with glacial solemnity. Christmas came and went without result. On January 12 a tournament was held, and in the course of it an incident occurred that led to a direct confrontation between Charles and the nobles. A bailiff trying to hold back the crowd of spectators struck the horse of the Duke of Infantado. Infantado, who was suporting Charles and Alba on the matter of the *sisa*, immediately called out, "Do you know who I am?" and was answered: "I know very well who you are; you are the Duke of Infantado." The enraged duke drew his sword and slashed the bailiff on the head, whereupon the bailiff struck Infantado's horse with his own sword, giving it a superficial wound. A general brawl appeared imminent. This was too much. A sixteenth-century court was a self-contained community with its own laws and a variety of officials to enforce them; the bailiff was thus a representative of imperial authority, and to attack him in the emperor's presence was to offend Charles himself. Rather than appear incapable of maintaining decorum in his own court, Charles ordered the *alcalde* to arrest Infantado. At this point Alba intervened. Visibly angered at what he took to be disrespect for Infantado's rank, he stepped forward with the Constable and blocked the arrest. Telling the *alcalde* that dealing with the duke was the responsibility of his peers, they marched him off to his quarters escorted by the rest of the nobles. The next day all seventy-four of them boycotted the session.[44]

It might be argued that Alba's action was a shrewd piece of political theater designed to reestablish his standing with the nobles, but this is unlikely. Though devious enough in dealing with the enemies of Spain, he was openly disdainful of such tactics on the domestic front and generally avoided them even in circumstances more tempting than these. His earlier defense of Garcilaso and a number of incidents in his later career show that he was consistently defiant when his own prerogatives and those of his class were involved, so long as exercise of a prerogative did not interfere with the broader goals of royal policy. Intellectually he may have justified this as compatible with a hierarchic system in which social roles were clearly defined, but his conflicting attitudes were eventually to cause him much trouble.

This time there were no consequences. Charles, unwilling to alienate the few remaining nobles who supported him, quickly pardoned Infantado, but this capitulation did not earn him the desired *sisa*.[45] Alba, Infantado, and their fifteen associates continued to support it, but the rest held firm and added a gratuitous, if traditional, lecture on the need for Charles to stay in Spain and reduce his personal spending. The Cortes ended with the crusade in jeopardy.

It was not, however, the failure of the Cortes that made Charles alter his plans, but a welter of new troubles in Germany and the Netherlands. In 1536 the imperial vice-chancellor, Matthias Held, had been instructed to calm the German Protestants. With what appears to have been habitual folly he tried to do so by forming a union of Catholic princes in order to threaten them. Thoroughly alarmed, the Schmalkaldic League began making plans for a preventive war as the Cortes of Toledo opened. Another emissary, the Archbishop of Lund, managed to smooth things over, but the price was a new round of religious talks, to begin in the coming year. Meanwhile in Flanders, Ghent chose this moment to rebel against Charles's sister, Mary of Hungary, and in the borderlands the new Duke of Cleves-Jülich, a nominal adherent of the emperor, began to intrigue with the French in the hope of reasserting the ancient independence of his house. Charles's presence was clearly needed, but his dreams of a crusade died hard. Only the loss of his empress in childbirth on May 1, 1539, and an impassioned but cogent plea from his sister brought him to his senses. He began making arrangements for a journey not only to deal with these vexations but to reach some agreement with his relatives on another problem whose solution was long overdue: the ultimate disposition of his inheritance.[46]

Grim though its initial auspices may have been, the trip turned out to be a gala vacation for all concerned. Still in the afterglow of Aigues Mortes, Francis I extended an invitation to pass through France, and Charles accepted with alacrity. With about twenty gentlemen, of whom Alba was the highest in rank, Charles proceeded to Fuenterrabía, where he was met by the Dauphin and the Duke of Orleans. Thus escorted, they traveled by way of Bordeaux and Poitiers to the castle of Loches, where they were greeted by Francis himself. Though confined to a litter, the king insisted on accompanying them for nearly two months, entertaining them sumptuously at each of the magnificent cheateaux along the Loire, at Fountainebleau, at Paris, and finally at St. Quentin, where he left them on January 20. It was a time of hunts, pageants, and feasts, uninterrupted by politics save for a concerted if unsuccessful effort to arrange a marriage between the widower Charles and the king's daughter Marguerite.[47] Brantôme has left us a capsule portrait of Alba in the midst of all this elegance and grandeur that agrees with what has been said before. He seemed, said the great raconteur, "in good fashion"—that is to say, well-dressed—but very cold and reserved, and in exceptional favor with the emperor.[48] Once again, this detachment does not seem to have cost him the friendship of Francis I. Alba passed into the Netherlands without further comment but with a diamond worth 4,000 ducats in his purse as the parting gift of a monarch who was perhaps his diametrical opposite in character and temperament.[49]

Once past the border, the pall of reality again descended. Nothing has been preserved of the duke's thoughts on France, but within three days of leaving he recorded his impressions of the Netherlands in a sardonic letter to the emperor's secretary, Francisco de los Cobos. In view of his later career, its contents are revealing and a trifle ominous:

> We, the poor little Spaniards, after we are out of France, feel that we are foreigners according to what we have found here. Men have come to the *cámara* now that I had thought dead twenty years ago. There are more folk at the alms-dish than at the table, so many that if Don Pedro de la Cueva and I had wished, we could have been there too without being seen among them.[50]

Three weeks later these negative impressions were reinforced by his experience at Ghent.

The Ghent rebellion was now more than two years old, having begun in 1537 with a refusal to pay taxes for the war of the preceding year. Mary of Hungary, desperate for revenue and jealous of her brother's prerogatives, had resorted to coercion, but when the magistrates wavered the populace rebelled. With fathomless stupidity, a new and more radical government then turned to the King of France just as the euphoria of Aigues Mortes had reached its height. Francis ignored this, but by 1539 revolt had spread like a contagion into the surrounding countryside and the economic life of the great city was at a standstill.

Charles's reaction was merciless. Quartering his troops upon the town, he declared it guilty of treason and deprived it of all rights and privileges. The leaders of the revolt were summarily executed and a fortress was erected to ensure obedience in the years to come.[51] It was a terrifying display of imperial authority and an object lesson not only to the Flemings but to Alba, who was an interested observer throughout.

After settling accounts with the city of his birth, Charles remained for some time in the Netherlands before moving on to the Diet of Regensburg, where the last faint hope of reconciliation between Protestant and Catholic died. Alba was present through much of this, but as he knew little of German affairs the role he played in them was inevitably minor. It is not even known when he left for Spain, but by September, 1541, he was at Cartagena, playing an important part in the unfolding of a new imperial adventure. He had seen much of politics as well as war, and was ready for a larger role.

III

THE COMMANDER

The attack on Algiers in October, 1541, was such a fiasco that Ossorio can hardly be blamed for denying that Alba was present,[1] but the duke was there, and in a critical capacity.

The genesis of the expedition was a curiosity in itself. While Charles haggled unsuccessfully at Regensburg, Suleiman mounted yet another campaign against the eastern fringes of his empire. Ferdinand was, as usual, hard pressed. It was essential that something be done to relieve him, but with the Germans recalcitrant, Spanish and Italian forces had to be used. Understandably, the Mediterranean components of his empire were unwilling to launch a second crusade on the faraway plains of Hungary, and Charles judged correctly that a diversion at Algiers would be more likely to gain their support. The season was already far advanced—he did not leave Regensburg until the first of August—and his advisors warned him that the Mediterranean in autumn was treacherous, but his earlier success at Tunis had made him reckless. It is also possible that Barbarossa's governor, Hassan Aga, had offered to surrender the city without a fight.[2] In any case, he determined to sail from Genoa for a rendezvous with the Spanish fleet under Alba before proceeding to Algiers in mid-October. This was Alba's first attempt to organize an expeditionary force on his own, and it was, at the very least, a memorable experience.

By the time he reached the staging point at Cartegena it was September 1, and the situation had already deteriorated to an alarm-

45

ing degree. Supplies were lacking, the soldiers were untrained recruits, and corruption flourished among both the sutlers and the officials who were supposed to control them.[3]

Some of this might have been prevented had the duke arrived earlier, but he was detained at Madrid by the Consejo Real, which with more wisdom than loyalty placed every possible obstacle in the way of the expedition.[4] He was thus forced to spend an unpleasant month investigating corruption, scrounging equipment, and restricting the activities of whores, great numbers of whom were flogged publicly.[5] Among the worst of his problems was the crowd of young nobles seeking renown through combat with the infidel. With few exceptions, they were novices who meant to crusade in comfort and whose large retinues and masses of gear astonished beholders. The duke, whose own habits remained fairly spartan, was undiplomatic. He ordered most of their horses off to Murcia because the local pasturage was insufficient, and ended by refusing to allow most of their servants and baggage aboard ship.[6] This was to some extent necessary, for when the transports at last came up from Málaga they were fewer than expected and already loaded up to the gunwales, but he might have been more tactful. As it was, a number of his peers were mortally offended, and at least one of them, the Count of Feria, was to be an enemy for life.[7]

Finally, on the last day of September, this convoy of innocents weighed anchor for the rendezvous at Mallorca and immediately ran into a flat calm. This was succeeded by a fierce levanter, and it was all they could do to reach Ibiza by October 13. It is a tribute to the skill of the fleet commander, Don Bernardino de Mendoza, that no one was lost, but further progress was impossible.[8] The emperor decided to go ahead without them, and sent word that they should proceed directly to Algiers.[9]

On October 21 they raised the North African coast about six leagues to the west of the city, but yet another levanter kept them from entering the harbor. The emperor's fleet, coming from the northeast, was able to land on October 22, but only two or three of the light, seaworthy *naos* from Vizcaya were able, thanks to their superior windward ability, to join him. Alba, with considerable foresight, had transferred to one of these craft and so arrived on time. The rest of his fleet rounded the point on October 24.[10]

They would have been better advised to put to sea. The city was quickly invested, with the Spanish vanguard under Alba seizing the commanding heights,[11] but around midnight the mistral against which the emperor had repeatedly been warned began. The fleet, as yet only partially disembarked, tried to claw its way off the lee shore, but to little avail. By morning as many as 150 ships were piled up on the beach or otherwise destroyed.[12] Charles raised the siege and withdrew to Cape Matifou, where a council of war was held on October 29, Alba's thirty-fourth birthday.

In retrospect, the deliberations of the council were the product of shock and panic rather than mature consideration. Charles and his admiral, Andrea Doria, were inclined to see the havoc wrought by the storm as a sign from God. Cortés, the conqueror of Mexico, who had come out of retirement for one last campaign, disagreed. He believed, probably with good reason, that enough of the army had been landed to take the city, and that this, whatever the risk, would be preferable to a dangerous and ignominious retreat. Oddly enough, the opinions of this great soldier were lightly regarded in Europe and he was ignored.[13] The survivors were embarked on November 1 and straggled back to Cartagena under appalling conditions of overcrowding and privation. Alba's opinion of all this was not recorded.

The entire expedition had been ill conceived, and the difficulties at Cartagena were not of Alba's making; indeed, in the brief period allotted he had done much to rectify them, but sixteenth-century campaigns involved lengthy preparations and this one had been undertaken almost on the spur of the moment. Fortunately, Charles was not the man to look for scapegoats. God had not favored his cause and he would spend no time in recrimination. Within months Alba had a far more important charge: the defense of the Spanish frontier.

It has already been noted that the meetings of Nice and Aigues Mortes had settled none of the basic points at issue between France and the empire. They had resulted in nothing more conclusive than a truce between exhausted adversaries, and the subsequent camaraderie showed only that Charles and Francis were heirs to a common chivalric culture. Inevitably, the disaster at Algiers and the failure of Charles's efforts in Germany revived French ambitions, but this time Francis gave advance notice of his intent. In January, 1542, his troops took Stenay, a strategically important crossing of the Meuse near Verdun, and Charles immediately ordered the strengthening of his borders both in Spain and the Low Countries. It was thought that Francis might attack on two fronts, and as Navarre seemed the most likely target in Spain, Alba was hastily dispatched to Pamplona.

To the Viceroy of Navarre, Alba's arrival must have resembled
the invasion it was intended to prevent. He was immediately ordered to provide a force of 7,000 foot and 500 horse, with 1,500 servants for the soldiers and supplies for four months. All of this was
to be done "without cost or annoyance" to the inhabitants, and
where it was necessary to quarter troops on the town, payment was
to be made in advance. Then the fosses were to be cleared and the
royal bakeries opened on a permanent basis. In the castle of Estella,
gun platforms were constructed and provisions stored for a garrison
of seventy. The gunpowder was buried in the patio. The artillerymen
were set to work fashioning gun carriages and ramrods, and a permanent guard was mounted on the gates and walls of the city with
orders to stop suspicious persons and send them to the viceroy for
questioning.[14] It was a magnificent performance, but the French did
not cooperate. By late spring it had become evident that their target
was Perpignan, on the borders of Catalonia.

Nothing daunted, the duke repeated his measures there—with
notable success. Armed with full powers to coordinate the defense
of the Pyrenees, and with fulsome if not always practicable instructions from the emperor at Monzón,[15] he settled down to await the
enemy. They came in August, 1542, with an immensely superior
force, under the Dauphin of France, the future Henry II. Alba's strategy was unexpected and entirely successful. To the intense dismay
of his officers he left a garrison at Perpignan and moved off to the
vicinity of Gerona, where he camped in the open. It was better, he
thought, to retain freedom of action than to be tied down without
possibility of advance or retreat. Moreover, the enemy would then
believe the Spanish army to be larger than it actually was and would
fear being caught between the forces. He was right on both counts.
Alba had only four *tercios* and six squadrons of cavalry, but faced
with a strong garrison at Perpignan and an indefinite number of
Spaniards lurking in the fields, Henry dithered and then withdrew.[16]
It was a clever, unorthodox, nearly bloodless defense, and it showed
what Alba could do when he controlled an operation from the
start.[17] Charles was now prepared to acknowledge him as the best
soldier in Spain,[18] but the next four years were to be curiously anti-
climactic, a succession of prestigious but insubstantial tasks that did
little to advance his reputation.

The withdrawal of the Dauphin ended the immediate threat to
Spanish territory, but the situation in the Netherlands continued to
deteriorate. With grave misgivings, Charles decided that he would

take command of the northern war in person, and began to ponder the task of setting up a regency to rule Spain while he was away. The results of his deliberations, embodied in the famous *Instructions* of May 1, 1543, effectively barred Alba from the larger European stage.

The *Instructions* were in three parts: a published segment describing the government over which his sixteen-year-old son Philip would preside as regent, a secret instruction in which he explained his decisions, and a third letter to be opened only in the event of his death or capture. This last was destroyed when his luck proved better than expected. The two surviving documents are nothing less than a blueprint for governance. Alba is mentioned only as one of several important court figures, but the emperor's comments about him are revealing. As some modern scholars have partially misinterpreted them, they will be examined in some detail.

There is no difficulty with the formal instruction. It simply appoints Alba captain-general of all forces in the Peninsula and gives him a seat on the Council of State while tacitly excluding him from Philip's innermost group of advisors.[19] The reasons for this exclusion are contained in the secret instruction, along with a concise if somewhat jaundiced portrait of the man in his broader political setting. For the sake of accuracy the following translation is more literal than elegant:

> The Duke of Alba wishes to join them [the inner council], and I believe that he does not go according to faction, but by what best serves his own interest, and as there are things in the government of the kingdom from which the grandees should be excluded, I do not wish to admit him, which will grieve him no little; I have found as I came to know him better that he has great ambitions and tries to advance himself as much as he can, though he appears pious and very humble and retiring, watch out for this as you are younger; you must guard against placing him or the other grandees very far within the government, because by every way they can, he and the others will try to gain favor that will later cost us dear, and even if it be by means of women, I do not think that they will cease to tempt you, of which, I pray you to be very much on your guard; in everything else I employ the duke, in matters of state and war make use of him, in this honor and favor him as he is the best we now have in these kingdoms.[20]

On the face of it, there is little here to astonish the reader. Alba was certainly ambitious and likely to be very much offended by anything that kept him from the levers of power. That he masked this with apparent humility is interesting only insofar as it shows him still capable of doing so at all. In later years this would not always be the case. Finally, the emperor's confidence in his military talents was implicit in the offices granted him by the formal instruction, and the duke's grasp of foreign affairs (*lo de estado*) ought to have been great, given his long exposure to them while in attendance on the emperor.

The true oddity of this assessment lies in a pair of misconceptions, one of them the emperor's and one the product of a modern mistranslation. The emperor's mistake lay in believing that Alba was untouched by faction. As a later chapter will demonstrate, he had already become associated with the *banda* headed by Francisco de los Cobos, and if the emperor did not see this he must truly have been blinded by the simplistic view of the grandees presented in the rest of his testament.

The other is almost trivial but has become widespread among English-speaking readers. In Brandi's widely read *Charles V* the above passage from the *Instructions* was rendered with much poetic license, and the emperor's general warning against the grandees was made to apply solely to Alba: "He will do his best to make himself agreeable to you, probably with the help of feminine influence."[21] To those familiar with the duke's private life the accusation of pandering takes the breath away, but of course, as the original indicates, this was not the emperor's intent.

The purpose in raising such an issue is not to protect the one virtue granted Alba even by his enemies but to preserve the coherence of his psychological portrait. This is doubly important in view of a second document that appears to level a similar charge. There is an eighteenth-century manuscript in the Biblioteca Nacional[22] that purports to be the copy of a letter from Cobos to the emperor dated February 6, 1543. Keniston, in his biography of Cobos, accepts it as genuine and prints it in full,[23] but its authenticity is extremely questionable. In the first place, the dates are wrong. On February 6, Cobos and the emperor were together at Madrid. Moreover, it supposedly answers a letter written by Charles from Palamós on January 15, but Charles was not at Palamós then, nor on the fifteenth of any other month in any year of his life.[24] Keniston suggests that it might have been written later, after June 29, and the date altered by secretaries because of its confidential nature,[25] but this is unlikely. The contents of the letter are such that its appearance at any time would have ruined its author. Its elaborate and artificial style bears no resemblance to the secretary's other writings. Perhaps most important, it is inconceivable that Cobos would have attempted to slander the man who was both his closest ally among the nobility and the executor of his estate. All of this, together with errors in forms of address and other matters of detail, points to a forgery of later date— possibly the 1570s, when a concerted effort was underway to disgrace the duke. If the emperor was suspicious of Alba it was as a grandee, not a pimp.

It may be, however, that there was something more definite and personal behind these suspicions than a generalized mistrust of the nobility. The emperor was embarking on a critical campaign, yet he chose to leave one of his best commanders at home. In itself this proves little, but Alba, too, was clearly upset, for he reacted in a way that was to become habitual whenever he thought himself ill-used. He began by complaining about his commission. It was, he thought, too restrictive and placed him under the effective control of the viceroys. If it were not changed he would refuse to enter the viceregal kingdoms even if they were attacked![26] Then he demanded an *ayuda de costa* to cover expenditures during the siege of Perpignan and haggled over the payment of his current salary and expenses.

There is a veritable flurry of letters on the subject, each more strident and petty than the last.[27] His complaints are not wholly invalid, for the Habsburgs expected noblemen to use their own resources and preferred whenever possible to avoid concentration of authority in hands other than their own. Other servants of the Crown raised the same issues, but the vehemence of Alba's letters is out of all proportion to his grievances. He was always careful with his own money, but on many later occasions spent handsomely in the course of royal commissions, protesting only when he thought that his personal, as opposed to financial, sacrifices were unappreciated. The exact cause of this first outburst is open to conjecture, but it clearly indicates a temporary disenchantment on both sides, and, as was so often the case with Alba, it set a pattern for his response to similar grievances in the years to come.

As it turned out, he need not have worried. The French did not attack Spain, and imperial arms enjoyed such success elsewhere that a contingency plan for Alba to invade Languedoc was never employed.[28] Instead, he found himself plunged into several months of festivities beginning with the marriage of Cobos's son to the Marquesa de Camarasa and ending with that of Prince Philip to Maria Manuela of Portugal.

The royal wedding was organized in part by Alba, who is said to have paid some of the expenses.[29] If this is true, it reinforces the belief that his complaints had nothing to do with greed, but it is possible that he was simply caught up in the enthusiasm of the moment. Certainly he tried to dominate the proceedings as though they were his own.

It is something of a paradox that this man who so often passed himself off as a simple soldier loved to organize festivals and court rituals of every kind and possessed an encyclopedic knowledge of the most arcane rules of protocol. This interest would one day find an official outlet, but even before he became Philip's majordomo his expertise was recognized. In later life it became legendary. When no one knew how to arrange Philip's entry into Portugal in 1581, Alba was consulted, and he answered as circumstantially and completely as he had about his military arrangements.[30]

In 1543 he adopted the role of an indulgent uncle, and enjoyed it thoroughly. In spite of accusations to the contrary, Philip seems never to have been a romantic, and his interest in women was minimal.[31] Nevertheless, Alba arranged an expedition to give him an early glimpse of his bride. The duke's residence at El Abadía lay only a mile or two from the main road between Portugal and Salamanca, where the wedding was to take place. A smallish house in the Italian style, with vast windows placed to catch the warmth of the setting sun, it was his favorite winter residence and over the years he was to spend heavily on improvements for it.[32] There they waited, and when the princess and her entourage appeared, they rode out with a party of horsemen to observe her from the not very satisfactory cover of some trees.[33]

After this gallant conceit they raced back to Salamanca, where Alba organized a *juego de cañas* (a tournament in which horsemen competed in teams) and not only provided extra-light lances so that the fragile prince would not be injured or fatigued but permitted the royal team to win against his own.[34]

On the day of the wedding, Alba, dressed in a fine mulberry-colored suit, served as best man. Unfortunately, he used this opportunity to create a major incident. Insisting that only he had the right to remain seated during the ceremony, he ordered all the benches removed save one, thus forcing the other nobles to stand and provoking a loud argument with the Duke of Medina Sidonia.[35] From their point of view it was poetic justice when the next day he organized a bullfight in which he was twice knocked from his horse and had to be bled.[36] It may have been on this occasion that a court lady wrote hopefully: "The Duke of Alba is going to kill a bull; or the bull him."[37]

In the midst of all this celebrating he did not neglect his military duties, but they were undemanding. It was not until the end of 1544 that he was once again involved, albeit marginally, in the larger issues of the day. The occasion was the unexpected triumph of imperial arms and the consequent Peace of Crépy. Though the Marqués del Vasto had achieved only a bloody stalemate in Piedmont, Charles had, with extraordinary daring, gathered an army at Metz, crossed the Marne, and marched on Paris itself.[38] The French were thrown into utter confusion, but Charles knew that he was badly overextended and accepted their offer to negotiate. As part of the subsequent agreement, the Duke of Orleans was to marry either the Infanta or the Archduchess Anna, with either the Netherlands or Milan as a dowry. The choice of which woman and which territory was left to Charles. French concessions were almost as grand, at least in aggregate.

The momentous decision between Milan and the Netherlands required lengthy consultation. Accordingly, the issue was laid before several bodies, including Philip's Council of State. In view of his later experience in the Netherlands, Alba's reaction is one of the great ironies of history. Cogently and with great force he called for the total abandonment of the Low Countries. His argument was rooted firmly in geopolitical realities. Milan, in his view, was the key to the empire. Without it, Charles could reach his other dominions only by sea, a perilous undertaking "if the king of England were not our friend." Milan controlled the Alpine passes and guarded the way to Naples and Sicily. If it were lost, Charles would be unable to protect the Netherlands, Genoa would be surrounded, and Naples would be dangerously exposed. The Netherlands, on the other hand, was virtually useless. In fact, it was a liability, for it was continually exposed to French attack and its population were far less loyal and obedient than they appeared. Alba acknowledged that the commercial value of the region was great, but with remarkable foresight doubted that this would compensate for the expense and difficulty of maintaining it.

Alba's opponents, led by Juan Pardo de Tavera, Archbishop of Toledo, were primarily concerned with what can only be called illusory short-term benefits. They believed that Charles's claim to Milan was relatively weak and wanted to avoid further embroilments so that they could concentrate on attacking the Moors of North Africa. Interestingly enough, Alba, the one-time crusader, now regarded adventures in Africa as chimerical. The lessons of Ghent and Algiers were bearing fruit.[39] This was not, apparently, the case with Charles who, preoccupied with the affairs of Germany, preferred to give away Milan. It was perhaps fortunate that Orleans died in September, 1545, making the question irrelevant.

The affairs of Germany were enough to preoccupy anyone. It had been apparent since Regensburg that the religious issue would not be settled by the agreement of theologians. Now it was equally obvious that politics would not succeed where reason had failed. Fearing the worst and aided by a generous subsidy from the pope, Charles prepared for war.

One of the first steps taken was to recall Alba from Spain and place him in charge of a commission that would lay the groundwork for the campaign. The period of obscurity was over. By January, 1546, Alba had arrived in Utrecht, where Charles received him into the Order of the Golden Fleece. The Fleece, or Toison d'Or, was the greatest honor the House of Burgundy could bestow, and Charles used it on this occasion to bind to his side such men as Cosimo de' Medici, Emmanuel Filiberto of Savoy, and the Duke of Bavaria. Not all of them were present, but of those who were, one should be mentioned in particular: Lamoral, Count of Egmont. Twenty-two years later, the solemn Spaniard who knelt with him at Utrecht would have him beheaded in the Grand' Place of Brussels.[40]

In April the court returned to Regensburg for yet another Diet. The attendant festivities resulted in the conception of Don Juan of Austria, but little else was accomplished. After many delays, the Council of Trent had convened in December, but the Protestants would not attend, and when the Catholics at Regensburg insisted on referring all issues to the council, the Diet collapsed. There were few open threats, but fighting broke out before the council was formally dissolved on July 24.

For all his efforts, Charles found himself unprepared to take the field in force. He had negotiated an accord with Ferdinand of Austria, Maurice of Saxony, and William of Bavaria, but neither the papal troups nor the German contingent under Buren had yet arrived. He was thus placed on the defensive from the start. By late August, however, the numbers had begun to equalize.

The conduct of the Danube campaign has long been the subject of controversy. Was it, as apologists claimed, the product of a deliberately Fabian strategy, or of sheer muddleheadedness and failure of nerve?[41] The correct answer, of course, is that it was neither. Like most campaigns it consisted of pragmatic responses to specific situations, though these responses were obviously developed within a broader conceptual framework. In retrospect it seems probable that the concept at work in 1546 was Alba's rather than the emperor's, for his entire career was an elaboration on themes first developed on the Danube, whereas Charles tended to revert to older methods whenever his general was absent.[42] This is also indicated by the apparent nature of the command relationship.[43] Charles was himself an experienced field officer, but on this occasion he seems to have left the tactical decisions almost entirely to Alba. The result was a bewildering series of maneuvers that bore little relationship to the emperor's normally headlong approach but appeared to derive from a new and disturbing vision of contemporary war.

The tactical developments of the early sixteenth century had been primarily defensive in character. A combination of pikes and arquebusiers could advance, but when it did so against a formation like itself, the casualties were usually appalling. This was primarily because when a formation was on the move there was no effective protection against shot, and when it was entrenched there was no way to break it. If the enemy occupied a prepared position, as Gonsalvo de Córdoba had done at Cerignola, the attacking force could be annihilated by firing at will. If they were not entrenched but roughly equal in numbers and training, neither side had an advantage and success depended almost entirely on who could absorb the higher casualty rate without flinching. To an intelligent captain this was clearly unacceptable. Soldiers were professionals, expensive to train and difficult to recruit. Considerations of humanity aside, it was folly to fight a battle if by so doing the victorious army was destroyed along with the losers.

As he advised the emperor on the coming struggle, Alba had before him a recent and terrible example of what could happen when an old-style battle was fought according to the latest methods. In 1544 at Cerisole in Piedmont, the Marqués del Vasto lost his reputation and half of an imperial army without achieving a decisive result.[44] It was to be the last battle of its type in the sixteenth century, and Alba was among the first to realize that such bloodbaths were inevitable until some new breakthrough in offensive tactics could

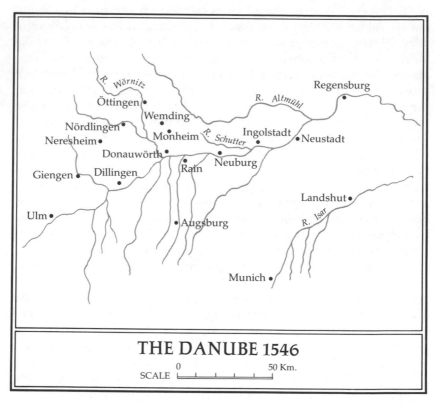

THE DANUBE 1546

SCALE 0 — 50 Km.

Map 2.

change the balance. For the rest of his career he would accept battle only if he possessed an overwhelming advantage. Under normal circumstances victory would have to be achieved by other means.

The campaign began with a Protestant initiative. Led by the experienced mercenary Schertlin von Bertenbach, they marched south to seize the Fern pass and disrupt the intended rendezvous between papal and imperial troops at Füssen. Schertlin was a first-class soldier and his troops were veteran *Landsknechten*. They had no difficulty in capturing the pass, but within days their own high command forced them to relinquish it. The Schmalkaldic League consisted of a number of towns and principalities whose only common interests were Lutheranism and fear of Charles. Anything Schertlin did could be overruled by the League's motley council of princes and town delegates, and in this case they began to fear that the cities of the upper Danube were dangerously exposed to imperial attack. This was preposterous, but they ordered Schertlin back to the river. Charles, who was outnumbered two to one, thought this presaged a frontal attack on Regensburg and withdrew to the comparative safety of Landshut on the Isar. There on August 13 his 15,000 papal auxiliaries under Alessandro Farnese arrived by way of Küfstein.[45]

Now that most of the imperial army had been allowed to gather without interference, the princes of the League dispatched a page and trumpeter with a declaration of war. Charles was scandalized by their presumption and refused to see them. Someone finally brought them to Alba, who observed that they were rebels and ought to be hanged on the spot, but as they were not responsible for the outrage he had decided to spare them.[46] Twenty years later in a similar situation he would not be so humane.

The imperial forces now consisted of approximately 30,000 infantry and 5,000 horse. The Count of Buren with 10,000 additional men, half of them cavalry, remained at Aachen watched by 15,000 Leaguers. With considerable skill he crossed the Rhine on the night of August 21 and avoided his pursuers by taking a roundabout route through Würzburg on the Main. Charles marched toward Ingolstadt to meet him: the 10,000 troops would be useful, and the money carried by Buren from the bankers of Antwerp was an even greater incentive.

Incredibly, the Protestants did nothing. The Elector John Frederick of Saxony wanted to stop Buren on the Main, but the Landgrave Philip of Hesse hoped to attack the emperor before reinforcements could arrive. While they bickered, Buren marched unhindered into Bavaria and Charles established himself a few miles east of Ingolstadt in a strong position chosen by Alba. Stirred to action, the Leaguers at last resolved to stop Buren. As he was expected to come toward Ingolstadt from the northwest, they slipped past their opponents and established themselves in a virtually impregnable position west of town. Thoroughly alarmed, Charles and Alba set off in pursuit.[47]

It was obvious from the first that little could be done. The army of the League had drawn itself up on what amounts to a peninsula formed by the Danube and the Schutter. As they faced northward, the Schutter and its marshes formed an almost impenetrable barrier on their front and right, while their left was guarded by a small hill on which they had placed their artillery. Behind them lay an extensive wood that stretched almost to the banks of the Danube, three kilometers away. The two armies were roughly equal in size, though the nearest imperial cannon still lay at Regensburg.[48]

As Alba immediately perceived, an attack on such a position would be both suicidal and unnecessary. In their eagerness to take advantage of the superb defensive qualities of the terrain, the Leaguers had allowed him to get between their forces and those of Buren. He had only to remain where he was to achieve the immediate strategic objective.

This fact soon dawned on the Protestants. On August 31, after a night made sleepless by an *encamisado* launched on their camp through the wood at the rear, they made an attempt to break out of the self-imposed trap. Moving their infantry forward in a half-moon formation, they began artillery bombardment of the imperial camp. It was a bloody business, in which Charles and Alba ran appalling risks to encourage the troops in the front lines,[49] but they had little choice. To pull back would have cost them their strategic advantage. After seven or eight nerve-wracking hours the guns fell silent, but there was to be no assault. At some point in the long afternoon the Landgrave appears to have realized that, as defenses, swamps and rivers are equally impassable from either side. To Schertlin's disgust, he ordered his men to pitch their tents for the night. Later that evening, it is said that Philip offered a toast "to those whom we have slain with our artillery," and Schertlin replied: "I do not know about those whom we have slain, but I know well that the live ones have not lost a foot of ground."[50] The great *Landsknecht* was right, but had he tried to cross the Schutter in the face of 35,000 imperial troops he would surely have lost his army.

That night Alba threw up earthworks, using his wagons as fascines. Dawn found the more exposed sectors of the imperial camp protected against enemy fire, and for the time being all bombardment ceased. After a day of skirmishing in which units of the League were badly mauled, Alba felt secure enough to try something new. On September 2, his men drew the attention of the Protestants by attacking a house they had fortified, while the *tercio* of Hungary and two regiments of Italians moved quietly upstream to Neuberg and annihilated the 3,000 Swiss who were guarding the League's artillery reserve.

By now it was obvious that there would be no battle, and all hope of intercepting Buren had vanished. To discourage curiosity the imperial camp was again bombarded on the morning of September 3, but by evening the Leaguers had gone. Stopping briefly at Neuberg, they fell back on Donauwörth, whence they could still control the approaches to Ulm and Augsburg.

Finally, on the fifteenth, Buren arrived at Ingolstadt. In most respects he was a fair representative of the Netherlands nobility. A good fighter but impetuous, outspoken, and possessed of a legendary thirst, he immediately fell foul of Alba, and as the campaign wore on became increasingly critical of his conduct of the war. For the time being, though, all went well. Neuberg was taken without a shot, and with only two companies of Germans, Alba personally seized the League's outpost at Rain.

From this point onward the course of the campaign is shrouded literally as well as figuratively in the mists of an inclement autumn. Moving on to Donauwörth, Alba reconnoitered the enemy camp and concluded that it could not be taken. The imperial army marched off to the northwest in heavy fog, camping on the banks of the Wörnitz between Wemding and Nördlingen. If their purpose was to draw out the Protestants by appearing to circle around and attack Ulm from the north, they succeeded. That night the Leaguers slipped out of Donauwörth completely unnoticed, thanks to the fog, and took up a position on the opposite side of the river.

It was Alba who discovered them, in the course of one of his predawn patrols. Like his *encamisados,* this habit of prowling about by night with a bodyguard of arquebusiers was fast becoming a personal military signature. It sometimes gained him startling advantages, but now nothing was achieved, for fog and darkness prevented him from discerning the layout of the enemy camp. As the murk lightened into an opaque dawn, the Prince of Salmona and his men exchanged shots with what may or may not have been an enemy patrol, and Buren was sent across the river with his cavalry. They skirmished briefly with someone but could see nothing and were soon recalled. That afternoon the Protestants withdrew as silently as they had come, and it is characteristic of the whole affair that for many hours no one seems to have known where they had gone.[51]

Concluding that their whereabouts were less important than the need to replenish his supplies, Charles marched back to Donauwörth, took it without incident, and drove straight for Ulm. The Leaguers shadowed him, marching on a parallel course but making no effort to interfere. On October 14, the two armies met at Giengen; again, no battle was fought. We know little of the circumstances or of the relative positions of the two forces, but the failure to engage caused much dissension in the imperial ranks. Buren in particular was incensed. He declared openly that, though he "was no Lutheran," he did not "believe in the emperor or duke either," and swore to remain drunk for fifteen days.[52] Alba and the emperor were themselves in bad moods,[53] but whether this *mala disposición* was due to a lost opportunity or to the grumbling of their troops is unknown. Not only had the soldiers been denied a battle, they were soon to be deprived of Ulm as well, for the garrison there was too strong to be overcome while the League was in the field.

The campaign was unraveling into a series of skirmishes fought against foragers in the mud and fog. On the eighteenth, Farnese and many of his Italians went home, but the army of the League was disintegrating faster than that of the emperor. Short of money and unable to fight a battle, by the end of the month the Landgrave was ready to give up. A week later Charles's brother Ferdinand and his ally Maurice of Saxony attacked the territories of the Elector, but for a time the League hung on. Finally, on November 27, the Protestants abandoned the field and marched north toward home. Because the messenger bringing news of the retreat became lost in the fog, there was no imperial pursuit. By the time Alba borrowed Buren's cavalry and took to the road it was too late. A victorious but dispirited army went to its quarters amid the worst snow and cold in years.[54]

The Danube campaign of 1546 was not a glorious passage of arms, but the conclusions drawn from it became the basis of Alba's military doctrine. The emperor had achieved undisputed control of South Germany without sacrificing his army, and though hotheads like Buren might have objected it is hard to see how a battle would have improved the situation. The secret of success had been the superior wealth and discipline that enabled the imperial army to outlast its enemies, and these were advantages that could be safely applied in other situations, since the forces of the Schmalkaldic League were in most respects typical of sixteenth-century armies. Taken individually, its soldiers and captains were brave and competent, but in aggregate they suffered from poor coordination between units and a divided high command. In battle they might be formidable. Faced with a war of attrition accompanied by night attacks and constant harassment, they were unable to formulate a concerted response and their army tended to disintegrate into its component parts. Morale deteriorated, and as the money ran out their defeat became inevitable.

In time these assumptions became commonplace and led to a tactical stalemate that paralyzed European warfare until the age of Gustavus Adolfus.[55] Ever since Clausewitz codified what he conceived to be the ingredients of Napoleonic success, military theorists have emphasized the offensive and reserved their highest praise for those who were able to shatter the sorts of restraints that fettered Alba and his contemporaries. Yet it is obvious that strategy and tactics are determined not only by military circumstances but by the political ends they are designed to serve. As the first of the great captains to absorb the lessons of Ceresole, Alba had little reason to go beyond them. He was, and remained throughout his career, the military agent of a great world empire. His aim was not to conquer new territories or to obliterate "national enemies" but to neutralize those who disturbed the shaky equilibrium of a heterogeneous and essentially conservative order. Duty and common sense alike demanded that this be done with as little risk as possible and with minimum expenditure of his soldiers' blood. Contemporary accusations of cowardice or excessive caution were meaningless, and were recognized as such by the wiser analysts of the day. His system, to be sure, had a terrible flaw, but it would not be made manifest for many years. In the meantime, the carping of such men as Buren interested him less than the barking of dogs. He never confused success with glory and would probably have found Napoleon incomprehensible.

Alba may therefore have been pleased with his autumn's work, but there was little time for self-congratulation. The Schmalkaldic snake was scotched, not killed, for amid the snows of January the elephantine Elector John Frederick of Saxony was waging a campaign of surprising effectiveness against the invaders of his ancestral lands. It was obvious that the imperial army would have to intervene, but first the south had to be secured and the troops restored to fighting trim. While Charles negotiated with the Duke of Württemburg, Alba, together with a prominent Frisian jurist, Viglius of Zwichem, arranged the capitulation of Augsburg, Frankfurt, and Ulm. He then turned his attention to his men, and by early March they were ready for the final act.

The speed and totality of the victory were astonishing. On or about April 10, the imperial forces joined those of Maurice and Ferdinand at Tischenreuth. The Elector knew of their movements but did nothing beyond crossing the Elbe in the hope of using it as a possible line of defense. He marched downstream along the eastern bank, arriving at the village of Mühlberg on the evening of April 23. Meanwhile, Charles and Alba had come up from the southwest and camped on the opposite side of the river.

The night was dark and foggy, but as usual Alba was abroad. Somehow in the predawn mists he located a peasant who showed him where the river could be forded and he either bribed or terrified the man into serving as his guide. The next morning, a Sunday, John Frederick attended services and breakfasted at leisure. Confident that the river would protect him, he remained blissfully ignorant of the preparations taking place in the imperial camp and did nothing to forestall them beyond placing a few armed men in boats to watch the opposite shore. By ten or eleven o'clock the Protestants resumed their march downstream, and the offensive began. Spanish arquebusiers, wading up to their armpits in the icy water, assailed the occupants of the boats, and when their return fire had ceased, other Spaniards swarmed out and boarded the boats like pirates, with knives clenched between their teeth. Charles thus acquired the means of transferring his baggage and supplies in perfect safety. Meanwhile, the bulk of the army made its way on foot or horseback through Alba's ford. It is a tribute to Alba's discipline and to the time-honored device of sending the cavalry across upstream to break the current that losses were minimal.

Once on the other side, the situation completely fulfilled Alba's requirements for a battle. The enemy was taken by surprise and his army was strung out in marching order along several kilometers of river bank. It was impossible to form them into any semblance of battle array in the time available, and in any case their artillery had been sent on ahead the day before. The Elector could do nothing but run for the heavily wooded hunting preserve at Lochau and pray that most of his men could take refuge there before the imperial vanguard cut them to pieces.

It was a vain hope. Mühlberg would be a hunt, not a battle, and Alba was still young enough to dress for the occasion. Clad in white armor and mounted on a white horse,[56] he led the assault and scoured the field for the Elector while his troops systematically massacred the fleeing Saxons. In this quest alone was he disappointed. When at length he appeared before the emperor, drenched, like his horse, in enemy blood, he learned that John Frederick had given his sword to a German knight, Thilo von Trotha.[57]

Years later, when his concern for personal glory had overcome gratitude, Charles tried to take credit for the victory,[58] but at the time he openly acknowledged it to be Alba's.[59] The duke was sent to escort John Frederick into his presence, and that night, it was the blackbeards of the *tercios* who guarded the prisoner.[60]

The battle of Mühlberg marked the turning point of the German wars but it was not quite sufficient to bring them to an end. Though Luther had died the year before, Wittenberg promised a sturdy defense, and Magdeburg, further downstream, appeared to offer an even greater obstacle to the emperor's designs. Only by threatening to execute their prince could Charles bring the Saxons to heel. The Wittenberg Capitulation of May 19 cost John Frederick his electorate and placed all Saxony under the rule of Maurice, but four days later, as Luther's city opened its gates, an imperial army under Erik von Calenburg was destroyed by the Protestants near Bremen. The loss itself was not irreparable, but there was reason to fear a conjunction between the victors and the Landgrave, whose intentions remained unknown.

It was perhaps fortunate for Charles that *der Grossmütige* had lost all taste for war. Beguiled by his devious son-in-law Maurice of Saxony, he entered into a series of negotiations that led straight to his downfall. It is possible that Maurice and his colleague, the Elector Joachim of Brandenburg, did not know what the emperor had in mind when they convinced Philip to come to him at Halle, but it is highly improbable. On the understanding that he would not be executed or imprisoned for life, Philip made his submission without receiving any sign of imperial acknowledgment. Alba then invited him to supper at his lodgings in the Moritzburg. After what must have been a very uncomfortable meal, he was taken to an adjoining room and arrested, as security for his good behavior.

Neither Charles nor Alba nor another rising statesman, Antoine Perrenot de Granvelle, Bishop of Arras, had any doubt that such a drastic step was necessary, nor was it precluded by the agreement signed two weeks earlier by the Landgrave. It was Maurice and Joachim who had convinced the gullible Hessian that *"ohne eivige Gefagnis"* (without eternal imprisonment) really meant *"ohne einige Gefagnis"* (without any imprisonment), and Alba and the bishop were appalled when the Electors kept them up until 2:00 A.M. protesting the detention of their fellow Lutheran. On balance these electoral ravings must be accounted political theater of the highest order, but Charles held fast. When he marched off to the Diet of Augsburg both rebel leaders were firmly in tow.[62]

The successful conclusion of the Schmalkaldic Wars was a milestone in Alba's career. He had shown himself to be one of the great captains of the age, developing in the process a conception of warfare that was to last a lifetime. Whatever doubts may have possessed Charles in 1543 had evaporated by 1547. Henceforth the saturnine Castilian would be trusted not only on the battlefield but with the most delicate political maneuvers. With Arras, he would be one of the great powers of the imperial court as Charles's reign moved uncertainly to its close.

IV

THE CAUDILLO

C harles V, though no genius, was a brave, conscientious, fundamentally decent man whose responsibilities were overwhelming. For thirty years he had shouldered them with dignity and common sense, but their intractability had taken its toll. At forty-eight he was old beyond his years, bone-weary and tortured by gout. As he presided over the endless wranglings of yet another Diet, he knew he could no longer delay settlement of his affairs.

His primary concern was the disposition of his vast inheritance. He had long since agreed to divide it, permitting his brother Ferdinand to assume the imperial title and possession of the Habsburg lands in Germany. Philip of Spain was to inherit the rest, including the Netherlands and Italy. Charles now began a series of fruitless negotiations aimed at returning the empire to Philip when Ferdinand died, but he was at the same time realistically concerned about his son's political development. Philip was now twenty years of age, a small, fair, handsome man with a retiring disposition and an outlook that had become wholly Spanish. It was time to introduce him to his subjects in the rich but turbulent Low Countries.

To prepare the ground for this visit, Charles decided upon two courses of action that were expected to be unpopular in Spain. One of them was to appoint his nephew Maximilian as regent in Philip's absence. Maximilian was the son of Ferdinand, King of the Romans, the man whose inheritance Charles was at that moment trying to divert. He was also as Austrian as Philip was Castilian, and therefore, in Spanish eyes, a foreigner. It is evident that the regency was intended as a sop,[1] but the possible reaction of this clever, enigmatic young man was as much an open question as was how he would be received by the Spaniards.

The other decision involved an aspect of the great cultural gap that separated Spain from the Low Countries. The dukes of Burgundy had accustomed their subjects to a degree of magnificence and ostentation in court ritual that remained the wonder of Europe until the days of Louis XIV, while Castile's origins as a frontier society were reflected in the simple, straightforward customs of its court. As King of Castile, Philip would have had to content himself with a relatively small handful of servants, a minimum of ritual, and a high nobility that wore hats in his presence. As Duke of Burgundy and Count of Flanders he would be the center of a rich series of observances based ultimately on the Mass and so elaborate that it required four courtiers to bring him a glass of wine.[2] Charles knew from long experience that his Netherlandish subjects would be appalled at the unceremonious functioning of his son's household and would scorn its simple dignity as mean-spirited and unworthy of respect. He therefore resolved to accomplish something far more serious than he could have imagined it to be: the reorganization of the Spanish court along Burgundian lines.

In January, 1548, Charles drafted his orders, together with yet another lengthy *Instruction,* and sent them off to Spain with Alba as his chosen messenger and deputy. The duke was not only to smooth the way for Maximilian but, as the new *mayordomo mayor,* to assume full responsibility for reorganizing the court.

The choice of Alba was in some ways obvious. His interest in protocol has already been noted. Beyond that, his organizational abilities were well known, his role at Mühlberg had earned him great prestige and, above all, he was indisputably Castilian. The grandees would resent any proposed change in their ancient customs but at least they could not accuse him of being personally a slave to foreign fashions.

In fact, this man who always wore his hat in the presence of kings[3] and who gave even his horses pointedly Castilian names[3] cannot have looked upon his assignment with relish.[4] At the same time he must have been aware that it opened up transcendent vistas of personal power. The *mayordomo mayor* controlled not only the rituals and discipline of the court but also its provisioning and many of its appointments.[5] With the augmentation of personnel required by the new ceremonial, his rights of patronage would be second only to those of the Crown. The possibilities inherent in this probably did not occur to him at first, nor would he be able to take full advantage of them in the short run, but in the years that followed it became obvious that Charles had created exactly the sort of monster against which he had warned his son in 1543: a nobleman with a power base that extended beyond his estates, and hence with a faction, or *banda*, of his own.

The immediate priority, though, was to get the scheme accepted. At Alcalá Alba caught up with Philip, who was returning from the Aragonese Cortes at Monzón. The Cortes of Castile was to be held at Valladolid, and as the two traveled together they discussed the best means of stifling what was sure to be vigorous opposition.[6] The regency of Maximilian and reform of the court lay well within the royal prerogative, but it was essential to avoid an unseemly public dispute. Accordingly, Philip decided to exclude the noble and ecclesiastical estates, convening only the representatives of the towns whose election was subject to interference by the royal *corregidores*. Even so, the meeting was strained. The Cortes took strong exception to Philip's intended departure and made no secret of its distaste for Flemish innovations. The nobles, if anything more obstreperous for having been excluded, vented their spleen on Alba, who was the only target of their rank within reach. Some even went so far as to ask him what his reward had been for so low a service. His reply, that it was not his idea but the emperor's and that he was merely transmitting the latter's wishes, met with ill-concealed disdain, and Ossorio tells us that he replied with "downcast eyes."[7]

All in all it was a wretched experience, but the results were preordained. By August 15 the court had been reorganized and Alba had in his possession the velvet-covered scissors-chair of the *mayordomo* and the keys to the palace. To Philip's apparent surprise, Maximilian was greeted with civility, and by October 1 the royal party was on its way.

Their route lay through Barcelona and from there by galley to Genoa. Before they could reach the ships tragedy struck. At Monteagudo, Alba learned that his eldest son, Don García, had died at Alba de Tormes of an unspecified malady. He had been eighteen years old. With a fortitude greatly admired by his contemporaries, Alba refused to permit mourning lest it delay the expedition, and went about his duties with no visible change in composure.[8] The episode added to the legend of imperturbability and iron character that was growing up around him, but inwardly it must have been a terrible blow. The chronicler Santa Cruz provides a clue when he says: "The death was taken badly by the house of Alba because it was the first knock given by fortune at the door of the duke."[9]

The remainder of the journey need not be chronicled in detail, though it consumed two and a half years and probably did everyone more harm than good. In an effort to introduce Philip to his future subjects, an endless series of tournaments, feasts, and triumphal entries had been arranged, but Philip hated travel, had no head for alcohol, and tended to faint at tournaments. The Netherlanders found him haughty and unimpressive, and he in turn found them drunken and vulgar.[10]

Alba, as majordomo, presided over many of these occasions, but what pleasure, if any, he derived from them is unrecorded. As always when he was at court, his correspondence dwindled to nothing, and it was scarcely a situation in which to vent his opinions in the presence of gossips. Much of this socializing was undoubtedly burdensome to a man who was even more dour and ascetic than his prince, but during those hectic months he laid the groundwork both for his relationship with Philip and for his future role as one of the great powers in Spanish politics.

In the Habsburg monarchy, absolutist in fact as well as theory, a career depended largely on the favor of the prince. It is therefore ironic that the long partnership between Alba and Philip II was neither smooth nor especially cordial. Alba had been something of a household figure for as long as Philip could remember. Like all the grandees he was officially referred to as *primo* or cousin, but behind his back the court called him *el tio*, "The Uncle."[11] This has long been an appellation for a political boss or *patrón*, but Alba's own conception of his role was truly avuncular. Twenty years older than Philip, he saw himself as the prince's guide. If the prince often accepted him as such, it was because Philip associated Alba in his own mind with the emperor. That he should have done so is not surprising. Alba had in fact been closer to Charles than any of Philip's other counselors, and when Charles had sent instructions to his son in 1548 it was Alba who brought them and explained their contents. In the trying and uncertain days that followed, Philip was inevitably forced to rely on Alba not only for guidance but for clues to the thinking of his revered father.

This almost tutorial situation formed the basis of their relationship for many years, though Philip found Alba's attitude increasingly annoying and presumptuous. He would often overrule or even rebuke his counselor,[12] but he rarely ignored him, for the duke was a true repository of the paternal verities. Moreover, his personal qualities tended to reinforce his message. A pasquinade posted in Valladolid at the Cortes of 1548 referred to him as "Duke Gravity."[13] Tall, somber, and ascetic, his physical presence was almost overpowering. Above all, he possessed the gift of absolute certainty. The young prince developed into a man of great thoroughness and considerable insight, but his habits of mind remained as elaborate and convoluted as his famous handwriting. Indecisiveness burdened him until his death, but in Alba he had an advisor who was rarely in doubt about anything, or so it appeared. Philip did not enjoy his company and may actually have disliked him, but he was indispensable not only for his military talents but for his ability to articulate Philip's own values in situations where they were likely to be mislaid. It was not exactly favor, but for all practical purposes it was nearly as good.

This peculiar and often strained association was one of the two pillars on which Alba's power rested. The other was that, in spite of many provocations, Philip never really lost his trust in the duke's military judgment or in the blunt honesty of his religious convictions. Even at the end of his career, when his advice on matters of state was increasingly ignored, his influence over military and ecclesiastical appointments remained immense. It is almost shocking that as late as 1581 Alba and his wife were able to reverse the appointment of the Dominican Provincial of Castile after it had been announced, substituting a candidate of their own.[14]

The immediate vehicle for the exercise of this power was the majordomo's office. Aside from a salary of more than 6,000 ducats per year, it gave Alba almost unparalleled access to the prince, a privilege he was sometimes inclined to abuse. He accompanied Philip to chapel and to all official functions, governed all matters of precedence, and arranged the audiences of ambassadors. These duties alone made him worthy of cultivation, but there were others. The court was a state-within-a-state that possessed laws and regulations of its own. On Mondays and Fridays the majordomo held judicial proceedings to resolve disputes and judge offenders, and the range of his discretionary powers, though subject to royal approval, was very broad.[15] Philip II was not a *roi fainéant* and took a lively interest in his immediate surroundings, but it was obvious to everyone that the duke was well placed to aid his friends and harass his enemies.

This capacity was further increased by his influence over court appointments. Under the new Burgundian system there were more than 1,500 of these, some remunerative and some purely honorary but all offering their incumbents access to royal favor. The right of appointment was Philip's, but as Alba was head of the household his recommendations on many of them inevitably carried great weight.

The duke was now the nexus of three key institutions: the court, the army, and the Church. It is little wonder that his correspondence contains a virtual avalanche of requests, recommendations, and letters of thanks, or that he quickly assumed a dominant position in Philip's government. No matter how selective or conscientious Philip might be in the area of appointments, the number of those who felt obliged to the duke grew geometrically over the years, as did the number of those who thought they had something to gain from him in the future. This rapid expansion of his clientage made him a true *caudillo*, a soldier with a large political following, but it did not necessarily constitute a danger to the state. For one thing, his ability to satisfy the demands of his clients still depended entirely on the continued favor of the king. For another, he had competition.

Ruy Gómez de Silva was an unlikely opponent for so formidable a character as the duke. A Portuguese, he had come to Spain as a page in the household of the empress but was soon transferred to that of her young son. Eleven years older than the prince, he was at first his playmate and then his confidant. As he grew to manhood, Philip increasingly appreciated his smooth, ingratiating manner[16] and absolute loyalty. There were no surprises here, no bitter complaints or vehement calls to duty, no patronizing references to what the emperor might do in similar circumstances—just a quiet, reassuring, intelligent young man who was above all an undemanding companion. If Philip knew the other Ruy Gómez, the ambitious, hard-eyed author of ruthless intrigues, he gave no sign. The former page had a positive genius for self-effacement and a delicate sense of how far he could go without embarrassing his master. The perfect favorite, he was a natural choice for *camerero mayor* (chamberlain).[17]

This office carried little authority but involved him in almost constant attendance upon the prince. He awakened him in the morning, put him to bed at night, and for twenty-five years was closer to him than any other courtier. An untitled foreigner, he had not, like Alba, been born with a host of clients nor did he enjoy wide connections among the nobility of Castile, but his close association with the prince quickly enabled him to acquire both. Within months of his appointment, many of those who sought the royal ear had attached themselves to his banner, and by the 1550s his following equaled that of Alba.

The arrival of Ruy Gómez as a major power was signaled by his marriage in 1552 to Doña Ana de Mendoza y de la Cerda, the only child of the Count of Melito. The house of Mendoza to which she belonged was comparable in prestige to the Toledos and far surpassed them in sheer weight of numbers. Though in aggregate their titles and revenues were impressive, the need to provide for their numerous progeny was even greater, and in 1548 they were poorly represented at the higher levels of court. It is hardly surprising that in the virtually landless favorite they saw the kind of opportunity that comes but once in a generation, and courted him with almost indecent haste.[18] The marriage was not consummated until 1556, for Doña Ana was only twelve on her wedding day—though she became a beautiful and formidable woman, her original role was to provide the favorite with an inheritance while binding him forever to the interests of some of Spain's greatest families.

The result was the eventual formation of the two great factions or *bandas* that dominated court politics until the scandals of 1579–1580. On the one side were Alba and the Toledos, including the duchess's brother Antonio, the Prior of León. Antonio was a valuable ally. Charming and unobtrusive, he served as grand equerry in the new court and later as a member of the Councils of State and War.[19] Then there were Alba's uncles. The most famous of them, Don Pedro de Toledo, the "iron viceroy" of Naples, died in 1553, but his son, García, Marqués of Villafranca, remained a staunch ally in spite of Alba's tendency to order him around.[20] This branch of the family had augmented its influence by intermarriage with the Italian nobility. García was married to Victoria Colonna, daughter and namesake of the famous intellectual, while Eleanora, his sister, married Cosimo de' Medici, ruler of Florence. At Rome, the family was well represented by another of Alba's uncles, Juan Alvarez de Toledo, Cardinal-Bishop of Santiago. After his death he was replaced by a more distant but equally loyal relative, Cardinal Francisco Pacheco Osorio de Toledo. Other members of the faction included the Enríquez de Guzmán family and, eventually, two men who were to become important figures in their own right: Francisco de Zapata, first Count of Barajas, and the wily Don Diego Cabrera de Bobadilla, third Count of Chinchón.

The *banda* headed by Ruy Gómez was larger, though it contained fewer men of conspicuous talent. Its core was the Mendoza family, but the degree of their participation varied. Most active was Doña Ana's father, who became Prince of Melito and Duke of Francavilla in the course of his long career as Viceroy of Aragon and Cataluña. The scholar-ambassador Diego Hurtado de Mendoza, his brother, the Marqués of Mondéjar, and the senior member of the clan, the Duke of Infantado, were also involved at one time or another in the squabbles of the court, and were eventually joined by the Duke of Medinaceli, the Duke of Béjar, and the Count of Feria.

It would be wrong to assume that these factions were in any sense fixed. Not only did their personnel change over the years, but individual members would occasionally support the opposition on a specific issue. Moreover, there were always courtiers like the influential Juan Manrique de Lara who followed their conscience or private interest as circumstances dictated. The cement that held them together was a curious amalgam of elements that defies facile generalization. Kinship ties were obviously important but not wholly determinative. Chinchón was distantly related to Doña Ana, and Bernardino de Mendoza, master of the royal galleys and brother of the Marqués de Mondéjar, was Alba's friend. His son (of the same name) served under the duke, eulogized him in his *Commentarios de los Paises Bajos*, and carried his policies into the next generation as ambassador to France and paymaster of the French Catholic League.[21]

It is equally incorrect to exaggerate the ideological differences between the two camps. Both J. H. Elliott and Gregorio Marañón have suggested that Alba's faction was Castilian and militant, while that of Ruy Gómez was imperial and conciliatory, though as both authors admit, Alba was militant on the Netherlands but conciliatory toward England.[22] Ruy Gómez was precisely the opposite. Elsewhere there is little to indicate that Mendoza viceroys were more respectful of local privilege than their Toledo counterparts, and it was Alba, after all, who introduced Burgundian ceremonial to the Spanish court. The confusion may be due in part to Marañón's belief that there was an historical basis for the rivalry, but his assertion that the house of Toledo had taken upon itself the *Comunero* sympathies of the Zapata is surely false.[23] As he himself admitted, no Toledo was actually involved in the *Comunero* rebellion, and Alba's association with Francisco de Zapata, first Count of Barajas, dates from the 1570s. As far as the Mendozas are concerned, the first decades of the century saw them, almost alone among the great nobles, as allies of the Toledos in their struggle to further the claims of King Ferdinand.[24]

More subtle differences may have played a part. The Mendozas had a family tradition of attachment to the New Learning that went far deeper and lasted longer than the brief flirtation of the Toledos. Moreover, as *adelantados* (governors) of Granada, the Mondéjar branch had advocated a measure of toleration for the Moriscos, and the first Marqués had even adopted some superficially Moorish tastes.[25] They were not heretics or even liberals, whatever that may have meant in the context of Philip's court, but by comparison with the Toledos there was always a touch of intellectual daring about them, a faint but unmistakable odor of brimstone and the pit.

The truth of the matter is that none of this was as important as the personal equation. Alba and Ruy Gómez were antithetical personalities, and though they managed, sometimes for weeks on end, to coexist in reasonable civility, the antagonism between them was deep and visceral. If a courtier got along with one, he would be unlikely to have much use for the other. In the end, their supporters were drawn by the same mixture of interest, kinship ties, and personal chemistry that has determined the makeup of political factions from sixteenth-century Spain to eighteenth-century England or modern Chicago, and their stance on any given issue was determined more by rivalries inherent in the situation than by ideological conviction.

What made this factionalism so virulent was the fact that it was not limited to the aristocrats. Parallel to these groups, though related to them, was a similar division among the secretaries. Under the conciliar system inherited by Philip II, much of the burden of day-to-day administration was handled by the royal secretaries and the secretaries of the various councils. These men not only funneled information and recommendations to the appropriate advisory bodies but summarized their deliberations and passed them on to the king. Closely related to them by training and background were the bureaucrats who administered the *contaduría* and *hacienda* and, by extension, the pay and logistics of the armed forces.[26] By the 1550s, if not earlier, they too had become divided into bitterly opposing factions, one of which was attached to Alba, the other to Ruy Gómez.

The root of this division lay in the method by which secretaries were recruited, trained, and placed in the royal administration. Generally speaking, a young man would be taken in by a powerful secretary and educated through a kind of informal apprenticeship. His responsibilities and access to useful information would be increased as his political skills developed, and ultimately he would be recommended for a place of his own. The more influential secretaries were thus patrons in their own right, with an implicit responsibility to support protégés who would then extend their master's influence in ever-widening circles throughout the government. As the great courtiers disposed of lucrative posts in their own households and enjoyed considerable influence over appointments in general, the success of a secretarial "school" depended at least in part on maintaining close relations with them.

Both major schools traced their ancestry to Francisco de los Cobos. Cobos and the duke had been close friends since the 1530s, when the secretary was at the peak of his extraordinary career and Alba was still largely an unknown quantity. The two men came from separate worlds and were very different in temperament, yet the one-time village boy from Úbeda and the great magnate were far closer friends than mere interest would dictate. When Cobos died in 1545 it was Alba who served as his executor and the protector of his widow against the numerous claims laid to his estate.[27]

Cobos was succeeded by his nephew, Juan Vázquez de Molina, who had three protégés of his own. One, Gonzalo Pérez, had been secretary to the humanist Alonso de Valdés.[28] The other two, Alonso de Idiáquez and Francisco de Eraso, were apparently created *ex nihilo*.[29] All three founded "schools" of their own, though the successors of Idiáquez need not concern us here. He was maneuvered out of the limelight by Gonzalo Pérez, and it was not until the collapse of the factions in 1579 that his son Juan emerged as a major power.[30]

Pérez, on the other hand, inherited nearly all of Cobos's supporters in Spain. Learned, touchy, and remarkably vindictive,[31] he nevertheless maintained close ties with Alba until a year or two before his death in 1566. Among his friends and accomplices was Gabriel de Zayas, another disciple of Cobos and future Secretary of State, who would become Alba's eyes and ears at court during his long years away.[32] His loyalty to the duke was unconditional. As Zayas told Alba on one occasion, "I am a man who must be grateful to Your Excellency until the Sepulchre, and to value the work of Your Excellency is my greatest renown."[33] It was not mere flattery. Other Alba partisans descended professionally from Pérez and Zayas were Juan de Albornoz and Esteban de Ibarra, the private secretaries of Alba and his son during their years in the Low Countries. Ibarra was in turn the younger brother of Francisco, another Cobos product whose genius for logistics made him truly indispensable and the man who more than anyone else helped Alba achieve his victories. There were others, but these are the best known.

Inevitably, the triumph of Pérez aroused the jealousy of Eraso, who had been left behind in Brussels as secretary to the emperor. Though he did not at first extend his considerable malice to Alba his hatred for Pérez was intense, and in the late forties he began to assemble a network of his own.[34] Among its leading alumni were Diego de Espinosa, the humble canon of Seville who rose to become president of the Council of Castile, Cardinal-Bishop of Sigüenza, and inquisitor-general, and the even more humble Mateo Vázquez de Leca, who became Philip's personal secretary and closest confidant in the later years of his reign.[35] Eraso attached himself to Ruy Gómez in 1555 and remained his chief ally until his disgrace ten years later. His position was then assumed by Antonio Pérez. Pérez was the son of Gonzalo, but for reasons that will become obvious he turned against Alba in 1566 and ultimately succeeded Ruy Gómez as the king's favorite. At this point Mateo Vázquez struck out on a course of his own that would remain independent of either faction until he triumphed over both in 1579. All this is admittedly confusing, but it serves as a reminder that, as in the case of the nobles, factional lines could be redrawn.

This group was probably less cohesive than the political heirs of Gonzalo Pérez but it was no less powerful. In addition to their numerous secretarial and conciliar offices they possessed great influence in the *contaduría mayor*, where many of the lesser fry took refuge in the 1550s and 1560s. The primary architects of this infiltration were Eraso and Ruy Gómez, who, improbably enough, became *contador mayor* (chief accountant) in 1556. As the *contaduría* was responsible for all disbursements, including those to viceroys and military commanders in the field, their efforts eventually made it possible to delay or even deny payment in situations where this kind of obstruction would create maximum embarrassment for their enemies. It is hard to believe that factional rivalry would be permitted to undermine campaigns launched by the king, but Alba was victimized in this way at least twice: in Italy in 1555–1556, and later in the Netherlands.

That this should be so indicates the importance of these alignments. For three decades they influenced Spanish politics—sometimes for better, sometimes for worse, but they were always a factor that must be taken into consideration whenever the policies of these years are examined. This is not to say that they were all-pervasive. Just as there were unaligned nobles there were unaligned bureaucrats, or perhaps more accurately, those whose allegiance lay with other, less powerful groups; but when all qualifications have been entered into the record it was the rivalry between Alba and Ruy Gómez that most influenced decisions at the highest level and attracted the bemused attention of foreigners. It was not a conflict of ideologies but of men and interests, rooted ultimately in the structure of Spanish society itself and extending to remarkably humble corners of the great estates from which its strength was drawn. If it led to endless conflict and intrigue, it also assured the king that he would always have at least two divergent opinions on which to base his acts. In an absolute monarchy, even such cold comfort as this cannot be rejected out-of-hand.

The factions, of course, did not hatch full-grown from the reorganization of the court but developed organically from it. They appear to have been mere embryos during the long progress through the Low Countries, but then the internal workings of Philip's entourage have been obscured by contemporary descriptions of clothing, ritual, and cheerless official gluttony. When the factions did come to the attention of foreign observers, in 1555, they were already quite mature, and there are indications of their influence at a much earlier date.

The most extraordinary example is the maneuvering that followed hard upon the death of Pope Paul III. The papal election of 1550 was a nine weeks' ordeal orchestrated largely by Cosimo de' Medici and his Toledo relatives in the face of dogged interference by Diego Hurtado de Mendoza, the imperial ambassador at Rome. When the conclave opened on November 29, 1549, the most likely candidate was Jacopo Salviati, Cardinal of Florence. Salviati was Mendoza's friend and Cosimo's maternal uncle, but Cosimo secretly hated him for his earlier involvement with the Florentine exiles. Accordingly he, Alba, and Pedro de Toledo poisoned the emperor's mind against Salviati while appearing to support him in public. Their purpose was ultimately to advance the candidacy of Alba's uncle, then Cardinal of Burgos, and they were at last able to secure a direct order from Charles telling Mendoza to work against the Florentine. Mendoza apparently did so with reluctance, but though Salviati fell short, Burgos did no better, and Alba openly accused the ambassador of undermining his cause out of personal interest. The idea of a Toledo pope was improbable from the start, but Mendoza had clearly preferred other candidates even as a second choice, and his conduct created much bad blood. The intrigue as a whole was far more elaborate than this brief summary indicates,[37] but whether it grew out of factional enmity or merely contributed to it remains an open question. In the end, the choice fell on Cardinal Del Monte. He was a compromise candidate very much in the pocket of Cosimo de' Medici, though not of the Toledos, and one wonders if Alba's problems were perhaps greater than he knew.

The incident was not forgotten. Alba's memory was long, and he had never liked Mendoza. The ambassador had a flippant, abrasive tongue, and his delight in teasing the duke was insupportable.[38] The Toledos worked long to undermine him, but the emperor, who must have known what was happening, appears not to have taken their accusations seriously after his first annoyance passed.[39] Alba, in any case, was soon busy with other things.

His ceremonial duties were time-consuming. In addition, the emperor was present throughout the tour and frequently demanded his counsel as he wrestled with the problem of succession and the endless difficulties created by the German Protestants. Finally, in the summer of 1550, the entire court decamped for Augsburg and yet another Diet characterized by wrangling, abuse, and intense political maneuvering. It was not until May 26, 1551, that a weary Prince Philip was allowed to go home. Alba went with him.

The long-awaited respite was destined to be brief.[40] While Alba relaxed on his estates, the situation in Germany deteriorated rapidly, and by the summer of 1552 it had become necessary to rescue the emperor from the worst predicament of his long career. The cause was, as always, complex. At Augsburg, Charles had advanced a plan to elect Philip King of the Romans after Ferdinand ascended the imperial throne. This would virtually have excluded Ferdinand's son Maximilian, though he was intended to succeed Philip in the unlikely event that he should survive him. The agreement had been wrung from Ferdinand under extreme duress, and Maximilian was understandably furious both with the emperor and with his father. The Electors were appalled, fearing the divisive effect of Philip's candidacy. His intense piety and his dislike for things German were already well known.

To make matters worse, the Council of Trent reconvened on May 1, 1551, and immediately began to issue decrees on communion, extreme unction, and confession that made all further compromise with the Protestants impossible. The Augsburg Interim of 1548 had been an attempt by Charles to paper over religious differences until they could be formally resolved by a council. Men had treated it as a joke but had done nothing as long as hope remained. Now that hope was gone, the princes saw before them the grim prospect of a fanatical and increasingly Spanish emperor leagued with a newly militant Church. They began to lay dark plans.

The core of the opposition was formed by Hans of Küstrin, Albert of Prussia, and John Albert of Mecklenburg. They soon gathered to their banner the devious but militarily powerful Maurice of Saxony, Albert Alcibiades of Brandenburg-Kulmbach, and the Hessians, and finished their work by concluding an alliance with the King of France. In April, 1552, they marched on Charles, who lay woolgathering at Innsbruck.[41]

The situation was perilous in the extreme. Charles had only a skeleton force at his disposal and could neither fight nor flee to the Netherlands, as the French had blocked the way. At the last moment Maurice offered to negotiate, but it soon became obvious that Charles would make no significant concessions, and two weeks later the remaining imperial forces were surrounded and captured in the Ehrenberg gorges. Now totally defenseless, Charles fled across the Brenner to Villach, an otherwise unprepossessing place that offered a choice of escape routes into Italy or Styria.[42]

Once again negotiations were resumed, but Charles now played for time. Though inconveniently distributed, his resources were immeasurably greater than those of the princes, and calls for assistance went out far and wide. Among those summoned was Alba, who came from Spain in great haste with 7,000 troops.[43] Ossorio claims that he had raised them largely at his own expense, pawning his household goods and redeeming a *censo* worth 8,000 ducats,[44] but there is reason to doubt this unusual generosity. If Ruy Gómez can be trusted, Alba had returned to his estates in high dudgeon, though "the prince had shown him favor enough."[45] On June 30, Philip wrote to his father recommending that the duke be given what he asks "so as not to have from him more importunities than I have already had, as these have been quite sufficient."[46] Apparently he was once again resentful over what he considered niggardly or disrespectful treatment and had been making exalted demands, but this was not at all incompatible with the sacrifices mentioned by his biographer. Alba was perfectly capable of pawning his furniture in such a dispute, both because he was as loyal as he claimed and because such an act would heap coals of shame on the heads of his ungrateful masters.

Unfortunately, his quick response did not bring him to a second battle with the Protestants. Maurice of Saxony may have been eccen-

tric but he was not a fool. He knew that the emperor was now beyond his reach and that it was only a matter of time before vast
powers were mustered on his behalf. Once again it was time to negotiate. After the usual second thoughts on both sides, an agreement
was reached several days before Alba and his hastily gathered troops
could arrive. Typically, Maurice did not even wait for the emperor's
signature. After signing the treaty himself on August 2, he became
annoyed with the protests of his troops, burned his own camp, and
went off to do battle with the Turks.[47]

The crisis was over, but there was still much to be done, for having escaped from one peril Charles immediately decided to cast himself into another. In the process of blocking the route to the
Netherlands, the Constable Anne de Montmorency had seized Metz
in the name of Henry II. The city, though scrupulously neutral in
normal times, was technically part of the empire and was of great
strategic and moral importance to Charles V. He resolved to win it
at once or die in the attempt.[48] Historians such as Brandi and Van
Durme blame Alba for encouraging him in this folly, but the Spanish
authorities argue that he did not in fact do so.[49] Unless one assumes
that Alba's military sense had deserted him entirely, the latter are
probably correct. The campaigning season was nearly over, and winter in those regions is notoriously harsh. Moreover, the Duke of
Guise was now governor and had used the summer to convert the
placid medieval town into a great modern fortress.

Alba knew all this, but his most immediate concern was the Margrave Albert Alcibiades of Brandenburg-Kulmbach. It is a measure
of his apprehension that he was willing to deal with such a creature
at all, much less conclude an alliance with him on behalf of the emperor, but he felt that the situation was too precarious to admit niceties of conscience.[50] Albert Alcibiades had not joined in the
agreement of August 2, but had spent much of the summer harrying
the lands of the Archbishop of Trier. He was a violent Protestant,
alcoholic and a bankrupt, who, like Christian of Brunswick in the
Thirty Years' War, lived by committing atrocities and threatening
worse in the hope that towns would pay him to stay away.[51] Now
he was somewhere in the vicinity of Metz with 15,000 men, a putative
ally of the French and as dangerous and unpredictable as a rabid dog.

Alba, who had gone before the emperor, made contact with the
Margrave during the first week of October.[52] With consummate skill
Alba played upon his greed and dissatisfaction with the French, dan-
gling before him the prospect of an imperial agreement that would

confirm his extortionate agreements of the preceding year. This was unconscionable, and it may even be that Alba and his master were negotiating in bad faith,[53] but their ploy worked. By the time Alba appeared before the walls of Metz on October 19, Albert Alcibiades was firmly in his pocket. To guard against surprises, a spy was placed in his camp,[54] but there was little need for concern. The Margrave was not so steeped in drink that he had forgotten the value of money.

It was now possible to concentrate on the siege. Alba had at his disposal about 4,000 infantry, an equal number of horse, and nine pieces of artillery.[55] Neither the emperor nor Albert Alcibiades had yet arrived, but knowing that his deadliest enemy was the approaching winter Alba opened fire on October 31 against the quarter just north of the Porte des Allemands. The result seemed to displease him and on November 2 he moved his batteries to a point south of the city between the Seille and the Moselle. The two rivers offered him better protection against sorties, and it may be that he thought that the walls in this section were weaker. On November 10 he began a sustained bombardment of the Pont des Mores. As Alba had left a party of Netherlanders at his original camp on the north, the city was now beset from three sides. On the twentieth, the emperor arrived, having been detained by ill health. His presence raised morale and brought the imperial forces to a total of nearly 50,000 men. Alba greeted him with three great salvos, but refused to waste ammunition: the ceremony was carried out with live rounds directed at the city walls.

At first the emperor's arrival seemed to bring results, but all was illusory. Abandoning his earlier target, Alba concentrated on the wall running westward from the Porte de Champenoise to the Tour d'Enfer at the southwest corner of the city. On November 24, an incredible 1,448 rounds collapsed the corner bulwark of the tower, and on the twenty-eighth a breach nearly twenty feet in width was finally opened. As the dust settled, the dismayed imperialists saw that behind it lay a newly constructed wall manned by a host of grinning Frenchmen. The Duke of Guise had ample reason to congratulate himself.

In the days to come, the breach was widened, but the inner walls made an assault impossible. It had been cold for weeks, but now winter came in earnest. By mid-December the snow was so deep that it impeded movement in the trenches, and the Italian and Spanish troops, many of whom were unequipped for the rigors of a northern winter, suffered horribly. Sickness set in and by Christmas even the Germans were beginning to die. Albert Alcibiades had lost half his men, and it was evident that a major disaster was in the making. It is perhaps inevitable that in the face of this inexorable decline the high command began to disintegrate. Hans of Küstrin, the chief author of the recent rebellion, had turned against his French allies, but with magnificent insolence now refused to fight under Alba's orders. It was, he thought, beneath his dignity as a prince of the empire. The Netherlanders too were unhappy, and Alba appears to have made few concessions to their feelings. Charles loyally backed his general, but the bickering only increased. On New Year's day, after a last futile attempt at mining, the emperor ordered a withdrawal and, exhausted in body and spirit, made his way to Brussels.[56] Many years later the Bishop of Arras—by then Cardinal Granvelle—would say that he could still feel the cold of Metz in his bones.

The failure of the siege did Alba's reputation little good. The Netherlanders and Germans long continued to nurse their wounded egos. The Venetian ambassador said that Charles had no good generals and that Alba "lacked the talents of a great captain."[57] A verse chronicle by one Jean Bauchert, recorder of the village of Plappeville, was openly contemptuous: "L'autre tiers fut menez par un homme ygnorant, / Duc D'Albe il s'appeloit, estant lieutenant."[58] Among professionals and those whose opinion mattered, no such hasty judgment prevailed. The French continued to view him with wary respect.[59] Charles, writing to Ferdinand, blamed the withdrawal on cold, snow, ice, and disease[60] and, as Griessdorf puts it, "could not have held Alba in higher regard if he had taken Metz and Paris, too."[61]

The plain fact is that the attack on Metz was every bit as harebrained as the earlier assault on Algiers, and for much the same reasons. Hastily planned, inadequately coordinated, led in part by captains openly hostile to the emperor, and launched at an impossible time of year, it was doomed from the start. Charles V was a great ruler. More honorable and steadfast than most of his contemporaries, he brought to his tasks a moral grandeur that men appreciated and would follow. He was also a fair judge of character, and his personal courage was universally recognized. His fault lay in a kind of fatalism that grew partly from a belief in the rectitude of his cause and partly from the *Weltschmerz* that ultimately took him to the monastery. In this case it led him to disaster among the snows.

Alba remained with him at Brussels for several months before embarking for Spain in the summer of 1553. He sailed from the Roads of Walcheren with a fleet of ten ships, and fought contrary winds and heavy seas all the way to the Cantabrian coast.[62] It was October before he joined Philip at Aranjuez. He was by this time thoroughly spent, both physically and financially, and though the prince gave him leave to winter at Alba de Tormes, his mood as expressed in his letters to Eraso remained bleak: "I promise you by the faith of a knight and swear to you by the Sacrament that my house and estate are in such a condition this winter that I have seen with my own eyes that it will be impossible for it to recover in my lifetime or in that of my son." He quailed at the prospect of new employment but knew that neither his ambition nor his stern personal code would permit him to avoid it. He hoped that he would be sent in a different manner from formerly—meaning at someone's expense other than his own—but acknowledged that "kings are born to do their will, and we, their vassals and servants, are born to do their will likewise, and I certainly more than anyone, because I never thought to have any other will than their own; if sometimes I have not gone by it, it is through not knowing it."[63]

The dreaded summons came in February, 1554, and he was as good as his word. Charles had been deeply dispirited by his failure at Metz and had largely abandoned the tangled affairs of Germany,[64] but he was capable of a last diplomatic coup. "That right Godly Imp," Edward VI of England, had died before reaching his majority, and the Protestant regency that governed in his name had perished with him. England was now ruled by Mary, the daughter of Catherine of Aragon—a plain, sad woman of thirty-six whose survival of an appalling childhood had been due largely to the strength of her Catholic faith. Through the efforts of his ambassador, Simon Renard, Charles was now able to strike a mighty blow at the French: the marriage of the Queen of England with the future king of Spain.

The ceremonies were to be held in England, and as majordomo Alba would have a large part in arranging them. He would also have the far more delicate task of minimizing friction between the Spanish delegation and its hosts, for the marriage was unpopular with many Englishmen, and even good Catholics feared that sovereignty would be lost by tying the island nation to the world's greatest empire. Protestants and crypto-Protestants were openly hostile. In a warm personal letter dispatched from Brussels on April 1 the emperor charged Alba with controlling the behavior of the entire court and especially of the soldiers and sailors, who would be confined to their ships for the duration. It was an all but impossible task, as the latter would be at the edge of mutiny and the rest subjected to constant provocations, but there was worse. In a postscript that is almost a *cri de coeur*, Charles conjured up painful memories of the Netherlands tour: "Duke, for the love of God, see to it that my son behaves in the right manner; for otherwise I tell you I would rather never have taken this matter in hand at all."[65]

Here, then, was a tall order. The duke carried it off fairly well, though he had little cooperation from anyone, not even from his wife. The royal marriage was, of course, a pathetic failure and Philip's sojourn among the English marked the start of much hard feeling between the two peoples. Moreover, in the pressure-cooker atmosphere of an alien land, the antagonism between Alba and Ruy Gómez burst into the open. Still, had it not been for the duke's stern control things might have gone far worse.

The fleet sailed from La Coruña on Friday, July 13, and after an uneventful passage dropped anchor at Southampton six days later. The English, already annoyed because Philip had refused to sail on one of their ships,[66] became more so when he chose to remain on board for twenty hours after his arrival.[67] When the prince finally came ashore, Alba accompanied him on a nocturnal visit to his bride in which he kissed all her ladies, but otherwise behaved well.[68] The wedding was without incident, but this calm was in many ways deceptive. It had not been achieved without effort.

The first and greatest of Alba's problems was housing. From the beginning he worked constantly with the Privy Council to find space for Philip's retinue, a task complicated by the need to protect them from the hostile English. In the end it was decided to lodge them only in royal houses or in the country, where their contacts would be limited, but even then problems arose almost daily.[69] Alba himself, with his wife and at least one of his sons, was allocated a modest house that was to many Spaniards little better than an insult in masonry.[70] Alba was also responsible for security, and as the Spaniards, too, were now on a hair-trigger, the task was formidable.

It is probably a tribute to Alba's reputation that serious incidents were few. His role as chief liaison officer in this very tense situation required more tact and diplomacy than one might have expected him to possess, but his manners had always been impeccable and his natural reserve may have been an asset, making him appear impartial. The experience also taught him a great deal about the English, with whom he seems to have got on surprisingly well. In later years he was frequently assigned to deal with them and even earned the approval of Dr. Man, perhaps the most difficult ambassador ever accredited to a major power by Elizabeth I.[71] At the very least, Alba learned enough about the country and its politics to stand virtually alone against the invasion schemes of the seventies and to provide more cogent opinions on English affairs than any of Philip II's other advisors.

The duchess was less tractable. After the wedding she was granted an audience with the queen in the Presence Chamber. When she entered, Mary rose to greet her, but the duchess fell to her knees and begged to kiss her hands. Mary then bent over, raised her, and kissed her on the lips. She then took her to the dais where there was but one chair. Mary seated herself on the floor, but the duchess, of course, refused to take precedence over her queen. Two stools were then brought in, but when Mary sat on one, the duchess sat on the floor, whereupon Mary also sat on the floor. Finally, both arose and sat on the stools for a long talk, mostly about the weather. This momentous conversation required an interpreter because Mary understood, but could not speak, Spanish, and Maria Enríquez knew no other language. After a bit, Mary wanted her to go back and rest, as there were a number of ambassadors to be seen, but the duchess wished to remain with the ladies-in-waiting. As luck would have it, the ambassadors were late, so they talked some more, but finally the duchess had to walk home, a good distance, accompanied by two countesses and "the old ambassador that had been at Corunna."[72]

That was the end. For some time the duchess refused to return to the palace and remained in haughty solitude in her own lodgings. She thought the English ladies were "of evil conversation"[73] and disliked the English custom of kissing on the lips,[74] but above all she seems to have been irked by the queen's well-intentioned effort to get rid of her. A classic case of cultural shock, it made Alba's life no easier. To complicate matters further, he then fell victim to one of those ailments that await many a foreigner on his first visit to England. On August 13 he wrote to Eraso: "I have been ill so long with pestilential catarrh, fever, and chills by night that in truth I have nearly gone crazy."[75]

Alba's burdens were indeed great, but they were destined to be short-lived. The record of his English adventures is necessarily incomplete—for contemporary chroniclers, like modern journalists, were forced to concentrate on surface manifestations and ignore the undercurrents—but though little mention was made of it at first, Alba's success was leading him into a political trap. By mid-winter he was Philip's chief spokesman, not only with the Privy Council but with both Houses of Parliament. The English were struggling with such thorny issues as the extension of the treason laws, to protect Philip, and the guardianship of hypothetical children in the event of their mother's death. Alba, as the ranking member of the Spanish court and an advocate of formidable persuasive abilities, inevitably assumed the dominant role. It was this combination of an increasingly visible presence with his powers as a faction leader that sealed his fate. He had become a mortal threat to the ambitions of Ruy Gómez, and it now appears that even Philip himself was becoming apprehensive. An intrigue was launched to remove him from the scene.

V

ITALY

The politics of Ruy Gómez are always difficult to follow. His sense of self-preservation was acute, and both his office and his instincts kept him in close proximity to the Crown. Since he therefore had little reason to commit his thoughts to paper, evidence about him is meager and secondhand. In the spring of 1555, however, he provided Francisco de Eraso with a glimpse of how and why Alba was sent away.

His motives for doing so are characteristic. After several years of quietly extending his influence, he was at last prepared to move openly against his rival, and he wanted Eraso's support. The powerful secretary had until now remained on outwardly good terms with Alba, but there must have been signs of tension in the relationship, for the effort to drive a wedge between them was well timed and wholly successful.

He began by intimating that the duke was no longer in Philip's good graces. Alba had, it seemed, been saying openly that affairs in England were not being handled with due care and that he himself held things together.[1] Whether this was true or was merely an idea planted in Philip's head by his chamberlain is uncertain, but it appears to have been believed. Philip was becoming increasingly suspicious of his majordomo and welcomed the chance to get rid of him. The excuse was not only honorable but heaven-sent. The English marriage had awakened the old French fear of encirclement, and they celebrated the wedding with a bloody and destructive attack on the Low Countries. By the end of 1554 they were driven back by Charles himself at Renty, but as usual they had been too clever to concentrate their energies on a single front. A great host under Brissac had seized much of Piedmont, including the key fortress of Volpiano, and another under Blaise de Montluc took advantage of a popular revolt to garrison Siena. The imperial troops were badly outnumbered, and with the opening of the new campaign season, Milan itself was threatened. The presence of a great captain was clearly required.

Philip, who was by this time holding up business so that Alba could not take credit for it,[2] persuaded his father to offer him the posts of Viceroy of Naples and Captain-General of Milan. The duke accepted, but with the greatest misgivings. He knew that the situation there was desperate and that nothing he could do would be likely to enhance his reputation. Moreover, he was aware of the role played by Ruy Gómez, who professed to be terrified at the prospect of his revenge. As he told Eraso:

> Now that the duke has spoken to me about the appointments to Naples and Milan, as I have written to you, and has assured me that he is eternally obliged to me for them, I am afraid that when he sees His Majesty he will not treat me as tenderly as he is accustomed to do when he speaks with you. Therefore I implore you to do what you can to protect me, for I certainly am afraid of him. He is a dead shot. May God be pleased to enlighten him and permit him to know his own failings.[3]

That Alba accepted at all is a fair measure of the problems of a *caudillo*. On the one hand, he could not have refused without hopelessly compromising his status as a soldier and loyal servant of the Crown. On the other, his family, with their extensive interests in Italy, saw in his appointment a once-in-a-lifetime opportunity for aggrandizement through nepotism. His sensitivity to these latter pressures is revealed in a wonderfully acerbic letter to his cousin Francisco de Toledo:

> What now has to be said is that my departure has been so retarded that I will not only be able to find the countess married, as you say, but will find her grandchildren frisking before my eyes. I am bringing Don Juan de Figueroa with me, who will be able to help us in the labors that lie ahead in this *maldita* of Italy. You are forewarned that many times I have been moved to return and pluck out your eyes for what you have persuaded me, that is to give thanks to those gentlemen who send me to go thither, but it is determined, and as I have ridden on the mare, I must hang on to her mane.[4]

Family and personal obligations are central to factional leadership, but only a patron who is also a great general can be placed in a forked stick of such formidable proportions. It is perhaps ironic that the military talents to which Alba owed his influence would also prove the weapon that his enemies could use against him.

It might be argued that anyone can be sent on a foreign mission, but military expeditions carry with them unique potential for catastrophe and disgrace. Knowing this, Ruy Gómez intended not only to remove his rival but to undermine him once he was in the field. It is to this end that he had directed his courtship of Francisco de Eraso.

His efforts were at first unsuccessful. The duke had always treated Eraso cordially and had given him no cause to risk the perils of an open break. It was not until June that an exasperated Ruy Gómez dropped all pretense of subtlety or restraint. Calling Alba "a rogue," he accused him of influencing the king to grant certain monastic revenues to Bernardino de Mendoza instead of to the secretary. To seal his case he included a letter from the Marqués de Mondéjar in which he claimed that "that dog Alba has bitten me, too."[5] Though otherwise unconfirmed, the complaint about the abbeys was quite plausible. As his letters to Eraso indicate, Alba was eager to retain the secretary's goodwill, but in a crunch Alba would have had to support Mendoza, a soldier and one of his own people.

In any case, Eraso was from that day forward a partisan of Ruy Gómez and the stage was set for events that nearly cost Alba his career and might well have led to the loss of northern Italy. Not content to have him away from court, these two conspired to deprive him of the money and supplies needed to complete his mission. From the standpoint of domestic politics it was a master stroke: Ruy Gómez sent his rival out on a limb and adroitly sawed it off. From the standpoint of the royal interest it was an act of irresponsibility bordering on treason.

The problems began before Alba set foot in Italy. He had originally hoped for an appropriation of 600,000 ducats, for he knew that the troops were expecting large sums of back pay on his arrival.[6] He would later discover that this staggering request fell short of the immense debt already contracted and that even had he received it he would have been 200,000 ducats in arrears and without anything whatever for the new campaigning season.[7] By ignoring past debts he could make do temporarily with a smaller amount, but the 200,000 ducats finally allocated to him was an irreducible minimum that would suffice only if larger sums were dispatched within a matter of weeks. Thanks to Eraso, he was nearly deprived even of that.

At first, his new enemy tried to delay matters by suggesting that even 200,000 ducats was exorbitant, as no more than 300,000 had been provided for all Philip's expenses.[8] This was too disingenuous even for the king. His stipend had never been intended to cover imperial emergencies, and Eraso was sent to float a loan on the Antwerp money market.[9] This proved to be an excruciatingly deliberate, if not leisurely, exercise, and on May 17 Alba himself arrived from England to see if he could expedite matters. He could not. Moreover, Eraso informed him in no uncertain terms that any monies received would be distributed as he saw fit and in accordance with the established procedures of the *contaduría mayor*.[10] Alba was livid, but there was nothing he could do. He went on to Augsburg for a conference with King Ferdinand, hoping that the necessary *cédulas* would catch up with him, but there was no sign of them and he moved on to Innsbruck. In the end he was forced to inform Philip that he would not enter Italy without the money in hand,[11] but the amount that finally reached Innsbruck on June 4 was 37,000 ducats short and much of the remainder had been specifically designated for the garrison at Casale. As Alba put it, "This horseshit of a little old man did nothing but pay off 120,000 in old debts."[12]

It is probably not surprising that Eraso and his henchman Domingo de Orbea also refused to pay the duke's salary.[13] The sum in question was only 12,000 ducats, but petty harassment had become the order of the day. Though in theory Alba had full control over all Italian appointments he soon found that he could not even obtain a formal commission for his own son. Fadrique, now seventeen, was rapidly becoming the victim of the paternal hopes once lavished on his dead brother, and Alba was determined that he begin his career with distinction. Someone, most probably Ruy Gómez, convinced the king that the boy was unsuited to a responsible post, and this judgment continued to haunt him in one form or another for the remainder of his life. Fadrique went to Italy only as a supernumerary companion to his father.[14]

It is to Alba's credit that these distractions did not seem to enervate him in the slightest. Though worried by his isolation, his deteriorating personal finances, and a serious illness contracted by the duchess,[15] he took aggressive steps to remedy matters on all fronts. At Naples, Bernardino de Mendoza was ordered to raise a subsidy from the local *parlamentum* and to investigate the possibility of borrowing from the Monte, a fund for retirement of the public debt. This last expedient proved fruitless, as the Monte had been depleted by previous administrations, and the subsidy, when it came, was late and disappointingly small.[16]

On the personal front, Alba embarked on a flurry of measures designed to increase the income from his estates. At Coria, a major development program was inaugurated involving new irrigation works and the planting of mulberry trees, and substantial improvements were also begun at El Abadía. As all this was expensive, it may be that his poverty was less burdensome than he claimed, but some of the improvements seem to have been financed by speculation in oil and other commodities.[17] It is a pity that so little is known of the management of his estates, for his instructions on this occasion reveal a solid grasp of such matters and a passionate interest in agricultural development.

The remains of his irrigation projects are still to be seen, but the problems of northern Italy proved less tractable than the parched earth of Extremadura. The French now held virtually every strong point from Valenza northwest to Ivrea, though their garrisons were necessarily scattered and imperial forces retained a precarious hold on several places behind their forward lines. The most important of these was the great fortress of Volpiano. Located only a few miles northeast of Turin, its value had become more symbolic than real. Though it was strong and ably defended, its garrison was too small to threaten the tide of Frenchmen that had washed over it and left it stranded. Without reinforcements it was unlikely to hold until autumn. From a purely strategic point of view its relief would be meaningless unless Alba could establish permanent control over the region between it and the borders of Milan, but from the standpoint of morale it was vital. When he arrived in mid-June he had only 38,000 troops, of whom 18,000 were tied down in garrison duty.[18] This meant that if he were to accomplish anything it would have to be with a field army of 20,000 demoralized, unpaid, and semi-mutinous troops with no common language and only the most tenuous of loyalties. If ever a campaign needed a focus it was this one, and the prospect of relieving their endangered comrades might well provide it.

There were, of course, some advantages on Alba's side, though they were not immediately obvious. If his troops were restive and he had little hope of meeting their demands, he was at least their only commander. His powers were virtually proconsular in both the civil and military realms, whereas the French command was divided

Map 3.

between Brissac and the Duc d'Aumale, who, as the summer wore on, disagreed increasingly between themselves as to what to do and how to do it. They were, after all, an occupying force in more or less hostile territory, and had to hold what they had taken with forces that inevitably dwindled from day to day. In general, Brissac was inclined toward caution while d'Aumale favored a more active role,[19] but the precise nature of their disagreements is unimportant. The fact was that the French campaign had lost its impetus before Alba left the Netherlands.

Siena, too, had returned to the fold, but this was a mixed blessing. Alba, as the man on the spot, was expected to adjudicate its possession between Philip and his own personal ally the Duke of Florence. Both sides naturally distrusted him,[20] and matters were further complicated by the emperor, who at one point wanted to grant him the right to approve any final agreement.[21] Alba wanted no part of the affair, but by the time Philip relieved him of responsibility for it, he was "like a mad friar with two fists full of sugar-plums, not knowing which to nibble on."[22] Moreover, though the capture of Siena removed one military threat it created another. Much of the credit for Montluc's surrender went to the imperial troops from Orbitello and Port' Ercole. In the minds of the French this increased the strategic importance of the two bases, and at their behest a Turkish fleet was on its way to destroy them.[23] Normally this menace could have been countered by the Genoese, but for a variety of internal reasons they were unable to put forth their usual effort,[24] and Alba could only pray that the Umbrian coast would hold.

The civil governments of both Naples and Milan were also in disarray and by mid-summer it was evident that the wheat harvest would fail.[25] It was thus little wonder that Alba prepared for the worst. It seemed almost prophetic that within hours of his arrival at Milan he was confronted by an unheard-of scandal in the house in which he was scheduled to reside.

The Prince and Princess of Ascoli were Spaniards of the de Leyva clan, heirs of the Antonio de Leyva who had been Alba's commander in Provence. As such they were fairly representative of the Italianate Spaniards whose prominence in the Peninsula increasingly annoyed its inhabitants. One of their ladies-in-waiting became involved in a torrid affair with Pedro de Mendoza, a captain of light horse who had taken to sneaking into the house by night. The princess discovered this and informed her husband, who ordered his chamberlain to lie in wait. On Holy Thursday, Mendoza was found in the house and was slightly wounded before escaping through an open window, but by then it was too late. The whole city was talking about the scandal and its reflection on the honor of the princess, who was widely thought to be the object of Mendoza's attentions. Mendoza, with the vanity and instinctive self-aggrandizement of his kind, encouraged this impression to the best of his ability.

Some days later the prince, who had been out of town, returned, and shortly thereafter a headless corpse was found buried in a sack in the garden. Inevitably, gossip declared that the remains were those of Mendoza, who had been found in flagrante delicto with the princess; but it was not so. Shortly after Alba's arrival, Mendoza was found alive and well in the town. On the night of the vigil of San Juan this was remedied by ten or twelve men of the de Leyva household, who invaded Mendoza's house, beheaded him on the spot, and slew several of his companions for good measure. As Alba put it: "This was a very great violence and a terrible case for the first to be offered me, as it was committed in my presence with the evildoers coming from the house in which I resided, and the prime movers of it being the Prince and Princess of Ascoli, Spaniards, my relatives, and persons of importance." Without hesitation, he locked both Prince and Princess in the castle.[26]

The episode was traumatic, but his evenhanded severity earned him much credit with the Italians and enabled him to begin his rule on a note of popular approval. Only one question remains to bedevil the hardened mystery addict. If the corpse in the garden was not Mendoza's, whose was it?

Alba remained in Milan until the fourteenth of July. Then, after inspecting the defenses of Pavia, he moved up the Po with his main army, picking off the smaller French garrisons as he went.[27] There was no effective opposition, but he could do no more than reinforce the garrison at Volpiano. The French, though divided in counsel, were numerous and controlled the entire region. As Alba said, they "go about as though they were two miles from Paris."[28] In an attempt to distract them he laid brief and fruitless siege to Santhia, but Volpiano finally had to be strengthened by 750 men under Lope de Acuña, who fought their way in through the French lines by night.[29] It was a brave and even brilliant action, but it accomplished nothing. The French responded with a furious assault, and on September 18, after a memorable defense, Volpiano fell.[30] At the same time it became obvious that nothing could be done to save Cherasco, Fossano, and Cuneo, the remaining imperial outposts in the upper valley of the Po.

It was fortunate that the season was far advanced and that the French commanders were on the point of doing violence to each other.[31] Both sides went into winter quarters, and shortly thereafter a truce was patched together at Cambrai. Lack of pay had now driven a number of Alba's units to outright mutiny, and by December he was forced to offer his son as hostage to the Germans. To their credit they refused this extraordinary collateral, but there can be little doubt that the truce, which took effect in February, was a godsend.

The campaign in Piedmont was neither a success nor the abject failure desired by Alba's enemies. He did what he could and emerged with his reputation intact, though some, such as Brantôme, said unkind things[32] and his opponents at court made the most of his setbacks. He might have made a serious attempt on Volpiano, but this would have involved him in a pitched battle against vastly greater forces. Had he won, the French would still have held Piedmont; had he lost, he would have lost Milan.[33]

In the end, the crisis ended through sheer lack of momentum, but though the Piedmont campaign was not the stuff of epics it holds a fascination for those who would understand Alba as a man. Up to this time his conduct in war had been scrupulous and even humanitarian. Not a hint of his darker side appears in earlier actions except, perhaps, for the gallows humor and inappropriately violent metaphors that occasionally invade his correspondence. Violence is there, and deep anger, but it is rigidly controlled. For a time in Piedmont that control may have slipped.

For reasons that are not immediately apparent, Alba insisted on the massacre of every French garrison that resisted him on his brief march up the Po.[34] When Brissac sent him a formal protest he called upon the laws of war, which as they were then understood permitted execution of any who refused terms.[35] Technically he was right, but such behavior was rare. Only weeks later the French shamed him by allowing the remnant at Volpiano to march out with full honors of war after a far more bitterly contested siege than anything yet seen by the duke in Italy. Worse, his cruelty served no useful purpose. To attempt to intimidate a stronger enemy by such means is simply mad. His own doubts were expressed in a letter to Antonio de Toledo: "God guide me: I have begun to make war as it has to be made because I hang and cast into the galleys dozens of those that they take for me alive, as I cannot with the light horse they kill,"[36] but this *cri de coeur*, if that is what it was, spared not a single Frenchman.

The fact is that when faced by true adversity Alba was likely to become brutal. He could fight against heavy odds and endure bad conditions with equanimity, but when given an impossible task in the field and undermined at home, a kind of despair settled upon him and the underlying ferocity of his nature emerged, with dreadful consequences. In all his long career, this only happened on two occasions. In Piedmont the deaths were relatively few and the repercussions minimal. Later, in the Netherlands, this tendency was to contribute heavily to disaster.

There is another, less ominous way in which Alba's brief sojourn in northern Italy reveals something of his character and his views on government and society. In January, 1556, after pacifying the mutineers almost entirely through his personal standing with the troops, he made ready to sail to Naples. While his galley awaited a favorable wind at Portofino, he dictated a memorandum on the government of Milan that demonstrates not only his interest in institutional reform but his understanding of Milanese affairs and the overall direction of his political thought. A thoroughly practical document comprising seventeen specific recommendations, its overall thrust is abundantly clear. The first eight deal with the reform of the senate, which, together with the tribunal of the Captain of Justice, acted as the chief court of the city. It had been established by Louis XII and its functions, as the duke points out, were essentially similar to those of the Parlement of Paris.

Little or nothing about its operations met with his approval. Eight of its twenty members were non-lawyers. These would have to go as they did not understand the law, introduced complications, and perpetrated grave injustices. Moreover, the procedures in use were appalling. The court should not be permitted to hear cases in the absence of the interested parties, nor should the *fiscal* (prosecutor) present cases in which he is involved. Delays should be limited to three, as processes were presently "immortal," and the senate should stop hearing cases that belonged properly to the lower courts. This matter of jurisdictional boundaries was especially worrisome. Alba felt that the senate was encroaching on Philip's administrative authority and that it could be constitutionally enjoined from doing so, "as they must yield to your claims as prince." Above all, they should not be allowed to name officials. The governor, in consultation with the senate and council, should submit a list for the approval of the Crown. Otherwise the senators would continue to pack city offices with their relatives and cronies.

The other recommendations are in much the same vein. Both the president of the senate and the Captain of Justice should be foreigners like the Podesti of Cremona and Piacenza. An archive should be established, treasury functions centralized, and a *fiscal* appointed to oversee the affairs of the *cámara*. *Ordinarios, contadores,* and other officials should be selected by the system currently used at Naples, and heroic efforts should be made to prevent relatives from serving on the same tribunal. The precise nature of these offices need not concern us, but the principles behind their proposed reorganization are clear and in accord with those later developed by Philip II. The primary goal is justice; the second, efficiency. In Alba's view these ends could best be served by centralization and the extension of royal authority. If this involved the modification of local tradition, so be it.

Marañón, among others, has seen this as "Castilianization," in contrast to the more "imperial" policies of those who, like Ruy Gómez, were prepared to tolerate a higher degree of local autonomy.[37] If this implies that Alba was attempting to impose Castilian institutions, it is false: from his recommendations it is obvious that he was prepared to copy Italian usage and retain structures that had no Spanish counterparts. If, however, it means that his views were in agreement with the thinkers of Salamanca and a majority of the Castilian governing class, it is correct: he believed that justice was rooted in universal principles and that it was both the prerogative and the religious duty of the Crown to maintain it at all costs. He was thus an uncompromising monarchist and centralist whose patience with local privilege was limited.

The other concern that informs his memorandum is a passionate desire to root out clientage and nepotism wherever they might be found. He may have been a mighty practitioner of both, but by this time few men living were greater experts on their more pernicious results.

For a while it seemed that a new career in administrative reform lay ahead, for though Alba could not stay to implement his suggestions in Milan, the political situation at Naples was perhaps even worse. The formidable Don Pedro de Toledo had been succeeded as viceroy by another of Alba's relatives, Cardinal Pacheco. Plagued by financial problems and lacking the implacable sternness of his predecessor, he had allowed the Neapolitan factions to run riot. By the time he returned to Rome in the spring of 1555 the administration had largely broken down and the treasury was empty. The *lugarte-niente*, Bernardino de Mendoza, subsequently tried to hold things together, but his nine months in office were a disaster. The old soldier was apparently naive in matters other than war, for he became hopelessly involved with the seductive Marquesa del Vasto and thus compromised his position as ruler of the city. A leading member of one of the great clientage groups that have always infested that troubled city, she had more in mind than honest adultery. Alba knew of this before he arrived in Italy and had attempted to set his old friend and comrade-in-arms back on the path of virtue and common sense. The effort failed, but as it represents one of the few instances in which the dour Alba tried to pass himself off as a man of the world, it is worth a brief quote:

There have not been two men who know each other better than we two. I know you for a little turtledove. Be careful that the Marquesa del Vasto does not bewitch you. She is the very devil there and I know for certain that she is dangerous and wants a part in the Kingdom. You may think, knowing me, that I write this as a turtledove also, but you are a great friend of fat matrons, and because of this run greater risks than I, even though I see myself in Milan lodging with her of Ascoli.[38]

As is usual with this sort of advice, it was ill received. Relations between the two friends grew strained, and when the situation at Naples continued to deteriorate, Alba was forced to protect himself by reporting it in some detail.[39] Mendoza never forgave him, but his opportunities for revenge were limited: he died in 1557, from wounds received at St. Quentin.

Alba's arrival in Naples was thus shadowed by a host of problems, most of them apparently unsolvable. The government was demoralized, the population hungry, and the countryside plagued with bandits. Like many others before and since, he was dumbfounded. The vast, sprawling city in its magnificent natural setting was perhaps the greatest in Europe, and the land around it seemed so rich[40] that he could not understand why there was "such want and poverty that there is almost nothing of lands or rents to sell in all the kingdom."[41] This last was a sore point, because something definitely had to be sold. The resources and goodwill of the Neapolitan parliament had been exhausted in 1555, and though the Monte showed signs of recovery its leisurely rate of growth made it almost useless as a milch cow. By the time Alba confiscated it again in June, 1556, it had accumulated only 25,000 ducats.[42] Compared to the massive sums owed to the imperial army this was scarcely worth mentioning, and all up and down the Peninsula the garrisons threatened mutiny.[43]

Once again Alba met his troubles head on. Thinking that there was little hope of money from Spain, he borrowed heavily from the Queen of Poland[44] and sent 180,000 ducats to Milan on his own personal note.[45] To clear the backlands of highwaymen, he dispatched companies of Spanish infantry,[46] and on at least one occasion followed the movements of a bandit by suborning his relatives.[47] The role of policeman was apparently agreeable to him, for he devoted a great deal of energy to it. The courts were encrusted with ancient and irredeemable corruption that would have required his sustained attention over many years, but their police officials were within his reach and he reformed them with a vengeance.[48]

In this his draconian approach paid dividends, but in other areas it proved an embarrassment. Deciding that the prevailing speculation in fiefs was harmful to the king's authority Alba ordered that none change hands without royal permission. Then, as he had no right to do such a thing, he was forced to send off a hasty plea for Philip's approval.[49]

It may be, of course, that he was simply forcing a decision, as the king's penchant for delay was already well known. That Alba was in fact capable of administrative foresight is shown by the fact that, as at Milan, he insisted on establishing an archive.[50] It would be pleasant to think that this fascination with archives stemmed from his old friendship with Cobos, the patron saint of Simancas, or from a kindly, if wayward, impulse toward historians, but the truth is more sinister, at least from the Italian point of view. There can be nothing more maddening than to assume a new post without hope of discovering the policies, precedents, or decisions of one's predecessors, and nothing more fatal to the assertion of local privilege than a permanent record of these transactions. There was no Spanish royal archive until 1545, but establishment of local repositories had been a feature of royal policy since the Cortes of Toledo in 1480. In this, at least, Alba was indeed extending Castilian precedent to other areas of the empire in ways that tended to compromise their autonomy.

These adventures in administration are interesting as a key to Alba's view of government, but they were not, of course, the reason for his being in Naples. As usual, his presence there was connected with war and rumors of war—this time with the most unlikely opponent imaginable.

The duke's arrival in Milan had coincided with the election of Gian Pietro Carafa to the chair of St. Peter. Carafa, who took the name Paul IV, was one of the guiding spirits of the Counter Reformation and a man whose views on religion were not unlike Alba's. Born to a powerful Neapolitan family, he had been a founder of the Theatines and had dedicated his life to reform of the Church along traditionalist lines. He had opposed the conciliatory policies of Contarini and was therefore entrusted with the revival of the Papal Inquisition by Paul III. There his enthusiasm for repression was so great that it spilled over into other projects such as the *Index librorum prohibitorum*. Tall, thin, and autocratic, with a savage temper and an apparent fondness for strong Neapolitan wine, he was utterly lacking in that saturnine quality that so often preserved Alba from the

worst excesses of his temperament. He was also an Italian patriot
and much influenced by his relatives, not all of whom were as honest as he.

Trouble began almost immediately after his election. The new
pope wanted desperately to free Italy from the barbarians, and by
barbarians he meant the imperialists. They ruled his native city, surrounded the papal territories both north and south, and protected
the more fractious of the Roman nobles. What was worse, they had
favored the Council of Trent, which was to him little more than an
attack on papal authority, and had opposed his own election.[51]
Clearly these sins were Babylonian. They were, he said, "rogues,
renegade Moriscos, children of the devil and of iniquity."[52] Philip
was "this little beast, begotten of that diabolical father [Charles
V],"[53] and he suspected him, incredibly enough, of Lutheranism.[54]

No one can blame Carafa for hating the Habsburgs, but by quar-
reling openly with them he once again allowed Italian interests to
take precedence over those of the Church. That, at least, is the most
charitable explanation available. It may be that nothing would have
come of it, but his malice was encouraged by his advisors, a mixed
bag of Florentine exiles, French sympathizers, and Neapolitan malcontents headed by his nephew Cardinal Carlo Carafa. A one-time
condottiere, the Cardinal had not allowed his elevation to the purple
to overcome his instincts. Quite simply, he wanted Siena for himself
and sought to get it by provoking a new Franco-Papal war against
the empire.[55]

The precipitant that crystallized all these elements was the affair
at Civatavecchia. The Sforza Count of Santa Fiore had long been a
supporter of the empire, but he had two brothers, Carlo and Mario,
who commanded galleys for the French. After the fall of Siena in
April, 1555, he finally prevailed upon these two to desert and bring
their galleys with them. This they did by persuading their French
crews to put in at Civatavecchia for repairs, and there another
brother, Alessandro, seized the ships and got them out of the harbor
by obtaining a letter from the papal governor, the Count of Monto-
rio. This was done through Lottini, the secretary of yet another
brother, Cardinal Guido Ascanio Sforza.[56] When the pope learned of
all this he arrested Lottini and issued a vehement protest to the
Spanish ambassador, but the galleys were not returned until September 15. Alba himself was largely responsible for the delay, as he had
taken great umbrage at the pope's behavior,[57] but the impression
created was sinister in the extreme and the papal advisors made the

most of it. They noted that some of Lottini's papers seemed to hint at Spanish intrigues and that the Colonna and Orsini were fortifying their strongholds at Paliano and Bracciano, respectively. Convinced that he was in danger, Paul IV concluded an agreement with the French on October 14.[58]

From this point onward, relations inevitably deteriorated. Imperial emissaries were arrested, posts were intercepted, and the ambassador, the Marqués de Sarriá, was insulted with studied regularity. In contrast to his reaction in the Civatavecchia crisis, Alba remained calm. He had no desire to make war on the Vicar of Christ, especially as that personage was so old that he might well "be found cold one morning." Even after the pope confiscated the estates of two of Philip's clients, Ascanio and Marc' Antonio Colonna, the duke advocated nothing more strenuous than economic and diplomatic sanctions.[59] His moderation, though exemplary, proved futile. The pope began to raise troops and strengthen his fortifications along the Neapolitan border. As Philip was becoming insistent on his rights, Alba had no choice but to draft an ultimatum that was a model of its kind. After listing the pope's crimes in detail, he vividly described the tragedy of war, and threatened "by the blood in my veins to stagger Rome with rigorous hands; and Your Holiness, even though you would be respected then as you are now, could not be free of the horrors of war or perhaps of the wrath of some soldier notably offended by the bloodthirsty actions done in plenty by Your Holiness."[60]

The text was presented to the pope by an emissary who apparently added some embroidery of his own. His Holiness declared that he wished he could deal with Alba "con la spadda e cappa," but what promised to be a classic tirade was cut short by an attack of diarrhea.[61] There was no other response and on September 1, 1556, Alba marched out of Naples with an army of 12,000 men.

Once again the duke was at war, but this was war with a difference, and he did not relish it.[62] Whatever his contempt for Carafa, the man was still pope, and as a pious Catholic Alba had no desire to do anything injurious either to the Faith or to his own soul, particularly since, as he had noted in his ultimatum, quarrels between Spain and the papacy had no place "in these times so full of heresies and harmful opinions." It was a situation of the sort most feared by the professional soldier: a war he would rather not win. For all his bluster Alba did not want to preside over another Sack of Rome, yet a way had to be found to bring the pope to his senses.

Accordingly he decided on a kind of *Blitzkrieg* against strategically important towns on the borders of Naples, to be followed immediately by an offer of peace. He knew that many of the cardinals were opposed to the war, and he hoped to exploit their dissatisfaction in the interests of an early settlement.

Within two weeks and in spite of heavy rains, Alba's military objectives had been achieved. Establishing himself at Anagni, he sent his cousin García de Toledo with Vespasiano Gonzaga to seize Bauco, Veruli, and Frosinone, whereupon half-a-dozen other places surrendered. To ensure that the point was driven home, the dispossessed Marc' Antonio Colonna led a foraging expedition to within sight of Rome.[63]

The situation in the Holy City was one of "indescribable confusion" and panic.[64] The cardinals—including Carafa, who, incredibly enough, thought this a good time to deal for Siena[65]—demanded that the pope hear Alba's proposals, and on September 16 he presented them. They were the essence of simplicity. His only condition for peace was that Philip be permitted to hold the newly occupied lands in trust for the College of Cardinals during the lifetime of the present pope. It is perhaps significant that the letter was addressed to the Cardinal of Paris and that Alba was careful to point out that he could conclude such an agreement without permission from the king.[66]

The offer was a blatant, though justified, attempt to separate the pope from his cardinals, and it nearly succeeded. At the urging of a special commission, the pope agreed to a conference between Alba and two cardinals, Carafa and Santiago (Alba's uncle), to be held at Grottaferrata on the twenty-fifth. Alba went in good faith and waited until 10:30 at night, but the cardinals did not appear. Paul IV had changed his mind.[67]

There was now no choice but to continue the campaign. Conventional wisdom dictated that his next objective be Paliano, a heavily fortified hill town a few miles from Anagni, but Alba decided to pass it by. Its garrison could defend the place but could do little against an invader if the invader chose to ignore it. Instead he descended on Tivoli. Tivoli was within an easy day's march of Rome and was virtually undefended, but it was more than a mere target of opportunity. Situated where the valley of the Aniene opens into the Roman Campagna, it dominates the road to the Abruzzi. The larder at Naples was almost bare and Alba hoped to supply his troops from this region while denying its somewhat meager riches to the pope.

Tivoli itself was quickly invested, but to secure the remainder of

THE ROMAN CAMPAGNA

MAJOR ROADS   SCALE   0   50 Km.

Map 4.

his supply route it was necessary to do something about Vicovaro, a smaller place 15 km upstream. Here Alba ran into trouble. The politics of the papal states were as complex as their geography, and no foreigner could hope to remain in the area for long without stumbling into some ancient vendetta. In this case, Alba in all ignorance dispatched Vespasiano Gonzaga to reduce Vicovaro. Gonzaga's father had been killed there a number of years before, and neither Vespasiano nor the townspeople had forgotten it. Knowing that he planned a massacre, they refused to surrender and mounted a spirited defense that was greatly aided by torrential rains. Finally, the duke discovered what was behind this unusual heroism and replaced Gonzaga immediately. Vicovaro laid down its arms with almost indecent haste.

The next few weeks were spent in virtually meaningless activities as Alba continued to search for a way to avoid using his strategic advantage. He asked the Venetians to intercede with the pope, and sent troops to interfere with whatever it was that another papal nephew, Antonio Carafa, was trying to accomplish in distant Ascoli, but his main achievement was to give the papal forces another sharp lesson in the art of war. Leaving his supplies unguarded at Tivoli, he wandered off toward Frascati in an attempt to draw them out and was rewarded by a demonstration of just how much his enemies had to learn. With wonderful innocence a detachment of cavalry galloped straight for the supplies and were captured almost to a man. Alba then circled back from Frascati and tried to engage a relief force under Cardinal Carafa with his main army. After a brief skirmish the cardinal scuttled back to the safety of Rome.

Incredibly, none of this seemed to make the slightest impression on the pope. After hanging about Tivoli until November 1, Alba moved to cut Rome off from the sea as well by taking Ostia. Though his purpose remained limited, in the sense that he would not attack Rome itself, Ostia was a potentially difficult objective. In the expectation, and perhaps the hope, of a lengthy seige, he constructed a boat bridge across the Tiber and set up an elaborate supply network based on Anzio and Nettuno. This took ten days. Then on November 17, after seven days of artillery bombardment, an assault was launched. It was repulsed with heavy casualties, as was a second attack later in the day. Alba can only have seen this as an unnecessary sacrifice to the vanity of an aging fool, but he kept his temper. He visited the wounded, seeing personally to their care, and when the fortress rather surprisingly gave up without a third assault, there were no reprisals.[68]

The season was now well advanced. Alba decided to return to Naples rather than press his advantage. The chronicler Andrea offers a number of unconvincing reasons for this,[69] but in fact it is the best of all indications that he thought of it as a limited war in which real victory was to be avoided. In the last week of November, he and Carlo Carafa met on the Isola Sacra, which separates the Tiber from the Fiumicino, and negotiated a truce that would expire on January 9. A half-hearted attempt to settle the larger issues foundered on Carafa's intransigence. Carafa claimed that Alba was merely defending his Colonna relatives and that if he wanted peace he would have to withdraw and beg it from the pope as a favor. Alba asked him if he would do such a thing if the shoe were on the other foot. Carafa answered that yes, he would, "to make amends."[70]

Not surprisingly, the truce expired three days before the agreed-upon time. Papal forces had spent the Christmas season building a fort above the village of Fiumicino. On January 6 they forced the Spaniards to abandon their position there, leaving Ostia surrounded and open to a siege. The fortress of Ostia was well provisioned and held a garrison of 500 men, but it unaccountably surrendered to Pietro Strozzi after the first assault. Its commander, Francisco Hurtado de Mendoza,[71] was almost certainly guilty of treason, and Alba later contrived his execution,[72] but the damage was done. The position of the combatants had been reversed. Now it was the duke whose garrisons were spread out over many square miles while Strozzi was free, as Alba had been in the preceding year, to concentrate on them one by one. Meanwhile, far to the north, even more ominous events were afoot. Belatedly redeeming his pledge to the pope, the King of France dispatched an army under the Duke of Guise. Entering Piedmont as Ostia fell, the French army began a slow but inexorable march along the northern slopes of the Apennines, the classic invasion route to southern Italy.

Faced with the likelihood of a combined French-papal attack on the kingdom of Naples, Alba and his council set about creating a plan for the defense. A number of his aides wanted simply to defend Naples and its environs, but Alba decided instead to fortify and garrison the Abruzzi. He reasoned that this important source of supplies should be retained if at all possible, and felt that by retiring within the borders of the kingdom he would lose the moral and psychological advantage gained during the preceding campaign. Accordingly, the Marchese of Treviso was sent to fortify Civitella, Atri, Pescara, and Chieti. Of these, Civitella was the strongest, and Alba hoped to hold the French there while inveigling Strozzi into a series of fruitless sieges in the Roman Campagna. As insurance he placed the main body of his troops at Venafro on the border of Naples. From this vantage point he could control the route to Rome as well as the longer road to Pescara, the Abruzzi, and, ultimately, the Marches.[73]

The plan was a good one, but it was perhaps fortunate that the French were slow and the papal forces relatively weak. The latter continued their attacks on Spanish garrisons, but though they had some notable successes, they were unable and perhaps unwilling to take advantage of these before joining forces with the French. Guise, meanwhile, had, according to plan, fallen foul of Civitella. After a leisurely march through the Romagna and down the Adriatic coast, he met his first serious resistance there and, realizing that he could not pass it by, decided to reduce it. He was still there in May.

The siege of Civitella was an heroic affair in which even the women took part, and it broke the back of the French invasion. Guise, who was nobody's fool, had long since begun to have doubts about the expedition, and this stubborn resistance tended only to intensify them. Not only were there no papal forces to aid him, he began to wonder if he were not being duped. From the beginning, Cardinal Carafa had wanted him to come by way of Siena, which made no sense at all unless that were the true object of the game.[74] Moreover, the pope had been very reluctant to grant him his price for the alliance: the investment of Naples in the name of Henry II, financial aid, and the appointment of more French cardinals.[75] In his present situation, these were bitter thoughts. He was faced with a determined enemy and untrustworthy friends. Even if Civitella fell he was still caught between the mountains and the sea and would have to reduce at least three more towns before opening the road to Naples. The odds against this were further increased when Alba abandoned Venafro and appeared at Pescara on May 10 with an army swollen to 28,000 men. To his credit, Guise decided to try them and sent a body of French to establish themselves at Giulianova on the coast. Though their position was strong and almost within shouting distance of the main French army, Alba's troops had no trouble in driving them out. On May 15 Guise lifted the siege.[76]

The rest was anticlimax. Guise withdrew to the plain below Nereto, and Alba countered by moving a short distance up the coast. The main reason for this was that the heat, filth, and insects were becoming unbearable in the camp at Giulianova, but Guise saw it as an attempt at encirclement and fled. On the principle that it is wisest to build bridges of silver for the enemy, Alba let him go.

Meanwhile, in the countryside around Rome, a vicious little war continued to rage amid overtones of ancient rivalry. Taking advantage of the concentration of forces in the Abruzzi, a papal army under Giulio Orsini sacked Montefortino and was moving against Pilla when it was driven off by Marc' Antonio Colonna. The vendetta, several centuries old, between the Colonna and the Orsini can only have added spice to Marc' Antonio's determination to regain his estates. He began to make a name for himself, taking town after town, and ultimately defeating Orsini in battle on July 27.[77] In all this, the suffering of the population must have been intense, for there was great destruction and a general paying off of old scores, but the pope remained indifferent. Bottled up in Rome with his allies in disarray, he sued for peace but would not restore the Colonna or surrender Paliano. Perhaps he was hoping for a French victory on the faraway borders of the Low Countries. If so, he was to be disappointed. On August 10 Henry II's main army was shattered at St. Quentin, and the more excitable of the Parisians began to flee the capital. Now even a madman could see that there was no hope, but Paul IV held firm.

Alba was dumbfounded. The war was over, but there seemed to be no easy way to convince the pope without attacking Rome, a desecration that was now more unacceptable than ever. Alba had spent most of the summer on the Adriatic coast, bringing grief to towns that had aided the French and observing the activities of Marc' Antonio Colonna. As everything had gone well, there had been no reason to intervene, and Alba had even disbanded some of his men. Now he returned to his old position between Rome and Paliano to ponder the next move.

On August 25, moving rapidly in spite of a light rain, Alba brought his entire army to the walls of Rome, where, brooding and ominous, it stood for an hour or two before vanishing back into the hills.[78] He did this purely as a gesture, without preparation and in full knowledge of the fact that Guise had returned and was lurking only a few miles away in the vicinity of Monterotondo. Nothing could more graphically have displayed his contempt for the enemy. The point was not lost on the pope, who moved at last, though not quickly and not very far.

Considering the relative strengths of the two parties, the negotiations that ended the war were remarkably complicated. The stubbornness of the pope and disagreements among his advisors led to endless trouble, while Alba's *caudillo*-like refusal to accept any settlement that did not protect his friends promised to interfere directly in the governance of the papal states. The leading figure in resolving these issues was Guido Ascanio Sforza, Cardinal Camarlengo, who was trusted by both sides in spite of his involvement in the Civitavecchia crisis two years before.

The pope began in his usual fashion, proposing terms that might have been appropriate had he won but which were in Alba's view wholly unreasonable. He wanted to retain Paliano and be left free to deal with the Colonna and their ilk as he saw fit. These were conditions Alba could never accept; he responded by laying formal siege to Paliano. At this point Camarlengo, who knew better than to deal directly with the pope, went to Cardinal Carafa and suggested that Paliano be placed under a trustee acceptable to both sides—an idea first advanced by Alba in November. Carafa responded with a tirade on Siena.[79] It took some time for Camarlengo to convince Carafa that Siena was both irrelevant and irretrievably lost, but in the end sanity triumphed, and an emissary was sent to Alba on September 2. Even then no specific offer was to be made: he was simply to discover what terms would be acceptable to the duke.

He found Alba in a foul humor, preparing to assault Paliano. After making the emissary wait overnight, the duke received him from his bed and told him that there must be a pardon for all participants and that most of the towns could not be returned without jeopardizing the security of Naples.[80] The news produced consternation, if not hysteria, at Rome. No one dared show Alba's letter to the pope, and the Venetian ambassador reported that there was talk of fleeing to Venice or Avignon.[81] In the end, of course, the parties simply agreed to another conference, but the road to peace was still far from smooth. Alba harangued the emissary sent to arrange the meeting and threatened to reconsider his refusal to assault Rome. On the same day Paul IV brought a brief of excommunication against Alba, but the cardinals dissuaded him from using it.[82] Finally, in a room hung with crimson velvet and surrounded by Spanish troops, a remarkably sensible agreement was hammered out. Alba would return the towns but destroy their fortifications, a trustee would be found for Paliano, and pardons would be issued to everyone on both sides.[83] Another war was over.

On balance, the two and a half years in Italy were among the triumphs of Alba's career, demonstrating clearly what he could do when his judgment was free to operate within the confines of non-ideological politics. He had begun at an enormous disadvantage, with mutinous troops, no money, and powerful enemies at home who undermined his every step. In spite of everything he had prevented a Spanish collapse in Piedmont and had then moved on to deal effectively with a delicate situation created by the Papal War. There his military talents and personal restraint averted what might have been an appalling tragedy, without in any way sacrificing Spanish interests. Paul IV was a true hero of the Church whose conduct throughout his career had been exemplary from the standpoint of Catholics like Alba. Even in his apparent dotage, when he seemed to fall victim to undue love of country and kinfolk, he was not wholly lost to the demands of the papacy, for such imperial sympathizers as the Colonnas and Sforza were a threat to the integrity of his office. It is hard to know which would have been worse: to have gratified the enemies of the Church by another Sack of Rome, or to have acquiesced in his more unreasonable behavior.

That Alba was able to steer a middle course is doubly remarkable when one considers his position. He was, after all, an Italian politician in his own right, with clients and allies throughout the Peninsula. Whatever he did led to accusations of personal interest, and his enemies seized gleefully on Cosimo's acquisition of Siena and Alba's spirited defense of the Colonnas as evidence of disloyalty to the king. To make matters worse, these events occurred in the midst of a lengthy suit brought by him against the Archbishop of Toledo over the tithes of Huéscar. Huéscar had been received in *encomienda* by his grandfather after the fall of Granada, thus giving him an hereditary, if disputed, claim to the tithes.[84] Just as he and the Pope were moving toward confrontation, Alba's uncle, the Cardinal of Santiago, was pressing this case in the Curia. Alba's caution was thus inevitably, and wrongly, seen as evidence of a secret deal, and the impression was strengthened when the case was settled in his favor.[85]

Under these circumstances it is a wonder that Alba could function at all, much less emerge with credit, but the resolution of the Papal War brought him wide acclaim. Even Brantôme, who never grasped the lesson of Ceresole and was highly critical of Alba's conduct in Piedmont, believed that in 1557 he showed himself to be a master of the art of war.[86] There was even praise from Henry II,[87] but it was his reception at the court of Philip II that mattered most. The Emperor Charles was gone. Living in retirement at Yuste, he was undoubtedly pleased, but it was now his son who controlled affairs, and Philip, according to the Venetian ambassador, was "in awe" of Alba.[88] The duke returned to Brussels in January, 1558, and was met by the entire court except Ruy Gómez, "who, from indisposition, real or feigned, did not go out of doors."[89] The duke, who knew how to be magnanimous and heap coals at the same time, thereupon went to see Ruy Gómez, but the chamberlain was not noticeably cheered by the visit. As the days passed and courtiers flocked to Alba's side it was rumored that his old rival would retire.

This rumor, of course, proved false, as did many others. It was said that Alba had demanded the duchy of Bari or the regency of the Netherlands, when in fact he wanted only to return to Spain with Philip. True, he said that he would retire to Alba although Alba no longer existed—an unsubtle reminder of all he had spent in the royal service[90]—but for all his complaints he had learned his lesson. Power lay in proximity to the king and, as a servant of his would later say, "The Duke of Alba was not made to wander in deserts."[91] This time the road home would be certain, but it would not be quick.

VI

THE PROBLEM OF
THE NETHERLANDS

The reason for the long delay in returning to Spain was at least worthwhile. Though he could not have known it, Alba's campaign against the pope was to be the last of that long series of conflicts known as the Italian Wars. For more than half a century the kings of France had pursued the chimera of an Italian empire. They based their hopes on a powerful army and on some rather dubious claims to Naples and Milan which in the aftermath of St. Quentin seemed highly academic. France was exhausted, its army in disarray. In Italy nearly all the French footholds were gone. Milan and Naples were under direct Spanish control, the papacy had ceased to be a factor, and all Tuscany lay in the hands of a Spanish client, Cosimo de' Medici. Henry II, encouraged by his mistress, Diane de Poitiers, and her allies of the powerful Montmorency clan, was finally ready to discuss a lasting European peace, and Philip, the outwardly victorious, agreed.

The result was the treaty of Cateau-Cambrésis, a watershed in the political history of the sixteenth century. In six months of hard bargaining the issues that divided France and Spain were settled one by one, and a new settlement was evolved that was to last with few alterations until the end of the century. Old suspicions remained, and hostilities still occasionally erupted, but in general the treaty marked a turning inward of the great European powers. In the decades to come, France was to be increasingly absorbed in a series of tragic civil wars, while Spain concentrated on maintaining the integrity of her empire.[1]

110

THE NETHERLANDS 1567

- - - - - BORDERS OF THE HABSBURG LANDS

SCALE 0 15 .... 105 Km.

Map 5.

Of those who negotiated the treaty, Alba was among the most active. The delegations on both sides were intended to be broadly representative, and as the leader of a court faction his presence was essential if the resulting treaty was to gain wide acceptance. It is not surprising, then, that he was joined by Ruy Gómez, the Bishop of Arras, William, Prince of Orange, and Viglius van Aytta of Zwichem, president of the Privy Council of the Netherlands.

In retrospect, this conjunction of personalities may have been highly significant. Alba and Ruy Gómez were enemies and would remain so, but Arras, soon to become Cardinal Granvelle, was another matter. This was the first time he had worked closely with the duke since Metz, and though their relationship on that occasion had been strained they formed an alliance at Cateau-Cambrésis that was to last (with periodic interruptions) until Alba's death. It was not a love match. Both men were arrogant and self-contained and may actually have disliked each other, but they were so frequently in agreement on policy that a bond of mutual respect developed which owed little to friendship or even trust.[2]

It was very different with the remaining members of the delegation. William of Orange was only twenty-six, a magnificent though somewhat frivolous prince who as yet showed no signs of becoming the indomitable Father of His Country. He missed most of the conference by dallying with a Flemish girl named Eve Elincx,[3] and Alba, perhaps understandably, concluded that he was a person of little substance. Viglius, on the other hand, was one of the most distinguished jurists of his age. Born in a remote Frisian village ten days before Alba, he had risen to preside over the highest judicial authority in the Low Countries and was known equally for his learning and his greed. Legal business prevented him from taking a major part at Cateau-Cambrésis, but years later he would serve Alba enthusiastically in another, grimmer task.[4]

For the French the leading negotiators were the Constable Anne de Montmorency and Charles, Cardinal of Lorraine. They hated each other personally as well as politically. Like Alba, Montmorency cultivated the role of a bluff, honest soldier, while the cardinal made no effort to disguise his subtle, devious nature or his great sophistication. The brother of Alba's old rival the Duke of Guise, he was a devoted Catholic, but his inordinate ambition and vast wealth caused many to regard him as a threat to the monarchy.[5] The Guise and Montmorency families had long been rivals, and it was perhaps inevitable that since Montmorency favored peace at almost any cost,

the cardinal tended to oppose it. They were assisted in their deliberations by Jean de Morvilier and Claude de L'Aubespine, two ministers and men of letters whose tasks were primarily secretarial.[6]

The story of the negotiations themselves, fascinating in a lugu-
brious way, has been told by Romier and need not be repeated here,
but Alba's role is worth noting. From the start he established a personal relationship with Montmorency that eased the talks and
opened lines of communication that might otherwise have remained
closed. On the shadowy but essential level of secret initiatives and
hidden compromise this friendship was second in importance only
to the initiatives of Christine, Dowager Duchess of Lorraine.[7]

Alba's other achievement was to negotiate the delicate issue of
Calais. The fate of this last English foothold on the Continent was
the obstacle upon which the treaty nearly foundered, not once but
several times. The French had seized Calais in the last major action
of the war and were understandably reluctant to give up a prize of
such great symbolic value, but Philip, who was still married to the
Queen of England, felt honor-bound to return it, as England's loss
had been incurred on his behalf.[8] During the first sessions held at
Cercamp in October, 1558, both sides were unyielding. Alba saved
the situation by arranging with Montmorency to postpone the discussion until a later date while the delegates plunged into the labyrinthine but more adjustable affairs of Italy.[9] At this point Mary died.
The conference adjourned in observance of her funeral and that of
Charles V, who had died in September,[10] but at least for a time her
death changed nothing. Philip, who now hoped to marry her successor Elizabeth, felt that a defense of English interests was more
essential than ever.

The break came when the delegates reconvened at Cambrésis in
February. When Elizabeth refused the Spanish marriage, the way
was opened to a negotiated settlement, though Philip could not
bring himself to abandon her entirely. He needed a friend in northern Europe and saw no point in driving her into the arms of the
French. The result was a face-saving solution that owed much to
Alba's skill and perhaps even more to his understanding of the island kingdom.

As majordomo in 1554–1555 Alba had developed a working relationship with the English. He understood them far better than did
other Spaniards, whose contacts had been largely social. Because of
this Philip permitted him to deal almost single-handedly with the
English commissioners at Cateau-Cambrésis.[11] It was a happy choice.

Alba knew that Calais was an emotional issue that posed grave dangers to an untried queen. He also knew that she lacked the resources to take it back and guessed that she was bright enough to know her weakness. A formula was needed that would leave Calais to the French without seriously compromising Elizabeth in the eyes of her subjects, and this is precisely what he set out to create.

After much acrimonious debate, the French were persuaded to send off a proposal that at first glance seems ridiculous but which provided Elizabeth with a way out of her dilemma. She was given a choice. If she should marry and have a son, and if that son should marry a daughter of either the king or the Dauphin, the son would have Calais. On the other hand, if these contingencies did not appeal to her, the French would simply agree to relinquish the town in eight years.[12] There was not much doubt as to which route she would take, but the choice itself, to say nothing of the proposed marriage, was of value to a woman who had been declared illegitimate by her own father and whose throne was far from secure. It was also pleasant to be offered either noble hostages or 500,000 crowns as security for the agreement. Elizabeth had little use for idle French gentlemen and knew that the money would be deposited in Venice rather than London,[13] but she also knew how to play the game.

On February 19 she told her commissioners to demand Calais "peremptorily" as long as Alba continued to threaten the French with war, but if he became reluctant they were to give in.[14] He must have been aware of these instructions, because a few days later Alba received the commissioners in bed, where he was once again recovering from an unknown malady. The war for Calais, he said, would be a war on two fronts, as the Scots would be certain to support the French. In those circumstances Spanish aid would be of little value.[15] No more needed to be said. A week later, though Elizabeth was still regaling her subjects with threats to "spend a million crowns a year on war,"[16] an agreement had been reached. The treaty was signed by the end of the month. Calais was irretrievably lost, but it would be eight long years before anyone could be absolutely certain of this fact; the hapless Mary, not Elizabeth, would bear the blame in the memories of Englishmen.

After the conclusion of the treaty on March 29, Alba, Ruy Gómez, and Orange, among others, made their way to Paris. There they would remain until August as hostages for the agreement, for there was a seemingly endless list of fortresses to be returned by both sides and a host of prisoners to be repatriated. There was also the projected marriage of Henry's daughter Elizabeth of Valois. The original intention had been to marry her to Philip's son Don Carlos, but when the English marriage collapsed it was decided that Philip himself should have her. An agreement was signed on June 21, and the wedding took place the next day, with Alba serving as proxy.

The celebration would long be remembered as one of the last in which the nobility of Europe met on friendly ground. Alba, who had until now astonished the Parisians with his costume of somber black, appeared before the Cathedral of Notre Dame in cloth-of-gold surmounted by an imperial crown. He was accompanied by his old rival Ruy Gómez, his future nemesis Orange, and Lamoral, Count of Egmont, whom he would one day kill. The new queen, her fragile beauty set off by innumerable jewels, was attended by her mother, Catherine de' Medici, and by her father, who held her hand. Tall, athletic, and in the prime of life, Henry had less than three weeks to live. Christine of Lorraine and Mary Stuart, the future Queen of Scots, held her train. Behind them was arrayed the entire cast of the civil wars to come: Montmorency, Guise, Bourbon, and Valois alike. After the ceremony, held on a platform erected before the west front of the cathedral, the entire party dined at the palace of the archbishop. Then, observing the custom of the time, Alba retired to the marriage chamber, briefly placed his arm and one leg across the bed, and left.[17]

The next few days were given over to feasting and tournaments. Alba seems to have developed a dislike for tournaments, or perhaps he had had a premonition. In any case, he told Throckmorton, the English ambassador, that "some ran well, some ran evil, but that in his judgment, none exceeded much the rest."[18] His opinion scarcely mattered. Henry II dearly loved jousting, and this was an opportunity for the greatest exercise of chivalry in living memory. On June 30, late in the afternoon, he insisted on running a final course against a young officer of the Scots guard. At the moment of impact his opponent's lance shattered and a splinter entered the king's visor, piercing his right eye. It was immediately obvious that it had damaged the brain, but the king was a man of unusual vigor and for a while it was thought that he might recover. Alba called in Vesalius, the greatest physician of the day, but it was too late. On July 10, Henry II died, leaving behind him four sons none of whom was old enough to rule.[19]

In a sense the death of the king sealed the peace of Cateau-Cambrésis as nothing else could have done. Such treaties had been made in the past and broken within months. This one would endure because France could no longer contemplate war. Francis II, a feeble, ungainly child, could not rule on his own, and by appointing the Guises as his regents Henry virtually forced their rivals into rebellion. Philip II was free, as his father had never been, to pursue his own concerns.

Of these, two were to dominate the first half of his reign. One was the Turk, whose depredations would remain a problem for many years to come. Alba, though he might have wished it otherwise, played only a peripheral role in these Mediterranean struggles and concentrated on the second great focus of Philip's policy, the Netherlands. Here he was to become involved in one of the most bitter of all historical struggles and earn the reputation that has dogged his memory into modern times.

For generations the various provinces of the Netherlands had defied the efforts of their masters to weld them into a workable state. Charles V, like his Burgundian predecessors, had attempted to centralize their institutions and tap their enormous wealth, but his efforts had met with little success. By the accession of Philip II this rich patchwork of contrasting languages, customs, and privileges had become all but ungovernable.

Chief among the problems was finance. Though rich, the Low Countries contributed little to the support of the Crown. What they did contribute came in the form of *aides*, taxes levied and collected by the Estates themselves for a specific purpose. Each *aide* had to be voted upon separately and each was likely to provide the occasion for new attempts to wring political concessions from the monarchy. The Estates had always been reluctant to support imperial ventures that appeared unrelated to their own interests. By the 1550s an unsettled economy and the interminable wars with France had made them stingy indeed, and this tendency was reinforced by something like a breakdown in the representative bodies themselves. Strident bickering between townsmen and the nobility over the latter's claim to exemption from the *aides* spilled over into non-fiscal matters and made cooperation impossible. The Crown could be certain neither of its revenues nor of effective action in any other area of government.[20]

The religious situation was equally difficult. As a cosmopolitan community heavily dependent upon trade the Netherlands had long been disposed to religious toleration and had been the source of a number of religious movements which the orthodox viewed with suspicion. Heresy flourished. Lutherans, Anabaptists, and, eventually, Calvinists found the teeming cities both a refuge and a source of converts. The magistrates frequently saw no reason to disturb them and the Church as it was then constituted seemed unable to answer the challenge.

There were only four bishops in the entire region, three of whom were located in the extreme south. Their dioceses had been established at an early date, and subsequent shifts in population had left the major towns without effective ecclesiastical authority. Charles V had attempted to get around this by establishing an inquisition, but large areas, including Brabant, were exempt from its authority. To make matters worse, the whole ecclesiastical hierarchy was at least nominally beyond the reach of the king. Three of the bishops were under the jurisdiction of the archdiocese of Reims, while the fourth came under the purview of Cologne. A number of towns were administered directly by these two authorities, while others fell into the dioceses of Trier, Münster, Osnabrück, Metz, or Verdun. Under these circumstances a unified religious policy would have been impossible even if the nobility had not, in practice, controlled the rights of nomination. With appointments made primarily for the financial or dynastic advantage of the great families, religious standards were appallingly low. The clergy of the Netherlands may not have been wholly corrupt, but in piety, learning, and zeal they were rarely a match for the heretics.[21]

To a monarch like Philip II such conditions were clearly intolerable. He believed firmly that it was the duty of the monarch to provide not merely governance, but justice and protection for the souls of his subjects. To fail in this, as he was obviously failing in the Netherlands, was to betray a sacred trust and imperil his own salvation.[22] Accordingly, one of his first concerns was to effect a complete reform of Church and State in the Netherlands.

The first step in Philip's program was to curb the power of the nobility, which he had first perceived as a threat during the Estates General of 1556 and 1558. The nobles had led the opposition to further subsidies for the French wars and had vigorously protested the continued presence of Spanish troops. Philip had—not unnaturally—concluded that their interests and those of the monarchy were irreconcilable, and in this he was probably correct. Whatever he did to increase his authority could only be done at the expense of their privileges and, therefore, their incomes. At a time when inflation had already eroded their financial position to an alarming degree he knew that he could expect serious resistance.

Characteristically, the king did nothing overt, but the arrangements he left behind when he returned to Spain reflected a determination to restrict noble influence. The major organs of government remained as they had been under his father, but they were placed under the control of persons unsympathetic to the nobility. The regency was given to his half-sister, Margaret of Parma, and the Bishop of Arras quickly assumed preeminence in the Council of State. Though talented, the bishop was hated as much for his arrogance and ostentation as for his bourgeois origins, and he seems to have returned the dislike of such figures as Orange and Egmont with interest.[23] The Council of Justice remained under the control of Viglius, while that of Finance was given to Charles, Count of Berlaymont. Both were dedicated royalists. Berlaymont, to be sure, was a nobleman, but his poverty and the need to provide places for his many children rendered him totally dependent upon royal favor.[24]

These appointments effectively excluded the nobility from access to the levers of power, for decisions were usually made by Arras, Viglius, and Berlaymont, acting as a *consulta*. Of these three, Arras was by far the strongest personality, and he may truly be said to have dominated the government: he was in constant communication with the king, and the regent seemed dependent on his counsels. It was all but inevitable that noble opposition would one day focus on this great minister, who was soon to unite Church and State in his own person.

If the organization of the regency was offensive to the nobility, the possibilities it opened up were truly frightening. They knew Philip's propensity for reform and were certain that he meant to change the judicial system and find some means of levying taxes directly. Depending on the type of levy involved, systematic taxation might or might not prove a threat to their position, but royalization of the courts would unquestionably remove an important source of their wealth and power. Philip was years away from implementing any such schemes but, as so often happens, the nobles were unwilling to let events take their course. Almost instinctively they obstructed the growth of royal power, out of fear of things to come.

Their concern was legitimized by the first great issue to arise after Philip's departure: the reform of the ecclesiastical hierarchy. There was nothing novel or unexpected about this. Sweeping reforms had been proposed by Charles V in 1551–1552, but owing to the manifold problems of these last darkening years, little was done beyond abolishing the French-dominated bishopric of Thérouanne. When he abdicated, Charles entrusted the completion of the task to his son, and in 1558 Philip had begun to move toward a resolution.

In outline, the plan was nothing less than complete reconstruction of the hierarchy on rational and dynastic principles. The Church in the Netherlands was to be removed entirely from the jurisdiction of foreign bishoprics and to be grouped into three provinces roughly according to linguistic and regional boundaries. The largest of these would be Flanders and Flemish Brabant, containing six new bishoprics (Bruges, Ypres, Ghent, Antwerp, Roermond, and 's Hertogenbosch) under the new archdiocese of Mechelen. In the north, new bishops would be created at Haarlem, Middelburg, Leeuwarden, Groningen, and Deventer and placed under Utrecht, which would be raised to archepiscopal status. The French-speaking regions were grouped under Cambrai and were to include Tournai, Arras, Namur, and St. Omer. The king was to have the right of nomination to all save Cambrai, and candidacy would be restricted to those with degrees in theology or canon law.

On May 12, 1559, the pope confirmed these arrangements in the bull *Super Universalis*, and a commission of five was appointed to work out the details. Specifically, the creation of dioceses *ex nihilo* is an expensive business, and it was essential to provide financial security for the new bishops. The commission completed its work with laudable dispatch. Bulls of circumscription were issued on March 11 and August 7, 1561. By their terms some revenues were to be transferred from Spanish dioceses, but most would be created by incorporating monastic foundations directly into the new bishoprics. Antwerp, for example, was to absorb the Abbey of St. Bernard's plus an annual contribution of 500 fl. each from the abbeys of St. Michel and Villers, while 's Hertogenbosch was to be funded almost entirely through incorporation of the Abbey of Tongerlo. In such cases full incorporation meant displacement of the incumbent abbot in favor of the new bishop, who would then assume both his duties and his revenues.[25]

The reaction to this scheme can well be imagined. The abbots protested to the skies, while those in Brabant went further and polled the universities of Paris, Bologna, and Cologne in support of their view that the incorporations were uncanonical. The *Joyeuse Entrée*, the document that had guaranteed the rights of Brabanters since Burgundian times, was invoked, and the nobles quickly rallied to support the beleaguered clerics.[26]

That they should have done so is hardly surprising. The nobles were themselves grievously threatened by the reforms, for they had hitherto controlled rights of nomination to many posts that would now revert to the king. A serious blow to their powers of patronage, it was greatly augmented by the new educational requirements, which effectively excluded their younger sons from high ecclesiastical office. They saw, too, that incorporation of the abbeys represented a purely political threat that was apparently intended by the commission. Three of the abbots were traditionally members of the powerful Estates of Brabant. If they were replaced by Crown-appointed bishops, noble influence on this important body would diminish correspondingly.[27] In view of all this, the transformation of the hated Arras into Cardinal Granvelle, Archbishop of Mechelen and primate of the Netherlands, was merely icing on the cake.

Opposition was not restricted to the nobles and their ecclesiastical friends. The Protestants, who knew full well the portent of these changes, were greatly alarmed, and ordinary citizens got the impression, inaccurate but understandable, that the Spanish Inquisition was about to be introduced. To add to the clamor, the northeastern provinces annexed by Charles V decided that the reorganization would compromise their autonomy and opposed the new bishops with such vigor that they could not be installed until Alba himself accomplished it seven years later.[28]

Granvelle, though he had not been directly responsible for the plan of reorganization,[29] found himself at the center of the storm. Strident cries for his removal came from every quarter and a scurrilous campaign of defamation was launched against him by Simon Renard, a former protégé.[30] At the head of the movement were the great nobles, led by Orange, Egmont, and Hornes. Though they avoided the excesses of the madcap Baron Brederode, who had taken to impersonating the cardinal in drunken masquerades, their bitterness was real. At the convocation of the Golden Fleece in May, 1562, a violent argument erupted between the malcontents and Granvelle's adherents Bossu, Berlaymont, and Noircarmes. It came as no surprise when the provincial Estates shortly thereafter rejected the regent's request for funds and when Horne's brother, the ill-fated Montigny, spent much of his first visit to Madrid haranguing all who would listen on the shortcomings of the cardinal.

In responding to all this, Granvelle once again demonstrated his subtlety and his grasp of Philip's character. Without giving way to resentment or open denunciation he made it abundantly clear that the opposition was a predictable response to royal policy and was at least partially influenced by personal considerations of a most ambiguous sort. Calmly, deliberately, and with an affectation of martyrdom, his letters to the king played upon the monarch's suspicions while he attempted, at least in public, to keep open the lines of communication between himself and the dissidents.[31] It was a masterful performance not wholly ungrounded in truth, but in the end it failed. The king had no love of insolent nobles and might have accepted his minister's version of events without question, had the whole issue not become involved in factional politics at home.

Alba had returned to Spain in August, 1559, fully expecting to take his place as Philip's leading counselor. He believed that his services entitled him to nothing less, and as Philip had recently granted him a *merced* of 160,000 escudos,[32] he had no reason to suppose that the king thought differently. It was therefore a shock to find that once again he was frequently excluded from the innermost councils.

The reasons for this were abundantly clear. The king may have been grateful to Alba but his gratitude did not make him love Ruy Gómez less. If the duke had any illusions about this it was because he had fallen victim to wishful thinking or to the self-serving flattery of courtiers. When Alba received his *merced*, Ruy Gómez was named Prince of Eboli, and there is no real evidence beyond gossip that he was at any time eclipsed in the royal favor.

Even more important was the ascendancy of Francisco de Eraso, now the king's chief secretary and the man upon whom he relied most extensively for the conduct of business. Rude, vindictive, and arrogant, Eraso hated Alba with a vigor undiluted by time. As he had somehow managed to remain on friendly terms with Eboli, these two indispensables found it easy to keep the duke at arm's length.

Alba found this intolerable, and it was only a matter of time before his resentment exploded in a scene that attracted much unfavorable comment. Finding the king closeted with Eraso, Alba pounded furiously on the door, demanding admittance. When they refused, he insulted Eraso in a loud voice. Then, complaining bitterly against the king, he retired to his estates.[33] It is a credit to Philip's patience that he smoothed things over and brought Alba back to court, but this acknowledgment of his importance changed nothing. The king disliked confrontations, and this display of bad manners bordering on *lèse majesté* could only reduce Alba's influence further.

This was doubly unfortunate, because just as Granvelle was fighting for his political life he was deprived of his most potent ally.

Alba was virtually ignored for the next three years, and Eraso, who remained high in Philip's esteem, hated Granvelle even more than he hated the duke. Granvelle had earned his enmity long before, not merely because he was a friend of Alba and of Gonzalo Pérez but because in the 1550s he had accused Eraso of corruption.[34] The accusation had borne meager fruit, but Eraso remembered. When he left the Netherlands in 1559 he left behind two associates who were instructed to report diligently on the bishop's activities, with special emphasis on any shortcomings for which he could be held responsible. Both these men, Alonso del Canto and Cristóbal de Castellanos, were *contadores* with access to much inside information, and del Canto was destined to play the role of gadfly with distinction.

Shortly after Eraso's departure, del Canto fell in with an Augustinian friar who was deeply concerned about Granvelle's failure to suppress heresy. Lorenzo de Villavicencio was disinterested, in the sense that he was not a partisan of either faction, but this only rendered him more effective. After a brief flirtation with heterodox ideas at Louvain he had become a conservative's conservative, bristling with suspicions and inclined to define heresy in the broadest possible terms. His reports, like those of del Canto, were carefully brought to Philip's attention by Eraso and in spite of their exaggerations did much to formulate the king's views on the Netherlands.[35]

In general del Canto and Villavicencio felt that Granvelle was less than enthusiastic in his enforcement of the placards against heresy, and that royal authority was threatened by his personal unpopularity. Both accusations were based on unrealistic expectations but, being zealots, neither of them had bothered to examine the alternatives. Granvelle may have been unwilling to prosecute for heresy in cases he could not win, but the nobles did not wish to prosecute at all. Many of them believed in something like religious toleration, and all were notoriously opposed to the extension of royal authority. Eboli of course knew this, as did Eraso. They maintained close contact with the nobles and seem to have shared their vision of a decentralized empire in which even religious policy would be determined primarily by local custom. Villavicencio and the king eventually realized this, of course, but their enlightenment came too late to save the cardinal.

During 1562 and 1563 Philip appears to have accepted Villavicencio's reports without serious question. They squared with his own concern for orthodoxy and a natural tendency to suspect his ministers, particularly those who were out of immediate reach. At the same time the nobles increased their protests, and the insinuations of Simon Renard began to trouble Margaret of Parma. At the heart of this web of intrigue was Eraso's old friend Cristóbal de Castellanos, by now a confidant of Renard and a close associate of the leading nobles.

The pressure reached its peak in the spring and summer of 1563. On March 11, Orange, Egmont, and Hornes withdrew from the Council of State and dispatched an ultimatum to the king: their return was contingent upon the removal of Granvelle. In July the Knights of the Golden Fleece demanded that the Estates be called, and Brabant refused to approve further taxes while the cardinal held office. Finally, on August 12 Margaret of Parma dispatched her secretary, Tomás de Armenteros, to Madrid. She had become convinced, apparently by Renard, that Granvelle had blocked her suit with the king over the Castle of Plasencia, and, with more justification, that his presence was making it all but impossible for her to govern.[36] Armenteros was to add the regent's voice to the chorus demanding removal, and he executed his commission with enthusiasm. With the cardinal gone, his own power would increase immeasurably.

When the secretary arrived at Monzón where the king was exposing himself to the ongoing grievances of the Aragonese Cortes, he found that his task was easier than anticipated. Granvelle was not yet without supporters, but the one whose influence and filed tongue were most to be feared was absent. Alba had retired to Huéscar, "a place of mine that I am not sure is in this world,"[37] and was to remain there until Christmas.

Huéscar was by all odds the most troublesome of his estates. Located in a remote district 150 km west of Murcia, it had been given to his grandfather Don Fadrique as a reward for service in the wars of Granada. Heavily Morisco in population, it seethed with discontent that was greatly augmented by the corruption of his governors. Taking full advantage of their isolated situation, they lined their pockets at his expense, and when he at length arrived after many years of neglect he found the community in a state of near-rebellion.[38] Believing that proper management of the town could bring him 30,000 ducats per year, he set forth to correct matters in his own way.

His departure from court was not, therefore, an open gesture of protest as it had been in 1560, but it was clearly related to his frustration over the ascendancy of Eboli. After the walkout of 1560 he had resumed his role as chief advisor on foreign affairs, but each evening after the day's business was concluded Philip sat down with Eboli for an hour or two and allowed himself to be persuaded that the duke's advice was in one way or another impracticable. The erosion of Alba's position was further demonstrated by the appointment of Juan Manrique de Lara as *mayordomo mayor* to the queen. The position had originally been held by the Count of Alba de Liste and was regarded by the Toledos as family property. On February 12, 1562, the count died of a dental hemorrhage and the post was temporarily assumed by Alba himself. He served in this capacity, apparently to the queen's satisfaction, until August, when Manrique de Lara was appointed instead of the family candidate, the Prior Don Antonio de Toledo.[39] In short, he remained painfully conscious of his lack of influence and felt that he was accomplishing little by remaining at court.[40]

Once arrived in Huéscar, Alba was, as he put it, more cut off from events at court than if he had been in Peru,[41] and his faction was left leaderless and thoroughly demoralized.[42] He continued to give his opinions by post, but it was a poor substitute for being on the spot meeting the arguments of Armenteros and the nobles head on. When the king asked him to comment on the proposed removal of Granvelle his reply was a model of frustration and rage that has been much quoted by subsequent historians: "Each time I see the dispatches of those three gentlemen of Flanders [Orange, Egmont, and Hornes] they move me to such choler that, if it were not much tempered, I believe that my opinion might seem to your Majesty like that of a madman."[43]

He had every reason to be upset. If a man can no longer protect his friends his usefulness as a leader is over, and Granvelle's case was far more crucial than that of Don Antonio de Toledo. Moreover, Alba believed as a matter of policy that removing the cardinal would be fatal to royal authority as well as to his own. He was convinced that the enmity toward Granvelle was based on his refusal to bow to the Estates, and as the Estates were the bastions of local privilege against the king, Granvelle or someone like him was essential to Philip's program of reform. In other words, if Eboli and Eraso favored a decentralized empire, Alba favored an empire directly controlled by the king, though not necessarily modeled on the institutions of Castile.[44]

Protest as he might, it availed him nothing. By Christmas Granvelle was doomed, and by March he was gone. Eraso had his revenge and the nobles were in de facto control of the Netherlands.

To Alba it must have seemed the low point of his career, but the triumph of his enemies was to be more transient than he imagined. Once in power, the nobles failed miserably to satisfy Philip's standards of orthodoxy and justice. Their aims were not his own, and both heresy and incidents of judicial corruption increased. It was then that Villavicencio and del Canto became like the sorceror's apprentice, for they continued to send voluminous reports that now reflected on Orange and Egmont rather than Granvelle. Villavicencio in particular had never been party to Eraso's schemes, and he was now more deeply offended by conditions than he had been before. By the time Egmont embarked for Spain in an effort to wring further concessions from the king, the worthy friar had progressed from dismay to an open attack on the orthodoxy of the noble junta.[45] Thus it was that the arrival of Egmont coincided with the beginnings of a reversal in Philip's policy. Ordinarily, reports from a single source would not have had such an impact, but they were the only disinterested reports available and they tended to cast doubt on the wisdom of Eboli's advice. Unfortunately, the king could not simply revert to Alba's position without grave embarrassment, and he may yet have been convinced that the duke's remedies were too extreme. In any case he decided to deal with Egmont on his own without consultation.

The mission of Egmont was in itself a prime expression of the nobility's hubris. Not content with their gains and unaware that the king's suspicions had been aroused, they dispatched the count to request a further extension of their authority. Specifically, they sought to add four more nobles to the Council of State and to divide the existing office of president into a presidency of the Council of State and a presidency of the Privy Council. The moment for this was propitious, as in the aftermath of Granvelle's removal Viglius had suffered a stroke and wanted to retire, thereby leaving the office vacant. Their other recommendations, as outlined in a memo presented personally by Egmont on March 24, 1565,[46] included an investigation of abuses in various councils and provincial governments and a relaxation of the heresy laws. The suggestion, originally made by Brantôme, that they also wished to renew the wars against France in alliance with the Huguenots is almost certainly false.[47]

Even without this their program was impossible, given Philip's attitude toward heresy and authority, but their choice of an emissary was worse. Lamoral, Count of Egmont, was handsome, charming, and good-natured, but extraordinarily naive. He was also extravagant and heavily in debt. When he arrived at court he had personal affairs to settle, and he was apt to confuse his personal cause with that of the Netherlands as a whole. Philip greeted him cordially, granted his personal requests, and sent him off believing that his mission had been successful. In fact, nothing could have been further from the truth. The king agreed to consider a reorganization of the government but pointed out that this was a complicated matter and would take time. He could appreciate Egmont's desire for the immediate appointment of new counselors, but until the larger issue was resolved such appointments would clearly be premature. On the all-important issue of heresy he did even less. Egmont had argued that the execution of heretics should be stopped, as it served only to create martyrs. Philip helpfully suggested that if that were the case the executions should be held in secret! He agreed that a general colloquy on religion might be held, but only if it were secret and much smaller than the nobles intended. He knew perfectly well that they hoped to use it to modify the placards against heresy, and this he would never permit.[48]

In short, the count returned to Brussels empty-handed, but in the roseate glow produced by the king's apparent favor he let it be known that Philip was prepared to make concessions. When on May 13, 1565, the king dispatched letters that set forth his true position, he cried to high heaven that he had been deceived, and the nobles believed him.[49] Another wedge had been driven between the Crown and its Netherlandish subjects, and in the process Philip's first attempt to make policy on his own had backfired. There was nothing left but to turn to Alba. As Villavicencio had noted, the policies of Eboli and Eraso had led only to an increase in heresy and sedition. The king's efforts had foundered on their own excessive subtlety. It was increasingly evident that only a strong line would prevent further deterioration of the royal cause. Alba had always opposed concessions, and now in retrospect he appeared to have been right, but there was something else afoot in the spring of 1565 that made his advice even more welcome. Eraso, after so many years of lording it over courtier and bureaucrat alike, was now under suspicion. An investigation was launched that found him guilty on nine separate counts of corruption.[50]

The investigation of Eraso owed little to Alba, but it was the final act in the duke's restoration to power. From early 1565 onward he was the dominant figure at court, and the king seems to have accepted his views without serious modification. Eboli was relegated to the thankless task of serving as majordomo to the increasingly difficult prince Don Carlos, and correspondence with Margaret was handled entirely by Gonzalo Pérez, an old ally of Alba, and by Villavicencio, a new one. The latter had returned to Spain shortly after the departure of Egmont, and his coming strengthened the king's resolve to act with greater severity. Both Eboli and Tisnacq, the Netherlands' representative at Madrid, were excluded from the deliberations; as often as not they were kept in ignorance of what had been decided. It was a complete reversal in the duke's personal fortunes and a revolution in Spanish policy.

The first sign of the direction things were to take was the appointment of Alba as the king's representative to the conference at Bayonne. This great set-piece of Renaissance diplomacy was the idea of Catherine de' Medici, who hoped to strengthen the tottering monarchy of her son through a closer alliance with Spain. For months Philip had postponed action on her requests for a personal meeting but in the end, at the urging of Eboli, he had reluctantly agreed. The shift at court occurred in the midst of preparations and in effect destroyed all hope of an expanded alliance between the two powers. The newly influential Alba thought it foolish to draw too near an unstable and, as he saw it, heretic-ridden regime, and was annoyed that the king had agreed to a conference.

Alba's primary concern was the relationship between the French Huguenots and the king's own heretics in the Netherlands. As a veteran of the Habsburg-Valois struggle he disliked the thought of a strong and united French monarchy and was doubly opposed to one that might tolerate Protestants, leaving them free to plot with their co-religionists in the Low Countries. He therefore insisted that any agreement with Catherine should depend upon her willingness to take arms against them, knowing full well that she was unlikely to do this.

This policy accorded with the deeper instincts of the king but it turned the conference into a purposeless charade. Philip refused to go and even intimated that the presence of his queen, Catherine's daughter, was improper, as heretics would undoubtedly be present. He finally relented on this point, but sent Alba as his substitute, along with Manrique de Lara, who though a partisan of Eboli could scarcely be excluded, as he was majordomo to the queen. When the Spaniards arrived, nearly a month late, the players spoke their lines and departed without attempting serious negotiations. Catherine talked of marriages and of a union between France and Spain to, as Alba sarcastically put it, "give law to the world." The duke responded by lecturing her on the evils of tolerance and by suggesting, none too gently, that she put her house in order. To Charles IX he spoke of *"niñerias,"* of war and the chase, and whenever possible he encouraged the pretensions of the more fanatical Catholics, notably Blaise de Montluc, whose vanity amused him. On two points, however, both he and Manrique de Lara were adamant: the present alliance was sufficient without further marriages, and there should be no talk of inviting the Huguenots to a general council of the French Church.

On this note, the meeting broke up amid general dissatisfaction on both sides.[51] Ironically, the Protestants of Europe were gravely alarmed by this diplomatic fiasco. They were sure that it portended nothing less than a crusade against them, and when the St. Bartholomew's Day Massacre erupted seven years later, they convinced themselves, against all reason, that it had been plotted at Bayonne.

There was in fact to be a crusade of sorts, but it was not to involve the French monarchy and would take place entirely within the dominions of Philip II. For the next eight years there would be no compromise with heresy or local privilege in the Netherlands, and the symbol of this policy would be the Duke of Alba.

The basic attitude of his faction was set forth in a memorial composed by Gonzalo Pérez in answer to the regent.[52] Keenly aware of the dangers of her position, she had replied to the letters of May 13 by supporting the claims of the nobles.[53] Gonzalo Pérez, of course, disagreed. The Inquistion and the edicts against heresy, he began, must be supported at all costs, and there should be an immediate investigation of corruption in the secular courts. In no circumstances should she call the Estates General, and efforts should be made to sow discord between Egmont and Orange. In the meantime, nothing whatever should be done to reorganize the government, though if it became necessary the Council of State might be enlarged as the nobles had requested by adding to it "loyalists" like Aerschot and Meghen. "And with this," says the document in a tone reminiscent of the duke himself, "we may predict that the nobles will affirm that no more members are required." Finally, there was the problem of Granvelle and Viglius to deal with. The president, though a known embezzler whose wits may well have been addled by his stroke,[54] was too important to let go. His request for retirement should be denied. Granvelle, on the other hand, could not return to his post, as the nobles would surely murder him. It would be best for him to go to Rome.

Owing to Alba's continued presence at court there is little or no correspondence to indicate his exact role in the formulation of this and later statements of policy, but we know that he spent the late summer and early autumn urging the king to respond firmly to what he saw as the regent's failure of nerve. It was an exasperating task. Philip agreed with the duke but could not bring himself to answer the letters. He knew that his response would create further trouble and doubted that his resources were equal to coping with it.

Finally, at the beginning of October, he convened a curious meeting of the Council of State. Only Alba, Don Antonio, and Gonzalo Pérez were present; the Eboli faction was excluded. It was decided that not only should the recommendations contained in Pérez's memo be adopted but that Philip himself must go to the Netherlands, though the date of departure was left unspecified. To soften the blow, it was agreed over the strenuous objections of Alba and Don Antonio that certain personal requests of the nobles should be granted, but still the king procrastinated.[55] Two weeks later, with Pérez driven nearly to distraction by the delay, he at long last exploded in a perfect flurry of letters in which Alba's advice became, with minor modifications, official policy. Some of them, notably to Egmont and Granvelle, were corrected by the duke himself.[56]

Philip might have waited a few weeks longer. His missives arrived in the Low Countries just as the nobility was gathering to celebrate the opulent wedding of Margaret's son Alessandro Farnese. The wedding provided them with a fine opportunity to air their grievances and they did so with enthusiasm, encouraged perhaps by Philip's own representative, Diego Guzmán de Silva. Guzmán de Silva was at this time ambassador to England and a strong partisan of Eboli. He sympathized openly with the rebels and may have given them the mistaken impression that the divisions at Philip's court might yet produce a shift in policy.[57] During the week of festivities that followed, a number of them drafted and signed the fateful *Compromise*, a document protesting the Inquisition and setting out their views on other issues.[58] Though sympathetic, Orange, Egmont, and Hornes abstained, but it was nonetheless a statement of historic significance, a declaration of independence the mere signing of which was two years later to be viewed as a capital crime.

Throughout the winter protests continued to accelerate as the terms of Philip's instructions were enforced. To preserve their popularity, Orange, Egmont, and Hornes resigned from the Council of State. Thousands of Protestants crossed the border into Germany or fled to England while propagandists trumpeted that the Spanish Inquisition was about to be established.[59] This was, of course, untrue, for as Philip had remarked several years earlier, "the one they have there is more merciless than the one we have here,"[60] but it was rapidly becoming a popular article of faith and the cause of much concern. It is hardly surprising that there were occasional disorders and that the life of Villavicencio, who had returned in October, was in constant peril.[61] Perhaps most serious of all was the growing willingness of a faction of nobles headed by Orange's brother, the Protestant Louis of Nassau, to consider the possibility of armed revolt.[62]

After lengthy consultations Orange persuaded this group that bloodshed might yet be averted and that the proper course would be to petition the regent formally for the redress of their grievances. He himself, with typical caution, declined to accompany them. On April 5, 1566, a great procession of 300 noblemen marched up the street to the palace of the dukes of Brabant where Hendrik, Baron Brederode, presented Margaret of Parma with the *Request*. It was a moment of great dramatic significance, worthy of the descriptions that have been lavished upon it by generations of historians.

The essence of the document was that the king's letters of October 17–20 were likely to produce open revolt and that to avoid this the Inquisition must be ordered to cease its activities immediately. All executions were to be suspended and a representation of the grievances of the Estates was to be forwarded to Madrid. When Brederode had completed the reading, the petitioners courageously passed before the regent, in a manner reminiscent of the cavalry maneuver known as the *caracole*, so that she could see them individually and take note of who they were.[63] The regent, whose nerves had been strained by the events of the preceding months, was visibly shaken. In an ill-advised attempt to calm her the loyalist nobleman Berlaymont is supposed to have uttered the words that gave the movement its name: "Et comment, Madame, votre Alteza a-t-elle crainte de ces gueux?"[64]

Brave words, but Margaret knew she could not afford to take them literally. After urging the Inquisition to use discretion she published a *Moderation* that effectively permitted the toleration of Protestants in those areas in which they had already become established. Though this satisfied no one in the Netherlands it came as a decided shock to Madrid. On July 26 Philip informed Montigny that the *Moderation* was totally unacceptable. Five days later he wrote to Margaret in a conciliatory tone but without conceding any significant points. He agreed to suspension of the Papal Inquisition and to issuance of a general pardon but insisted on retaining the episcopal inquisitions and exempting religious crimes from any pardons whatsoever.[65] Shortly afterward, in a bizarre secret ceremony at which Alba was present, Philip absolved himself of compliance with even these modest changes.[66]

By the time these letters reached Brussels in mid-August, the Calvinists were engaged in an orgy of hedge-preaching and proselytizing, egged on and indeed openly protected by the nobility. It is surely no coincidence that receipt of the letters was followed by a great outburst of iconoclasm that destroyed images and church property throughout the Netherlands and which, though ultimately repudiated by the nobles, may well have been encouraged by them at the time.[67]

The news of the *Beeldenstorm*, as it was called, broke over the Woods of Segovia like a thunderclap. Believers in the psychosomatic theory of physical ailments will be gratified to learn that virtually the entire court was stricken with one illness or another. The king was felled by his usual headaches and by fevers of uncertain origin. Alba contracted gout, the first known attack of a disease that was to afflict him heavily, especially in times of stress.[68] All eventually recovered, but it was now clear to the convalescents that drastic measures were needed.

Much, however, had changed at court during the preceding year. Alba was still the dominant figure but alignments were changing in ways that made his dominance less complete. Most important was the disaffection and death of Gonzalo Pérez. In August, 1564, Pérez had written an almost savage letter to Granvelle complaining that Alba had tricked him in the matter of a *capelo* (cardinal's hat) but that he was preparing a "nephew" to avenge him.[69] The nephew was of course his son Antonio, who in deference to his father's clerical status had not originally been acknowledged. The origin of this quarrel is obscure, but the most reasonable conjecture is that Alba somehow thwarted Pérez in his well-known desire to be named a cardinal.[70] He certainly had the power to do so, given Philip's respect for his views on ecclesiastical patronage and his contacts at Rome, but if he did his reasons are unclear. No man living had a better claim on his favor than Pérez, and though there may have been an earlier squabble of some sort the outrage and sense of betrayal in Pérez's letter argue against it. In the end it may simply have come down to a matter of conscience. The secretary was undeniably talented, but no one had ever called him holy.

The matter seems to have been smoothed over or tacitly ignored during the period in which Alba and Pérez worked together on the letters of October, 1565. Their proximity must have been an added source of tension in an already strained atmosphere, but for the secretary at least, there would be no hope of escape. His own view of the crisis in the Netherlands was on record as coinciding with Alba's, and the king now shared it. To change sides would have been unthinkable even if the Eboli camp had welcomed him with open arms. Above all, his health was beginning to fail. He knew that he did not have long to live, and his last winter was devoted almost exclusively to securing the future of his son. He was determined that Antonio should succeed him as secretary of the Council of State, but in this too Alba opposed him and by so doing brought their quarrel once again into the open.[71]

The duke's motivation is fairly obvious, though it was a situation that factional leaders dread. Antonio's rival for the secretariat was Gabriel de Zayas. The claims of Zayas, who had supported the duke with scrupulous devotion for twenty years, could not be ignored. Moreover, Alba cannot have been unaware of Pérez's anger and may even have known of his threat. The vindictiveness of the secretary was legendary. Only a fool would have ignored the slightest hint of disaffection, the barest whisper of gossip. Antonio Pérez was well trained but young and inexperienced. He was also a "debauched youth"[72] whose loyalty to Alba was questionable. The duke threw his full weight behind Zayas.

Pérez died in April. In December of the following year Philip resolved the issue of his replacement by dividing the office between its two claimants.[73] It was a decision worthy of Solomon, but Alba had made a bitter and subtle enemy who from that day onward favored the Prince of Eboli and ultimately succeeded him as favorite.

The loss of Pérez and the defection of his son were made worse by the simultaneous appointment of Diego de Espinosa to the Council of State. Espinosa had long been Eboli's protégé, and in spite of his personal zeal as inquisitor-general he joined the Count of Feria in supporting a policy of moderation.[74] To balance this, Juan Manrique de Lara deserted to Alba's camp in July, 1566,[75] as did the king's confessor, Bernardo de Fresneda. It says much about the atmosphere of Philip's court that his confessor's defection was prompted by jealously over the rise of Espinosa.[76] Even Eboli himself was making a comeback. Though still much preoccupied with the demented Don Carlos, he was attending council meetings with greater regularity.

The net result of these maneuvers did not initially weaken the duke's position. The events of August merely strengthened Philip's conviction that Alba had been correct from the start, and the reconstitution of the Eboli faction neither delayed nor altered the implementation of his policies. Instead it exerted a subtle but definite force on the process by which Alba was ultimately forced to become the executor of his own schemes.

The shock produced by the iconoclastic disorders and by the *Accord* with which Margaret once again capitulated to the nobles took some time to wear off. Philip kept to his bed through much of September until Alba, in exasperation, accused him of malingering and threatened to leave court so that he would not be blamed for the consequences of inaction.[77] At the end of the month Philip wrote saying that he would come, but no date was given and the matter of the *Accord* was passed over in silence.[78] It was not until October 29 that more concrete measures were discussed in council.

There have been a number of accounts of this meeting, none of them wholly convincing. The best is that of Ossorio, Alba's first biographer, but even this is disfigured by imagined speeches in the style of Thucydides. Apparently, the meeting was begun by Eboli. He argued that extreme remedies were not required and that it would bemean the king to go in person. All that was needed to restore confidence was to dispatch a Spaniard of "clemency and goodwill." Eboli seems to have believed that the extent of the disorders had been exaggerated but that a show of force would be met by force, a point of view that contained obvious inconsistencies. It would not have appealed to a king determined to uphold royal authority, but his final point struck home. Philip, he said, was needed in Spain, especially in view of the condition of his only heir, Don Carlos.

Alba replied that Spain would keep. He knew as well as Eboli that certain of the nobles had threatened to resist Philip's coming by force of arms, and with characteristic bluntness declared this to be treason. Both Church and State were in mortal danger and only an anointed king had the personal authority to restore order. Philip must go in person, accompanied by a capable general, and once there he should not be too gentle. The events of recent years had shown that clemency would be taken for weakness. The evil must be rooted out entirely before reconciliation could take place. As was usual in such cases, he invoked the sacred memory of the emperor—one can almost hear him say "que está en cielo"—and declared that he would have had no doubts as to what course should be followed. It was, in short, a typical Alba performance.

At this point Manrique de Lara suggested, perhaps disingenuously, that as a precaution a general should go first, and that Alba would be perfect for the job. His words, remembered later, were then almost lost in an impassioned tirade by Feria, who defended Eboli in the most extreme terms. He was rudely interrupted by the usually phlegmatic Antonio de Toledo, whereupon Philip, who hated these scenes, abruptly adjourned the meeting.[79] On the following day Philip announced that he would be ready to depart in the spring of 1567.

The king's resolution was genuine enough, but almost as soon as it was made he began to fret about complications. Another meeting of the Cortes loomed on the horizon and vehement opposition to his leaving could be expected from that quarter. Don Carlos, too, was a worry. It was now obvious that his irrationality, his sadism, and his utter lack of discipline rendered him unfit for the throne, and Philip was beginning to doubt the possibility of conceiving another heir.[80] At forty, his own past record was not reassuring; moreover, Isabel of Valois was in delicate health. There was in any case much wisdom in the remark of Manrique de Lara. Would it not be better for a general to go first and suppress the insurgents, leaving Philip to appear as a peacemaker bearing pardons for all? Clearly this was the clever thing to do, but he was not certain that Alba was the perfect choice. The duke had turned fifty-nine on the very day of the council meeting, and he was aging badly. A visiting Englishman once estimated his age as eighty and was astonished to learn that he was twenty years younger.[81] He was also a Castilian and rightly hated by the Netherlanders as an enemy of their interests. It would have been much better to send someone like the Duke of Savoy or even Margaret's husband, the Duke of Parma, but both apparently refused to go. In the end there was no choice. On November 29, with great reluctance and foreboding, Alba agreed to undertake the mission.

If ever a man had been trapped by his own rhetoric it was he.[82] He had nothing to gain by the appointment and much to lose. It was not simply a question of personal convenience, though he dreaded the journey and knew that it would afflict him in both health and pocket, but of more serious considerations. Once he was out of Spain the influence of Eboli would increase and he would be helpless to counter his intrigues. The memory of 1554 was still green. He had gone to Italy to deal with an unpleasant and perhaps hopeless situation only to have Ruy Gómez undermine him in ways that might have led to disaster. His reputation had survived but it had taken nearly a decade to recover his influence. There was no reason to suppose that the situation now would be any different. Eboli would criticize his dispositions, block his funds, and generally obstruct matters while appointing friends and relatives to posts that might otherwise have gone to the Toledos. Alba's supporters, aware of this, urged him to stay.[83]

Even had there been no Eboli, there was ample reason to stay at home. Alba had never sought popularity. His proud, irritable disposition freed him from this besetting sin of weaker spirits, but he was jealous of his reputation. To serve as hatchet-man, suppressing the revolt so that Philip could appear as an angel of mercy, was good for the king but would expose Alba to much calumny and to the possibility that as a final sop to public opinion he would be repudiated entirely. His finest letters on the ingratitude of princes were yet to be written, but he was under no illusions on the subject and could not have expected much in the way of reward.[84]

Alba accepted only because there was no choice. He could not retract his arguments in council, for he believed in them wholeheartedly, nor could he deny that he was the only plausible candidate for the job. Not even his enemies spared him. At some point in that chaotic November Eboli and his followers reversed themselves and enthusiastically supported his appointment.[85] Whether they did so because further obstruction was useless or because they saw in Alba's departure new and glorious opportunities for mischief is hard to say. The answer would seem obvious were it not for their attempts to substitute Eboli even after the final decision had been made. The only evidence of these intrigues is, of course, the rumors recorded by ambassadors,[86] and it may be that these were nothing more than "leaks" intended to maintain Eboli's credit with his friends in the Netherlands, or wishful thinking on the part of Tisnacq and Montigny. In any case the duke was confronted by unanimous support which he could not contest, but he agreed only on condition that Philip should promise to come within a few months. If there was anything worse than repudiation it was the chilling possibility that he would be left to harvest personally the crop of resentment he expected to sow.

Fateful is not a term to be used lightly by the historian, but the decision to send Alba to the Netherlands with an army fully deserves

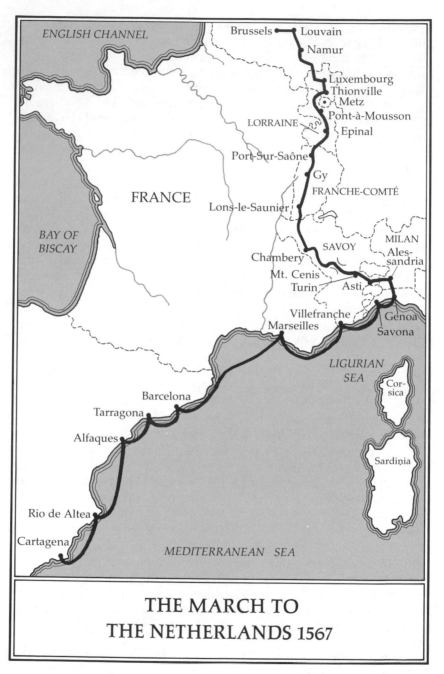

THE MARCH TO
THE NETHERLANDS 1567

Map 6.

that adjective. Taken amid factional intrigues and entered upon with real foreboding by its principal author, it opened the door to one of the great holocausts of early modern times. Yet, for all that, it need not have been a mistake. The events of 1564–1566 convinced both Alba and the king that neither royal authority nor religious orthodoxy could exist in the Low Countries without their active intervention. In this they were probably correct. To have followed Eboli's advice might well have avoided eighty years of disastrous conflict, but such a peace could only have been won on terms unacceptable to Philip and perhaps to a majority of his people. By their standards, reassertion of authority was essential but need not have led to catastrophe. Though the original plan was not without merit and even cunning, as if to justify the duke's suspicions its key provisions were never implemented. Deliberate intrigue and unavoidable contingency made all his nightmares come true, leaving him and his strategy suspended, as it were, in mid-air. Alba's involvement in the Netherlands was to be an unmitigated personal tragedy and, more important, a debacle from which Spain was never fully to recover.

VII

THE REGIME
ESTABLISHED

Trouble began almost immediately. Alba was given full control over the preparations for his march to the Netherlands and, with his usual concern for detail, he plunged into a mass of calculations and correspondence. Routes were discussed, ships and transport secured, supplies purchased, and commissions drafted for the officers. With the foresight born of long experience he tried to anticipate every contingency. What if the French should attack him on his march or the Turkish fleet come out to divert resources to the Mediterranean after he was fully committed in the north?[1] The broad outlines of the campaign were developed by the end of December, but he could not depart until four more months had passed.

This delay has been attributed to the intrigues of his enemies,[2] but it is more likely that formidable problems in logistics were at fault. Four to six months seems to have been the time span normally required for assembling an expedition of this size, and as always there were unforeseen delays, such as the loss of twenty-nine of his vessels in a storm off Málaga. The intrigues against him were numerous and virulent but largely ineffective. The papal nuncio reported that a scheme had been hatched to send Eboli on ahead to make peace while Alba waited in Italy,[3] but there is little to indicate that Philip took this seriously.[4] There were also secret documents that found their way by mysterious routes to the Netherlands, and a harebrained plot by Don Carlos to escape from court and flee to Brussels, but few of Alba's orders were contermanded and his dispositions were for the most part left intact until after his departure. It is all but certain that officials connected with the Eboli faction disrupted his preparations by traditional bureaucratic means and that Eboli did what he could to create friction over salaries and appointments, but it is unlikely that he wanted to prevent the departure. Instead, his plan seems to have been a reprise of 1554. The duke should go, but under conditions that rendered success unlikely.

Alba was aware of all this and infuriated by it. After his departure he had his secretary Juan de Albornoz draw up an extraordinary list of grievances, presumably so that he could meditate upon them at leisure.[5] The duke was, after all, a man who liked to nurse his wrath. Chief among his complaints was one that would become a *cause célèbre*. He had asked that his son, Don Fadrique, should be permitted to go to Flanders, but instead the king deported him to Oran for secretly contracting marriage with a lady of the court, one Doña Magdalena de Gúzman.[6] The duke eventually secured his release, but his exile was the first act of tragedy that would blight the careers of both father and son and bring endless satisfaction to the enemies of their house.

The remainder of the complaints are a catalog of lesser harassments: interference with his prerogative in the matter of military appointments, and the usual disputes over pay and expenses. It was bad enough that "they had sent him to serve without giving him a *merced* or a single *real* of *ayuda de costa*," but they shortchanged him of half his salary as well. Though it was not mentioned in the list, Alba was also denied what he considered adequate *entretenimientos* (maintenance grants) for his personal staff of officers.[7] Once safely arrived in Italy, he defiantly issued a warrant for nearly double the sum originally granted, but similar measures could not avail where larger amounts were at stake.[8]

Perhaps most annoying of all was the detailed instruction he received on the eve of his departure. Written by the disgraced Eraso, of all people, it provoked an acid and wholly justified response from the duke, whose patience with king and civilian advisors alike was by this time exhausted.[9]

While none of this is likely to have impeded his departure, it vividly illustrates the petty and venomous atmosphere in which the preparations took place. The situation became so intolerable that a formal reconciliation had to be arranged between Eboli and Alba, but although they dutifully embraced both knew that nothing had changed. Even more bizarre was the conduct of Don Carlos, who is said to have attacked Alba with a dagger.[10] In such circumstances it must have been a relief to turn once again to the complex but soluble problem of transporting an army across half of Europe.

The selection of a route to the Low Countries was determined by a number of factors both political and geographical. The sea route was not considered, partly because of the hazards involved but largely because most of the troops to be transported were garrisoned in the presidios of Italy. Though Alba had in mind a force of more than thirty thousand men, he intended to bring only the *tercios* of Naples, Lombardy, Sardinia, and Sicily, with the remainder to be recruited in Germany and the Low Countries. This meant that the march would be undertaken by an estimated 8,646 infantry and 965 light horse—though in the end the cavalry came to number nearly 1,200. With servants, camp followers, and equipment, provision would have to be made for 16,000 people and 3,000 horses, a modest enough figure that reflects Alba's determination to hold noncombatants to a minimum.[11]

The most logical route would have been through France, but the French refused him passage on the sensible ground that the presence of a Spanish army might upset their delicate religious peace. A second possibility, to float down the Rhine in comfort, was ruled out by the implacable hostility of the Calvinist Count Palatine of the Rhineland. This left only the difficult option of devising a route through the neutral or friendly territories that lay along the French border.

After much consideration it was decided to route the troops through Piedmont and Savoy by way of the pass of Mount Cenis and into the Franche-Comté, carefully skirting the lands of Calvinist Geneva, whose citizens would be in a state of predictable alarm. The Franche-Comté was part of Philip's patrimony, but even here great care had to be exercised to avoid the free city of Besançon. From St. Loup, which was to become a major staging point in later years, the army would pass into the neutral territories of the Duke of Lorraine and from thence into Luxembourg by way of Thionville.

As Savoy, Lorraine, and Liège were all in the hands of independent, albeit friendly, powers, diplomatic missions had to be undertaken to avoid offense and secure free passage. The French, too, had to be reassured, and Don Francés de Alava was forced to calm a nervous Charles IX even after the march had begun. Nothing was done about the Genevans, though it was assumed that they would require watching—as would the French, who ultimately dispatched an army to shadow Alba's movements.

The diplomatic maneuvers were time-consuming, and the geography of the route created problems unrelated to politics. Though Mount Cenis Pass and other parts of the road were used by merchants and even possessed some fully equipped resting places, there was doubt that it would be adequate for the transport of an army. Don Juan de Acuña Vela had been sent to reconnoiter the route immediately after Alba's appointment, and on the basis of his report an engineer and 300 pioneers were sent to widen the track from Novalesa to the pass. They were accompanied by an artist whose paintings of the terrain would, it was hoped, facilitate further planning.[12]

Alba and his commissary-general, the redoubtable Francisco de Ibarra, lavished this painstaking care on every aspect of the preparations. Local guides were retained, maps drawn up, and river crossings prepared in advance. Most important, a series of *étapes* (supply depots) were set up along the entire route, each one a day's march from the last, and contracts were let for provisioning the troops at every stage of the journey. These were friendly territories and foraging would be forbidden on pain of death.

This, then, was the Spanish Road, Alba's creation, which, with some modification in *étapes* but few in basic procedures, would last until it was closed by the Duke of Savoy in 1622. Upon it, the military communications of the empire would come to rely.

On April 17, Alba took leave of the king and departed for Cartagena, where Gian Andrea Doria waited with a fleet of thirty-seven galleys. He took with him his new confessor, the Tridentine theologian Alonso de Contreras, and one of the royal physicians, Juan Muñoz de Benavides.

The first stages of the journey were anything but auspicious. Just out of Cartagena the fleet was delayed by strong levanters and *tramontanos* that blew them back and forth as though, in Alba's words, "we were in a spherical ship."[13] The weather moderated slightly, but it was still a difficult crossing, with unplanned stops at Nice and Savona. Alba thought it a great tribute to Gian Andrea's skill as a navigator that they were not forced into a French port, and believed that the experience was responsible not only for a recurrence of his gout but for a severe case of the tertians as well.[14] When they arrived at Genoa on May 24 they had been nearly a month in passage.

The duke, feeling his age, remained at Genoa several days before moving on to Alessandria, where he consolidated his plans and held a muster on June 2. Another relapse of fever kept him at Asti until June 15, but from that point on the enterprise moved forward with the smooth certainty of a python enveloping its prey.

To avoid crowding and disorder at the *étapes* the army was divided into three segments each marching a day apart, the vanguard under Alba, the battle under his son Don Hernando, and the rear under Chiappino Vitelli. Discipline was rigid. When three horse arquebusiers stole some sheep belonging to a peasant, Alba ordered them hanged and immediate restitution made. Only one was actually executed, for the Duke of Lorraine intervened with what his subjects may well have regarded as a spirit of excessive goodwill,[15] but the point was made and contemporaries stood amazed. No army since antiquity had been so well disciplined, so well equipped, or, by the prevailing standards of military aesthetics, so elegant.[16]

Alba, of course, did not agree. His letters are from the very first a litany of complaint. The infantry were not all Spaniards; many were, he claimed, "of I know not what nation" and whatever they were, they did not look good to him. "The largest company is eight ranks of boys without beards or shoes." Discipline was, in his view, nonexistent.[17] Moreover, he had to contend with the obstructions of Eraso's old crony from Brussels, the *veedor* Cristóbal de Castellanos. This official was refusing to pay the Germans who were to rendezvous with Alba in Luxembourg.[18] The duke's comments graphically reveal his state of mind on the eve of the most delicate mission of his career:

> Yesterday I received a letter from Castellanos, a copy of which will be shown to you by Antonio de Lada, and it has put me in such a choler that I have taken the line with him that if he comes near I will have him shot, because it seems to me that he is not content to be *veedor* and *contador* and general of the artillery but wishes to be captain-general and has raised the devil of a fuss so that they write me from Flanders that it is said publicly among the Walloon soldiers that . . . they will not let me enter their country.
>
> This Castellanos is a great friend of Egmont. I fear that it is his persuasions that have created these bestialities even though he is a proper ass, as are all the officials they have sent there.[19]

He was also annoyed by the king's new insistence on detailed reports but, as Zayas told him, this was not without its advantages. Now that Philip had reorganized procedures and everything had "to go by so many *arroyos*," chaos was endemic and he was more dependent on his secretary than before. In the process of straightening it all out Zayas felt that he could be of more service than ever to such friends and patrons as the duke.[20] Alba does not appear to have disagreed.

Still, there seems little doubt that this truculent and incautious mood sustained him until his arrival in Luxembourg and beyond. Nothing else can explain his greeting Egmont with the words "You see here a great heretic,"[21] or the increasing asperity of his letters to Madrid. He was able to pass off the remark to Egmont as a joke, and Egmont accepted it as such, knowing from past experience that the duke was fond of gallows humor, but the incident is nonetheless revealing. Alba was, after all, an elderly man in poor health undertaking an unwanted assignment among people he neither liked nor understood. Believing that the king would shortly come to relieve him, he underestimated the complexity of that task and tended to see himself purely as a policeman come to restore order and root out heresy. As a result, political sensitivity was abandoned as irrelevant, and his personal feelings were allowed to surface.

In only one area did Alba restrain his increasingly habitual irritation: the necessarily delicate relations with Margaret of Parma. During the panic of the preceding year Margaret had requested that a captain-general be sent,[22] but in the intervening months she had come to believe that such a step was no longer necessary. Her attitude was perfectly understandable. With the aid of Meghen and Noircarmes she had been able to quell the disorders that followed the iconoclasm and felt, quite rightly, that a military emergency no longer existed. The appearance of Alba and his army was therefore as ominous to her as to her quondam subjects. She feared reprisals that would undo her successful work of pacification and foresaw that his very presence would constitute a severe challenge to her own authority. His patent was purely military—she appears to have been unaware of a second patent, which granted him civil authority in case of an emergency,[23]—but she knew that in cases of this sort civil and military authority were virtually undistinguishable. Who would raise money for Alba's troops, handle the political ramifications of their quartering, and determine their use now that the danger of open revolt had passed? The possibilities for conflict were infinite.

It was at one time fashionable among historians to denigrate Margaret of Parma. A stout, unattractive woman with a discernible mustache and a tendency to weep openly in moments of political stress, she was neither loved nor respected in her own time, but neither was she a fool or the simple pawn of her advisors. With moderation reminiscent of Catherine de' Medici or Elizabeth of England, she seems to have realized that the problem of the Netherlands required a certain flexibility, and if she opposed the open triumph of heresy and noble self-interest she was no less wary of the iron-handed repression foreshadowed by the coming of Alba. She knew that she could not openly thwart the king's will, but from the week of Alba's departure she, no less than Eboli or Castellanos, began to lay obstructions in his path.

First she offered her resignation. When it was not accepted, she complained about the introduction of foreign troops.[24] Then several letters were required before she would instruct Castellanos to pay the Germans. Alba, who knew full well that certain nobles had once threatened to oppose Philip's coming with force, did not wish to be met by Netherlandish troops when he arrived in Luxembourg. Margaret opposed him in this as well. Endless difficulties were made over the discharge of garrisons in Luxembourg and Antwerp, and arguments were mustered to prevent the transfer of Alberico Lodron's Germans to the place of rendezvous.[25] When the duke finally met the regent on August 22, Margaret immediately complained that the quartering of his troops would be a hardship to the poor.[26] Throughout all this Alba remained the soul of courtesy, venting his displeasure only on Castellanos *in absentia*, but it was obvious that the two would be unable to work together for long.

The final breach came after the arrest of Egmont and Hornes. In spite of repeated warnings and the ominous circumstances attending Egmont's first interview with the duke, these two innocents had remained blissfully unaware of their peril. Measuring their own behavior by its motivation and apparently unaware that the traditions of the Spanish court were wholly unlike their own, they were confident that they had done nothing treasonable and that their orthodoxy was unquestioned. They could not imagine that Philip and Alba had from the start seen them as the key to a noble conspiracy or that it had long ago been decided to make an example of them.[27] After all, had not Philip repeatedly assured them of his favor and goodwill? Their view of the relationship between the nobility and the Crown was essentially feudal. They did not seem to realize that in Spain the king had become a being of an entirely different order, intolerant of even loyal dissent from his nobles and no longer bound by the conventions of chivalry in his dealings with them. Orange, more astute and more politically imaginative than his colleagues, shared none of their illusions; he took the opportunity of Alba's arrival to visit relatives in Germany.

The arrest was a curious replay of twenty years earlier, when Alba had arranged the capture of Philip of Hesse. As in military affairs, he saw little reason to change the methods evolved during his formative years. On September 9 the two counts were invited to a banquet given by Alba's son, the Prior Don Hernando. Toward the end of dinner, the duke, who was not present, sent an invitation to the company asking them to come to his lodgings and advise him on the plans for the new citadel he proposed to build at Antwerp. Sometime after their arrival, he excused himself, pleading illness, and left them arguing at the table. As the meeting broke up, Sancho Dávila asked Egmont to remain behind, and when they were alone demanded his sword. Compliance was assured by the sudden appearance of an armed body of Spanish soldiers, and Hornes was stopped as he made his way across the courtyard. The two were imprisoned separately in rooms at the top of Alba's house, and there they remained for two weeks until they could be transferred to the citadel at Ghent.[28]

Margaret was outraged. She believed the men innocent and saw the duke's failure to consult with her before their capture as an affront to her authority. Her complaints to the king were now truly bitter, but Alba was unmoved. He could not have consulted her without compromising the security of the plot, and the immediate results of his action were otherwise gratifying in the extreme. The arrests had badly frightened the nobility and served notice to the population at large that no one was beyond the reach of the king's justice. Papers found in the possession of the two men's secretaries not only illuminated the events of recent years but were in Alba's view highly incriminating.[29] True, it would be necessary to explain all this to the emperor, the Duke of Cleves, and the chapter of the Golden Fleece,[30] but on the whole Alba was satisfied and looked forward to compiling a dossier on his victims at leisure. "I remain," he said, "in the greatest contentment in the world that it has all been done with such quietude and tranquillity."[31]

The regent might have spared herself the effort of complaint. Realizing on the basis of her earlier letters that nothing more could be gained by retaining her, Philip accepted her resignation on September 13. By October, Alba found himself the de facto ruler of a region nearly as populous as England and a good deal wealthier.

It was a situation for which he was totally unprepared. The removal of Margaret freed him to allocate resources and organize judicial proceedings as he pleased, but at the same time it forced him to organize a government. Given the circumstances, this was extremely difficult. There were no truly useful models to follow: the governmental structures of the Netherlands were almost wholly discredited in Spanish eyes and the Castilian alternatives, though no doubt congenial to Alba, would surely be resisted as an alien intrusion.

The problem was compounded by the temporary and somewhat ambiguous nature of Alba's authority. Though he had been charged with the implementation of vast reforms should the opportunity arise, he believed that he would be gone in six to nine months. There was therefore little incentive to develop sophisticated administrative procedures, and in any case his own perception of his role was essentially proconsular. He was to suppress heresy and rebellion in preparation for the arrival of the king. This effectively precluded development of a permanent administration with strong local ties, while it encouraged ad hoc arrangements that could easily be dismantled when the time came to repudiate them.

The result was a kind of military dictatorship that satisfied no one, least of all the duke. Though he bore the military title of captain-general, his powers were those of a regent or viceroy unrestrained by the presence of an *audiencia*. The *audiencia*—a court combining administrative with judicial functions that was perhaps the central institution of the Spanish dependencies in the New World—might well have checked Alba's frequent abuses of power, but the Netherlanders had continually opposed its establishment. They were thus left with nothing but their own weak and, to the Spaniards, untrustworthy Estates. The captain-general remained free to trample upon the rights and customs of the country as necessity or his own impatience demanded. Alba's authority, of course, was dependent on the will of the king, but the king was far away. If the duke wished to conceal something or even to ignore a direct order, as he did on more than one occasion, he could usually get away with it.

His system of government, if it can be called that, was a direct outgrowth of these circumstances. It was above all intensely personal. Like his royal master, Alba immersed himself in a host of petty details and found it increasingly difficult to delegate authority in any rational or systematic way.[32] This was due not to personal preference but to his distrust of the existing administration and of the inhabitants of the Netherlands as a whole. With some justice, Geoffrey Parker has characterized this attitude as the product of a Master Race mentality,[33] but though Alba's preference for Castilians needs no further comment it would be unwise to attribute it to racist theory. The government of the Netherlands had been corrupt and inefficient for many years, and there was good reason to doubt the loyalty and religious zeal of its servants. Alba's suspicions were exaggerated, but this was because he sensed with terrible clarity that the values of the society he governed were not his own and were therefore dangerous. Like many other Spaniards, he was suffering profoundly from cultural shock.[34] Eventually he came to trust certain of Margaret's counselors—notably, Viglius, Berlaymont, and Noircarmes—but even this trust remained limited, and when he was forced to rely on traditional institutions at the local level he did so with reluctance and foreboding.

What he really needed, or so he thought, were Spaniards, but these were never available in sufficient numbers. He pleaded and complained,[35] but in the end he fell back on the small coterie of bureaucrats who had accompanied him from Spain. His administration became one in which business was conducted by a handful of men, most of whom were as isolated from the surrounding community as he was himself. This meant that they were usually disliked, misinformed, and understaffed, yet their isolation did not protect them against corruption.

No man could be expected to handle this immense burden of work by himself: ever larger portions of it were delegated to Alba's immediate subordinates. This was done without establishing formal administrative procedures, because throughout his governorship, replacement and the arrival of new administrators seemed imminent. As the months stretched into years the duke's secretary, Juan de Albornoz, became a figure of enormous power, often acting for his master much as the latter acted for the king, and distinctions among governmental functions became hopelessly blurred. The army paymaster, Francisco de Lixalde, ultimately controlled finances at many levels, not only paying the troops but raising the money by means of *asientos* with Antwerp bankers,[36] most of whom were themselves part of an ever-narrowing circle of Genoese friendly with Albornoz. Ordinarily, such arrangements would have been audited by the *veedor* or inspector-general, but this official, one Galíndez de Carvajal, was denied access to the treasury by Lixalde and resigned in 1569.[37]

He was not replaced until 1572, and by then it was too late. Lixalde's accounts had achieved such monumental complexity that a thirty-year investigation by the Contaduría Mayor de Cuentas failed to unravel them.[38]

Complaints abounded, and the *contador* Jerónimo de Curiel was the source of many of them. Curiel had served under the regent and was associated with Eraso, but his objections do not seem to have been inspired entirely by faction. He evidently opposed procedural informality of any sort and feared—rightly, in this case—that it would lead to trouble. He often refused to honor expenditures without a direct order from Alba, and he created difficulties both great and small.[39] Zayas, who was always alert to the cabals of Alba's enemies, thought Curiel was a good man who was simply doing his job,[40] but there were other accusations in which faction undoubtedly played a part. Among them was a "relation of abuses" dated September, 1571. Containing little more than malicious rumors and insubstantial allegations, it is apparently the work of Antonio Pérez.[41]

There were, of course, genuine and massive irregularities in Lixalde's affairs, some of which were due to corruption. It is thought, for example, that between 1567 and 1572 he pocketed the contributions deducted from the soldiers' pay to support military hospitals. If so, the sum involved exceeded 40,000 ducats, and there is no reason to assume that this would have been his only venture in creative bookkeeping.[42] At the same time, the administrative procedures that allowed him such wholesale skimming created other problems that owed little to malicious intent. An example of what Lixalde had to face cropped up just prior to Alba's departure. Lixalde found himself short 100,000 ducats and wrote to Albornoz in a panic suggesting that everyone should come to an agreement in their accounts before Alba's successor could demand an audit.[43] Apparently Alba's major-domo and the Castellan of Antwerp, Sancho Dávila, had spent the money on some military necessity without warrant and without informing anyone. The paymaster, who should have had full control over all such expenditures, was left holding the bag. In the end he covered the shortage with a loan from an Antwerp banker named Gramoy and talked Alba into declaring it a legitimate expense,[44] but such maneuvers would not have been necessary or possible had there been effective controls. Lixalde undoubtedly had a sharp pen and light fingers but he was also trapped in an administrative nightmare. Had he been honest, the chaos would not have been less.

In all of this Alba was worse than useless. Far from heeding Lixalde's pleas to reduce his responsibilities, he sought to increase them by giving him control over all sources of Crown income in the Netherlands.[45] This extraordinary scheme failed when the Council of Finance complained to Madrid, but it indicates once again the duke's determination to bypass local institutions. When, inevitably, Lixalde fell under suspicion Alba was unmoved. Such accusations, he said, were part of the job, and in any case he neither understood the financial system nor did he greatly care so long as the troops were paid.[46] Alba's attitude toward accounting was in fact notoriously cavalier. When a deficit of 12,000 fl. appeared in the accounts of confiscated rebel goods he told his brother-in-law that "the devil could not find it," and that in any case he was more interested in "the perpetuity from the Indies that they may wish to give me."[47] Yet, for all his levity, it is worth noting that he required detailed reports from Lixalde throughout the first winter of his rule, abandoning the practice only when he became convinced of the paymaster's ability.[48] The basic problem was not the duke's tendency to pose as a gruff, simple soldier but his refusal to trust the natives and his consequent inability to develop an administrative organization. The army had to be paid. This was the basic fact of life on which all else depended and to which all other considerations were secondary. He would have preferred a better system, but lacking it, he was prepared to ignore the bureaucratic niceties. This view was shared by his commanders.

If Lixalde's problems were an outgrowth of circumstances and Alba's penchant for ad hoc procedures, so too were the controversies that surrounded Albornoz. A native of Cuenca and protégé of Zayas, he had become the duke's secretary in 1565, just as the latter was emerging once again into the political limelight. Clever, witty, and a glutton for work, he was only too happy to ease the burdens of his master. His attachment to the duke was genuine, but he was not a man to ignore the wealth and power such an attachment could bring. Overbearing and servile by turns, his control over so many aspects of state business earned him a host of enemies.

The chief among them were Jerónimo de Curiel, who seems to have been impartial in the universality of his dislikes, and Francisco de Ibarra. The reasons for their enmity are not clear. Ibarra was perhaps the oldest and most valued of Alba's men; they had served together in Italy. The quartermaster's genius for logistics, as well as his absolute loyalty, had earned him a secure place in the Alba regime. Whatever may be said of Curiel, faction was not at issue here. It is probable that by controlling access to the duke and thus interfering in the everyday business of government Albornoz had thoroughly offended these two professionals, while his habitual levity would have been intolerable to the dour and somewhat priggish Curiel. The depths of hatred aroused by the secretary may be indicated by the fact that Ibarra and Curiel were themselves mortal enemies who had worked for each other's removal since the beginning.[49]

These festering resentments came to a head in the autumn of 1569. The nasty incident that resulted tells us perhaps more than we care to know about the atmosphere of Alba's little court. It was common gossip that Albornoz had been investing the king's money for his personal gain at Antwerp.[50] The truth behind this and similar accusations may never be known, for an investigation into the secretary's affairs was curtailed abruptly after his return to Spain.[51] In any case, by October 22, 1569, Albornoz was convinced that Francisco de Ibarra had prepared *informaciones* against him that would be taken to Spain and laid before the court.[52]

In the meantime, rumors had attracted the attention of Alba's son, the Prior Don Hernando, who in the interests of his father decided to investigate. He went first to Ibarra, but the quartermaster claimed to know nothing and refused to discuss it further. After some persuasion Hernando got him to raise the issue with his younger brother Esteban de Ibarra and with Curiel. Esteban drew up a memo on the subject, which he gave to Curiel. Somehow a copy of the document fell into the hands of Albornoz, who complained so bitterly to the duke that the latter ordered Curiel to Brussels to examine him about it.

This was apparently Alba's first inkling that something was afoot. Never a sociable man, he had grown increasingly reclusive after 1568, when it became obvious that the king would not come. Keeping to his quarters, he dined alone and saw as few people as possible. No one knows what Curiel told him, but on leaving the Hôtel de Jassy that night the *contador* was set upon and wounded with a knife.[53]

Curiel lived, but Albornoz was exultant. The secretary had been writing to Zayas and even to Alba's wife, slandering his detractors and pleading desperately for protection. The attack on Curiel was to him a judgment of almost biblical significance,[54] but was he responsible for it? From the distance of four centuries he seems the most likely candidate, especially as the would-be assassins were known to him,[55] but at the time matters were more opaque. Curiel's enemies were so numerous that the Ibarra brothers and even Don Hernando were suspect—the latter because Curiel had written to court with manic proceduralism that Hernando's investigation usurped ducal authority.[56] The duke was furious, but nothing was ever proved, and, ominously, no further investigation of Albornoz was attempted while he remained in Brussels.

Given Alba's personal rectitude, his willingness to tolerate such goings-on is at first glance astonishing, but it was rooted in the very nature of his administration. Seeing themselves as a temporary government of occupation, many of his Spaniards tried to profit as best they could from an unpleasant situation. When they did so Alba had no choice but to cover up their transgressions, lest scandal discredit both Spain and the royal cause. It was a natural and patriotic, if not necessarily intelligent, response.

This, then, was the household government that sought to cleanse the Netherlands of heresy and reform its political life. Though inadequate in almost every respect it would survive Alba and serve as a model for subsequent governors until the reforms of the 1690s.[57] With it the duke would attempt great things, not always with success.

The broad outline of his policy was dictated by instructions brought from Spain. He was to establish a military presence, punish those responsible for the disorders of 1566, and restore religious unity. When this had been done, a general pardon could be issued, and Alba could presumably go home.[58] The first part of the program began before he reached Luxembourg, with the disbanding of local garrisons at Antwerp and elsewhere, and culminated in the quartering of his troops "on towns which have sinned."[59] It was finally decided that citadels should be erected throughout the country. In May, 1567, Margaret submitted a list of towns requiring them that included Antwerp, Valenciennes, Amsterdam, Flushing, and Maastricht.

Of these Antwerp was obviously the most important. Alba lavished so much personal attention on its construction that it is tempting to think that he saw in it a kind of personal monument. If so, it was indeed worthy of a soldier whose ego was equal to his accomplishments. Incorporated into the southern wall of the city between Kronenbourg and St. Joris gates, it was pentagonal, with a bastion at each angle named for himself—"Duke," "Ferdinand," "Toledo," and "Alba," with the fifth graciously called "Paciotto" after the Italian engineer who designed it.[60] The walls themselves sloped inward from the moat at an angle of perhaps thirty degrees from the perpendicular and were surmounted by rounded parapets with open-topped embrasures. The main gate faced the city to the north and was built in the classical style. Upon entering the visitor found himself staring into the muzzles of an artillery battery. On his left was a church, on his right a substantial brick building that served as headquarters. On each of the remaining sides, against walls of earth faced on the exterior with brick and stone, were double ranks of barracks sufficient to house the entire Antwerp garrison. In the broad open space at the center were trees and, after the campaign of 1568, a famous and extraordinarily tasteless statue of the duke himself.[61]

Alba believed it was "the most beautiful *plaza* in the world,"[62] and he traveled to Antwerp to inspect it whenever he could spare the time. He pored over the plans, worried about details, and tried to oversee various aspects of the construction himself. Not surprisingly, Paciotto abandoned the project in disgust and returned to Italy without permission,[63] but he was replaced by Bartolomeo Campi and the work went on. When the terrible inundations of September, 1569, dislodged a fragment from the "bastion's curtain near the point" Alba had himself carried from his sickbed and rowed through the moat to inspect the damage,[64] and when the citizens of Antwerp balked at the mounting costs he extracted 400,000 fl. from them with threats.[65] This loving care resulted in a citadel that was indeed a masterpiece, invulnerable to war—if not to political change: finding themselves temporarily without a Spanish garrison, the resentful Antwerpers demolished the part of it facing their city in 1577.

Alba's enthusiasm for fortification was matched by his vigor in pursuing those whose grievances had led to the outbreak of 1566. The sudden arrests of Egmont and Hornes were directed toward this end, as was his virtual kidnapping of Orange's eldest son, the Count of Buren. This young man, who was evidently intended as a hostage for his father's good behavior, was taken from his studies at Louvain and conveyed to the Spanish court with full honors, and there he remained for twenty years, in apparent contentment.[66] Other suspected leaders—including Anthony van Straelen, the burgomaster of Antwerp—were taken, but most of the chief figures were able to make their way abroad, together with thousands of lesser folk who had either been implicated in the disorders or whose religion made their lives and fortunes potentially forfeit.[67]

This exodus naturally affected the persecution launched by Alba within days of his arrival. Historians have generated much confusion about his policies on this score, but the reality was fairly simple. He meant to extinguish opposition, whatever its source, to royal authority, and since neither he nor Philip could conceive of royal authority without religious unity his target included not only noble malcontents and rioters but consistorial ministers and all those whose religious beliefs seemed to imply opposition to the Crown.[68] As Van der Essen noted, the Spanish claim that they were interested only in the suppression of rebels was disingenuous.[69] Alba was no inquisitor, though he sometimes expressed a desire to be one,[70] but like many men of the sixteenth century he made little distinction between rebellion and heresy and was inclined to accept a profession of Calvinism as *prima facie* evidence of disobedience. He had, however, no intention of conducting a twentieth-century-style purge. As Brantôme has him say, his purpose was "to fish for and to take the trout and salmon and let the sardines go,"[71] a quote that has the ring of accuracy, given the duke's liking both for fish and for concrete metaphors. His own letters reiterate the theme in more prosaic terms.[72] He was, for example, much concerned about the refugees, "seeing the great harm that these Estates will receive from the departure of the soldiers, officials, and other little people whom I have always understood that Your Majesty wished to use with clemency and *misericordia*, as with people deceived and who have sinned through ignorance."[73] His answer to the problem was to issue a "reassuring" placard, but few were reassured, and it may be because of this that his net seemed more finely meshed than he may have intended. Only the sardines were left.

The mechanism devised by Alba to find and punish the enemies of the Crown was a special tribunal known as the Council of Troubles. Popularly called the Council of Blood, its operations and Alba's part in them have done more to blacken his reputation than any other episode in his long career. The idea behind the Council was hatched in Spain before Alba's departure and had the full approval of the king. It seems to have been one of those notions for which no individual can be held responsible, the product of a collective decision based on apparent necessity. Something had to be done, and it was clear to everyone that the existing courts were unable to do it.[74] Their loyalty, like that of the administration, was suspect and they were bound by procedural rules that might prove inconvenient. To be effective, a tribunal would have to be independent of local influence but it would also have to be free of these constraints. It was for this reason that when Alba established the Council in the first week of September, 1567, he took the extraordinary step of reserving all final decisions for himself. His reasons were brutally straightforward:

> The first that, now knowing its members, I might be deceived by them, the second, that the men of law only condemn for crimes which are proved; whereas your Majesty knows that affairs of state are governed by very different rules from the laws they have here."[75]

Within a month, the pressure of business had forced Alba to modify this edict by permitting the council to convict automatically all those who signed the *Compromise*, but to the end the final word remained his.

These suspicions, arising, like his administrative problems, from an indiscriminate distrust of all Netherlanders, were belied by events. The council set to work with exemplary enthusiasm, and in spite of Alba's complaint that its members were covering up the deeds of their countrymen[76] it showed neither independence nor mercy. Given the composition of the group, this was a foregone conclusion. Five of its members were local: Noircarmes, Berlaymont, Jacob Hessels, and two others chosen in consultation with Viglius, a man whose loathing of the Beggars and their Calvinist allies was notorious. Of the other two, Juan de Vargas was a Spaniard and Luis del Rio a Netherlander of Spanish descent. Del Rio was a loyal nonentity; Vargas alone among the members of the tribunal possessed the full confidence of the duke.[77] This is in itself revealing, for Vargas was by all accounts a rather dubious character. A former *oidor* of the Chancellery of Valladolid, he had left Spain pursued by at least three damaging lawsuits, one of which accused him of violating a ward.[78] In addition, he knew neither French nor Flemish, which prevented him from understanding the documents placed before the council and made it necessary to hold the sessions in Latin.[79] In spite of this Alba relied on him extensively, attempted to have the suits against him quashed,[80] and even recommended him for a position on the Netherlands Council of State.[81] Vargas must have understood the function of political trials with a clarity worthy of his master.

Under this central tribunal were subordinates who conducted investigations at the local level and forwarded their denunciations to the council for action. Their number was initially modest—by the end of 1567, only fifteen had been appointed—but it grew rapidly, until by the end of 1569 there were about 170, engaged in ferreting out sedition with the aid of malicious neighbors, jilted lovers, and disgruntled business competitors. Twenty-six more were appointed before the council closed its books in 1576, but these appear to have been replacements.[82] All were, of course, natives, and like the council itself they did their job with élan. It is sometimes forgotten that the revolt of the Netherlands bore many of the characteristics of a civil war and that, as in all communities, there were many scores to settle. In spite of his worries, the duke never lacked Netherlanders who were prepared to cooperate enthusiastically with his most repressive measures.

The policies followed by this organization had been laid down by the duke and were simplicity itself. Signers of the *Compromise* were to be executed. Otherwise, the placards were to be enforced to the letter. By April, 1568, Alba had decided that he wished to see only those cases in which there was evidence of wrongdoing not covered by the placards.[83] As there had been a great flurry of these edicts in recent years this decision must have eased his workload enormously. The additional leisure was badly needed: not only was he beginning to prepare his campaign against the resurgent Prince of Orange, but the first trickle of denunications had become a flood. Investigators tended to submit them in batches, and in the preceding week 395 had come in from Ypres alone.[84]

Confiscations were a more complex issue and an important one, for Alba was mindful of the enormous expenses his expedition had incurred. Receivers of confiscated goods were appointed on a regional basis, but they immediately ran into difficulties. The goods of the condemned were to be seized in their entirety; what, then, should be done about their families? Alba rather ungenerously agreed to leave widows and orphans with a moiety if they were in danger of starvation, but insisted that, to prevent fraud, their names should be submitted to the council and their status verified. Those whose providers were in exile got nothing.[85] Then there was the problem of money owed to the condemned by municipal governments. The duke ruled that it had to be paid to the Crown but stipulated that restitution could be made on a case-by-case basis if irregularities were found.[86] Confiscated arms were to be inventoried and sent to the arsenals at Antwerp or Amsterdam, where they could be used by the army or sold, and ships were to be disposed of promptly at a fair price. It was a hard, greedy policy, but it was successful. The confiscations may ultimately have provided more than 450,000 badly needed florins in annual rents.[87]

The results achieved by these policies constituted a veritable reign of terror, though it was nothing like the holocaust envisioned by later historians and pamphleteers.[88] A total of 8,957 individuals were condemned between 1567 and 1576, but thanks to the general exodus that preceded Alba's arrival only 1,083 were executed and another 20 banished.[89] Still, the overall impression must have been terrifying, because the vast bulk of cases were settled within a four-year period, with the largest number of executions occurring in 1568–1569. This concentration, with its adverse effect on public opinion, was yet another consequence of Alba's belief in the imminent arrival of the king. He felt that he had to act quickly if the land were to be secured and confiscations maximized before issuance of a general pardon.[90]

There was yet another reason for the widespread impression of indiscriminate terror. Most of those executed were either artisans or people whose place in society was so humble that their occupation was never recorded. This was due partly to the fact that those who could afford to leave or knew themselves to be hopelessly compromised had long since escaped, and partly to the internal dynamics of the council's organization. As we have seen, Alba never intended to go after the small fry, but denunciations solicited by the state are never the monopoly of a single class. An agent who received an accusation, even if it involved the most insignificant wretch in the district, had little choice but to forward it to Brussels, for if he did not and someone else did, he would be dangerously compromised. Moreover, there was always the hope that preferment might be gained from a show of enthusiasm, so the council was inevitably flooded with denunications, and it could scarcely ignore evidence of treason simply because the perpetrator was an unemployed drifter. If people got the idea that no one was safe, they may have been right.

It is difficult to avoid the conclusion that if the Council of Blood did not fully deserve its name, it was not for want of trying. Subsequent persecutions and massacres have somewhat dimmed its horror, but it was a sensation at the time, and its portrayal in the pages of Dutch historians like Hooft, Bor, van Meteren, and de Thou left an indelible impression on later ages. Motley's description of Alba and his sinister henchman Vargas condemning thousands of innocents while a drowsy Hessels mutters *ad patibulum, ad patibulum* in the background is unlikely to be forgotten by English-speaking readers, and, with the exception of the grossly inflated figures, it is not even really unfair.[91]

The council executed more than a thousand persons, most of whom probably represented no clear danger to anyone. It condemned seven thousand more with only the thinnest pretense of legality, and would have executed them as well, had it been able to catch them. Alba organized the council, appointed its members, and reviewed its verdicts, intervening impatiently whenever one of the judges suffered a momentary attack of legal scruples. It was in every sense his court, and he ran it like his administration—as an extension of his personal authority unhindered by law, custom, or formal procedures.

It would be tempting to call it the first of the political tribunals and give the duke full credit for introducing one of the more appalling features of modern life, but to do so would be gravely anachronistic. In the minds of Alba and most of his contemporaries the council had many ancient and medieval precedents. It was the king's duty and that of his lieutenants to suppress rebellion. If the events of 1566 constituted rebellion, and Alba believed they did, his actions were no different than those of Charles V at Ghent in 1540 or of the dukes of Burgundy on numerous occasions during the fifteenth century. English history, up to and including Elizabeth's contemporaneous suppression of the Northern Rebellion, is replete with similar examples of royal justice, some of them little inferior to Alba's in number of executions.[92]

Why, then, are the persecutions of Alba remembered when these others are long forgotten? First, Alba's side lost. Those he condemned became the founding martyrs of a new nation, and history is notoriously written by the victors. Even for those who cannot read there is Breughel the Younger's unforgettable *Massacre of the Innocents*, in which Alba, with long, forked beard, piercing eyes, and vulturine posture, watches as Spanish soldiers slaughter the children of a peaceful village.[93] Second, the emergence of the Netherlands as a nation, like the events that immediately preceded it, had a religious and even ideological dimension. This has become inextricably confused with the purely political question of royal authority with which the council was nominally involved. Alba knew this at the time, and the religious convictions of some of the rebels no doubt strengthened his resolve, but it did nothing to alter the fundamentally traditional nature of his objectives. The council had no authority over heretics nor did it seek to pry into the minds of its intended victims. It was concerned with deeds, and though heresy would be dealt with in good time, the task would be undertaken only by those who could legally define it: the clergy.

In the eyes of contemporaries, the real fault of the council was that of Alba's administration as a whole. It was excessively personal in character, organized according to no rational principle, and openly contemptuous of existing law. It was, therefore, unjust. This would have been true even if its individual judgments had been impeccable, but they were not. When the time came to scrutinize Alba's actions this weighed more heavily against him than anything else, for the king loved justice as he loved his authority, and even in the case of traitors had difficulty in accepting the rough judgments of what must have resembled a military court.

VIII

WILLIAM OF ORANGE

T hroughout the winter of 1567/68 Alba proceeded as though his control over the Netherlands were undisputed, but he was at all times painfully aware that this was not the case. Over the German border at his castle of Dillenburg, William of Orange was preparing to return.

As the greatest of the nobles who had eluded Alba's net, William was the obvious leader of any potential resistance, but as the result of his cautious behavior in 1566 his efforts to organize resistance met with suspicion or indifference. The Calvinists were at best luke-warm; some of the more famous, such as Philip Marnix, Lord of Sainte-Aldegonde, refused to support him at all. They apparently believed that the rising of 1566 would have succeeded had he supported it openly, and tended to view William as the betrayer of their cause.[1] Given his role in the suppression of the troubles it is hard to blame them, but in fact he had never abandoned his opposition to the policies of Philip II.

More enthusiastic were a group of nobles that included his brother Louis of Nassau, the counts of Culembourg and Hoogstraten, and a mixed bag of lesser figures. Though loyal and even inspired, they were a wild and obstreperous lot, profoundly disturbing to the sober element of the population whom Orange needed to impress. One of his major problems was to keep them within the bounds of reason while at the same time stirring up a people thoroughly cowed by the speed and severity of Alba's repressions. The

159

Netherlands still held individuals brave enough to send him money, but there was no discernible groundswell of opinion on his behalf.

By November, 1567, it was obvious that support would have to be found elsewhere, and several Protestant princes of the empire, including the Landgrave of Hesse, were invited to Dillenburg to help celebrate the birth of William's son Maurice. They offered their congratulations and much verbal encouragement but little in the way of tangible aid. Predictably, the emperor remained noncommittal.

It was a discouraging time, but the winter eventually produced more than the sickly child whose military genius would do so much to bring final independence from Spain. Gradually the contributions of dissenting Netherlanders and French Huguenots accumulated, and with more speed than might have been expected an army was gathered in the vicinity of Cologne.

Alba was aware of these developments and took steps to counter them before the new year. After two boatsfull of arms were seized at Nijmegen on their way to Orange, the duke dispatched a force of 3,000 men to the border of Cleves and protested to the emperor. Mercenaries were hired in Germany and sent into Luxembourg under Mansfeldt while Aremberg, who had been sent to aid Charles IX against the Huguenots, was ordered to remain at Cateau-Cambrésis until further notice. "It would be a bad joke," said the duke, "to put out a fire in a neighboring house when your own is beginning to burn."[2] Reports of increased activity among the Forest Beggars also disturbed him. These rural partisans of Orange, the land-based counterparts of the notorious Sea Beggars, had not been fully suppressed, and when they killed two priests near Ypres he revealed his nervousness by sending 900 men to arrest them.[3] By March he was fretting over the shortage of money, strengthening garrisons from Walcheren to Groningen, and planning to hire as many as 6,000 Swiss to supplement his troops.[4]

His apprehension was fully justified. By April, Orange commanded a force far larger than Alba's, and his plan, if properly executed, might well have posed a serious threat to the Spanish regime. Its essence was to force Alba to do battle on two fronts. One army, under Orange, was to invade the southern Netherlands, in the vicinity of Maastricht, and march westward to join a contingent of Huguenots then being recruited in France. A second, under Louis of Nassau, would simultaneously cross into Groningen and Friesland from the territories of the sympathetic Count of Emden. Orange fully expected that the countryside would rally on his behalf, but even if it did not it was hard to see how Alba could meet such a concerted attack.

Unfortunately, William soon found himself on the horns of a dilemma. His army, though large, had not yet reached full strength nor was its provisioning to his satisfaction. Cautious to a fault, he hesitated to commit himself. At the same time he could not allow too much of the campaigning season to pass without taking action. His soldiers were, for the most part, not patriots but German mercenaries who had to be paid monthly or they would return to their homes. He had raised a great deal of money and contributed 100,000 florins of his own, but it was not enough to keep an undisciplined and increasingly demoralized army in camp through an endless summer.[5]

His solution to the problem reveals that whatever his political talents, William was at best an amateur soldier. Sacrificing the element of simultaneity on which his plan depended, he sent his brother Louis off to the north with perhaps 12,000 men while dispatching a much smaller force under Hoogstraten toward Maastricht. His reasoning seems to have been that Hoogstraten would create both a diversion for Louis and a bridgehead for William's own crossing of the Maas at a later date, but neither purpose was accomplished. Hoogstraten fell ill on the eve of departure and was thus spared for a more ignominious fate.

Hoogstraten's successor, Jean de Montigny, Lord of Villiers, crossed the border on April 20 with only 3,000 men and invested Roermond. To his chagrin, the place refused to surrender. As neither he nor the defenders had any artillery he tried to burn the gates, but this proved a slow process. In the meantime Alba reacted with lightning speed. Seeing a small, isolated force within easy reach he sent Sancho de Londoño to deal with it much as a man might swat a fly. Londoño's army, though even smaller than Villier's, was something of an elite corps. Consisting of five companies of veteran Spanish infantry, three of horse under Sancho Dávila, and a small detachment of German pikemen under Eberstein, it was led by men whose names, like that of Londoño himself, were already becoming legendary.

Villiers, who until the week before had served as William's quartermaster-general, did not bother to check their credentials but fled to Erkelenz and then, perhaps seeking a more defensible position, doubled back toward Dahlheim. He was wise to do so, but not quick enough. Londoño caught up with him between Erkelenz and Dahlheim and in a matter of moments destroyed half his force, including its full complement of cavalry. With what remained Villiers retreated in good order to Dahlheim along a narrow, difficult path and entrenched himself before the village. It mattered little. The Spanish cavalry were slowed by the difficulty of the route, but in the end they were not needed. His five companies of Spaniards outnumbered even by Villiers's remaining troops, Londoño carried the trenches in less than half an hour, leaving only a handful of survivors to take refuge in Dahlheim with their commander. These, too, were soon captured. Villiers, no hero, divulged what he knew of Orange's schemes to Londoño, who immediately forwarded them to Brussels. The first southern offensive was over. The Spaniards had lost 20 men; the rebels, 3,000.[6]

Villiers's expedition was a pointless waste of good men and a thoroughly inauspicious beginning for a war of liberation. It followed hard on the failure of an attempt to assassinate Alba, and these two blunders within a single month may well have discouraged some potential supporters of Orange. The botched assassination alone was enough to give anyone pause. A large, ill-sorted group of civilians and one-time soldiers had planned to gather in the forest of Soigny outside Brussels and from there to mount a frontal attack on Alba's guard. Well-primed with drink, not one but several of the conspirators gave the plot away and thereby saved their compatriots from almost certain annihilation, but the damage was done. Their leader was apparently a retainer of Egmont's named Chiarlot, and Orange himself may have known nothing about their designs, but once again his competence was called into question.[7]

Affairs went better in the north, at least at the beginning. Louis of Nassau crossed into the Netherlands on April 24 and seized the castle of Wedde, which belonged to Aremberg, the royalist Stadholder of Groningen. He then established camps at Wedde, Dam, and Slochteren and attempted to increase his force by recruiting from the local population, many of whom were Protestants. Alba, informed of these movements by Aremberg's lieutenant, Zegher de Grosboeck, immediately dispatched Aremberg with five companies of his own and a small body of cavalry to join the Count of Meghen with a similar force at Arnhem. Neither was to attempt anything separately. It was Alba's intention that they should await the arrival of the *tercio* of Sardinia under Gonzalo de Braçamonte, which was expected to arrive by sea at Harlingen.

Aremberg succeeded in joining forces with Braçamonte, but owing to a brief mutiny over the soldiers' pay Meghen was delayed. In the meantime Aremberg and Braçamonte had made contact with the enemy near Dam on May 22, and as they had been told by Meghen that he would arrive the next day, they apparently decided to take the offensive. Unfortunately for them, Louis of Nassau moved with unwonted cunning. Around midnight he abandoned his camp at Dam and took up a position three leagues away, near the monastery of Heiligerlee. From the defensive point of view it was an excellent choice. When Aremberg arrived the next morning he found his enemy ensconced on a slight eminence surrounded by the bogs, lakes, and ditches so characteristic of this waterlogged region. Wisely, he chose to attempt nothing more ambitious than a skirmish or two while awaiting the arrival of Meghen.

Here the celebrated fighting ardor of the Spaniards betrayed him. Emboldened by Louis's apparent retreat of the previous night, they could not be held when a troop of skirmishers, apparently by pre-arrangement, fled back toward the main squares of the rebel army. Taunted with accusations of cowardice by the soldiery and even by Braçamonte, who ought to have known better, "he yielded to the braggart humor of his soldiers, which he had not, like Alba, learned to moderate or to despise."[8] He allowed the Spaniards to rush forward; they quickly became mired in the deep, scum-covered pools of a peat bog, and were picked off at leisure by Louis's musketeers and ultimately dispatched *en toto* by his pikemen.

With the vanguard destroyed, it was relatively easy to dispose of the others. Louis had concealed a part of his force behind the flanks of the rise on which his main army was situated. As Aremberg's rearguard advanced to the aid of their comrades they were engulfed and almost instantaneously destroyed by this contingent, leaving Aremberg himself to perish in heroic hand-to-hand combat against hopeless odds. By the time Meghen arrived it was all over, and there was nothing for him to do but take refuge in Groningen.[9]

The battle of Heiligerlee was an encouraging victory for the followers of Orange, but in real terms it accomplished little. Alba, when he learned of it, was furious. In his report to the king he lamented Aremberg's death as a great loss but added that he ought to have been able to ignore the folly of his troops. As for the latter, he ordered Meghen to prevent them from taking refuge in Groningen, "not only because of their shameless flight" but because they had upon capture taken an oath not to fight against Louis for three months.[10] This last was normal procedure in sixteenth-century warfare, but the duke had already cast his baleful eye on the *tercio* of Sardinia for what he considered its lack of discipline on the march north. The days of the unit were numbered.

Obviously it was necessary to take the field in person, but first there were other matters whose conclusion had long been deferred. The work of the preceding winter had yielded a rich harvest of noble prisoners, any one of whom might in an emergency prove dangerous to royal authority. Alba thought well of his chances, but no man appreciated the uncertainties of war more than he. If he should lose, or even if he should win but be carried off by a stray shot or other accident, the problems of his successor would be greatly augmented by the presence of men so widely regarded as popular heroes. His responsibility was clear. On May 28 he issued an edict of banishment against Orange, Louis of Nassau, Hoogstraten, and the rest of the nobles who had fled in the preceding year. On June 1 eighteen other nobles whose convictions had already been secured from the Council of Troubles were executed at the Horse Market in Brussels, and on the afternoon of June 5, before a weeping throng in the Grand'Place, the counts of Egmont and Hornes also perished by the headman's sword.

Their execution sent a thrill of horror throughout Europe. Men were disturbed not only because of the exalted rank and past services of the victims but because they were almost certainly innocent, in a legal sense, of any wrongdoing. At worst, they had been dabblers in revolution, complaining against the new order but unwilling to forswear their loyalty or take arms against the king. Lacking the intelligence of William of Orange, they had misjudged the temper of Philip II, and they paid for this obtuseness with their lives. But in one respect Philip and Alba were made to pay as well. It seems probable, with the wisdom of hindsight, that both of these men could have been won back to the Crown with little difficulty. As it was, their judicial murder accomplished little save to convince a host of others that no man was safe and that Philip was indeed a tyrant in the classical sense: vengeful, capricious, and unnecessarily cruel.[11]

Ironically, this diverged only slightly from the impression that Philip and Alba were trying to make. They wanted to demonstrate to the nobility that no one was beyond reach, and Alba had been openly delighted at the panic caused by the arrests.[12] They were, after all, friends of Orange and the most prominent, if not necessarily the most enthusiastic, supporters of the noble cause. They had also, it seems, been remarkably indiscreet. As Alba wrote of Hornes's papers, "there is scarcely any sort of thing that we have not found."[13] For months his agents had been gathering material, and the accumulated evidence was, by the rough standards of the Council of Troubles, enough to convict them several times over.[14] It would not, of course, have been acceptable in an ordinary court of law, but this, as Alba had already noted, was irrelevant. The biggest problem was their membership in the Order of the Golden Fleece. According to its rules members could be tried only by their peers. Philip had thoughtfully provided Alba with a patent to bypass this requirement,[15] but the duke was still careful to hunt up precedents, particularly in cases of *crimen lesae maiestatis*.[16]

All this took time, but by mid-April Alba had informed the king that he was ready to pronounce sentence. As he did not think it appropriate to do so during Holy Week and was sensitive to accusations that he was providing "the justice of Peralvilla" (a town in La Mancha where the local Hermandad had proverbially been given to summary lynchings), he had decided to put it off.[17] Now there was no more time. On June 3 the prisoners were brought under heavy guard from their lodgings in the citadel of Ghent and housed in the Broodhuis, the guildhall of the crossbowmen facing the Grand'Place. The following day Alba examined the material placed before him by the Council of Troubles and, declaring that the documents proved the men party to the conspiracies of Orange, condemned them to death. Shortly after five the next afternoon Egmont died as he had lived, with courage, style, and fundamental incomprehension. The moving letter written by him to Philip on the morning of his death reveals not only his loyalty but also his real confusion as to why this dreadful fate was about to befall him. When the sword swung the duke, standing upon the balcony of the Hotel de Jassy, wept—as well he might,[18] for he could remember hunting and gambling with Egmont in happier days, and if he remembered too, that it was Egmont who had given Philip the great victory of St. Quentin, thoughts on the gratitude of princes cannot have been far from his mind.[19] Shortly thereafter the dour Count of Hornes met his death with equal composure, and the crowd, weeping and cursing, came forth to dip their handkerchiefs in the blood of martyrs.[20]

These final tasks can only have been disagreeable in the extreme, as the parallels between Alba's own career and that of Egmont were too obvious to be ignored, but the man who years before had been unwilling to halt a march because of the death of his eldest son delayed only long enough to complete his arrangements before marching to do battle with the victorious Louis of Nassau. Among those final arrangements was a letter on behalf of Egmont's widow that is worth quoting:

> I have great compassion for the Countess of Egmont and the poor people who are left. I beg Your Majesty to take pity on them and make them a *merced* with which they can sustain themselves, because in the dowry of the countess they do not have enough to sustain them for a year, and Your Majesty will forgive me for giving my opinion before I am ordered to do so. The countess is taken here for a holy woman, and it is certain that since her husband was imprisoned there have been few nights when she and her daughters have not gone forth covered and barefoot to visit many places of devotion in this city, and before now she had a good reputation, and Your Majesty could in no way in the world, given her virtue and piety, fail to give her and her sons something to eat.[21]

Finally, on June 25, he rode out of Brussels to rendezvous with the *tercio* of Naples at Mechelen. Stopping only long enough to hang a soldier for disobeying orders, he proceeded to Antwerp, primarily to see that his great citadel was in order, and arrived at s' Hertogenbosch on the second of July.

Before him lay the Water Line, the system of three great rivers that was to prove so crucial a factor in the campaigns of the 1580s. Now it was undefended, a mere problem in logistics which Alba solved in characteristic fashion. His son Don Hernando and Francisco de Ibarra were sent ahead with a company of light cavalry to arrange for provision of boats and repair of bridges. As in 1567, *étapes* were established along the several lines of march. The force was then divided and ordered to cross the Rhine, the Maas, and the Waal at widely separated points to avoid the confusion inevitable when large numbers of troops are funneled into a single crossing point. They were then to proceed to Deventer for a general muster on July 10. That all were present and accounted for on the appointed day is in itself a minor miracle of planning and discipline. Fifteen thousand men with their baggage and impedimenta had covered an average of more than sixty miles and crossed three major rivers in less than a week.[22]

From Deventer the march followed the route taken by Aremberg nearly two months before. On July 14 the duke was at Rolde, "three long leagues" from Groningen and without any clear idea of the enemy's position or intentions, thanks to the hostile silence of the peasantry. He soon learned that Louis had established his camp on the northern outskirts of Groningen, and on the following day marched his troops through the heart of town without stopping. He meant to give the rebel host a foretaste of the doom that awaited them.

According to his established custom the duke led the reconnaissance himself. He soon discovered that Louis was entrenched on the opposite bank of the Groningen-Dam canal. A broad wooden bridge crossed the stream, defended by a brick house which had been fortified and stocked with combustibles in case the bridge had to be destroyed. Louis apparently knew, as Alba later noted in his report to the king, that it was a good bridge, but "as useful to one as to the other."[23]

The afternoon was warm and sultry, and it was nearly evening before the repeated provocations of 1,500 Spanish skirmishers could draw the reluctant rebels from their positions. Louis's men, in a semi-mutinous state over the usual question of pay ever since their victory at Heiligerlee, showed little desire to risk themselves against Alba's veterans. As a result, Gaspar de Robles with his troop of Walloons was able almost without opposition to seize another fortified house on the enemy's left flank. Finally, at about 6:00 P.M. Alba decided to draw them out with a feint on the bridge. The ruse succeeded beyond all expectation. A large body sallied forth to protect the all-important crossing but were met with such a ferocious counterattack that they panicked and fled back into their encampment, spreading fear as they went. The duke, who had cautiously held his own men in check during the long afternoon, now released Chiappino Vitelli and 2,000 Spaniards in pursuit. Though the retreating troops had the presence of mind to fire the bridge it did them little good. The Spaniards rushed across the burning structure and gave chase with their clothes and beards aflame. Others simply swam the canal, some holding their horses' tails and pricking them forward with a lance. Faced with such a vision, the enemy made no attempt to hold their prepared positions, and for some hours the Spaniards hunted them at will. It was 10 P.M. before Vitelli could gather his men and lead them back to camp.

The victory was encouraging, but it was neither total nor in the long run significant, except perhaps as a harbinger of things to come. Louis had lost more than three hundred men to the Spaniard's ten, but he was able to regroup and move off toward the east. Alba, pleased but no less cautious than before, returned to Groningen and laid plans for pursuit. During the night the burned bridge was re-

built, and on the following morning Vitelli and his 2,000 arquebusiers were sent on ahead to shadow the fleeing rebels and harass
them if possible. Alba followed with most of the Spaniards in the
van and the Walloons and Germans in the rear. He left the 1,500
sent by the Duke of Brunswick to garrison Groningen together with
a small band of German infantry, as he had concluded that in a country as sodden as this cavalry would only be a major impediment to
his march. An even worse impediment was that he did not really
know which direction to take. It was as though Louis's army had
evaporated in the morning mists that hung over the desolate landscape of bog and fen. When a troop of mounted arquebusiers finally
located them on the banks of the river Ems, Alba moved eastward
with caution, passing Heiligerlee and Wedde and by the evening of
July 20 arriving at Rhede in what is now West Germany.

It was here that the duke discovered a bit of what must have
seemed miraculous good fortune. Rhede, or Reydem as it is called
in Dutch, is a small and otherwise unprepossessing place, but in
those days it had the merit of being the northernmost point at which
the Ems could be crossed by bridge. It was in fact the only place at
which Louis could hope to cross into imperial territory, and not only
had he not done so, but he had not even bothered to garrison it
against the possibility of such a retreat. The Spaniards were speech-
less with amazement at this strategic gaffe. When they discovered
the whereabouts of the rebels, their amazement turned to elation.
Louis of Nassau had led his men into a trap from which there could
be no escape.

The village of Jemmingen, now called Jemgum, is located on the
western bank of the Ems about 25 km north of Rhede and about 5
km downstream from the present town of Leer. The river here is a
tidal estuary that sweeps in a wide northwesterly curve downstream
until it meets the Dollard. Jemmingen is thus located on a peninsula
with the Dollard on the west and the Ems on the north and east. In
Alba's words, Louis had posted his army "in the bottom of a sack."[24]

The reason for this suicidal error is unclear. No one has ever
credited Louis with genius, but he was an experienced commander
who should have been above such a sophomoric mistake. The only
conceivable answer is that he wanted to place his mutinous troops
in a position where they would have to fight or die. They had long
been without pay, and even located as they were, almost literally
between the devil and the deep blue sea, they were perfectly capable
of threatening mutiny and desertion right up to the commencement
of action. Headstrong, courageous, and not overly wise, their com-

mander must have felt that this desperate act was his only chance to maintain the northern front and provide the diversion that would be needed by his brother who, incredibly enough, was still idling in Germany. Whatever his reasons, he had entrenched his 10,000 infantry in two large squares with Jemmingen to the rear and the deep, swift-moving tidal currents of the Ems to their left. His small force of cavalry was stationed on the right, and the narrow road that formed the only entry to his camp was guarded by two ravelins full of arquebusiers, one on each side, and five pieces of artillery. If Louis had a chance of survival it lay in exploiting the nature of the land, but even here, though he realized the possibilities, he was fatally hesitant. The region around Jemmingen is crossed and recrossed by drainage ditches and canals. As the land is low, sluice-gates are necessary to keep the sea out at high tide, and Louis hoped to exploit this by opening the gates and flooding the area around his camp. His misfortune was that he did not begin to do so until the morning of July 21, and by that time the Spaniards were upon him.

The news that Louis was planning to inundate the land left no time for delay. Early on the morning of the twenty-first Alba left Rhede for Jemmingen under a heavy cloud of fog that burned off as the day advanced. As he went he took care to seal off every possible avenue by which an enemy soldier might escape. The vital bridge at Rhede was fortified and garrisoned with Germans, and arquebusiers were stationed at every bridge, village, and other strategic point in the vicinity. This was to be a massacre, not a battle.

In spite of these preliminaries, the duke and a handful of followers had arrived within sight of the enemy camp by 8:00 A.M. The Spanish van was still two hours behind. For the duke, the wait must have been painful indeed, as the rebels were already destroying the sluices and the water in some areas was rising rapidly, but when 1,500 arquebusiers and a detachment of noble volunteers, or *particulares*, finally arrived they had little trouble in driving Louis's men back into their camp. Louis, predictably, counterattacked in force, but the Spaniards held on until reinforcements appeared and drove the rebels back a second time.

It was at this point that Alba apparently decided to use a variant of the plan he had found so useful at Groningen. In addition to being well suited to employment against badly disciplined troops, it comported with the fact that his own men were strung out along the road to Rhede and would not be present as an army until much later in the day. Accordingly, he moved the same detachment that had saved the sluices closer to the enemy, hoping to draw them into ever more serious skirmishes. Louis's men were at first understandably cautious, but as the day wore on and the bulk of the Spanish forces did not appear they grew less so. This was, of course, precisely the duke's intention. By midday most of his detachments had arrived, but as they came up he placed them off to the right of the raised roadway, where the numerous dikes hid them from the enemy camp. In the meantime skirmishing became more intense. Londoño and Julian Romero, hard-pressed, called repeatedly for reinforcements. The duke, who for psychological reasons had not informed them of his intentions, repeatedly refused. Finally, after sending out a reconnaissance party in boats that quite naturally failed to locate the Spaniards hidden behind the dikes, Louis concluded that the main body of the Spanish army had not arrived and that it would be possible to break out if he made a sally in force.

It was the moment for which Alba had been preparing throughout the day, and it came none too soon. Increasingly nervous over the rising water and the appearance of a threatening raincloud, the duke was steadily increasing the pressure in the hope of drawing Louis out before he should be forced to fight in an element for which, lacking boats, he was totally unprepared. When at 1:30 P.M. Louis and his men marched forth in full panoply, it must have seemed the answer to a prayer. The conclusion was foregone. Discovering Spaniards in all sorts of unlooked-for places, the rebel army turned and fled before it had covered 300 yards. Again, as at Groningen, they were pursued by Spaniards who carried their trenches and ravelins, turned their own artillery upon them, and chased them through the camp, the village, and the fields beyond until there was nothing to do but plunge into the waters of the Ems in a desperate attempt to escape.

Few routs have been so complete or have been followed by such wholesale butchery. Throughout the long afternoon, the remnants of Louis's army were hunted down like animals. Those who fled to an island in the river were followed there next morning at low tide and slain. It is estimated that 7,000 lost their lives. The result of the battle was known almost immediately when the burghers of Emden saw the hats of the vanquished floating by the hundreds out to sea. Estimates of Spanish fatalities, on the other hand, range between seven and eighty. Louis of Nassau, after valiantly trying to rally his men, escaped across the river by swimming until he was picked up by a boat and carried to safety.[25]

Like Mühlberg, Jemmingen was more chase than battle. The duke had risked a full assault only because his enemy was at so great a disadvantage that victory was assured. It was accounted a major triumph, but Alba, his eye as always on the larger canvas, knew that the second phase of the campaign was unlikely to be so easy. He retired in haste to Groningen and began his preparations, not knowing, and perhaps incapable of believing, that William would wait until September to make his next move.

There was much to be done. The *tercio* of Sardinia had completed its record of iniquity by venting its disappointment over Heiligerlee on the civilian inhabitants after Jemmingen. As the men involved were a mere remnant of the original force, and as the unit had been involved in severe disciplinary problems since the march from Italy, Alba decided simply to abolish it and distribute its remaining troops among the other *tercios*.[26] There was also the problem of security in the north as a whole. On June 27 the king had ordered Alba to seize Emden if he could do it without offending the emperor. "For more than forty years it has been another Geneva and the receptacle for the heretics of Frisia, Holland, and other parts of my estates."[27] As long as it held out it would be a staging point for future invasions and piratical raids, a prediction borne out when, in 1571, together with Delfzijl, it became a major base for the Sea Beggars. Alba recognized the threat, but beyond ordering the construction of a citadel at Groningen he did nothing. The king's order had reached him only after he had left for Utrecht and was in any case impossible to obey. An attack on Emden would have wasted valuable time and created major difficulties not only with the emperor but with a host of German princes. As it was, Alba's brief incursion into imperial territory at Jemmingen raised a diplomatic tempest that had not subsided by Christmas time.[28]

Another potential source of difficulty was the Huguenots. While the duke marched northward to deal with Louis, a force of 2,500 under the Seigneur de Coqueville had entered the region of Hesdin along the French border. They had been driven off by the Count de Roeulx and been slaughtered almost to a man by the French Catholic governor of Picardy, the Maréchal de Cossé, but the full extent of the Protestant forces and the nature of their intentions remained unclear.[29] There was even some doubt at this time about William. On the off-chance that he might use his army to regain his old possessions in the Franche-Comté, Alba was forced to send money to its governor, François de Vergy, for the purpose of hiring Swiss.[30]

Money, at least, was not a problem. To Philip the projected invasion was a personal assault on royal authority by a discredited if overmighty subject. He was therefore prepared to spend whatever was necessary,[31] and neither Eboli nor all the bureaucrats of Spain could have prevailed against him. It was a novel situation and one that to some extent determined Alba's strategy, but he was still outnumbered by the horde gathering in Germany, and there was no more time for recruitment. His shortage of cavalry was especially critical. If, as seemed likely, Orange decided to attack near Maastricht and then move on to the great cities of Brabant, his superiority in this branch would give him a clear advantage on the open, relatively level fields. When Alba communicated these fears to Philip, the king told him not to worry: God would intervene on his behalf.[32]

At times, though, God's favor seemed far away. William continued to dither, and as the weeks passed Alba's health began to deteriorate alarmingly. Throughout the autumn of 1568 and well into the following year he would spend much of his time in bed or in a litter, wracked with fevers, diarrhea, and the symptoms of gout. The exact nature of this illness or series of illnesses cannot be diagnosed from the descriptions available, but it was of concern to the duke and his officers.

Fortunately, there was another side to the ledger. After extensive lobbying Alba had at last secured the release of his son Don Fadrique from Oran. The king had not reduced the term of exile but had finally agreed that the young man would be more useful to his father in the Netherlands than to the commandant of a post that was at least temporarily out of harm's way. Fadrique arrived at Utrecht shortly after Jemmingen and was immediately given two companies of arquebusiers and a personal guard. To Philip's undisguised horror, he was soon given command of the entire infantry as well.[33] This appointment provided much fodder for Alba's enemies at court and was, in fact, wholly unjustifiable given the young man's lack of experience. Still, Alba was convinced that it was a risk worth taking. Fadrique badly needed to develop a reputation for something other than intrigue and matrimonial misadventures. He also needed restoration to royal favor. What better way to accomplish all this than to give him a significant role in a campaign which, for all Alba's worries, was expected to turn out well? It was especially tempting because the son would be operating under the benevolent gaze and protection of the father rather than under the command of someone who might not be willing to cover his mistakes.

Privately, Alba seems to have doubted his son's capacities. At 31 Fadrique was neither stupid nor, as events would show, incompetent as a soldier. He lacked the restless ingenuity his father brought to war, the constant and aggressive search for hidden opportunities, but so did nearly everyone else. The real problem seems to have been some hidden defect of character, a flaw in judgment, perhaps, or even simple bad luck. Fadrique was one of those men for whom nothing ever seems to go quite right. Alba sensed this and so did the king, but the reasons for it can only be guessed. His father, of course, was an overpowering character. It may be that the son of a man who could intimidate kings found it difficult to trust his own judgment or to cast off the crushing burden of his heritage. In any case, his arrival at Utrecht provided his father with a golden opportunity. If he did poorly, the damage could be controlled. If he did well, he could be given an exaggerated share of the credit.

There were other causes for satisfaction. William had been gracious enough to remain in Germany for a month and a half after Jemmingen. Had he moved immediately, the consequences might well have been disconcerting. Moreover, the duke remained confident that his army, though small, was better than that of his opponent and that he was himself the better general. On the evening before he took the field, Alba wrote to the king: "I will always attend to the greatest necessity and look for the occasions on which to demonstrate that few men can sometimes have great effect."[34] It was both a prediction and the key to his strategy.

On September 11, William crossed the Rhine and moved toward the border. Alba was ready for him. Anticipating that Maastricht or Roermond would again be the most likely target, he had been at Maastricht for two weeks with 5,500 horse and between 15,000 and 16,000 infantry.[35] Orange's army was substantially larger: approximately 9,000 cavalry and more than 20,000 foot.[36] For nearly a fortnight they wandered about on the east bank of the Maas seeking a crossing. William sought permission to cross the territories of Liège, but the bishop refused. Finally, on the night of October 6, under a full moon, Orange suddenly turned and forded the Maas near the castle of Stokhem, his cavalry standing upstream to break the force of the current while the infantry waded across in water up to their necks. Within hours a herald was sent to request that prisoners be exchanged rather than executed during the forthcoming campaign. He found Alba encamped, with an eye toward historical parallels, at Keiserslagen, the old *Castrum Caesaris* where Julius Caesar had established an operational headquarters in ancient times,[37] but he was unable to deliver his message. Under the rules of war as they were then understood, rebels did not enjoy the rights extended to ordinary combatants. Alba had him dragged from his horse and hanged on the spot.[38]

William's hopes of success depended upon provoking a battle as soon as possible. Though he possessed significant numerical superiority, time was on the side of his adversary. It was well known that discipline and regular pay won more campaigns than pitched battles did, and Alba had been among the first to incorporate this fact into his strategy. More than twenty years ago, in the Danube campaign, he had merely shadowed the princes of the Schmalkaldic League until their army broke up in disarray, and he was quick to perceive that the present situation was not entirely dissimilar. He knew that Orange's mercenaries would become less and less effective as autumn turned to winter and the prince's slender purse became more and more frayed. If Orange had the good sense to seek a battle, Alba must on all accounts avoid it. As in 1546, he would hound his enemy, marching at his heels, never losing contact, but drawing back if Orange aimed a kick in his direction. Such a strategy would not only weaken the invader but make it virtually impossible for him to move against the great cities of Brabant. The relatively exposed position of Brussels, Mechelen, and Louvain was never far from Alba's mind, and he was determined to keep his enemy in the open fields, away from the rich centers of population with their vast resources and uncertain political temper.[39]

To implement this strategy the duke adopted the novel innovation of traveling in the vanguard with the pioneers. He would thus be in constant personal contact with the enemy and aware of his position. If William encamped or became belligerent Alba could make his own dispositions and, as the pioneers were with him in the van, fortify himself without delay. He knew that in this kind of warfare William would always possess a slight time advantage, and he wanted the bulk of his army to be capable of moving up into prepared position on short notice. To protect himself against cavalry and to cover his arquebusiers should a major engagement develop, he carried some new inventions by the Italian engineer Bartolomeo Campi. These were folding screens of cord strung inside stout wooden frames that could be laid across the ground to entangle the feet of galloping horses.[40]

These snares may have accomplished little, but the overall strategy succeeded in achieving its objectives. That it did so is a tribute to Alba's mastery of the art of war, but William's indecision and relative lack of military experience undoubtedly helped. Though he tried from the outset to precipitate a battle he proved wholly unable to draw the duke into a position that might have given him some hope of success. On October 8 for the first time the two armies met face-to-face in battle order, near the village of Eigenbilzen on the outskirts of Maastricht. Orange, apparently believing his position weaker than Alba's, withdrew after some desultory skirmishing and seized Tongeren. Instead of attacking as William had hoped, Alba moved to the west of the town and camped near Borgloon on the main road to Brussels. Determined to force an engagement, William marched out to meet him, but the wily duke abandoned his position, circled around the main body of the rebel force, and reoccupied Tongeren, thus blocking their most direct line of retreat. In military affairs at least, William was cautious to a fault. His own will to fight evaporated in the face of this strategic development.[41] He drifted off into the area around Sint-Truiden, where he remained for several days in apparent perplexity. Learning that a detachment of Huguenots under the Sieur de Genlis had penetrated the Ardennes and was marching northward to meet him, he finally decided to continue onward and rendezvous with them at Wavre, 27 km from Brussels.

In the meantime his force was beginning to disintegrate, as Alba had predicted. Neither the country people nor the towns were prepared to receive or aid him in any way. They seemed, in fact, to be rallying to support Alba. Their behavior was, as Albornoz put it, "like the young wife of an old man who runs to embrace him when thieves enter the house."[42] In truth, they resented Orange's Germans, who were looting at will, and feared the reprisals of the duke. Orange, in an attempt to improve the situation, ordered his men to stop plundering but succeeded only in stirring up an ugly riot between the Germans, who refused, and the French-speaking troops, mostly Gascons, Walloons, and Lorrainers, who were prepared to obey. He was able to bring the incident under control, but not before his sword-hilt stopped a bullet presumably meant for someone else.[43] Morale, in short, was extremely low: money was running out, food was scarce, and the troops were intensely frustrated by Alba's tactics, which forced them to move into and entrench a new camp every night while Spanish skirmishers kept them on edge with endless sallies and ambuscades.

Alba, of course, had problems too. At times scarcely able to lift his head from the litter, he must have had difficulty in concentrating on the innumerable complexities of the campaign. He must also have been filled with misgivings at seeing his enemy about to join a second army within a single long day's march of Brussels. He need not have worried, for the journey to Wavre proved more costly than Orange had anticipated.

In order to reach his rendezvous with Genlis William had to cross the river Geete, which formed the border between Brabant and the territories of the independent diocese of Liège. It is not a broad stream, but its banks near the village of Jodoigne were steep and slippery from the autumn rains. Orange reached the place on the afternoon of October 16, and Alba's men, marching to the north along a converging route, stumbled upon his right flank at about 2:30 P.M. Rather than give battle with only two hours of daylight remaining, Orange withdrew to strong positions, and by so doing probably saved his army. Alba, less cautious now that Brabant was endangered, had cunningly prepared an ambush for him in a nearby wood.

In fact, the two commanders seem temporarily to have reversed their strategies. If Alba was prepared to risk a battle, albeit only if the advantage was overwhelmingly his, Orange was now doubly anxious to avoid it. His men were in doubtful condition, and the royal forces lay squarely across his line of retreat. He was no longer sure that his superior numbers would alone constitute a decisive advantage, and was desperately eager to make contact with Genlis. The extra manpower would be useful, and the boost in morale might well prove invaluable. With this in mind he decided to cross the river by night as he had crossed the Maas two weeks before. The difference, of course, was that this time he would have to cross under Alba's very nose, and this could not be done without sacrifice.

William's plan was to protect the main body of his troops by placing his arquebusiers, nearly 3,000 of them, in the village on Alba's side of the river together with a few companies of reiters. They were to cover the roads that led to the crossing and keep the Spaniards at a distance until the maneuver was complete. All went as planned, and by morning this rearguard stood alone on the right bank of the river.

It should hardly be necessary to say that they were then slaughtered almost to a man. It does not seem to have occurred to Orange that the duke would attack in force. If it had he would not have committed so vital a part of his force without providing some means for its safe retreat. Alba deserves no credit for the massacre. He merely did what any sensible commander would have done. Companies of arquebusiers were placed both above and below the village along the riverbank, while a force of about 4,000 horse and foot under Don Fadrique made a frontal attack along the roads to the east. The defenders, under Hoogstraten and the Seigneur de Louverval, were in effect surrounded. The cavalry reinforcements Orange attempted to dispatch were unable to recross a river whose steep and muddy banks had been turned by the Spanish into a deadly shooting gallery. By this time, Spaniards had even circled around and infiltrated the left bank, which Orange had unaccountably failed to secure. The rearguard fought with exemplary courage, but in the end more than 2,000 of them perished.[44] Hoogstraten, too, was lost. He shot himself by accident, and the wound, becoming infected, killed him in a matter of days.[45]

This engagement was the largest single action of the campaign. It was a major setback to William because, though the main body of his army was left intact, he had lost his arquebusiers, the most important single element in a war based on skirmishing. Worse yet, the sacrifice had been pointless. When he arrived at Wavre he found that the vaunted force of Huguenots was smaller than expected, ill equipped, and encumbered by a horde of women and children. They would be of little use against Alba's veterans and the additional mouths would further increase his already appalling problems of supply. Orange knew his chance had passed. He had been unable to force a battle, not a single town had offered its support, and the disorders in his own camp were becoming uncontrollable. There was nothing to do but return to Germany.[46]

With Alba at his heels Orange retraced his march until he reached the Maas. To his dismay, he found that the rain-swollen river was no longer fordable. Once again he requested permission to cross at Liège, and once again the bishop refused. Wearily, his now starving and mutinous troops turned and made for the uncertain hospitality of France. Continually harassed by Alba's skirmishers and suffering miserably from hunger, they wandered through the endless rains of November until on the seventeenth they crossed the border at Cateau-Cambrésis, looting and burning churches as they went.[47] There Alba halted. He remained at Cateau-Cambrésis with his army while the redoubtable Cossé took up the work of harassment. Charles IX, then in the midst of his third civil war against the Huguenots, had reached a stalemate with Condé along the Loire. Determined at all costs to prevent a juncture between Orange and his adversary, he went so far as to permit Alba to draw upon the French countryside and, if necessary, the walled towns for sustenance.[48] But he need not have worried. Orange was finished. His Germans refused to fight against the king of France, the weather continued to deteriorate, and the Loire was far away. On December 6 Alba wrote: "The army of the Prince of Orange . . . goes now on the road to Germany, as undone as it deserves and in such a way that he and the rest of his accomplices will remain undeceived from this time onward about returning to disturb the estates of His Majesty."[49]

The duke was certain that royal authority had been established on the firmest of foundations, but he was wrong. Orange may have been thoroughly discredited, his health impaired, and his fortune wasted, but he was by no means destroyed. There was an implacable stubbornness, a strength of purpose about the man that Alba, who had known him only in his irresponsible youth, did not perceive. Orange would return, and in the end it would be his cause and not the duke's that triumphed. It is therefore only reasonable to ask whether Alba's conduct of the campaign was appropriate. There were certainly many at the time, especially among his officers, who thought not, and their criticisms struck a nerve. As the duke, still suffering from gout and fever, made his way back to Brussels, his mood was far from elated. "I remain with so little health and such little hope of having it, thanks to the contrariness of the land, that I am pained to think I may be unable to finish serving His Majesty in this business as I wish."[50] And for the first time in his life he gave the carping of his soldiers the dignity of reply. "Not the least of a soldier's problems is that both those who are soldiers and those who are not wish to judge actions according to their humor, and they are not content that a victory has been accomplished, but each one wishes that it had been done in the way that seems best to him."[51] He believed that he had reason for vanity, as he had overcome difficulties that could not possibly have been understood "by one who had not put his hands in the wounds,"[52] and was even prepared to attribute his conduct to divine guidance,[53] but the vehemence of his protests betray him. Second thoughts are natural in such circumstances, but if he had them he was right to reject them. Orange's army was as thoroughly obliterated as if it had lost a battle, and no matter what he had done there would have been very little hope of laying hands on the prince in person. Still, as Alba lay fighting the sickness within him and dreaming of the trout at El Abadía,[54] he must have wondered if perhaps, just perhaps, the head of Orange might now have been joined with those of Hornes and Egmont on iron spikes in the Grand'Place instead of being left to meditate further treason at Dillenburg.

Something, at any rate, was clearly amiss, for the duke celebrated his return to Brussels with a major lapse of political judgment. After entering Brussels in a triumph reminiscent of Charles V's entry into Milan, he commissioned a statue of himself to be erected in the citadel of Antwerp. This incredible monument, which bore a strong resemblance to an earlier statue of Charles V by Pompeo Leoni, showed him in full armor trampling upon figures representing Sedition and Heresy. The inscription referred to him as "the greatest servant of the king." Cast from cannon captured at Jemmingen and executed with some skill by the sculptor Jonghelinck, it offended everyone. To many in the Netherlands it was a gloating reminder of their subjugation, while to the Spaniards it was an arrogant and tasteless encroachment on the glory of the king.

Alba's enemies made much of this at the time, and it has been used ever since as evidence of his vanity, arrogance, and insensitivity. On the surface, at least, it would be very difficult to dispute this verdict, but the facts in the case are by no means clear. To begin with, the involvement of Benito Arias Montano must be considered. The indefatigable humanist had come to the Netherlands to supervise a favorite project of Philip's, the publication of the Antwerp Bible. He was also expected to help in the search for heretical books and to select volumes for the library at El Escorial. While there he struck up a remarkably close friendship with the duke, and it was he who devised the symbolism of the statue, gave Jonghelinck his instructions, and may well have suggested the project in the first place.[55] Though an admirer of the duke he was no mere timeserver, and it has been suggested that he thought of it as a monument not to Alba the man but to the idea of Christian monarchy for which he stood.[56]

Then there is the assertion repeated by the Conde de la Roca that it was erected by prior agreement with the king. By taking full responsibility for the repressive aspects of his regime, Alba was thus able to take upon himself the odium that might otherwise have attached itself to Philip.[57] Though this notion had been ridiculed by Ossorio, it has been accepted by a number of recent authorities as compatible with Alba's mission and with the possibility that Requesens asked for and received the duke's permission before removing the statute in 1574. The result is a dilemma. Which is more incredible: that Alba should have committed such a folly in the face of royal displeasure, or that, as Ossorio put it, the king should have agreed to such a "puerile and ridiculous" gesture?[58]

As Alba himself sheds no light on the matter, conjecture must again fill the gaps. To begin with, the statue is clearly an aberration. Alba was capable of great arrogance, but it normally took forms different from this. He might brag of his achievements in private correspondence, stand rigidly on his privileges, and treat lesser mortals with undisguised contempt, but his commissioning of the statue defied norms of behavior that he had never previously questioned. Its very existence indicated that something was terribly wrong.

That something was perhaps the greatest misfortune to befall Alba in his entire career. After he returned to Brussels, fuming at the impertinence of his critics and in the midst of what, for all he knew, might be his last illness, he learned that the king had decided not to come to the Netherlands and relieve him.

Philip's decision was not based on personal timidity or on the intrigues of Eboli, but on a distressing conjunction of events that left him no choice. In January, 1568, he had been forced to confine his only son and heir, Don Carlos. The behavior of the youth had always been strange, and as he grew older he became increasingly dangerous to himself and others. On July 24 he died, primarily as a result of his excesses. In October the queen, Elizabeth of Valois, also died, and on Christmas Eve, 1568, the Moriscos of Granada rose in a bloody revolt that would last two years and prove extremely difficult to suppress. To leave his country in turmoil and to undertake a perilous journey when there was no one to succeed him was unthinkable.[59]

Alba did not question this, but he knew that his worst fears had been realized. He was now truly abandoned in a cold and cheerless land, unable to protect himself from his enemies and cut off from the sources of his power. Soon he would be unable to govern. His policies had earned him a rich harvest of resentment, and the king's failure to repudiate those policies would drive many to desperation. At the same time any attempt to modify them would be distrusted or, worse yet, taken as a sign of weakness. Alba was, in other words, hopelessly imprisoned by the role he had originally been sent to play.

His first reaction was to fall into a kind of depression aggravated by physical weakness. During the first months of 1569 he isolated himself in a sickroom atmosphere, drawing his ailments around him like a cloak. In time his health returned and, to some extent, so did his spirits, but the process was slow. Almost a year later, he wrote to the Bishop of Orihuela:

I tell you that there are many nights that I am troubled by the thought that I will not awake; if this is done when I have no disquiets and restlessness, well it would be for the soul, but I also see those who are there. I believe it is best for a man to seek out the many honored people who await us in the other world.[60]

More practically, he clamored to be replaced, knowing as he did so that the chances were slim. There was simply no one else available for the job.[61]

It was in this atmosphere that the statue was commissioned. The idea was probably hatched in the course of a conversational evening with Arias Montano and the decision taken without consulting the king. Its purpose, at least arguably, was to provide a graphic symbol of legitimacy for a regime that badly needed it. Alba, "the greatest servant of the king," had subdued rebellion but now stood ready to embrace his fellow subjects. In the symbolism of the statue, rebellion was underfoot but his own head was bare and his sword sheathed. His baton hung loosely in his left hand, and on the pedestal were a shepherd and two empty suits of armor hanging from an olive branch.[62] The imagery was ambivalent and the conception inappropriate, but it symbolized perhaps better than anything else the character of Alba's regime after 1568.

It was also the first real indication of his declining political judgment. After 1568 Alba was under enormous stress. For the most part he bore up well, but in moments of crisis his irritability and his almost willful failure to understand the country betrayed him. He could still think creatively about war and diplomacy, but as far as the Netherlands was concerned, his resilience was gone. It was almost as though his loathing of the place and his misery at being there prevented him from looking beneath its surface. As a result, he tended to fall back on instinctive responses that owed more to his upbringing and the traditions of his house than to political reality. He might carry on like this for a time, but catastrophe was inevitable.

IX

ENGLAND'S PROTECTOR

Throughout the grim winter that followed his defeat of Orange and for several months thereafter, Alba seems to have concentrated much of his remaining energy on the conduct of foreign affairs. It is almost as though he sought relief by plunging into an older game whose rules were familiar to him. Since the diplomatic situation had begun to deteriorate it was perhaps well that he did so.

Ironically, most of the troubles that surfaced in 1568/69 resulted from Alba's own presence in the Netherlands. His appearance there with the main body of the Spanish army created a diplomatic revolution by shifting the center of Spanish power from the Mediterranean basin to the shores of the North Sea,[1] and the failure of Orange made it appear that the shift was permanent. For different but equally cogent reasons England, France, and the empire all saw in this turn of events a threat to their stability and even to their very existence.

Though their fears were largely unwarranted at least in the short run, they were certainly understandable. England had been accustomed to think of France as her natural enemy and had, since Cateau-Cambrésis, maintained her ties with Spain as carefully as confessional differences and the instincts of her seamen permitted. Still, she could hardly be expected to view the presence of a great Spanish army on her threshold as anything but a threat. Both Elizabeth and her secretary William Cecil were fully aware that Spanish friendship was based on Philip's desire for a counterweight to France and were inclined, if anything, to exaggerate the strains this association placed upon his conscience. Even if Alba meant no harm for the present—and this was by no means certain—there was the future to consider. With the Netherlands secure and France neutralized by her civil wars, might he not turn his attention toward deposing Elizabeth and replacing her with Mary Queen of Scots? It was a possibility no statesman could afford to disregard.

Such thoughts were far from Alba's mind, but Cecil could not have been sure of this. Relations between the two countries had been unusually troubled of late. If English privateers harassed Spanish shipping in the Channel, English merchants were actively persecuted in Spanish ports. In November, 1567, negotiations over the marriage of the Archduke Charles to Queen Elizabeth had broken down over the archduke's demand that he be allowed to hear Mass privately in his quarters. Finally, during the summer of 1568, Philip had expelled from Madrid the English ambassador, Dr. John Man, and had recalled his own envoy, Guzmán de Silva, an advocate of Anglo-Spanish friendship despite his ties to Eboli. The explanation for these acts was innocent enough, but Cecil, hampered by poor information and surrounded by men whose religious bias caused them to put the worst possible construction on Philip's behavior, regarded them with suspicion and alarm. In truth, Man's Protestant chiliasm and contempt for Spanish sensibilities had rendered his presence intolerable. It had been folly for Elizabeth to appoint this blustering academic in the first place, but Philip's timing in the removal of Guzmán de Silva was a blunder of equal scope. The diplomat had himself asked to retire, pleading ill health and financial distress, but by granting his wish in the midst of the squabble over Dr. Man's expulsion Philip succeeded in creating a very sinister impression. He compounded the error by appointing as de Silva's successor Don Guerau de Spes, another partisan of the Prince of Eboli who for tactlessness and fanaticism was very nearly the Catholic equivalent of Dr. Man.[2]

Unfortunately, this *contretemps* over ambassadors had effects more far-reaching than a simple increase of tension between the two monarchies. It left England without a resident-ambassador in Spain, and this made it difficult, if not impossible, for Cecil to discover what was happening at Philip's court. Had Man done his job or had he been provided with a successor, the English might have known that Alba and his faction were as determined as ever to avoid trouble with England and that their views were, at least for the present, those of the king. As it was, this breakdown in representation left Elizabeth and her counselors in a vacuum, prey to their worst fears and to the promptings of the extremists in their midst. On the other side, Philip and Alba were equally ill served by Guerau de Spes. By openly associating with the adherents of Mary Queen of Scots he cut himself off from the sources of information that would have been most useful to his master. Thus at a critical point in their relations each kingdom was left in almost total ignorance of the other's intentions and, by the law of self-preservation, tended to assume the worst.

It is sometimes easy to forget how small and weak Elizabethan England must have seemed before the might of a colossus like Spain. With no army to speak of, and a navy which, while promising, was still far from the standards of 1588, she appeared, to nearly everyone but Alba, ripe for the plucking. In this Cecil was at one with those other non-soldiers Eboli and Granvelle. He was certain that England needed the protection of an alliance, but with whom? France, he thought, was out of the question, for together with the rest of Elizabeth's council he believed that the Catholics would eventually triumph there and make common cause with Spain. The only acceptable alternative was a Protestant league combining England with the Lutheran states and the Calvinists of France and the Netherlands. Here he parted company with his fellows. If the council had underestimated the complexity of French affairs and forgotten the hostility that continued to inform Franco-Spanish relations, they were not about to overestimate the power of European Protestantism. A majority, including the resolutely Protestant Leicester, urged a policy of reconciliation with Spain and marriage of the Queen of Scots to the Duke of Norfolk. Elizabeth, characteristically, rejected this out-of-hand. She would neither abandon Cecil nor see her chief rival married to one of the greatest nobles in the land. In any case she seems to have viewed the chaos in France with less passion and more insight than any of the others, and she was not unduly alarmed at the prospects of an alliance between Spain and France.[3] The result was that, for the moment at least, England's policy lacked direction. England remained an enigma and an annoyance to the Spaniards, but one that required the most delicate of manipulations if open hostilities were to be avoided.

The situation in France was even more perplexing. As might be expected, each of the factions in that troubled country reacted differently to Alba's arrival, but the reaction of the Huguenots was so rapid and so violent as to precipitate what has been called the Second War of Religion. Tensions between the two faiths had been increasing for some time, and in July, 1567, the edict of Amboise was amended to prohibit Protestant worship in the Ile de France. This had apparently been done to prevent riotous outbreaks by the notoriously Catholic Parisians,[4] but the Huguenots perceived an ominous connection between the amendment and Alba's northward march along the borders of France. They were in any case closely connected with their brothers in Flanders and the Walloon towns and were understandably concerned on their behalf. The arrests of Egmont and Hornes provided the spark that set their military enthusiasm aflame. It happened to occur while not one but two Huguenot synods were in progress, and if any doubt remained that the evil prophecies of Bayonne were about to be fulfilled it was obliterated by the news that the 6,000 Swiss who had been shadowing Alba on his march were now, by order of the king, on their way into France.

The Protestant reaction was immediate. At the end of September Condé attempted to seize the person of the king at Meaux, but failed and moved off to besiege Paris. Catherine de' Medici and her son had no alternative but to reply in kind. Their immediate reaction was something akin to panic. They were desperately short of troops and knew it would take time to recruit them in Germany. It is also apparent that they misjudged the difficulties to be encountered by Condé in attempting to cut off supplies to a city the size of Paris. Their urgent request for aid from Alba can be explained in no other way. Though the Huguenots would never have believed it, the last thing in the world Catherine wanted was to introduce Spanish troops into France. Her misgivings were only increased by Alba's first response, a prime example of the duke at his most annoying. After commenting that had she followed his advice at Bayonne, this would never have happened, he delivered a long lecture on how the French monarchy should conduct its affairs.[5] When the French ambassador protested, Alba concluded that he (the ambassador) "besides being a beast, . . . must be a very great heretic whom I could wish to baptize in another manner."[6] In spite of this and in spite of his reluctance to leave the Netherlands unguarded, Alba finally offered to come in person with the main body of his army for a period of no more than thirty days.[7] By then, it was the end of October and, to her enormous relief, Catherine was able to refuse him with due expressions of gratitude. Her own levies had at last come up, and Condé had yet to make significant progress in his designs against Paris.

If the queen mother was thrown off balance by the audacity of Condé and tempted by the proximity of Alba's army, the house of Guise was driven to near-desperation. Had the attempt at Meaux been successful or should the Huguenots take Paris, their position would be hopeless. Already compromised by their connections with Spain, they were now prepared to offer almost anything in return for aid. For months, the Cardinal of Lorraine under the alias *Verbum Domine* had been informing the duke of events in France. Now he dispatched his chaplain to Brussels with the offer of several border fortresses in return for Spanish aid. He concluded with the astonishing suggestion that "if the king were lost" Philip himself might inherit the Crown of France through his marriage to Elizabeth of Valois. "The Salic law," he said, "was a joke, and could be smoothed over by force of arms." This was going too far. The duke was openly incredulous, and imprisoned the chaplain until Esteban de Ibarra could verify the truth of the matter.[8] Ibarra returned with full confirmation and more. On November 3 the cardinal wrote directly to Alba, offering Burgundy and much of Picardy and Lorraine to Philip if Charles IX were overthrown by Condé.[9] He had apparently concluded that the Spaniards were too shrewd to be cozened by the offer of the throne.

Alba was willing to occupy the border fortresses if the situation became desperate enough to require it,[10] but the contingency never arose. On November 10 the siege of Paris was broken at St. Denis, and Condé retreated, with most of his army, into the region between Sens and Troyes. Knowing that he expected to be joined by another force of 6,000 Germans now marching through Lorraine, Catherine again asked for Spanish troops. Alba agreed to send the 2,000 arquebusiers she requested and added the 1,400 horse he had stationed at Cateau-Cambrésis the previous month, though he very much doubted that they would be of any use.[11]

He was right. The Germans were already in France, and on December 28 they joined the Huguenot army at Dessay. Both sides were once again faced with a stalemate. Neither had adequate financing or an overwhelming desire to continue the campaign in the dead of winter. To Alba's disgust the queen mother offered to negotiate, and after much wrangling the treaty of Longjumeau was signed on March 26, 1568. More a truce than a treaty, it lasted only until September, when the growing militance of the French Catholics and the desire of Charles IX to prevent cooperation between Condé and Orange precipitated yet a third War of Religion.

The events of 1567/68 offer a superb illustration of the difficulties involved in developing a Spanish policy toward France. There was not one France but three, and none of the parties could be regarded as fully predictable. The Huguenots would always be hostile to Spanish interests, but what form might that hostility take? They might do no more than continue to bedevil France, or they might attack the Netherlands on behalf of their co-religionists. Alba boasted that "if the Huguenots wish to come and take the title of Count of Flanders, they will find their reckoning,"[12] but in truth the prospect made him extremely reluctant to commit troops outside his borders. Even more worrisome was the prospect that they might make peace with Catherine. As their leadership was at this stage primarily motivated by political considerations, and as Catherine and her son were themselves flexible in matters of religion, this was a distinct possibility. The Guises, on the other hand, were unimpeachably Catholic, and their power was greatly augmented during the summer of 1568 by the appearance of local Catholic leagues in every corner of France. But here, too, the leadership was suspect. The Cardinal of Lorraine, at least in Spanish eyes, had shown himself on numerous occasions to be both imprudent and treacherous, and though he was in a sense their natural ally, both Philip and Alba were inclined toward caution in dealing with him.[13] There was also a certain reluctance on their part to support a faction that might find itself in rebellion against an anointed king.

The ideal solution would have been to support Charles and his mother, if those two will-o'-the-wisps could have been brought around to a strong anti-Huguenot policy. This was, unfortunately, impossible. Catherine was justifiably fearful of the Guises and of Spain, and aid in this quarter could not be expected to produce more than transient results. From the correspondence it seems that Philip and Alba never quite grasped the logic of her position. In letters intended for their eyes only they railed against her folly and rather disingenuously ignored the dangers their chosen policy presented to French autonomy. At Mons in December, 1568, Alba wrote: "Your Majesty cannot imagine the bad government they [Charles and Catherine] conduct, thinking to deceive the whole world; I have not seen a man or a horse that I think capable of doing anything worthwhile;

they negotiate purely like children. I pray to God that I am deceived, but I fear some great prodigy, and to see how forgetful they are of God makes me fear it even more."[14]

The other major power with which Alba had to deal was the Holy Roman Empire. The chief source of troops for Protestant and Catholic armies alike, it was a garden that required constant tending, and throughout his time in the Netherlands Alba was forced to devote a disproportionate amount of his effort not only to correspondence with Vienna but to worrying about the activities of a dozen lesser princes. The independence of these rulers and the religious differences between them were sources of endless complexities which European statesmen had long appreciated and understood. No one could seriously doubt that the Protestant states would protest Alba's policies and aid William of Orange as best they could. It was true that Orange could expect little more than verbal encouragement from some of the Lutheran princes, but others, like the Calvinist Count Palatine of the Rhineland, were another matter. Moreover, Alba was fully aware that neither the emperor nor the other rulers of Catholic Germany were prepared in 1568 to upset the delicate balance of imperial politics by interfering either with their Protestant counterparts or with the Netherlandish situation itself. This was something he would try to change, but the main obstacle to attaining a more favorable balance in imperial affairs was the disturbing attitude of the emperor.

The father and uncle of Maximilian II had been forced, on occasion, to accommodate themselves to the Protestants, but there were many who thought that Maximilian himself did so even when it was unnecessary. His protests over the Jemmingen affair had been excessive and based on what can only be described as malicious exaggerations.[15] He had opposed Alba's coming and since then had "abominated the proceedings here more than any Prince in Germany."[16] Much of this obstructionism was undoubtedly rooted in his fear of contributing further to imperial disintegration.[17] As Alba put it in an unusually bitter letter: "He has always seen fit to take into account the lords and private persons, and even his domestic servants. And after they began to swarm, what they have always hatched among them is that Your Majesty was advised that they had complained to him [the emperor] of Cardinal Granvelle and of the bad manner in which affairs were conducted here."[18] But there were other, darker, suspicions afoot. Maximilian had been partially educated by Lutheran tutors and was thought by many to be a crypto-

Lutheran himself. It has even been suggested that he might have converted had he not been a possible heir to the Spanish Crown.[19] Whether or not these conjectures were justified, it was obvious that Maximilian would oppose Alba so long as he could do so without attacking Philip.

This, then, was the situation as it appeared at the end of 1568. Orange, though still at large, had been defeated and the last vestiges of armed resistance in the Netherlands crushed. New outbreaks were always a possibility, but the crisis seemed to have passed. The situation in France, on the other hand, remained highly unstable, and there was great potential for mischief-making by both the English and the Germans. Alba's primary concern was therefore two-fold: to protect his lines of communication via the Channel and the Spanish Road, and to prevent, if possible, any further military co-operation among the Huguenots, the German Protestants, and his own local dissidents. These objectives would have to be met without recourse to Spain and with reduced resources owing to the outbreak of the Morisco Rebellion in Granada. Adventures were clearly out of the question.

In practical terms this meant that Alba would have to maintain peaceful relations with England and tread warily in dealing with the French. He could not afford to commit troops outside the Low Countries unless the Catholics were in mortal peril, and Catherine was in any case the least trustworthy of allies. Committed as she was to achieving a balance between her overmighty subjects on both sides, any success she might have would be of little value to Spain. Alba might intervene to prevent the final triumph of the Huguenots, as he had been prepared to do in October, 1567, but short of this the queen mother could look forward to little more than a surfeit of free advice. With regard to the empire, Alba, like Philip, believed that an improvement in relations could be secured with little expense or risk. Elizabeth of Valois died October 5, 1568, leaving Philip once again a widower. He was now free to seek the hand of one of Maximilian's daughters, a match that could be expected to tie the emperor more closely to Spanish interests. At the same time Alba would encourage the development of a league among the German Catholic princes as a counterweight to the Protestants, and if necessary smooth the way for both projects by offering Spanish pensions to the emperor's more recalcitrant counselors.[20]

These were conservative policies, typical of Alba's approach to international affairs. Knowing perhaps better than anyone else the difficulties and uncertainties of a military campaign and profoundly aware of the weaknesses in his own position, he was willing to accept moderate gains in return for modest risks. He was not lacking in zeal, nor had his loathing of heresy abated in the slightest. It was merely that he, unlike the pope and sometimes the king, was keenly aware of human limitations and not overly confident that God would provide for those who failed to look out for themselves. His policy was both sane and flexible, but he was to find in the years following his defeat of William of Orange that even such a moderate and unassuming course was difficult to maintain. During much of the next three years he was to be seriously distracted from his main task of reforming the Netherlands by unexpected difficulties in foreign relations.

The first of these distractions began while he was still on the road from Cateau-Cambrésis to Brussels, and like most of the rest, it proceeded from England. In mid-November five Spanish ships bound for Antwerp ran into trouble in the English Channel. Battered by an autumn gale and pursued by Huguenot privateers, four of them put in at Plymouth, while the fifth made for Southampton. On board was a total of £85,000 (approximately 285,000 ducats) intended for Alba's troops, and perhaps another £40,000 that was carried without license and did not, therefore, appear in the bills of lading.[21] Once in port they found themselves trapped. Pirates and privateers blocked access to the sea and were even attempting to enter the harbors. Guerau de Spes, the newly appointed Spanish ambassador, duly requested an armed escort for the money and Elizabeth agreed. To this point, there was nothing extraordinary either about the situation or the actions of the parties involved, but as the days passed and the escort did not appear de Spes grew worried.

On December 28, Elizabeth informed him that, far from providing an escort, she had decided to keep the money for herself. This was an extraordinary turn of affairs. England and Spain were, officially at least, on friendly terms, and friendly states simply did not do such things. Even today the explanation of her actions is by no means clear. There is every reason to believe that she originally intended to return the money but was convinced by Cecil, and perhaps by the Genoese merchant Benedetto Spinola, to do otherwise. It was Spinola who revealed to her that the money was not Spanish but a Genoese loan that would remain Genoese until it was delivered at Antwerp. The Genoese, moreover, were perfectly content to lend the money to her rather than to Alba if she so desired. Whether they took this position because, as Alba himself suspected, they thought Elizabeth the better risk,[22] or whether Cecil suggested it to them is unknown. If Cecil did in fact suggest it, they would have been hard put to refuse, as their privileges in England were dependent on royal goodwill. In any event, their behavior provided Elizabeth with a justification, not a motive. Though she and her secretary clearly underestimated the vehemence of Alba's reaction, they must certainly have realized that taking the money involved serious risks. She needed it for a variety of reasons, but her financial situation was not desperate, and Elizabeth was never one to construct her budgets on the hope of a god-given windfall. It is equally hard to believe that she acted out of pique over the dismissal of Dr. Man or in revenge for the defeat of John Hawkins at San Juan de Ulloa, of which she could not have had trustworthy reports until a month after the decision was made.

A more probable explanation is that, by creating a crisis over the payships, she and Cecil hoped to achieve two objectives: to embarrass the Duke of Norfolk and his friends on the council, and to weaken Alba's position by depriving his troops of their pay. Norfolk, Pembroke, Arundel, and even Leicester were beginning to make a serious nuisance of themselves with their demands for Cecil's removal, the marriage of the Queen of Scots—preferably to Norfolk—and a conciliatory policy toward Spain. Elizabeth and Cecil may well have felt that a tiff with the Spaniards would undermine the credibility of their arguments while reinforcing those of the beleaguered secretary. Far more important was their concern over Alba's ultimate intentions. From the beginning Cecil had tended to exaggerate the dangers posed by Alba's appointment, and his fears were reinforced in September by a dispatch from Sir Henry Norris, the English ambassador in France. Drawing, no doubt, upon Huguenot sources, Norris had told him flatly that if Alba succeeded in Flanders he would invade England.[23] This was but one of a long series of false alarms, most of them inspired, as this one seems to have been, by attempts to gain more active English support for the Protestants on the Continent. But now that Alba had indeed driven Orange back into Germany it must have seemed prudent to prepare for such a contingency. If Alba's troops were mutinous for lack of pay there would be little cause to fear an invasion.

Whatever Elizabeth's reasoning,[24] Alba's response came with uncharacteristic haste. Egged on by the belligerent de Spes, he ordered that the goods and persons of the English in the Netherlands be seized "with all the gentleness and good treatment possible" and suggested that Philip should extend the order to the English in Spain itself.[25] It was a serious mistake, for it provided Elizabeth with an excuse both for retaining her prize and for confiscating the goods of Philip's subjects resident in England. As the Netherlandish trading community in England was large, this amounted to a much greater sum than that confiscated by Alba and provided her with further incentives to avoid a settlement.[26] That the duke should have done such a thing is perhaps indicative of the strain placed upon his temper by ill health and by concern over his position in the Netherlands. About the only good thing that can be said of it is that he did not follow the rest of de Spes's advice and attempt an immediate invasion of England.

When Alba finally came to his senses it was only to compound his error with a premature attempt at reconciliation. The vigor of his initial response was apparently more than Elizabeth had expected, and there is reason to believe that she was preparing to send an envoy to smooth matters over.[27] Before she could do so Alba, alarmed at the effect of her counterseizures and fearful of her control over the Narrow Seas, sent the Councillor Christophe D'Assonleville as an emissary of his own. By so doing he seems to have convinced her that she held the better hand and thus set in motion a comedy of errors that was not to end until 1574. D'Assonleville, who was by this time aware of the queen's initial fears but not of her subsequent resolution, took a threatening tone and for his pains received a tour of her armory. Philip then wrote, without consulting Alba, a letter so accommodating that the duke feared she would never come to terms; had it not been for a major shift in English policy two years later, he would have been right. As it was the Spaniards were left only with two rather meager sources of hope: the damage that would be done to the English cloth trade through the closure of the Netherlands ports, and the possibility of a revolt by the Catholics in Elizabeth's Privy Council. The first vanished when Cecil rerouted the cloth shipments through Hamburg, and the second was, as Alba knew in his heart, little more than wishful thinking.

The issue of the payships was to drag on throughout the remainder of Alba's term as captain-general, and while relatively unimportant in itself, it served as a barometer of Anglo-Spanish relations during those years.[28] Thanks largely to the insistence of Alba, Spanish policy remained consistently pacific where England was concerned, but Elizabeth and Cecil could neither be certain of this nor could they develop a consistent long-term policy of their own. As always, their calculations were bedeviled by the situation in France and the threats posed to their government from within.

Cecil's preference, in contrast to that of the majority of the council, had always been for a policy based on an alliance of European Protestants.[29] Seizure of the payships may be seen as a momentary triumph for that policy, but events in France during the following year tended to call it increasingly into question. The death of Condé at Jarnac on March 13, 1569, and the year and a half of bloody but inconclusive struggles that followed caused Elizabeth to draw back from open aid to the Huguenots[30] and might have forced her to reappraise her relations with Alba had it not been for the unfolding of a Catholic conspiracy headed by the earls of Northumberland and Westmorland in 1569–1570. There is little need to describe that muddle-headed rebellion except to note that it served to increase the queen's suspicion of the Spaniards. Part of this was due to the irrepressible de Spes, who had to be cautioned on several occasions to avoid inflammatory contact with the dissidents,[31] but Alba himself must share the blame for unintentionally strengthening the English impression of Spanish complicity.

The immediate response to D'Assonleville's mission had been to refuse any negotiations with Alba and to insist on dealing directly with Philip, though how this was to be done was never specified. Alba fell back on the expedient of negotiating informally through a Genoese merchant named Tomaso Fiesco. Fiesco was a smooth and able operative, but the duke came to suspect, apparently with good reason, that he was more concerned with maximizing Genoese profits from the affair than with protecting Spanish interests.[32] Accordingly he dispatched Chiappino Vitelli to England in October, 1569, just as the details of Norfolk's plans were becoming known. It was apparently hoped that Vitelli could ferret out the true state of Fiesco's negotiations while at the same time gaining intelligence on the military strength of Elizabeth's opponents. Alba had long since decided that de Spes was irredeemably foolish and distrusted his glowing reports of the queen's imminent overthrow by the Queen of Scots.[33] Vitelli, of course, failed to get past the customs officers at Dover. The appearance of so prominent a soldier convinced the English that an invasion might well be in the offing;[34] together with the mouthings of de Spes, it made a rapprochement unthinkable.

It was not until the following March that a thaw once again seemed possible. On the eighteenth of that month Alba reported that the queen seemed anxious to reach an accommodation, "not out of virtue but out of fear of this accord with France." She had even gone so far as to send four small boats into the Scheldt laden with fish, general merchandise, and her own safe-conduct. The duke did nothing to impede them, though as he said, "I have laughed enough over the safe-conduct."[35] The reasons for her newfound goodwill were essentially as Alba had perceived tnem. The discussions that were to end in the Peace of St. Germain were underway, and the English had reason to fear that the final terms would be unfavorable to the Huguenots. The Protestant successes of the preceding summer had been great enough to call forth a royal request for troops from Alba—a request he had denied in spite of orders to the contrary from Philip II[36]—but these gains had been largely frittered away during the autumn. Now Cossé was preparing to dislodge the Huguenots from La Charité. If he were to succeed the Protestants would be cut off from direct access to German troops and money and their overall position would be gravely weakened.[37] It was at this point that Elizabeth stopped her arms shipments to La Rochelle and made overtures to Alba.

Her concern was in fact both excessive and premature, but whatever advantage Alba hoped to gain from it was dissipated by a new masterpiece of misplaced zeal, this time perpetrated by Pope Pius V. On February 5, just five days after the Northern Rebellion had gone down to final defeat, he published a bull of excommunication against Elizabeth for heresy. It was the culmination of a campaign to raise the Catholic powers on behalf of the Queen of Scots. Four months earlier, on November 3, 1569, the pope had issued a brief to Alba, not Philip, urging an attack on England.[38] This had earned him the resentment of the king[39] and a sarcastic reply from the duke which ought to have laid the matter permanently to rest. Writing to Zúñiga, the Spanish ambassador at Rome, he explained that the pope and Granvelle had informed him that the time was now right to deal with the affairs of England,

> about which His Holiness, whose zeal for the service of God is so great and whose intentions are so holy that we could rightly judge them to be of heaven rather than of earth, rambles. If our sins did not impede God's work no one could doubt that without thinking of any human means we could set forth with entire confidence on an enterprise of this quality, but as the world has such a part in us His Holiness ought not to marvel that we wish to avail ourselves of human means. On these, in the fewest possible words, I will tell you what I can offer.

Essentially, he said, the whole thing was impossible because it would require three armies: one to conquer England, one for protection from the King of France, "who never lacks for offending the things of His Majesty," and a third for defending the Netherlands from the Germans, who would certainly invade them to create a diversion. If the King of France wished to invade England it would be the same in reverse, further complicated by his inability to govern in his own kingdoms. Finally, to join with France in a common effort would be Naples all over again, "and the memory of the example of Naples is very fresh."[40]

Alba was probably right about the pope. One whose inspiration came from anywhere but on high would have been discouraged by such an outpouring of gloom, but Pius V was undeterred. Without knowing that the revolt had begun, much less come to a bloody and ignominious end, he rushed forward with the excommunication in the vain hope of spurring Catholic Europe to greater efforts. The result was a curious piece of work from nearly any point of view. In his haste he not only allowed the document to go forth riddled with errors and non sequiturs,[41] but he failed to consult the Catholic princes or even notify them that an excommunication was in the offing.

Both Philip of Spain and the Emperor Maximilian complained bitterly of the bull and forbade its publication in their domains. Alba was fully in accord with their views. In a letter to Juan de Zúñiga he laid out the case against the bull with his usual clarity. It was, he said, the "right medicine" but applied at the wrong time. The English Catholics were now in no condition to do anything against an armed and ready queen, and even if they were the Spaniards could do little to help them. The king's resources were stretched dangerously thin owing to the expenses incurred in the Netherlands, France, Malta, and above all in this "present embarrassment in Spain" (the Morisco Revolt). To publish the bull at such a time was "the total ruin and destruction" of any attempt to deal with the English question.[42]

It was perhaps fortunate for the English Catholics that Elizabeth herself took a more nonchalant view of the matter than either Alba or the more militant of her advisors. Still, tensions increased considerably, thanks largely to an unfortunate conjunction of circumstances. The bull made its first appearance in England in May, fastened to the door of the Bishop of London by an Englishman who had received his copy from one Roberto Ridolfi, a Florentine merchant.

Ridolfi, in turn, had received it from de Spes's chaplain.[43] Given the origins of this incident it is not surprising that Philip's assurances of continued goodwill, transmitted not through de Spes but through Francés de Alava in Paris, received little credence. When it was discovered that Alba was assembling a mammoth fleet, incredulity gave way to a moment of genuine alarm.[44]

In truth Alba was gathering a fleet that would eventually number some ninety vessels, but its purpose was quite different from that assumed by Elizabeth's agents. In his continuing efforts to tie the emperor more firmly to his interests Philip had succeeded in arranging a marriage between himself and the emperor's daughter Anne of Austria. It was Alba's task—a frustrating one, as it proved—to arrange her transportation to Spain. A large armada was deemed necessary, for England's intentions remained as opaque as ever, and even if those intentions were benign the perennial threat from Huguenot corsairs remained. The English, who had no mischief in mind whatever, quite naturally assumed that Anne's journey was being used to cover preparations for an invasion, and Guerau de Spes, with his usual manic perversity, encouraged them in this belief.[45]

By the time the invasion scare passed the French had brought their third Civil War to a close. To the surprise and delight of the English, the treaty of St. Germain was remarkably favorable to the Protestants and its signing inaugurated a period of strong Huguenot influence on royal policy that was to end only in the St. Bartholomew's Day Massacre of 1572. Relieved, at least temporarily, of the specter of Spain and France united against her, Elizabeth could now see no reason to accommodate Spain. Instead, she drew nearer to France, even to the point of inaugurating her strange courtship with the Duke of Anjou. From the Spanish point of view all hope of accommodation seemed irretrievably lost, and thus it was that when Cecil and the queen felt themselves most secure they began for the first time to drift into what might have become real peril. For three years they had misread Spanish intentions. Now the self-fulfilling nature of their prophecies became evident. Philip II and his councillors began serious discussions on the possibility of an invasion.

The reasons for this turnabout may be sought in three related conditions: frustration over the vagaries of English policy; real concern over the position of the English Catholics; and the continuing struggle for factional supremacy in the Council of State. The resolution of the problem reveals much about Alba's attitudes and methods and even more about the nature of his authority in the Low Countries.

Frustration, at least, was inevitable. If Elizabeth knew nothing of Spanish intentions and therefore tended to assume the worst, the Spaniards were little better off. They had a resident ambassador, but that ambassador had so discredited himself by openly supporting the queen's enemies that he was virtually under house arrest. No one of real consequence would have anything to do with him, and when he did happen to stumble upon a bit of useful information his fanaticism led him to distort it beyond recognition. It was perhaps fortunate that after his advice led to the debacle over the payships his shortcomings as a source of intelligence were recognized. One of Alba's comments is typical: "In that of England I can extract little light from what Don Guerau has written me, as Your Majesty will be able to see by his letters."[46] It was to become a kind of refrain. The result was a series of curious and potentially dangerous misconceptions about the queen and her government that were fostered partly by lack of information and partly by Alba himself. As he was, largely by default, Philip's chief source of advice on English affairs, his attitude is worth examining in detail.

At bottom, the duke's analysis was rooted in the same incomprehension with which he confronted the dissidents of the Low Countries. "Things are seen every day," he said, "which are so devoid of reason that I know not what can be assured."[47] But if Elizabeth's policies seemed irrational on the surface, he could no more afford to act on this assumption than Elizabeth could afford to assume that his were benign. The key to his attitude is found in a letter to the king written in April, 1569. He begins by observing that her ministers encourage her in obstructing a settlement, and though she always seems to want peace, "such great seizures together with the constant piracies" indicate something else. Her refusal to deal with him as Philip's representative, the detention of Guerau de Spes, "and many other strange behaviors which she uses give sufficiently vivid testimony that she has some other secret intention." He advises that nothing be done, but concludes: "And in truth, it is a great indignity and insupportable, especially from a woman so obligated to Your Majesty."[48]

Elizabeth's ingratitude and the malice of her counselors, whom Alba elsewhere calls "the most miserable subjects and most pertinacious heretics in the world,"[49] had become uppermost in his mind. It seemed to him that she could gain nothing by harassing Spain and that she was morally obligated to refrain from doing so by the fact that Spain had since 1559 protected her from the designs of the French. That she behaved as she did could be explained only by a wicked perversity, whether her own or that of her counselors. As all were heretics this was not, in Alba's mind, wholly unexpected, but it led him into a miscalculation. Heresy, as we have seen in his policy toward the Netherlands, was simply beyond his powers of comprehension. He saw it as the result of a deliberate preference for evil over good and assumed that those who held heretical opinions would prefer evil in other things as well. Nothing, therefore, was more natural than that he should attempt to bribe Leicester and Cecil in an attempt to resolve the issue of the payships.[50] Such tactics may well have been effective with some of the emperor's counselors, notably Lazarus Schwendi,[51] but Alba's attempt to utilize them in this case is a measure of his despair.

The reception of these opinions in Madrid can be imagined. Though Alba continued to insist that direct action was unwise, his reports can only have led Philip to the conclusion that it was not possible to conduct relations with England on an amicable basis. When this gloomy assessment was added to Philip's deep and abiding concern for the faith and for the tribulations of the English Catholics the pressure to act was substantially increased.

Throughout 1569 and 1570 Philip's sense of responsibility was artfully cultivated by a steady stream of English and Irish visitors to his court. To a man, they stressed the sufferings of the Catholics and of Mary Queen of Scots and urged the invasion of either England or Ireland, depending upon their nationality or degree of optimism. From Philip's letters it is clear that they made an impression.[52] Once again Alba, though he regarded their schemes as nonsense, may unwittingly have strengthened their case by his importunities on behalf of English refugees in the Netherlands[53] and by his outspoken sympathy for the dethroned queen. In fact, it seems that the plight of this lady, whom he had known in happier times at the court of France, caught his imagination much as it was to scramble the wits of more romantic souls throughout Catholic Europe. His comments at the time of Norfolk's rebellion have the ring of genuine emotion: "I fear for that poor lady; God take her in his hand and guard her."[54] "They have much straitened the Queen of Scotland; it makes me [have] the greatest compassion in the world."[55]

Philip shared these sentiments to the full and, like Alba, he was aware that Mary's plight was of central importance to Spanish policy. As long as she lived she provided a rallying point for English Catholics and a potential excuse for intervention in English affairs. If Elizabeth were to do away with her, Spain would be the loser. The situation, then, was extremely discouraging in the closing months of 1570, and it is not surprising that Eboli saw in it the possibility of reviving his schemes for the conquest of England. In Alba's absence he had the ear of the king, and his opinions were reinforced by those of his ally de Spes and by Jerónimo de Curiel, who complained of Alba's inactivity in terms reminiscent of Villavicencio's earlier denunciations of Granvelle.[56] When Granvelle added his support to the proponents of invasion Alba was left as the lone and decidedly uncomfortable defender of nonintervention. It required only the emergence of an opportunity for the issue to be brought to a head. This was soon provided by Roberto Ridolfi, the man who had previously been involved in the publication of the bull.

The Ridolfi Plot is one of the most famous of the schemes by which Elizabeth's enemies, with childlike naïveté, sought to achieve great results with small means. Its origins are unclear. Whether it was generated by Ridolfi himself, by Guerau de Spes, or, as seems most likely, by a process of fermentation at work among those who frequented the house of the Spanish ambassador, it stands as a monument to misconception and incompetent execution. For this Ridolfi must bear the blame, for it was he who almost single-handedly put the plot in motion. Busy, scurrying, an incurable optimist with a loose tongue and a penchant for recording his dealings on paper, he was a novice in international politics and woefully ignorant of conditions in England. From the start he overestimated the strength of the opposition to Elizabeth, underestimated her ability to deal with it, and completely misread the situation of Spain in regard to both.

That he was given any credit at all was due largely to wishful thinking on the part of Mary, Norfolk, the pope, and Eboli's faction at the court of Spain, but other factors, in retrospect unconvincing, nevertheless served to strengthen his case. One of these was that if the Spaniards were alarmed at the English détente with France and the marriage negotiations with Anjou, the English Catholics were truly desperate. The prospect of an Anglo-French alliance would dash their hopes of overthrowing the queen or even having the Catholic Mary succeed her. The time to strike was now, before a French marriage could be arranged, and there was every reason to suppose that Spain would aid them in force. After all, such a marriage would be nearly as great a disaster for Spain as for the English Catholics; in Philip's own self-interest, it could not be tolerated.[57]

If these considerations inspired confidence among the English

Catholics, Philip was soon presented with what looked like a glorious opportunity to fulfill their expectations. John Hawkins, that fearless seadog and enemy of all things Spanish, offered through an intermediary to desert to Spain with a substantial fleet. He was, of course, acting with the knowledge of Cecil, now Lord Burghley, in an apparent attempt to entrap Mary and de Spes, but Philip was wholly deceived and saw in the appearance of Hawkins's agent a God-given chance to protect an invasion fleet against English interference.[58]

On March 25, 1571, having obtained the support of Norfolk and Mary and after compiling a long and partly imaginary list of English supporters, Ridolfi embarked for the continent to ensure the cooperation of Alba, the pope, and Philip II. His plan was to ask for a force of 6,000 Spaniards to reinforce the troops that would be gathered by the Catholic nobles. This invasion force, he thought, might land either at Harwich, which he placed in Norfolk, or at Portsmouth, which he conveniently relocated in Essex. At Brussels he received his first and only rebuff, though characteristically he seems not to have recognized it as such. Alba was polite but noncommittal and said he would refer the matter to the king. In fact Alba opposed the scheme from the beginning. It was not simply that "from the hour that Roberto Ridolfi arrived here I took him for a lightweight and greatly feared the danger of the persons involved in that negotiation,"[59] but because for the past two months he had been engaged in long consultations on the subject of an invasion and had once again decided firmly against it.

On January 22 Philip had written a long, bitter letter to Alba—nearly twenty pages of complaints against Elizabeth for "breaking our ancient friendship," seizing the payships and the goods of Flemish merchants, "making corsairs of her subjects," and mistreating Guerau de Spes. It was a clear reflection of his frustration and of the degree to which Eboli had influenced his thinking. Philip concluded that he had a clear moral duty to do something about the situation even if "human" as opposed to Christian wisdom counseled prudence. This last was probably a reference to Alba's earlier arguments, but the king nevertheless requested his opinion again.[60]

Before replying, the duke covered himself by placing the matter before the Netherlands Council of State. When his answer left Brussels on Februrary 23 it appeared, therefore, to be a unanimous corporate decision but was in essence no more than a detailed and subtly tailored version of Alba's letter to Juan de Zúñiga of the year before.[61] Even the condescending tone remained. Everyone, he said, was agreed that the king would be fully justified in taking arms against Elizabeth, but the problem remained of how to go about it. "The principal means must come from God as Your Majesty very virtuously and piously suggests, yet as He works ordinarily through the means that are given to men, it appears necessary to examine what methods are needed to execute his intention. The first, and what can in no way be forgotten, is money, which is the nerve of war." The cost would be enormous, not only for the army but for a fleet, "as one cannot get there by any other road," and there was money enough in Brussels only for ordinary expenses. Though he left it to Philip to decide if there was money enough in Spain, it was clear that he knew there was not.

Other obstacles abounded. Aside from the hazards of the campaign itself, it was as true as it had been at the time of the Northern Rebellion that France would intervene if Spain acted unilaterally and that a joint expedition "could not escape falling into great disputes and difficulties." The threat from Germany not only remained but had grown worse since the breakdown of Alba's effort to form a league of Catholic German princes. As he had reported on December 14, the emperor, by insisting on the exclusion of the Low Countries, had brought negotiations to an end, thus preventing the formation of an effective counterweight to the Protestants.[62]

Finally, the duke raised an issue which was by no means understood or fully appreciated at court and which indicates that, if he was often baffled by the queen, he understood her Catholic subjects well. "I omit," he said, "another doubt that I have, that, though the Catholics of England may beg succor, I have understood that they do not wish it so greatly as to put themselves in danger of being reduced by it to the subjugation of a foreign prince." He concluded on behalf of the council that war should be avoided in favor of secret aid to the partisans of Mary and continued negotiations for the return of the confiscated goods.

Ridolfi, of course, was unaware of this earlier exchange and departed with a light heart for Rome, where his plans were received with universal applause. By the end of June he was in Madrid. Here, too, he received a favorable hearing. On July 14 Philip ordered Alba to invade England.[63] That he should have done so has been nearly as incomprehensible to historians as it was to Alba. The duke had not taken Ridolfi seriously, commenting only that he had seen him and found his plans without substance.[64] The king knew that Alba opposed the idea and, thanks to the tremendous authority conferred upon him by distance, was in a position to obstruct it indefinitely. Worse, there was reason to believe that the plot had been discovered. Charles Bailly, a servant of Mary's confidant the Bishop of Ross, had been arrested with a packet of incriminating correspondence and put to the question. De Spes, with incredible complacency, assured Philip that the papers had been returned to him before Burghley could see them, and that Bailly knew so little that torture would be useless.[65] In fact, Burghley knew enough to break the back of the conspiracy, and the cautious Philip suspected as much. He was even beginning to doubt John Hawkins. He had learned that both Hawkins and his agent George Fitzwilliams were in close touch with Burghley, and though Hawkins had offered his ships with the stipulation that they be manned largely by Spaniards, these new revelations were cause for alarm.[66]

In view of all this, the reasons for Philip's decision to go ahead are open to conjecture, but it is at least possible that he never intended his order to be carried out. His chief concern may have been to retain credibility with the English Catholics, a need that had been heavily stressed by Feria and, presumably, by his ally, Eboli.[67] If he refused openly, all hope of future cooperation would be lost, but if he agreed to aid them and the plot collapsed before Alba organized an invasion, they would have no one to blame but themselves. He did not want them to destroy themselves and urged de Spes to rein them in,[68] but it is significant that no provision of money accompanied the invasion order.

Still, if this was Philip's thought, the duke was unaware of it, and indeed the advantages of such a course seem never to have occurred to him. His reaction was predictable. After thanking God that he had been born the vassal of such a pious prince, he reiterated the arguments of his earlier letters and added two more which were intended to strike close to the heart of a parsimonious and home-loving ruler. If, in spite of all arguments to the contrary, Philip should wish to go ahead with this scheme, it would be necessary for him to come in person to the Netherlands to cope with the inevitable French invasion. Moreover, a great sum of money must be sent immediately to put the Germans in *Wartegeld* (a kind of short-term retainer to hold them in readiness for war). He hoped he would be forgiven for delaying the execution of the royal order until he received a reply. In the meantime he would keep the matter secret even from his own counselors. As he had recently learned that

Bailly's arrest had been followed by the arrest of Ross himself, he had taken the liberty of telling Guerau de Spes to burn all his correspondence with the English conspirators.[69]

On August 30 Philip reiterated his order, with an important modification: if it appeared that the enterprise would endanger the English Catholics, it should be postponed.[70] Two weeks later he anticipated his captain-general's response by telling him that though he was convinced that the scheme was God's cause and that he was determined to put it into operation, Alba could in effect use his own judgment.[71] The crisis, if it had been a crisis, was over.

The consequences of this fiasco were not as serious as they might have been, but they were bad enough. Norfolk was imprisoned, and in January, 1572, he was executed. Mary was spared—to the great annoyance of the Commons and many of Elizabeth's counselors—but her personal circumstances were much straitened. In December Guerau de Spes was finally expelled for his rudeness and incessant plotting. As the king said in one of his marginal notes, "This is bad business, and I fear it is [bad] not only now but for the future, and if it is thus, no number of victories over the Turk can console me for it . . . and I fear that we are guilty of its being in such bad terms."[72]

That it was not worse was due largely to forces beyond the king's control. Put simply, Burghley was beginning to have doubts about his own policy. Louis of Nassau had put forth a scheme for a joint attack on the Low Countries by England, France, and his brother William, now lining up support in Germany. If the enterprise succeeded, France would get Flanders and Artois, England would take Holland and Zeeland, and the rest would go to Orange under the empire. On the surface this looked like the fulfillment of Burghley's dreams, but he began to worry about the consequences of having France in control of the entire Channel coast and about the difficulties involved in defending Holland and Zeeland once they were acquired. Success would present problems, and the possibility of defeat had recently been enhanced by the victory of the Spanish and Venetians over the Turks at Lepanto on October 6, 1571. Even the French, who had initially approved the project, began to draw back. If the Spaniards and their allies could defeat the hitherto invincible Turk and conspire with the likes of Norfolk, what might they do to France, where the Guises posed a greater threat to the monarchy than any that existed in England?[73]

Slowly the Anglo-French détente began to unravel. The Anjou marriage was shelved, ostensibly over religious issues, and Elizabeth showed little interest in an alternative arrangement with Anjou's brother Alençon. After much dickering a treaty of alliance was signed at Blois on April 14, 1572, but its curiously imprecise terms were highly favorable to England. Elizabeth received a general guarantee of protection by France without committing herself to support France against the Spaniards.[74] In the meantime, Burghley had informed Alba that he was ready to come to terms on the question of the payships. The issue was not settled until 1574, after rebellion had once more broken out in the Netherlands and Alba himself had returned to Spain, but the offer was an indication of changing winds. On March 1, in response to Alba's repeated protests, Elizabeth expelled the Netherlandish privateers from her Channel ports, and when on August 24, 1572, the French monarchy reversed itself and attempted to destroy the entire Huguenot party, further cooperation between the two nations became impossible. Spain had evaded the catastrophe that Alba's policy had attempted to prevent, but it was an exceedingly narrow escape.

X

THE REFORMER

D iplomacy, if conducted sensibly, is a matter of small gains offset by small losses, an attempt to maintain a state of equilibrium in which catastrophes are either mitigated or, with luck, avoided entirely. It is easy to see why Alba found it a congenial and even enthralling diversion in an otherwise dark time, but its arcane rituals could not blind him to the fact that events in the Netherlands were rapidly coming to a head. As we shall see, Elizabeth's expulsion of the Sea Beggars unwittingly precipitated their seizure of Brill, thus touching off what must be regarded as the true revolt of the Netherlands. It remains only to ask how a people who had ignored the appeals of Orange in 1568 were brought to open and largely spontaneous rebellion by 1572.

Ironically, the immediate answer lies less in Alba's arbitrary government and religious persecutions than in his attempt to place the taxation and governance of the Netherlands on a rational basis. As will be remembered, part of his original mandate had been to reform certain aspects of the government, and the need for these reforms was in no small degree responsible for the disorders that had brought him to Brussels. Specifically, he was to provide a uniform legal code for the provinces, to rationalize ecclesiastical administration according to the bull *Super Universalis* of 1559, and, above all, to devise some equitable means of taxation.[1] Guidelines were provided only in the ecclesiastical sphere, and even there the means were left entirely to his discretion.

His problems were in a sense those of an occupation government. How could the legal and administrative foundations of a state be laid by a regime that was itself temporary, extralegal, and extremely unpopular? The duke's instruments were, if anything, worse than most, but even before the defeat of Orange he had begun the task of state-building with considerable relish. Much of what he did was of course flawed by the means used to achieve it, and in the north, at least, all the reforms were washed away by the deluge of 1572/73, but the importance of his efforts has been recognized by historians.[2]

The legal reforms need not be described in detail. Though they could not have been achieved even temporarily without Alba's military presence, he was no lawyer. Realizing the difficulties involved, he left the matter to the jurists of the central councils. Shortly after his arrival the king wrote to ask if it would be good to place all of the provinces under "the same law and custom." The duke's answer reveals that he was by no means as insensitive to the local situation as some have thought: "If Your Majesty looks well at what must be done, you will see that it is to plant a new world, and would to God that it could be planted anew, because to take away customs long established in a people as free as these, is, and has always been, a very laborious matter." In view of this, he went on to say, some people had already been asked to see if they could create an *"orden de policía* that would be useful and most agreeable to the humors of the country."[3] The result was the Ordinance of the Penal Law, published in the autumn of 1570. Even authorities otherwise unsympathetic to the duke have judged it an excellent piece of work, providing protection against arbitrary rulings and procedural guarantees for the rights of subjects.[4] Unfortunately, it did not survive the Alba regime.

Alba's reorganization of the Church, on the other hand, was to form the basis of ecclesiastical organization in the Netherlands for centuries to come, and though he was by no means the originator of the plan he contributed far more than the force necessary to impose it on a largely reluctant clergy. That he was able to do so is a tribute to his unquestioned devotion to the Faith and to the king's wisdom in recognizing that in this, at least, his advice was untainted by ulterior motives of any kind.

When the duke arrived in 1567, little had been done to implement the reforms promulgated eight years before. It would be no exaggeration to say that the ecclesiastical structure of the region was in even

Alba de Tormes today. The ruins of Alba's castle are at left. Photo by Brooke S. Maltby.

Alba, c. 1550, artist unknown. Collection of the Dukes of Alba, Liria Palace, Madrid.

Alba in 1557, by Antonis Mor. Courtesy of the Hispanic Society of America, New York.

Don Fadrique de Toledo, artist unknown. Collection of the Dukes of Alba, Liria Palace, Madrid.

Garcilaso de la Vega. Engraving, from *Retratos de Españoles Ilustres con un epítome de sus vidas* (Madrid, 1791).

Charles V in 1548, by Titian. Alte
Pinakothek, Munich.

Doña Ana de Mendoza y de la
Cerda, Princess of Eboli. From
V. Carderera y Solano, *Iconografía
Española*, vol. I (Madrid, 1855).

Philip II in 1554, by Titian. Museo e Gallerie di Capodimonte, Naples.

William of Orange in 1555,
by Antonis Mor. Staatliche
Kunstsammlungen, Kassel.

Margaret of Parma, by
Antonis Mor.
Gemäldegalerie, Berlin.

Anton Perenot, Bishop of Arras (later Cardinal Granvelle) in 1549, by Antonis Mor. Kunsthistorisches Museum, Vienna.

Don Hernando de Toledo (Alba's illegitimate son), by Antonis Mor. Kunsthistorisches Museum, Vienna.

The Statue of Antwerp. Engraving, from P. C. Hooft, *Neederlandsche Histoorien* (Amsterdam, 1642).

greater disarray than it had been in 1559. A beginning had been made in erecting the new dioceses, but owing to the refusal of the abbeys to incorporate themselves into the system and the compromise accepted by Margaret of Parma in 1564, the reorganization was incomplete. In the four eastern dioceses of Roermond, Leeuwarden, Groningen, and Deventer, bishops had been named but were prevented by local unrest from taking possession. A somewhat similar situation existed at Antwerp where the original appointee, Philip Nigri, had died in 1563. The leadership of the town remained unalterably opposed to the appointment of a successor, on the theory that a reforming bishop would be bad for business,[5] and between 1563 and 1565 the diocese was administered by Cambrai. Since that time it had been governed jointly by Mechelen and 's Hertogenbosch, an arrangement highly satisfactory to the Protestants but frustrating to those who hoped for an effective Catholic presence in what Alba referred to as "a Babylon, confusion and receptacle of all sects indifferently."[6] Finally, Bruges too was unoccupied, but only because Petrus Curtius had died shortly before Alba's arrival, having enjoyed relatively untroubled possession since 1561.

Of the remainder, only Tournai, Arras, Ypres, St. Omer, Utrecht, and Middelburg were without serious problems. Namur was relatively secure, since the annexation of the Abbey of Brogne in 1567 had provided some hitherto unavailable funding. The rest were in confusion, with Mechelen perhaps the worst. Granvelle was technically in possession as Archbishop and Primate of the Netherlands, but he was still in Rome and with the Brabant abbeys successfully resisting incorporation the see was virtually without resources. It was also without Brussels or Louvain, which remained within the old dioceses of Cambrai and Liège, respectively. At 's Hertogenbosch the able Sonnius continued to survive, as he had since 1561, without the promised income from the Abbey of Tongerlo or any other funding of importance, but at Ghent Cornelius Jansenius was unconfirmed by the pope after three years' delay, largely because, as there was no funding, he had been unable to take possession. Lesser problems were experienced at Cambrai and Haarlem. The latter had a bishop, Nicholas van Nieuwland, but he was old, sick, and incompetent. Cambrai, on the other hand, was perhaps too well organized. Maximilian de Berghes had ruled effectively since 1558, but the king was having difficulty in securing the right to nominate his successors. Since Cambrai was an archdiocese and the chief see of the Walloon provinces, this was a major issue—one on which the

Crown was destined to lose: the cathedral chapter steadfastly preserved its right of nomination, losing it only to Louis XIV more than a century later.[7]

As a result of all this, it was virtually impossible to come to grips with heresy. Alba could drive the Protestants underground by sheer force, but without an effective episcopate he was powerless to root them out. No one was more conscious of this than he.[8] Within six months of his arrival he informed the king that steps should be taken to enforce the Bull of 1559 in its entirety.[9] Philip of course agreed, but there were numerous obstacles to an immediate settlement. Not the least of these was that a number of the original appointees had died or become incapacitated, and from the Spanish point of view there were few suitable replacements. This was not due primarily to distrust of the Netherlanders but to the exceptionally high standards of Philip and his captain-general. All too often, if a man were found whose ability and holiness qualified him for a diocese, he was unwilling to accept it. Philip's long courtship of Guillaume de Poitiers is a case in point. Having rejected St. Omer in 1561, he refused the offer of Bruges in 1568 and was finally, if reluctantly, allowed to pursue his meditations in peace.[10] A diocese in the troubled Low Countries was no plum, and it is not surprising that great difficulties were experienced in finding anyone willing and able to be thrown into such caldrons as Antwerp.

To the basic qualifications of learning, piety, and willingness to serve Alba added another of his own which shows that, once again, he was more sensitive to local concerns than his reputation might indicate. When the king suggested that Bruges be given to either Jean Ghéry or Jean Straetman, Alba argued strongly against both on the grounds that neither spoke Flemish and that diversity of language was one reason for detaching the diocese from Tournai.[11]

When these difficulties are added to the basic problems of funding, incorporation of the Brabant abbeys, and the delicate task of replacing the incapacitated, it becomes evident that Alba's reform of the Church was more than a simple implementation of earlier decisions by military force. One can only agree with Father Dierickx that the reorganization of the ecclesiastical hierarchy of the Netherlands was one of Alba's greatest contributions as an administrative reformer.[12]

The process began on March 31, 1568, when Philip, in response to Alba's letter of the preceding month, dispatched a long instruction ordering the installation of all bishops and the incorporation of the

Brabant abbeys according to the original bull. It would have been easy to obey had it not been for the vacancies at Bruges and Antwerp. Philip suspected that Guillaume de Poitiers might refuse Bruges and suggested that, if he did, it might be given to Driutius, the bishop-elect of Leeuwarden and a native of West Flanders. As this would leave Leeuwarden vacant the duke was instructed to look for a candidate who knew Friesland. If Poitiers were to accept, Driutius should have Ypres and Rithovius, the then bishop of Ypres, should have Antwerp. Poitiers of course refused, and Driutius was only too happy to barter the wastes of Friesland for the amenities of Bruges, especially since the revenues of the rich abbey of Ter Doest were promised him when the abbacy should fall vacant in the following year. Rithovius, on the other hand, categorically refused to expose himself to the tumultuous burghers of Antwerp, remaining snugly at Ypres and putting his great "science," as Philip had called it, to safer uses.

In spite of these obstacles all was in readiness by autumn. Alba's choice for Leeuwarden fell upon Cunerius Petri, who accepted, and orders were sent for installation not only of Petri but of the bishops of Groningen, Roermond, and Deventer. Ironically, William of Orange was at least partially responsible for the ease with which these changes were introduced. Had it not been necessary to fortify the eastern borders of the Netherlands in order to fend off his projected invasion, resistance might have been more widespread. Alba himself was aware of this, for he used this opportunity to expand Mechelen and 's Hertogenbosch to the full. Both these dioceses were intended to include those parts of Philip's estates that lay within the boundaries of the independent bishopric of Liège. This had naturally been opposed by Liège, but with his territories overrun by Alba's troops and threatened by Orange's undisciplined horde the bishop's protests were relatively subdued and went unheeded.

These successes were paralleled at Ghent, where Cornelius Jansenius at last found himself in possession, with an annual income of 3,000 fl. from the abbey of St. Peter. To complete the settlement, Alba at Philip's suggestion extracted a further 2,000 fl. from the hapless abbey, 1,000 to fill the vacant provostry of St. Bavon and 1,000 as a pension for the inquisitor-general, Pieter Titelmans. This left only Antwerp unoccupied, and once again the redoubtable Sonnius proved his worth by stepping into the lion's den. Alba had argued that only he had the intelligence and strength of character for the job.[13] Sonnius justified his confidence, not only by coming in spite of age and a personal attachment to the city of his birth, but by refusing the 3,000 fl. recently acquired from Tongerlo.[14] Sonnius's place was taken by Laurent Metsius, the Dean of St. Gudule at Brussels.

The search for appropriate candidates was, of course, only one aspect of a complex process. As he scoured the countryside for pious churchmen Alba was also wrestling with the problem of the Brabant abbeys. This had long been a bitterly contested issue, but it must be admitted that by 1568 the duke himself had become the chief obstacle to its solution. The king's original instructions were clear.[15] Mechelen, Antwerp, and 's Hertogenbosch were to be constituted immediately according to the original bulls and without regard to the compromise effected by Margaret of Parma. This meant that the Abbey of Afflighem would be incorporated into Mechelen, Tongerlo into Antwerp, and St. Bernard's into 's Hertogenbosch. St. Bernard's posed no difficulty, as it had long since fallen vacant and its revenues had as an emergency measure been divided between Sonnius and Granvelle in 1565.[16] Afflighem and Tongerlo were occupied, but Alba was to launch an investigation to discover if either abbot had obtained his office by simony or other uncanonical means. If Arnold Motmans, the abbot of Afflighem, passed scrutiny he was to be given St. Peter's of Ghent as consolation; if the abbot of Tongerlo were innocent he would be permitted to remain on payment of an annual contribution of 3,000 fl. to the see of Antwerp. The idea of an investigation may have come from Granvelle, who had known since 1565 that the Abbot of Tongerlo was a simoniac,[17] but the king's suspicions were prophetic in the case of Motmans as well.[18] Both were ultimately dispossessed, but in the meantime Alba had created some complications of his own. In June, 1568, for reasons that are by no means clear, he attempted to secure a moderation of these orders and began pursuing incorporation by an entirely different route.

The essence of Alba's plan was that the existing abbots should be allowed to remain in office with full administrative authority over everything save what pertained to the bishop's donations. This was a sort of *via media* between the full incorporation envisaged in the bulls and full independence secured by contributions to the bishops as set forth in the compromise of 1564. In addition, Alba wanted to transform the monasteries' contributions from fixed sums of money to percentages of their gross revenue, on the theory that inflation would otherwise increasingly lower the value of the donations.[19] The reasoning behind this second proposal requires little explanation: like every other sixteenth-century nobleman, Alba was an expert on the declining value of fixed rents.

His purpose in modifying the larger terms of incorporation is less obvious. Granvelle saw in it an attempt to limit his own powers as primate of the Netherlands and protested vigorously to both Alba and the king. He argued that the plan would result in maladministration, partly because control over the abbeys would be divided and partly because, in the case of Afflighem, the present abbot had done more harm in four years than his predecessor, the Bishop of Tournai, had done in forty, though the latter "was not the most temperate man in the world himself." Moreover, the present pope was an admirer of Paul IV and would therefore be ill disposed toward altering the original bulls. It was dangerous to request a change, but now even a papal rejection would present difficulties. Alba had referred the matter to Rome without prior consultation. If the pope refused the new proposal the Brabanters would blame Granvelle for the rejection, and as everyone knew, he had enemies enough without this.[20]

The cardinal may have suspected that his old ally had turned against him, but this was not the case. Alba had no reason to antagonize Granvelle at this point, and his motives in suggesting the change were in all probability unrelated to court politics. In fact, his purpose appears to have been twofold. On the one hand, he sought to prevent a repetition of what had happened when the Abbey of Egmont was incorporated into the diocese of Haarlem.[21] There maladministration by corrupt and incompetent bishops had created an endless series of scandals and disputes. Alba knew perfectly well that as long as Granvelle lived there would be no such problems but that after him

> there might come a prelate who neither gives the monks anything to eat, nor provides the necessary hospitality, nor repairs or sustains the house as it should be, and with this remaining at the disposition of the bishop, it is a perpetual dispute and difference between the bishop and the monks, and a terrible vexation in that they and the prelate will occupy themselves without being able to attend to anything else that touches the office of the one or of the other.[22]

This was a legitimate concern, and the only one that Alba himself mentioned in the subsequent dispute. There was another, perhaps more important, problem, which he preferred not to discuss openly.

By April, 1568, he owed his troops more than 3,000,000 fl. in back pay but he had only 150,000 fl. in hand. He knew that summer would bring a costly campaign and that there might be little in the way of contributions from Madrid. Accordingly, he had proposed a one-time levy of one percent on all movable goods as an *ayuda de costa* and had broached for the first time the subject of a permanent sales tax, the soon-to-be-infamous Tenth Penny.[23] Predictably, resistance was substantial. The duke might bully the Estates unmercifully but he could not act on financial matters without their approval, and, as he had said less than two weeks before his plan for the abbeys was dispatched to Rome, "I have put all my honor and authority into following this [the introduction of the taxes] with all my resources."[24] When he wrote this, he was experiencing particular difficulties with the Estates of Brabant and Holland[25] and may well have sought to modify the incorporation of the abbeys in order to smooth the way for his fiscal proposals.

If this is true, it need not be regarded as a cynical subordination of religious interests to the exigencies of finance. Aside from the fact that the situation was desperate enough to imperil his entire regime and with it the religious principles it embodied, the duke undoubtedly believed in the arguments he advanced to Granvelle. Still, he was capable of acting from purely secular motives if the need were great. In April, 1569, after his plan for the abbeys had been rejected by the king, he asked that the incorporations should be delayed until after the Brabant Estates accepted his tax proposal,[26] a further indication that this had been uppermost in his mind from the start.

Having originally accepted the scheme, Philip changed his mind in the face of Granvelle's arguments. He could not see that a divided administration would be better than one controlled by a bishop, nor did he wish to become involved in endless broils with the notoriously unreasonable Pius V.[27] On March 12, 1569, he ordered Zúñiga to press for the enforcement of the bulls, "purely and simply," but not before Granvelle, hearing that Philip had agreed with Alba but unaware that he had since reconsidered, lent his support to the duke's compromise.[28] Alba, never a graceful loser, took advantage of this contretemps to express his amazement over Philip's acting contrary to the advice of Granvelle himself,[29] and in the following year he achieved the incorporations.

With the resolution of this problem, reorganization of the hierarchy was essentially complete. The only remaining problems were at Haarlem, from which it was essential to remove the ailing and incompetent Nicholas van Nieuwland, and at Deventer, where the newly installed bishop, Jean Maheu, suffered an incapacitating stroke. In both cases Alba offered the incumbents a pension on condition of their retirement, replacing them with Godefroid van Mierlo and Aegidius de Monte (Gilles van den Berghe), respectively. These were both excellent appointments, but in a sense van Nieuwland had the last laugh. He demanded a pension of 1,200 fl., three times what the more worthy Maheu had received. Alba, who was scandalized by this outright extortion, sent the protonotary Pedro de Castilla to talk him down to 600 fl. He found the old sinner in bed, "from which it takes three persons to remove him," and decided that they could afford to compromise on 1,000 fl, as he was likely to die at any moment. This so cheered the bishop that he experienced a miraculous recovery and lived on in great comfort until 1580.[30]

It was a small enough price to pay for the completion of such a major reform. Alba had not only concluded the reorganization begun ten years before but through his persistent attention to ecclesiastical matters he had done much to ensure that the new hierarchy would be among the best in Europe. This, in itself an important achievement, was only a part of the larger work he had in mind.

Scarcely a single aspect of ecclesiastical affairs escaped his attention. The regular clergy no less than the secular were in disarray, and by January, 1568, he had made serious efforts to reform them. The king had requested the re-edification of the Carthusians. Alba responded by delegating the task to Alonso de Contreras.[31] At about the same time and on his own authority, he asked the pope for a visitation of the Dominicans and Franciscans. It is characteristic that when a Franciscan visitor did arrive with briefs not only for this purpose but for investigating the Inquisition as well, Alba refused to allow him to interfere with the latter. Such a task, he thought, required "a cardinal, or someone of that quality."[32] In short, his concept of reform remained typically Spanish and regalist.

This attitude is doubly evident in Alba's dealings with the Jesuits. In September, 1570, they requested permission from the king to abandon their college at Tournai and relocate in Antwerp. Philip referred the matter to Alba, who responded indirectly by way of Antonio de Toledo, "because these fathers are numerous and have many intelligences, and I do not wish them to hate me as they are very hard enemies." After providing a brief but comprehensive history of the Spanish community in Antwerp and the Jesuits in particular, he advised against relocation. Though they could undoubtedly perform great services elsewhere, their persistent threats to royal authority made them a hazard in the Netherlands. Not only had they already established themselves at Antwerp without asking leave from Alba or the bishop, but they had "murmured about the justice being done here" and opposed the levying of taxes in order to curry favor with the people.[33] To the end, Alba remained incapable of separating the interests of Church and State. This was not due to stupidity or to a blind confusion of ideals but to the conviction that Catholic hegemony in the Netherlands depended ultimately on the maintenance of absolute royal authority. If he was wrong it was in his understanding of the term *absolute*.

The banning of books was pursued with even greater enthusiasm. To enforce the rulings of the Council of Trent, Alba established a commission whose task it was to compile a list of condemned books. The bishops and other interested parties were invited to submit selections of their own. When they had produced what the duke called "a very copious catalog," he dispatched agents, including Arias Montano, to visit the bookshops and seize works containing *"la doctrina de los muchachos."*[34] The printers of such texts, if they were not already in exile, were haled before the bishops and examined. It was a most successful campaign, and Philip was delighted. He informed the duke that his dispositions would be the model for those in Spain.[35]

Alba also inquired into the state of the universities. He was impressed with Louvain but recommended salary increases for the faculty at Douai so that "the university will be well provided and have learned men without their trying to go elsewhere." He noted that something should be done for the University of Dôle in the Franche-Comté; it was, he said, very poor, but important because it was surrounded by heretics.[36] These ecclesiastical reforms, though widely resented, were successful in the sense that they survived the Alba regime and greatly strengthened the position of the Church.

The duke's fiscal policies, however, were an unmitigated disaster. They not only proved impermanent in the extreme but were a major factor in precipitating the general rebellion of 1572. Much has been written about the celebrated Tenth Penny, but all too often the true nature of the tax and the process by which it was imposed have been obscured by partisanship and oversimplification. It was not in its final form a simple *alcabala*, or ten-percent levy on all commercial transactions, nor was it in any sense the unmodified product of Alba's "military," economically untutored mind. It was instead the product of a long series of discussions among Alba, the Council of Finance, and the provincial Estates, and the result was less burdensome than a similar tax levied successfully by William of Orange after the duke's departure.[37] Neither the tax nor the opposition it provoked can be understood without a detailed explanation of the circumstances that surrounded it.

As we have seen, the financial condition of the Netherlands government in 1567 was little short of disastrous, and drastic measures were essential. At the very least it was necessary to develop a permanent source of revenue to stem, and if possible reverse, the alienation of royal property and to eliminate the manifold abuses that had grown up in such areas as marine insurance and currency speculation. Alba was granted extraordinary latitude in achieving these ends, but the range of available options was severely limited by inviolable custom and the economic ignorance characteristic of his generation. Confiscations increased the royal patrimony,[38] insurance was placed under the control of an *administrador general de seguros*,[39] and currency speculation was forbidden by placard in 1571,[40] but the question of permanent revenue could not be solved by such heavyhanded means.

The first steps toward a solution were tentative indeed. After several months of "attempting to understand the government, but gingerly," Alba asked the Council of Finance to suggest ways in which the financial problems could be ended. A month later the councillors returned with the traditional and unimaginative suggestion that a one-percent tax be levied on all movable property as an *aide*. The duke agreed, as he expected it to cover most of the 3,000,000 fl. in current debt, but noted that this did little to provide for the future. Accordingly, he proposed for the first time on April 13, 1568, that an *alcabala* of ten percent be imposed on all transactions as a source of perpetual revenue and that it be supplemented by a five-percent tax, the Twentieth Penny, on all sales of real estate.

There was an immediate outcry that this would be harmful to the merchants, but the duke replied "saying that it was the best expedient I knew and the one most equal to all sorts of people."[41] This was the crux of the issue and the first of many points at which historians have gone astray in their portrayal of the conflict between Alba and his ministers. It was not ignorance or the supposedly opaque quality of the military mind that led the duke to prefer the *alcabala*, but the conviction that no segment of society should be exempt from the burden of support. Where the wealthy were already sheltered from most forms of taxation, only a sales tax could prevent the entire burden from falling upon the poor.

At first glance such concerns might seem unusual in an aristocrat, but Alba was also a royalist, and fiscal egalitarianism had long been part of royal policy. Both the Castilian *alcabala* and the unsuccessful *sisa* of 1537 had been defended in similar terms. Alba had himself supported the latter, to the intense disgust of his fellow nobles. Religious conviction and an aristocratic distrust of merchants may also have been involved, but whatever the origins of his opinion, he held it with characteristic tenacity. When a scheme was presented to raise an equal sum of money by taxing marriages, baptisms, and successions in the collateral line he firmly rejected it as oppressive to the poor.[42]

In fact, the duke's mind was already made up. He intended to have the *alcabala*, in one form or another, at all costs, but for the moment he decided to let the matter rest. The treasurer, Schetz, raised "100,000 objections in an hour," even after Alba suggested that first transactions be exempt as a concession to trade, and as Schetz was "the chief *cabrón* they all adore" he thought it best to proceed with caution.[43]

Alba knew he had to interest the nobles and financiers in his proposal and hoped to do so by providing them with a role in the management of the tax,[44] but it was not until November 4 that the Councils of State and Finance approved a resolution setting the Hundredth Penny and the Tenth Penny, as the taxes had come to be called, before the provincial Estates.[45] In the meantime, Orange's invasion had been launched and Alba had been in the field since July at a monthly cost of 260,000 *escudos*.[46]

The duke was apologetic about the expenses and resented in his very soul the obstacles raised by his counselors,[47] but the king could provide little comfort. On Christmas Eve, 1568, the Moriscos of Granada rose in the second rebellion of the Alpujarras, and on January 10 Philip was forced to write:

> There remains not a single expedient for obtaining a *real*, and thus I strongly implore you and order you with the love, attention, and diligence with which you alone look after the things of my service to arrange the matters of the *hacienda* in those estates in such a way as to supply all their costs without [our] having to send more money there, because, aside from there being none, as has been said, it would be taken very badly in these kingdoms even if there were some, to see it sent there for ordinary expenses as in the past, now that the war is over.[48]

It was a refrain to be sounded frequently in the months to come.

So great was the need that Alba decided to contravene the king's orders and call the Estates together as a group rather than meeting them separately, as he had originally intended. He felt that if he could call them into session for a single day he could prevent them from expressing their discontent over other issues, but that if he met them separately, distance and bad weather might cause the affair to drag on indefinitely.[49] On March 21 the taxes were proposed and Alba visited each delegation individually to hear their reaction.[50] He was optimistic, but his optimism turned out to be premature. Once they had returned to their homes, the members began to create difficulties. The strongest opposition, oddly enough, came from predominantly agricultural Artois, but there was general agreement that the Tenth Penny would be the utter ruin of trade.

By the end of June, 1569, Alba was beginning to agree,[51] but he had staked his prestige on the issue and felt that he could not back down without imperiling royal authority.[52] The impasse was finally broken when he suggested that if the Estates accepted the *alcabala* in principle, he would agree to an *encabezamiento* of the tax.[53] *Encabezamiento* was a process by which a tax would be collected by a town or province on the basis of a figure agreed upon in advance. In other words, it would be not unlike a traditional *aide* collected in the traditional ways by the local authorities. In the meantime, the Estates had agreed to the imposition of the Hundredth Penny, thus alleviating the immediate financial crisis.

Philip was delighted with the *encabezamiento*.[54] Alba too seemed pleased, as it enabled him to get down to "give and take," now that royal authority had been asserted.[55] The wonder is that the duke seems not to have thought of such a compromise until October. After all, the Castilian *alcabala* had been in *encabezamiento* since 1525![56]

The "give and take," as Alba called it, lasted until the following summer, when the Estates accepted a proposal sent to them by the Councils of State and Finance. It was agreed that the *alcabala* be placed in *encabezamiento* for two years at the sum of 2,000,000 fl., or 1,000,000 per year. This represented a victory for Alba, as the Estates had originally proposed that the sum be paid over a six-year period. But if the collection period was shortened the fundamental character of the *alcabala* had been changed. While admitting that the full tax would produce a sum "that it would be madness to say," the duke noted that many of the states could meet their quotas by collecting only a sixtieth, an eightieth, or even a hundredth of the total value of transferred goods.[57] Moreover, though it was agreed that the

Hundredth Penny could be imposed again in six years if there were an invasion, none of these arrangements was in any sense perpetual.

The compromise, then, was successful only in the short run. It produced what one modern historian has called *"les années des vaches grasses,"* the years 1570–1571, in which the government of the Netherlands was truly solvent for the first time in living memory,[58] but these profits were accompanied by costs as heavy as they were intangible. By compromising as he did, Alba gave the impression that the question of a perpetual tax was negotiable, when nothing, in fact, could have been further from the truth. Worse yet, he seems to have believed that the Estates had agreed to such a tax in principle, a claim they later denied.

This misunderstanding, which may not have been innocent on either side, was much aggravated by the ducal state of mind. Negotiations had been lengthy and difficult and had driven a wedge between him and his ministers that was to remain until the end. As his secretary Albornoz said: "In bringing the matter to this point, I can assure you that the duke has lost more sleep than I have hairs on my head, because what has passed in negotiating with these men can neither be imagined nor thought, [their] being contrary to all the things that have to be done for the service of His Majesty." He felt that they had been "put to cape and sword" by the country as a whole and by none so much as the very ministers whose task it was to execute the policies.[59]

The experience deepened the sense of isolation Alba had felt since arriving in Brussels and encouraged an already pronounced tendency to think of himself as a kind of Childe Roland, cut off from the succor of his king and surrounded by paynims. Not only had the Netherlanders resisted his own and the king's authority, they had gone so far as to threaten him, saying that the tax could cause rebellion within the states and encourage invasion from without. His response, delivered at white heat, reveals the development of a siege mentality and the continuing erosion of his political good sense:

> I responded that they should understand that in the same way that His Majesty sent me here to cut off the heads of the disobedient and those that had raised the country, I could cut off [the heads of] those who disquiet me in this other way, and when all the world was lost, I could break the dikes and inundate it all, because His Majesty would prefer a country lost and drowned to one preserved rich and disobedient.

After somewhat regaining his composure, he added that such a course was unlikely where the king had so many good vassals but that it would be easier for him than continuing the negotiations, as "I have studied forty-nine years on that faculty."[60]

There was almost certainly an element of bluff in all this, but it was a threat born of real exasperation and it forced his counselors to face the alien and essentially unsympathetic nature of his rule. They acceded to his wishes, but the lines were drawn and communication all but ceased. After all, they were not simple Quislings but men who believed that royal authority and the welfare of their homeland were inseparably joined. Now they had either to reject this cherished belief or assume that Alba did not truly represent the king's will. When the issue arose again in April, 1571, their resistance was more obdurate than before.

The *alcabala* was due to expire on August 13, and it seemed probable that discussing its replacement might take months. If the counselors had hardened in their views, so had the duke. He remained convinced that effective royal authority depended upon maintenance of a perpetual tax, and the experience of the preceding year had dramatically reinforced this opinion. By February, 1571, every penny of the 4,000,000 fl. produced by the *alcabala* and the 3.3 million produced by the Hundredth Penny had been consumed by the army, whose pay was—as usual—in arrears. The debt to the German mercenaries alone had come to nearly 5,000,000 fl. Alba feared that if there were an invasion he would be unable to defend himself. The bankers refused to loan him money against a second Hundredth Penny; by the agreement of 1569 it could not be levied until 1575, and four years was beginning to look like a very long time.[61]

A long, bitter wrangle was inevitable. It began, as expected, in a complete deadlock. The councillors, led by Berlaymont, argued that the Estates had never agreed to an extension of the tax and, having met their quotas, would insist on negotiating the matter from scratch. Alba replied, "not without choler," that they had plainly agreed to a perpetual *alcabala* and that he had done no more than commute it temporarily by accepting the *encabezamiento*.[62]

The stalemate lasted for more than a month. The councillors had learned that Alba's recall was imminent and hoped to prolong matters until the arrival of a more sympathetic successor. Viglius in particular was so heartened that he became the chief spokesman for the opposition, a turnabout so complete and so unprecedented that it shows more clearly than anything else how swiftly the tide was running against the duke. Alba was painfully aware of this[63] and his melancholy deepened, relieved only by ever more frequent bursts of rage.

The councillors' opposition was understandable in other terms. They saw that a perpetual tax would forever deprive the Estates of the power of the purse and feared that even the machinery of collection would fall into the hands of Spaniards. Alba was notoriously opposed to tax-farming, and the collection of the Hundredth Penny under the aegis of superintendents named specifically for that purpose and responsible directly to the duke filled them with trepidation.[64] But when all is said and done, the chief responsibility for the debacle must rest firmly with the duke. Since long before the discussions actually began he had favored a severely modified *alcabala* in which all transactions save the last would be exempt. He had become as convinced as any Fleming that full imposition of the tax would ruin the country and was even prepared to entertain proposals that would exempt specific categories of merchandise,[65] but by a miscalculation of truly heroic proportions he appears to have given no inkling of this to anyone but the king and Albornoz.

That this was deliberate may be seen in Viglius's account of the meeting of April 21. After Alba's outburst against Berlaymont he had ordered Schetz to proceed with the collection of the *alcabala* forthwith, an order that was of course evaded.[66] It was not until May 29 that he took Viglius aside after a particularly violent row and said that he actually agreed with him but preferred that the rest of the council not be aware of it. The Frisian was dumbfounded, but after some thought he concluded that Alba was preparing to put forth another opinion without appearing to contradict himself.[67] In fact, Alba proposed an extensive "moderation" at the next meeting of the council, but the modifications were those he had suggested to Philip months before.

The only reasonable conclusion is that without thinking of the hazards involved Alba had decided to use the ancient tactic of beginning a negotiation with outrageous demands that he never expected his opponents to accept. Unfortunately, such tactics were wholly inappropriate to his situation. He was unpopular, even hated. His councillors and much of the population had come to see his regime as both alien and unreasonable and were convinced that the king agreed. Why, after all, was he being removed? In these circumstances the only possible result of such maneuverings was to inflame public opinion and stiffen the resistance of even the most cowardly of politicians. It was an error in judgment for which he, the people of the Netherlands, and the harried taxpayers of Castile were to pay dearly.

Whatever his intent, the conversation with Viglius must have broken the deadlock, for by June 22 a compromise of sorts had been reached. The councils agreed to collection of the tax on a percentage basis but insisted that it be moderated to avoid injuring commerce.[68] The nature of the moderations was disclosed in the placard of July 31.[69] The tax would be imposed at ten percent but all transactions save the last, the point at which the merchandise reached the consumer, would be exempt. The Twentieth Penny, an impost that had aroused little opposition, would be collected at the same time.

It is worth noting that this time the Estates were not consulted, they were informed. Alba had at last carried his point that when the Estates accepted the *encabezamiento* they had agreed in principle to a perpetual tax. In a letter to the Estates General dispatched on the very day the placard was published he told them that the quotas were to be abandoned, but as they had not yet been filled in their entirety the new imposts would be held back until the present collections were complete. The provincial Estates were to provide an individual accounting of how much they had already taken in.[70]

If Alba had any illusions about the acceptance of his compromise they were soon dispelled by a violent and all but universal outcry. The most vocal opposition came from the small tradesmen of Brussels, who ultimately preferred to close their shops rather than submit, and remained firm even when he threatened to send troops and hang them in their doorways.[71] More ominously, the Estates claimed that there was no royal warrant for the taxes but that they had been purely Alba's idea from the start.[72] Alarmed, the councillors began laying their grievances directly before the king and Hopperus.[73] Though they had come to terms, and a *merced* had even been requested for Schetz as a reward for his cooperation,[74] they were still unhappy with the terms[75] and public opposition made them fear for the future when Alba should be gone.

In short, further compromise was essential. Alba knew it and in August had told Arias Montano that he intended to introduce further modifications. He feared that if he did not there would be a general emigration of artisans to such heretical places as Hamburg and Emden. A number of drapers had already left Louvain, and Alba was concerned, it seemed, as much for their souls as for the economic consequences of their exodus.[76] On September 23 he wrote to the king suggesting that the tax on articles imported from abroad should be eliminated and the rate lowered substantially from the existing ten percent. As in May, the councils were not advised that he had specific concessions in mind; they were told only that the whole amount must be carried at the outset and if the Estates wanted changes they should come and negotiate, as he had suggested in the original placard.[77]

In October 21, 1571, in answer to a remonstrance from Holland, the new moderations were announced. The Tenth Penny would in effect become the Thirtieth Penny, as the rate dropped from ten percent to three and a third percent.[78] Unfortunately for Alba, the change came too late. By persisting in his negotiator's tactic he had convinced both the Estates and the people that he was vulnerable to their protests and could be forced to alter his position in the face of popular resistance. They concluded, quite naturally, that further opposition might lead to new concessions and clamored more loudly than before. Worse yet, they assumed that his initial insistence on ten percent had been genuine, and that if he could lower the rate to three and a third percent he could also raise it again when circumstances were more propitious. In this they may have been right, for he had indeed mentioned that possibility to Philip.[79]

Alba's blunder in making unreasonable demands and then turning the initiative over to the Estates was thus extremely serious, and the king then compounded it by giving the Netherlanders the best reason of all to resist him and his taxes to the uttermost. In the midst of all this uproar, on September 24, 1571, he chose to announce the appointment of Juan de la Cerda, Duke of Medinaceli, as Alba's replacement. Though Medinaceli, through a variety of mishaps, would not arrive for another nine months, his moderate reputation preceded him and the prospect of a new regime led many to believe that if they could hold out a bit longer the whole policy might be reversed. If Alba had been isolated before, he was now entirely abandoned.

In its final form, then, the Tenth Penny was anything but destructive of trade. It was, in fact, a relatively modest tax that would produce substantial revenue without causing serious hardship to anyone. It was also less regressive than most sixteenth-century taxes, in that the burden would be universally borne. The poor would probably have paid more than their share, but they would not have had to pay it all, and the rich were to some extent protected by its perpetual character from the more traditional raids on their capital. As it was never collected, it is also unreasonable to claim that it contributed to the economic difficulties of 1571–1572. The increasingly violent opposition must therefore have been due to other causes.

Probably the greatest of these was concern over the establishment of a precedent, but there were others. The regime itself was extremely unpopular. As an alarmed Don Francés de Alava reported at the beginning of 1572, the entire population was anxious for the duke to depart. All they could think of, as he put it, was *"Vaya, vaya, vaya."*[80] Alba had made no effort to ingratiate himself, and his unbending Hispanism was as offensive as the autocratic nature of his rule. There was also a strong undercurrent of religious feeling, not only among the large number of crypto-Protestants but among all those who shared in the generally tolerant attitude that had so long been characteristic of the Low Countries. If few had resisted his persecutions, fewer still had approved, and the general restiveness was intensified by a sharp economic downturn that reached its lowest point just as Alba had the misfortune, or bad judgment, to introduce his taxes.

The depression of 1571–1572 was at least in part another of those periodic slumps that had become characteristic of economic life in the Netherlands, but it was made infinitely worse by the depredations of the Sea Beggars. Operating from the English Channel ports and to a lesser degree from Emden, they played havoc with shipping and periodically threatened the lesser coastal towns. There was little that Alba could do. The naval forces at his command were wholly inadequate, and though he knew as well as anyone that command of the sea was essential he also knew that Philip could not possibly provide him with a decent fleet. He could repel limited attacks, as his fleet had done off Delfzijl in the summer of 1571,[81] but the larger problem was insoluble. Trade languished, insurance rates skyrocketed, and exchange rates became steadily less favorable as businessmen grew increasingly pessimistic. By February, 1572, Antwerp's once bustling wharves were all but deserted.[82]

Under these circumstances the country had become a reservoir of rage and frustration, with the frustration only serving to deepen resistance to Alba's policies. Contemporary memoirs such as the *Dagboek* of Jan de Pottre and the *Kroniek* of Godevaert van Haecht are filled with accounts not only of dire misery but of increasingly open denunications of Alba's authority. The famous "Ghent Paternoster" beginning "Hellish father who in Brussels doth dwell / Cursed be thy name in heaven and hell," is a fair sample.[83] This is why there is no point in discussing the merits of the Tenth Penny as an economic measure. It had become the symbol of a thousand grievances, the rallying point around which nearly everyone could find common ground. The winter of 1571/72 was unusually bitter. When the ice melted it required only that someone raise the sluices to unleash a flood of revolutionary activity. As so often happens, they were kicked open largely by accident, but the timing was perfect.

Elizabeth of England had at long last decided to mend her fences. Her new relationship with the French was disappointing, there was little to be gained by annoying Alba further, and the Hanseatic League was complaining. As a gesture of goodwill she expelled the Sea Beggars from their lair at Dover.[84] Their leader, Lumey de la Marck, was a study in himself. A bloodthirsty, hard-drinking nobleman, more pirate than national leader, he had sworn never to cut his hair or beard until the death of his kinsman Egmont was avenged. With a fleet crewed by men as hirsute and desperate as himself he had terrorized the narrow seas, making little distinction between friends and enemies of his presumed cause.

Now he was very much at a loss. For nearly a month he wandered aimlessly until the hunger of his men forced him to take refuge. His original intention was apparently to put in at Enkhuizen, which he believed to be Protestant in sympathy, but adverse winds prevented him from rounding Den Helder. He dropped down the coast, and on April Fool's Day, 1572, appeared before the small town of Brill with a fleet of twenty-four ships. Hungry, disorderly, and ill-equipped, his was not an impressive force, but to the citizens of Brill it appeared sufficient. When Lumey somewhat hesitatingly demanded their surrender they fled almost to a man, leaving a mere handful of defenders to watch as the Beggars burned the gates and entered the town. There was no resistance, and the next few days were devoted to the congenial business of desecrating churches. By Lumey's orders,[85] thirteen priests who had stayed behind with their parishioners were tortured to death.

It was not a great action nor were its perpetrators fully aware that they were touching off an heroic struggle that would consume decades and the lives of thousands. The capture of Brill was in many respects the beginning of the Dutch revolt, and Alba, though he did not at first realize it, had reached the crisis of his career.

XI

THE DELUGE

I f in retrospect the seizure of Brill was one of the great events of Netherlands history, at the time it seemed far less dramatic. The immediate reaction of nearly everyone involved was one of uneasy embarrassment. Even Lumey, having seized the prize, would have let it go had not his fellow Beggar Guillaume de Blois, Lord of Treslong, persuaded him to keep it. The raider's instinct told him to victual his ships, steal what he could, and put to sea, but Treslong, whether more prescient than his leader or simply overtaken by nostalgia (his father had been governor of the place), insisted that they remain. This decision, though it would bear amazing fruit, produced no joy at Dillenburg where Orange, cautious and pessimistic as ever, grumbled that it was all premature.[1]

Alba, too, did not at first realize the importance of the stroke. Something of the sort had long been expected[2] and indeed had nearly come to pass at Delfzijl in the preceding summer. He had no way of knowing that this was not just another raid, and Brill was after all a small place on the edge of nowhere. Still, given the level of popular uproar he was in no mood to take chances. He raised additional companies of Walloons under de Capres and Cristóbal de Mondragón and offered garrisons to important towns in Holland and Zeeland. His major concern was, as always, money. He told the king that he was "without a *real* under heaven," and though he expected to smooth matters over, he knew that things could become very ugly if the "native princes" stirred themselves.[3]

Aside from Treslong, the only one who seemed to realize the possibilities and act accordingly was Louis of Nassau. After his defeat at Jemmingen, Louis had gone to France, where he served as his brother's emissary to both the Huguenots and the Sea Beggars, many of whom were operating out of La Rochelle and the Breton ports. His purpose was to consolidate the alliance with the Huguenot leader Coligny so that, when the day of liberation arrived, the rising of the Low Countries could be supported by a French invasion from the south. William, as before, was to raise an army in Germany and move simultaneously from the east—it was hoped, with better timing and greater success than in 1568. These arrangements were incomplete in April, 1572, but Louis felt that the circumstances demanded action. Prematurely or not, the Beggars had achieved a beachhead in the north, and in France Coligny and the Huguenots had achieved temporary dominance in the counsels of Charles IX. To a man of strong faith and little caution such things can be taken as signs, and he set in motion a plan that would worry Alba far more than anything that might happen in the fens and sandy wastes of Holland.

As if to prove him right, the Beggars began to meet with success beyond their wildest dreams. Alba's offer of garrisons set off serious internal struggles in each of the towns involved. All possessed a vocal minority that favored the Beggars, but the magistrates in general were against them. This was partly because some of them had supplanted the exiles of 1566–1567 and feared that a Beggar triumph would bring the return of their old rivals. Others, and perhaps a majority of the citizens themselves, were horrified by Lumey's atrocities and saw little point in trading one group of rapacious fanatics for another. The town governments were therefore prepared in most instances to admit Alba's garrisons, while those who favored the Beggars opposed them with every means at their disposal. In town after town this meant an appeal to the Beggars themselves, who were only too happy to provide their version of protection.[4] By midsummer a majority of the towns in Holland and Zeeland had declared for the prince of Orange, though there were some major exceptions. Inspired by these events, Count van den Berghe appeared on the northeastern border with a small but enthusiastic army and quickly terrified the magistrates of Gelderland and Overijssel into submission. North of the rivers Orange had triumphed without lifting a finger.

Alba knew that these appearances were to some extent deceptive. He still held a number of important cities, including Amsterdam and Middelburg, though the burghers of Amsterdam infuriated him by refusing a garrison. They were loyal, they said, but needed no Spaniards, for their own militia was proof against any contingent of Beggars.[5] Moreover, Bossu, as *Stadholder* of Holland, was able to recover Rotterdam by a trick while at the same time managing to extract a subsidy from the Estates of Holland.[6] It was apparent that Orange's support was still very soft and that of all the towns taken by his adherents only Flushing, which controlled the entrance to the Scheldt, was of major strategic importance. At first this was his greatest concern, as its Beggar garrison was almost immediately reinforced by French and English volunteers. With her usual brass, Elizabeth told him that this was merely to protect Spanish interests.[7] Later he concluded that it was her response to the Ridolfi fiasco,[8] but it scarcely mattered: long before he could act he was distracted by a far greater loss. On May 24 Louis of Nassau, at the head of a small army of Huguenots, captured Mons.

This prodigy was achieved by a comedy of errors, but its consequences were serious. On the preceding day Orange's followers within the town had been secretly armed by Antoine Oliver, Alba's cartographer and a double agent whose true loyalty lay with the rebels. The plan was that Nassau should enter the city with a handful of followers and proclaim the revolt, whereupon Oliver's fifth column would arise and open the gates to some 1,500 Huguenots lurking nearby. Unfortunately, when Louis and his friends rode into the sleeping city an hour before dawn, yelling and firing pistols to give an impression of greater numbers, nothing happened. Oliver's men did not appear, nor for that matter did the Huguenots, who had lost their way and had to be retrieved by the intrepid count himself. They managed to reach the city before the drowsy burghers could close the last of the gates, but the magistrates then refused to declare for Orange or accept the new garrison. This embarrassing *contretemps* was relieved only when substantial reinforcements arrived under the French commanders Genlis and de la Noue, who had just succeeded in gaining, and losing, nearby Valenciennes in a matter of hours.[9]

Scarcely a landmark in the history of warfare, the capture of Mons nevertheless placed Alba in an almost untenable position. Aside from opening a second front, it was the last real stronghold on the road from Paris to Brussels and the perfect staging point for a full-scale French invasion. The duke, whose thoughts never wandered far from the improbable doings at the court of France, knew that such a thing was entirely possible, as the Huguenot leader Coligny was now high in the favor of Charles IX and was said to believe that a war with Spain would strengthen his position. Charles, it seemed, had no real desire for war, but he could not repudiate his counselor without risking another Protestant revolt or at the very least admitting to the world that he had lost control of his own government.[10] The expedition of Louis of Nassau might therefore be seen as a *fait accompli* by which the reluctant king could be forced into committing his army on Orange's behalf.

Alba's situation, then, was as follows. Most of the country north of the Water Line was in the hands of the Beggars, and if their grip on the towns was often insecure their control of the sea was undoubted. The south, though it remained grudgingly loyal, could expect a major French offensive at any moment while, beyond the Rhine, William of Orange was once more amassing forces for a descent on Brabant. To meet these variegated threats Alba had only the core of his army—some 7,000 men, long unpaid and widely dispersed in garrisons throughout the country—and a fleet numbering fewer than 30 vessels, most of them small craft manned by sailors whose pay was also in arrears.

The reason for this scandalous lack of preparation was purely financial. The millions raised in 1570–1571 had been used to cover the debts incurred by Margaret of Parma and during the campaigns of 1568. The wrangle over the Tenth Penny had effectively blocked any further revenue from the states themselves. Alba's requests for subsidies from Spain had at first been ignored and, more recently, met with demands that he account for the four million ducats already spent.[11] This last was a measure of the growing influence of his enemies at court, and though it came from Cardinal Espinosa rather than the king it was indicative of a set of problems more intractable than those presented by the rebels.

Alba knew that whatever was the outcome of this latest debacle it could only discredit him. The Eboli faction, encouraged by the outcry over the Tenth Penny, had redoubled their intrigues and now their every prophecy was fulfilled. The duke's policies had driven the Netherlands to revolt as predicted, and even if he won the battles to come his ideas could no longer be regarded as the basis of a permanent settlement. He could assume that the king was annoyed, and by the end of the summer it was rumored that the House of Toledo was finished at last.[12]

This was a dismal prospect for the long run, and it had immediate implications as well. The Ebolistas could be expected to argue against sending him further support, either financial or military, on the grounds that it would only make matters worse. After interminable delays Medinaceli was finally on his way. Let him make peace and issue a pardon, as further bloodshed would simply widen the breach. Moreover, vast sums had already been set aside for the League against the Turk. To divert men and money to Alba would prevent Don Juan of Austria from following up his glorious victory at Lepanto. Philip was not yet ready to follow such advice, but Alba had no way of knowing that and the news from court was uniformly discouraging. It was beginning to look as though he would have to cope with these disasters using his own meager resources and with his successor at his side complicating everything he did. God alone knew what that might portend.

The duke's ill-wishers, and they were legion, may be forgiven for thinking the old man was overwhelmed by this series of catastrophes. At first there was little sign of movement at the Hôtel de Jassy. Morillon tells us that as each new disaster was announced Alba waved it off with an airy "*No es nada*," and implies that his wits were temporarily addled by misfortune.[13] In fact, nothing could have been further from the truth. It is a measure of this man's immense inner resources that at the age of sixty-five, with his most important mission in ruins at his feet, his letters took on a new certainty and vigor and even his health seemed to improve. It is hard to escape the impression that after so many endless months of wrangling, backbiting, and maneuvering, a call to action even in such unfavorable circumstances came as a relief. Whether they knew it or not, Orange and his followers were confronting an opponent who was still their equal in courage and tenacity and was far ahead of them in cunning and military talent. If he moved slowly at first it was because there was much to be done.

The first necessity was, obviously, to find troops, but this required money. It is a measure of his desperation that without informing the king, Alba arranged through his Italian connections for the dispatch of 200,000 ducats from Cosimo de' Medici. Philip was understandably annoyed at this presumption and the Ebolistas made much of it in the months to come,[14] but Alba was past caring. The money enabled him to call out Frundsberg, Eberstein, and the other

German captains whom he had long kept on *Wartegeld* against just such an emergency.

His other major problem involved the French. It was imperative for him to discover their intentions and restrain them, if possible, by diplomatic means. Even before the seizure of Mons he had been demanding assurances of nonintervention, and French affairs continued to take up much of his time and attention. But though assurances were indeed forthcoming, the situation remained so fluid that he could never relax his vigil.[15] In the end, this gnawing uncertainty determined his strategy for the campaign to come: Mons would have to be recovered at all costs even if this meant temporarily abandoning the north and allowing Orange to roam the provinces at will. It was a painful but necessary decision. He had no choice but to concentrate his forces, as numerical inferiority prevented him from fighting on more than one front. By going to Mons he could not only hope to relieve that city but to block a French invasion if it should occur, thus isolating the Beggars and depriving Orange of his primary objective. Unfortunately, in June, 1572, he was so short of men that even this modest scheme was beyond his capacity.

On the day before Mons fell, the unsuspecting duke had dispatched Don Fadrique to the island of Walcheren for the purpose of relieving Middelburg. This important provincial capital and episcopal seat lies only a few miles from Flushing. It was hotly besieged by the Beggars, who knew that without it their control of Zeeland was insecure. The seizure of Mons forced him to recall Fadrique and his troops, leaving the inhabitants of the island to their own devices—which in this case meant a civil war pursued with remarkable bitterness and tenacity until 1574. Abandoning Middelburg meant that he could no longer hope to secure the Scheldt, but it did not at the same time give him the means for a full-scale assault on Mons. The best that could be done was to send Fadrique, Chiappino Vitelli, and Julián Romero with 4,000 men to cover the place against attempts at reinforcement or victualling. A holding action pure and simple, it was meant to gain time until Alba could gather the rest of his forces and undertake the siege in person.

Fadrique arrived before Mons on June 23, and with an eye to the French he set up his headquarters south of the city, at Bethlehem Abbey. The following day he fortified a house on the road to Maubeuge and put garrisons into St. Ghislain and Bossu, thus covering all the routes open to the French. With one troop of light cavalry at Bavay and another under Bernardino de Mendoza at Maubeuge he was well protected against surprise attack but without heavy artillery could do little against the town itself. The next three weeks were devoted to a series of inconclusive skirmishes, the heaviest of which occurred on July 11 when a party of townspeople came out to harvest the wheat accompanied by 600 arquebusiers and some 70 cavalry. They were driven back, but Vitelli and several other officers were wounded. On the same day a number of local women were caught spying on the Spanish camp. Amid general merriment, Fadrique ordered them to be sent back to town with their skirts cut off above the knee.[16]

On the fourteenth, Fadrique learned that an army of Huguenots recently recruited by Genlis had passed Cateau-Cambrésis on its way to Mons. Though this force was reputedly almost three times the size of his own he resolved to take the offensive and marched off to meet it with the wounded Vitelli leading the vanguard from his litter. After several false starts caused by Fadrique's apparent reliance on local intelligence sources as opposed to proper reconnaissance, battle was joined at the village of Quiévrain on the afternoon of the seventeenth. Fortunately for the Spaniards, Genlis's force consisted not of the 10,000 foot and 2,000 horse reported by a credulous peasantry but of between 6,000 and 7,000 arquebusiers, about 800 cavalry, and no pikes whatever. It was even more fortunate that Genlis had, if anything, done less in the way of reconnaissance than his opponent did. The result was a textbook lesson in the shortcomings of unsupported musketry. After two hours of trading fire with Fadrique's much smaller contingent of arquebusiers, the Huguenots allowed the prospect of an easy victory to draw them out of a good defensive position in the village. They seem to have been unaware that the skirmishers were backed by a square of pikes or that the woods surrounding the gardens of Quiévrain contained nearly 1,500 cavalry, both light and heavy. They poured out of the village in good order and their opponents simply fell back, leaving them face-to-face with a solid mass of determined pikemen. At that moment, the concealed horse charged from both flanks. Within minutes, the entire Huguenot army was dead or in scattered flight.

The invading force was totally destroyed. Approximately 3,000 French were killed and another 600 were captured, including their commander, Genlis. The toll might have been even higher had not darkness halted the pursuit but further efforts were really unnecessary. No one can estimate how many of those who escaped found a shallow grave in some village midden or woodlot, but, as in 1568, it was said that the peasants gave ample evidence of their zeal for the service of His Majesty.[17]

Back in Brussels, Alba was able to control his delight. If the victory bought time it also increased the likelihood of open war, and he immediately dispatched an emissary to see whether Charles would avow Genlis.[18] At about this time he also learned that Orange had crossed the Rhine, and, to complicate matters further, this was the week Medinaceli chose to land at Sluis after a narrow escape from the Sea Beggars. It is little wonder that the duke's customary thanks to God were tempered by the hope that He would be as generous in the weeks to come and that Philip and his courtiers would do no less. "I have need," he said, "of all the help they can give this old bird."[19]

Of all the problems confronting the "old bird," those created by the arrival of Medinaceli were by no means the least. Alba received his successor with open arms and told Espinosa that he was delighted by Medinaceli's arrival,[20] but in reality the situation was equivocal in the extreme. Medinaceli was not a known enemy and his personality was not unusually abrasive, but if his merely waiting in the wings had critically undermined Alba's authority his presence could hardly do less. There was, of course, no question of Alba's immediate departure, for the new governor had little military experience. What, then, would be the official relationship between the two dukes? Given Alba's autocratic nature and Medinaceli's inexperience, the answer to that question was fairly obvious. Alba would order things to suit himself and Medinaceli would trail along behind.

Needless to say, Medinaceli's resentment grew as the weeks passed. He had already been annoyed because Alba had failed to warn him that Flushing was in rebel hands, and did not accept the explanation that two boats had been sent but had missed the fleet.[21] In this he was almost certainly wrong, but his suspicions put him into a state of mind that could only be aggravated by Alba's reluctance to share information or seek his counsel.

The inevitable tension was further magnified by disagreement over two issues on which Alba held strong if not intransigent views: a new pardon and the repeal of the Tenth Penny. A general pardon for those who participated in the Beggar's rising had been discussed almost from the start, and on July 21 Philip dispatched two possible versions to the dukes for their opinion.[22] Alba procrastinated, and in the end, as we shall see, came to favor a restrictive document that would not have been in the best interests of his successor.

On the matter of the Tenth Penny he was adamant. He knew as well as anyone that some form of accommodation was essential, but he had gone through too much to abandon the project without a struggle. From the beginning he insisted that the tax could be dropped only after it had once been collected. This perverse notion was based on two arguments, neither of which appealed to Medinaceli or the king. The first was, like many of Alba's political ideas, apparently an outgrowth of his experience with military discipline. He feared that if the king backed down without first demanding obedience, his authority in other areas would be irretrievably lost. A firm exponent of the "give them an inch" school, he even tried to convince the local authorities that if they failed to enforce the tax they would find themselves unable to take a "strong hand" with such problems as vagabondage. The second argument was more legalistic but perhaps more sensible. If the tax were withdrawn uncollected it would be taken as a precedent that could be applied to all regular levies in the future.[23]

Philip would have none of this. On June 29 he dispatched a letter ordering that the Tenth Penny be abolished in exchange for an outright grant of two million florins.[24] Two months later the duke was still demanding his concession from the Estates; if the letter was received—as it ought to have been—it was not acknowledged.[25] The struggle over the Tenth Penny, very much alive, could only have strained relations between the man who had staked his reputation on it and the one whose task it was to reconcile the Netherlands to the Crown. By the time the two dukes left to besiege Mons a facade of cordiality remained, but large cracks were beginning to show.

The dukes arrived at Mons on August 27 with 36 heavy guns and about 8,500 troops to join the more than 4,000 commanded by Don Fadrique. Though not large, it was a highly professional force led by such veteran mercenaries as Frundsberg, Eberstein, and the Bishop of Cleves, who in spite of his ecclesiastical office rode in full armor with a brace of pistols at his side. The Germans were supplemented in turn by Spanish contingents, including that of Don Rodrigo de Zapata, withdrawn from their garrisons in the north. The recall of Zapata from his lair at The Hague was in itself a measure of Alba's need, for Zapata, almost alone, had provided encouragement to the royalists since the taking of Brill. For more than three months he had waged a hair-raisingly successful guerrilla campaign in reverse, harassing the Beggars and disrupting their communications; but as he could not be reinforced he and his men were living on borrowed time and would be safer as well as more useful at Mons. Joining with Alba's nephew, Don Hernando de Toledo, he arrived in Brussels on the twenty-third accompanied by more than 4,000 Catholic refugees.

In the meantime Orange was making his way across Brabant with 20,000 men. His grasp of military science had improved but little in recent years and he did not make the rapid dash for Mons that might have secured the campaign. Instead, after taking Diest, Louvain, and Mechelen, he wasted precious days besieging the ridiculous castle of Weert, only to abandon it in the face of staunch resistance by twelve Spaniards, thirty Germans, and a handful of Walloons.[26] After that, his journey to Mons was leisurely, but at least he was on his way.

Alba's arrival was thus overshadowed by the gloomy prospect of finding himself caught before the walls by Orange, a second French invasion force, or both. Within hours, half of this threat was unexpectedly dispelled. Before the camp could settle itself for the night, his emissary Gomiecourt arrived from Paris with the news that a great massacre of Huguenots had taken place only three days previously. If the St. Bartholomew's Day Massacre gave Alba "an excessive contentment," to use Mendoza's phrase, it was with good reason. Much has been made of his unseemly rejoicing over the murder of some 5,000 Protestants, but in this case at least his joy was born of relief as well as bigotry. The massacre now appears to have been a last desperate attempt by Catherine de' Medici to keep her son from being dragged into a disastrous war with Spain. By ordering the assassination of the Huguenot leaders she had hoped to rescue Charles from the dilemma created by Coligny and Louis of Nassau, and in this she succeeded. The enthusiasm of the French Catholics may or may not have exceeded her intentions, but it was at least certain that there would be no French invasion of the Low Countries.[27]

Characteristically, Alba's first response was to encourage his soldiers in a noisy celebration for the benefit of the besieged garrison.[28] His second was to complain that the deed had been done not for the glory of God but for private ends.[29] Yet for all his apparent coolness he saw in the carnage at Paris the hand of God protecting him from the French and leaving him free to deal with Orange, a prospect he could now savor with a degree of relish.

The siege of Mons commenced formally on August 30 when Alba placed his battery of thirty-seven guns against the south wall of the city, from the gate of Bertemont to the tower of St. André. Throughout the first day's bombardment, and indeed for much of the siege, he insisted on remaining in an exposed position among the guns where in the first few hours the new *veedor* sent out with Medinaceli and another officer were killed at his side. In the meantime, with a concern for hard intelligence that might well have been emulated by his son, he sent out parties of light horse to shadow Orange. Learning that his enemy was coming by way of Nivelles, he tried to delay him by felling trees and digging ditches across the line of march while Monsieur de Capres and his Walloon cavalry were sent to St. Symphorien on the Charleroi road to cover the eastern approaches.

These maneuvers were, of course, subsidiary to his main concern. Trees and ditches notwithstanding, Orange would be there shortly, and Alba would find himself defending a battery exposed to the fire of the city's artillery on one side and the attacks of the rebel army on the other. As his force was the smaller of the two, he was reluctant to take the offensive, for fear that Orange might overwhelm him or get between him and the city. Unfortunately, the site of Mons made a defensive strategy difficult if not impossible.

The city itself was roughly pentagonal in shape and bordered on its southern and western sides by two small rivers, the Haine and the Trouille. The most likely points of entry for Orange's host were the Porte du Parc on the west by the suburb of Jemappes, the Porte de la Gueritte on the road to Charleroi, and the Porte de Bertemont itself. Bertemont was, to be sure, the site of Alba's main battery, but it was overshadowed by a hill to the southeast which, if occupied by the enemy, would make the camp indefensible. Jemappes too was dominated by a hill separated from that of Bertemont by a broad plain in which the citizens of Mons had their gardens. Whoever controlled it would control Jemappes and with it the Porte du Parc and another gate at the city's southwest corner. The problem, then, was to man and fortify these two hills, provide an adequate defense for the main camp, and at the same time cover the Porte de la Gueritte and the northeastern side of the city. As Alba's force was smaller than that of his opponents, this meant that at none of these points could he achieve a concentration of force sufficient to repel a full-scale assault.

His answer to this conundrum was, in Mendoza's eyes, brilliant, but it was also risky and showed a measure of contempt for the military talents of Orange. The approaches to the two eastern gates were fortified by M. de Capres, who left behind a token force and went with the rest of his troops to Jemappes. The Porte de la Gueritte, in turn, was covered by a larger unit under Monsieur Licques, who hovered a few hundred yards to the south. The hill overlooking Jemappes was given to Medinaceli, who with the help of Bartolomeo Campi constructed a star fort of five bastions at its summit and staffed it with two cannon from the battery and two companies of German infantry. Frundsberg and Eberstein took the hill of Bertemont with the bulk of the cavalry and a squadron of Spanish infantry spread out along its base in the plain. The key to all these dispositions was three mobile reserves composed of nearly all the arquebusiers at the duke's disposal. One unit, under Rodrigo de Zapata, occupied an abbey immediately outside the Porte du Parc; another, under Julián Romero, was to keep an eye on Medinaceli's position and intervene if necessary. The third and by far the largest contingent, headed by Don Fadrique, was stationed in the main camp ready for dispatch to any part of the surrounding area.

On September 8 it was discovered that Orange was camped a half-day's march to the east. Alba, who had personally laid out the defensive lines in front of all his squadrons, spent the night supervising the digging of trenches and the positioning of his guns. Some were left in position against the walls of Mons, and others were turned outward toward the open plain onto which, as expected, Orange and his army emerged late the following morning.

Orange immediately brought his own guns to bear and began a long-range bombardment of the duke's position while the batteries of the beleaguered city opened up on the other side. The Spaniards were thus in a crossfire, but, due either to the range or the incompetence of the rebel gunners, damage was minimal. Alba was enjoying himself hugely. While his own artillery blazed away in both directions, his infantry skirmished off and on until nightfall put an end to the deadly game. As he told the king, "it was one of the most beautiful days I have ever seen."[30] Refreshed by his first taste of combat in four years, he spent the evening catching up on his correspondence.

His opponent was in a quandry. Orange had no stomach for a direct assault on Alba's camp, especially as he knew that Frundsberg and Eberstein were waiting on their hilltop for the chance to swoop down on his flank once he was committed. He decided to move off toward Jemappes, and when morning came found himself in a race with Fadrique to see who could get there first. Fadrique arrived to find the rebel vanguard beginning to infiltrate the suburb but was able to throw them out before they could invest it. By this time the rest of the arquebusiers had arrived and a general skirmish ensued. Orange attacked in force, only to be repelled by a hail of musketry directed in person by Alba, who appeared in a disreputable cassock of plain blue and without his armor. The prince retired in good order to Frammeries, about 5 km to the south, and spent the next day licking his wounds and wondering what to do.

Only one hope remained: to try his luck at the Porte de Gueritte. When on September 12 Orange marched off in that direction he was met once more by Fadrique's flying squad of arquebusiers and the cavalry of Bernardino de Mendoza. After the obligatory skirmish he encamped a short distance away, and here he met his downfall. Alba, who seems to have been growing impatient, reconnoitered the enemy camp in person. Finding that it was poorly guarded, he decided on an *encamisada* to be carried out by a party of picked troops under Julián Romero.

The device succeeded beyond all hope. In the small hours of a moonless night Romero was able to achieve complete surprise. Men were killed in their sleep or by their own comrades, who struck in panic at anything that moved. Horses plunged and bucked through the camp, terrified by the war-cries of the Spaniards and the flames from the burning tents, while numbers of the prince's men were drowned in a mere rivulet into which they fell while trying to escape the carnage. When the morning dawned, grey and cheerless, the rebel army had vanished save for the three hundred corpses found amid the abandoned baggage. Legend has it that Orange himself would have been taken but for the vigilance of the little dog whose carved portrait now rests at the foot of many of his statues.

Orange's retreat was as disorderly as this collapse suggests. His troops, their morale shattered, soon came to realize that they would be paid only in securities of dubious value, and mutinied. It was with great difficulty and amid serious threats to his own person that he reached the shelter of the Rhine. His brother, Louis of Nassau, now bedridden with fever and commanding a garrison that saw no further point in resistance, could only surrender. This he did on September 21, his troops marching out with full honors of war and taking with them those citizens who were compromised by their adherence to the revolt. Louis himself, carried in a litter because of his illness, was courteously received by Medinaceli, and even Don Fadrique sent his compliments. Alba himself did not appear.[31]

The duke granted these generous terms not out of the goodness of his heart but because he was in a hurry. With Orange out of the way and the French no longer a menace, he hoped to force the capitulation of the northern towns before the onset of winter. Thus he simply could not afford a lengthy siege. For this reason he was prepared to ignore both the French king, who wanted him to execute the Huguenots en masse, and the laws of war that gave him the right to do so. More painfully, he had to set aside "the personal hatred that I have for this man [Louis of Nassau]," because to do otherwise would tie down his army and take no account of the overall loyalty of the citizens of Mons.[32]

It was a moderate and statesmanlike decision. Mons was spared, though Noircarmes in his capacity as Bailiff of Hainault inevitably discovered and executed citizens whose collaboration with the rebels seemed dangerously enthusiastic, but this was not to be a model for Alba in the months to come. Instead, the duke was about to embark upon a policy that would blacken his reputation even further and shatter the slim remaining hope of reconciliation between the king and his subjects.

Policies of deliberate frightfulness, or, as the Germans say, *Schrecklichkeit*, remain popular today in spite of a vast weight of evidence indicating their almost universal failure in the past. The bombings of Guernica, London, and Hamburg all tended to strengthen resistance among the survivors, yet thirty years later it was thought by many that bombing Hanoi would have a different effect. In the sixteenth century there was, of course, no formal theory of *Schrecklichkeit*; indeed, a continuing though much attenuated allegiance to Christian principles and the laws of war tended to militate against it. In practice, however, commanders resorted to terror with great frequency, partly because the concept of deterrence through fear was as deeply rooted in their culture as in our own and partly because the law of war acknowledged its legitimacy in certain specific cases. Rebels, for example, fell entirely outside its provisions, as did soldiers fighting in an undeclared war or in a war declared by someone whose legal authority to do so was unacknowledged; hence the "legality" of Charles IX's request for the massacre of the Huguenots at Mons. It might be argued that the law of war was an unenforceable convention to be ignored with impunity, but this was not the case. As M. H. Keen points out, the law was also a code of behavior for the upper classes and thus was buttressed by the most powerful of social sanctions.[33]

Alba's decision to make an example of certain towns *pour encourager les autres* was taken within this framework. No one then alive was more expert in the laws of war or more determined to abide by them as a matter of class pride and as an expression of his allegiance to that higher order for which he fought. To him, as to many of his contemporaries, the laws of war were as immutable a part of the divinely established order as church or king, and he had scrupulously observed them for more than half a century. It therefore seemed only natural that men who were rebelling against the very structure of God's universe should not be entitled to benefit from its protection. He would not, and did not, do anything contrary to God's law, as he saw it, at Mechelen or at Naarden or even in that dark and bitter winter to come before the walls of Haarlem, but what he did was nevertheless wrong.

It was wrong not because the world was changing and the history of that autumn would be written by those who had rejected his views, but because he had forgotten that terror if it is to be effective must be balanced with mercy. In this Alba was at one with other commanders before and since, and his self-deception was cut of the same cloth. He had long since convinced himself that his opponents were less than human, perhaps even diabolic in their inspiration. More than ever he believed that heresy was at the root of everything and would hear nothing of Tenth Pennies, local privileges, or any of the other grievances that had been advanced as possible causes of the revolt.[34] These views were reinforced by the atrocities committed by the Beggars, and in particular by their systematic torture and execution of priests. Alba, like most of the Spaniards around him, was profoundly shocked by these things and by the insults offered to holy places, to symbols of ecclesiastical authority, and even to the Host itself.[35] Surely such creatures were devils, not men, and could lawfully be treated as such.

Then there was his own personality. For all his iron control Alba had always been a man of violence, in whom anger stirred constantly beneath a surface of melancholy calm. His fondness for bloodcurdling metaphor and his delight in combat reveal it no less than his untimely outbursts in the presence of the king. Like many who see their lives as dedicated to the service of others, he harbored a deep resentment that appears in nearly every one of his many letters to friends and allies at court. Composed equally of the suspicion that he had denied himself too many gratifications and of the certainty that his sacrifices were unappreciated, it served to keep him in a state of controlled rage that, at its most productive, was the source of his enormous energy. Now, surrounded by heretics and crypto-heretics and abandoned, as he saw it, by king and court, he hoped and even prayed for an excuse to bring down upon the heads of these traitors what he saw as the judgment of a righteous God.

His first and most obvious target was the city of Mechelen. This thriving community, the administrative heart of ecclesiastical reorganization and site of the royal cannon foundries, was in Alba's view a major center of disaffection. He believed that its citizens had frequently called upon Orange to invade the Netherlands and that they alone had voluntarily raised troops on his behalf.[36] When the prince arrived they opened their gates without awaiting a demand for surrender and had then aided him in the ignominious retreat from Mons. Even now, with their champion once again in full flight, they remained defiant, holding firm behind their own hastily raised militia and a thousand troops drawn from his disbanded army. Alba was certain that if an example were not made the reduction of the rebel towns would be an "infinite business,"[37] and Mechelen, with its psychological and strategic importance, was ideally suited to this purpose. As for scruples, the duke had long since convinced himself that the city's recent insubordination was "God's permission" to punish it for evils committed during the iconoclasm of 1566![38]

Promising his largely unpaid army the spoils of the town, he left Mons on September 23. Thanks to torrential rains that washed out the roads and mired his baggage carts, the ordinarily brief march consumed nearly a week, but on the twenty-ninth Fadrique invested the suburbs of Mechelen, and Cressonière began the task of rebuilding bridges destroyed by the defenders. On the thirtieth the duke placed his batteries and demanded that the town redeem itself either by killing Orange's mercenaries on its own or by casting them out to be slaughtered by the waiting Spaniards.[39] Without waiting for the decision of their hosts, the garrison fled under cover of darkness, leaving the town virtually defenseless. In the confusion no response was made to Alba's demand, and after a brief and almost bloodless assault the town was given up to three days of murder, rape, and systematic looting.

With the destruction of Mechelen, the land south of the rivers was pacified, and Alba moved off in high spirits to Nijmegen, where he established his headquarters. There could be no doubt that his policy was working. Louvain and Termonde had surrendered on merely hearing of his threats against Mechelen, and when the news of his terrible vengeance spread beyond the confines of Brabant other towns followed suit. Alba had every reason to believe that

Gelderland and the northeast would soon be his. Then, as he said, "If it pleases God, I will arrange to reacquire Holland and Zeeland."[40]

The only potential obstacle of any size at this point appeared to be Zutphen. This small city on the east bank of the Ijssel was the strategic key to the northeastern provinces. No geographic barrier separated it from the vast expanse of the north German plain. A garrison, once established, could effectively block Alba's access to Overijssel, Groningen, and Friesland while continually replenishing itself from the inexhaustible manpower of the empire. In the preceding weeks the town had also assumed a symbolic importance, for it was there that William of Orange surfaced once again. Twice defeated and unaccompanied save by a token force of supporters, he had reentered the Low Countries for the last time. With that grim, almost fatalistic tenacity that was so much a part of his character he had refused to acquiesce in what lesser men might have seen as the verdict of history. Raising his standard again at Zutphen and leaving behind the bulk of his remaining force as a garrison, he marched westward into Holland. Alba probably saw this pitiful rearguard of 800 men as an attempt to secure his communications and a line of retreat, but if so he was wrong. For Orange there would be no more retreat. He would go to Holland, and there, as he told his brother John, "I will make my sepulchre."[41]

His departure did not save the city. From Nijmegen Alba dispatched Don Fadrique northward, with orders to leave no man alive if resistance was offered.[42] The city fathers, emboldened by the presence of Orange's men, held fast, but their courage was rewarded by the treachery of their protectors. Zutphen, with its high, thin medieval walls and its moat already frozen in mid-November, was indefensible—a fact obvious to soldiers if not to aldermen. After two days' bombardment by Fadrique's paltry three-gun battery, most of the garrison made good their escape through a gate by the riverside. Seeing this, the Spaniards immediately seized the virtually undefended town and repeated the outrages they had practiced at Mechelen the month before.[43] To further demonstrate the futility of resistance, Fadrique, on his father's orders, burned much of the city after the soldiers had satisfied their greed and lust.[44]

Once again, the sack of Zutphen achieved the intended result as an object lesson. Town after town sent in its declaration of loyalty and begged forgiveness for sins past, and Count van den Bergh took horse for Germany. By the end of November, only Holland and parts of Zeeland remained loyal to the prince. To crown his triumphs,

Alba learned at this time that there was hope even in the wastes of Zeeland. On October 20, a force under Cristóbal de Mondragón had waded across several miles of estuary at low tide, in waters sometimes rising to their chins, and had relieved the important town of Goes. Alba likened this, somewhat inappropriately, to the parting of the Red Sea,[45] but his enthusiasm was forgivable: it was an extraordinary feat of arms and a fitting climax to a successful year. What had begun in disaster was ending in triumph. The "terror," as he himself called it,[46] was a manifest success, and victory seemed near at hand. He had no way of knowing that the revolt was still in its infancy.

XII

HAARLEM

The turning point was Naarden. Before the destruction of this small and otherwise unimportant place, the duke's campaign, though brutal, had been a success. After it, everything seemed to sour at once. It was not that the behavior of his troops on this occasion marked a change in policy, nor did it reveal anything about his intentions that should not already have been known. It was significant only because it finally convinced the rebels of Holland that they had two stark choices: to fight or to die. Until then, terror had been successful because it appeared discriminate—towns that submitted, albeit from a distance, were not sacked. In the case of Naarden it was believed that a surrender had actually taken place and that the destruction of the town was therefore an exercise in frightfulness for its own sake. This perception may or may not have been rooted in a misunderstanding of events, but it was persuasive. The truth is now in any case obscure.

All accounts agree that after sacking Zutphen, Fadrique and his army marched westward through the snow toward Amsterdam. Stopping at Amersfoort, he sent a company of soldiers on to Naarden, the first rebel town across the borders of Holland, and demanded its surrender. The town government made the dangerous mistake of refusing compliance for more than a week while it sought help from other rebel communities in the area. When none was forthcoming they resolved to seek terms, but Fadrique, thinking that a show of force might encourage the waverers, refused them until his army was at the gates. At this point, all similarity among the various accounts disappears.

According to the early Dutch historians, none of whom was an eyewitness or even a contemporary, the Spaniards graciously accepted an offer of surrender and pledged themselves to protect the lives and property of the citizens. Then, when they were within the gates, they turned and slaughtered the inhabitants without exception.[1] Mendoza, who was present but whose inclusion of a legalistic apology for the sacking of rebel towns leaves him open to charges of special pleading, has an entirely different version. According to him, the sack occurred because, after offering resistance, the townspeople agreed to parley with Noircarmes and Cressonière but, by prearrangement, those within the town opened fire during the conference, provoking the Spaniards to a frontal assault.[2]

Alba, writing from Fadrique's reports, does not mention a parley. He claims that the town held a garrison of about 300 troops, all of whom wanted to surrender, but the burghers forced them to remain.

> Seeing that it was necessary to cure this affair with iron . . . the Spanish infantry gained the wall and killed the soldiers and burghers without any man born escaping, and set fire to the town in two or three parts, and Your Majesty may be certain that it has been the permission of God to blind them thus, because they proceeded as I have said, and the town so weak that no men in the land would have dared to defend it but those whom God has wished to blind in order to give them the punishment that they have so much merited, and I am pleased about it because the example is made in such a miserable place and [amid] such great heretics. God grant that the rest may learn from it and that it will not be necessary to carry with them to the end and go from town to town with the army of Your Majesty.[3]

Allowing for the fact that both Alba's and Mendoza's accounts are self-serving, though in different ways, and that the Dutch version is equally distorted—Hooft even accuses the Spaniards of cannibalism[4]—it is possible, with liberal infusions of guesswork, to construct a narrative of the affair. By the time Fadrique arrived at Naarden he and his men were almost certainly on a hair-trigger. The place had the reputation of being, as Alba put it, "the crucible of all the Anabaptists,"[5] and the long delay while help was sought from Orange and his lieutenants could only have convinced them that these folk were treacherous and ill-intentioned. On the other side, it is too much to expect that the townspeople were all of one mind. Even a "crucible of Anabaptists" has its loyalists and trimmers as well as the usual complement of fanatics ready to face martyrdom in God's cause. It is not improbable that while the saner members of the community sought a decent capitulation, a handful of diehards fired a few rounds from the crumbling walls, thus giving the Spaniards the excuse they needed to repeat the horrors of Zutphen and Mechelen.

That, of course, was the problem. Alba and his son were consciously seeking provocation, and they found it. The technicalities of the case were as usual virtually irrelevant, because what happened was less important than what was believed. The accounts published by Hooft, Bor, and van Meteren are only reflections of a tale that had long since passed into folk history. In all fairness, no one, Dutch or Spanish, has denied that the sack was both horrible and complete. The beleaguered rebels in Enkhuizen, Alkmaar, and Haarlem thought Naarden had surrendered in good faith and been destroyed. Given that belief, they had no choice other than to fight to the end, without quarter and, if necessary, without hope.

In spite of this the beginning of the siege of Haarlem went well enough from the Spanish point of view. After leaving the smoking ruins of Naarden, Fadrique made his way to Amsterdam, where he found a blockading fleet of rebel vessels stuck fast in the ice. The Beggars had thrown up embankments on the ice around their ships and sent out parties of arquebusiers on ice-skates to break up Spanish attempts at reconnaissance. A few brief skirmishes convinced Fadrique that his men could do little against soldiers on skates. He resolved to forget the ships for the time being and concentrate on the problem of Haarlem, though Alba—characteristically—ordered several thousand pairs of the novel device to be held against future necessity.[6]

Haarlem was essential to Alba's plans because of its geographic situation—which was, as is so often the case in that shifting and watery land, very different from its setting today. First of all, it is necessary to visualize the Ij not as a narrow ship channel but as a broad estuary of the Zuider Zee that virtually isolated North Holland from the main landmass of the Netherlands. Only a narrow strip of dunes and marshland separated its headwaters from the open sea. At the southern end of this strip lay Haarlem, controlling the vital land passage from north to south. The city itself was relatively weak, with medieval curtain walls, but its site made investment difficult. To the west was a narrow stretch of pastureland abutting the sand dunes and beaches of what is now Bloemendaal. To the south lay an open region that was in 1572 controlled by the Beggar garrisons at Leiden and Delft. To the east, toward Amsterdam, stretched a broad, rather shallow lake, the Haarlemmermeer, which has since been drained. Created many years before by an incursion of the North Sea, it extended from Spaarndam on the north to Sassenheim on the south, and from a few yards east of the city's walls to what is now the further edge of the air terminal at Schiphol. The city was therefore accessible from Amsterdam by only one route, a narrow causeway or dike running between the Ij and the Haarlemmermeer.

For a time it appeared that this hazardous passage might be opened voluntarily. A pair of magistrates offered to surrender the city at Amsterdam on December 3 but their efforts were repudiated by the townspeople, who proceeded to fortify the village of Spaarndam at the western end of the causeway.

It was at this point that the weather intervened on behalf of the Dutch. For weeks the country had been in the grip of a hard freeze. The Haarlemmermeer, like the Ij, was frozen solid and troops could maneuver upon it at will. This rendered the new fort at Spaarndam less secure than it might have been, but no sooner had Fadrique begun his preparations for an encirclement than a fierce westerly gale brought a thaw and winds so strong that men were blown off the causeway into the water. In the end the fort was reduced only when a submerged dike was discovered leading from the Spanish end of the causeway to the village of Spaarnwoude on the Haarlem side. It was very narrow, and the Spaniards had to wade across it through knee-deep water and broken ice but, miraculously, no one was lost to the fifteen-foot depths on either side. Thus surrounded, Spaarndam fell in a matter of hours and the way to Haarlem was open.

Losing no time, Fadrique completed the encirclement of the city on its three landward sides by December 12. There was a brief interval in which a relieving force sent up from Delft under Lumey de la Marck was annihilated in a blinding snowstorm,[7] but on the eighteenth Fadrique began a bombardment of the walls near the gate of the Holy Cross. With a long string of successes behind him, he was supremely confident. After only three days of rather inconclusive battering, and to the dismay of several of his captains, he ordered a frontal assault on the ravelin that protected the gate. The assault was repulsed with heavy casualties, and the next three weeks were devoted to the construction of an elaborate network of covered trenches leading into the ditch at the ravelin's base. The Haarlemmers defended their position with everything from pikes to molten lead, but on January 17 the ravelin was carried and the Spaniards found to their chagrin that a terreplein had been created around the gate beyond. It was becoming apparent that this would not be another Zutphen.

Some minor successes were registered during these weeks but they were more than offset by almost insoluble difficulties. If the loyal militia of Amsterdam succeeded in destroying a rebel column sent to cut Fadrique's lines of communication at Naarden, other rebels managed to find their way with food and ammunition across the Haarlemmermeer. The bitter cold had returned, the lake was frozen, and even during the short winter days, freezing fog and frequent snowstorms hid the movements of the Dutch supply sleds.[8] Though Fadrique did not yet know it, one of the longest, most bitter sieges of the sixteenth century had begun.

Meanwhile, at Nijmegen, Alba was involved in battles of another kind. The feud with Medinaceli, submerged during the summer under the flood of cordialities occasioned by his arrival, was out in the open by fall. Unable to assume office and generally ignored by Alba, the new captain-general poured out his grievances to the king.[9] Philip in turn wrote to Alba, telling him in effect to be pleasant to his successor, but he got back little more than expressions of innocent puzzlement. He had, Alba said, been friendly to Medinaceli and consulted him on everything. He knew that his successor had complained about certain minor matters that were not in any case his fault, but he thought he had been satisfied—and so forth.[10] To Diego de Zúñiga in Paris Alba ventured some light sarcasm, implying that the inexperienced Medinaceli was unhappy with the speed of military operations. "I, as I am now old and tired of managing armies, cannot go any faster, and thus, so as not to remain in Holland stuck in one of their canals, I have [sent] Don Fadrique with the men."[11]

Zúñiga was, of course, no friend, and Alba had to tread warily. The full measure of his bitterness and contempt was poured out in a letter to his old confidant, the Prior Don Antonio. There was "no more choleric or stupid man in the country" than Medinaceli. His outbursts in council were unpardonable and his continual attacks on Alba made it necessary for him to defend himself, which was a great and unnecessary effort. All in all, Medinaceli was nothing less than a punishment from God. In his own hand, he added one of those ironic homilies of which he was so fond:

> Don Bernardino de Mendoza had in his company a *forzado* named Trujillo, and this Trujillo was a great buffoon and bought a slave in order to give him his liberty, and we called to the slave and told him that he

should quarrel with his master, and when he did, he gave his master the bravest buffets you could think of and afterward many kicks, and this Trujillo, for all the other did, did not touch him, but told him: get along, dog, as I do not wish to maim you, and in this way passed all the days in the world; now I am with this gentleman to whom I cannot raise a hand without crippling him. . . . God help me to finish the enterprise.[12]

This letter too found its way to the king, for Alba was not averse to "leaking" his opinions when their outright expression might be considered disrespectful.

Medinaceli returned to Spain at the end of November, but by this time the endless squabbling and the rigors of the campaign had taken their toll. Not only were Alba's enemies at court provided with useful new ammunition but the duke himself fell ill of a serious but undiagnosed ailment and remained confined to his bed at the Golden Eagle in Nijmegen until mid-January. At the end of February he was still sick but could at least attend Mass and conduct a certain amount of business. This was fortunate, because a major diplomatic question had been left unresolved and Orange's activities now threatened to bring it to a crisis.

Shortly after the revolt at Flushing, Elizabeth of England had sent three hundred men under Captain Thomas Morgan to strengthen the Beggar garrison. Her reasons were, as usual, mixed. She was upset that Philip had not responded to her request for a settlement of the embargo and may have hoped that this gesture would remind him of the continuing uncertainty of Anglo-Spanish relations.[13] At the same time she was under considerable pressure from Parliament to intervene against the popish oppressor.[14] The Flushing expedition was a relatively simple and inexpensive way to accede to their demands without risking anything of importance. Neither of these considerations, however, may have been as important as the need to keep the French from gaining control over the roads of Walcheren. A band of Huguenots was already on the scene, and it is significant that they objected strenuously to the coming of the English.[15]

These purposes were of course unknown to Alba. He fretted continually over Flushing and bitterly lamented the lack of a fleet with which to recapture it.[16] The queen had informed him that she was holding the place for Spain,[17] but he had every reason to believe she was lying. Why, if her intentions were benign, did she replace Morgan with the more adventurous Sir Humphrey Gilbert and send him off to aid Orange in his attempted relief at Mons? The English got no further than Sluis, but this was due to incompetence rather than deliberate intent.[18] Then they assisted in the "ignorant, poor siege of Goes"[19] that was broken by Mondragón's famous crossing of the Ooster Schelde at low tide. By this time the Dutch were disgusted and sent their allies packing, but Alba could be forgiven for wondering if the queen might yet lend more open support to the rebels.

These suspicions crystallized in January, when Orange sent a mission to England in search of aid. Alba had as yet no doubt that the royal cause would triumph in the end but was worried lest English intervention increase his already insupportable expenses. Worse, if Elizabeth helped the Beggars now, she would undoubtedly give them refuge when Alba finally drove them from the Netherlands and would encourage them to prey upon commerce thereafter.[20] He had no choice but to renew negotiations on his own initiative, and after a minimum of debate reached agreement with Burghley on March 15, 1573.[21] The embargo was lifted and the parties swore eternal hostility to each other's enemies, leaving Orange more isolated than before, but Alba could take little pleasure from his success. One major worry had been removed, but another, more serious concern had arisen to take its place. Haarlem not only failed to yield as expected but was showing signs of becoming an epic siege on the antique model, a Numancia among the snows.

Since his success on January 17, Fadrique had accomplished little. Though he now held both ditch and ravelin, he could make no headway against the parapet newly erected before the gate of the Holy Cross. He sealed off the townward side of his ravelin with sandbags and attempted to dig mines under the gate, but the rebels met him with countermines and in a series of dreadful struggles fought deep within the earth his miners were driven back with heavy losses. Frequent enemy assaults on his own camp were repelled with little difficulty, but there seemed to be no way to prevent supplies and reinforcements from reaching the city. The weather continued to be the worst in living memory, and every blizzard or freezing fog brought out long lines of supply sleds from Leiden and Sassenheim. Already some of the officers were suggesting that the siege should be lifted.

To forestall them Fadrique ordered a full-scale assault on January 31. From the accounts of this action, which are unusually imprecise, the idea seems to have been foolhardy. The men had to swarm down into the ditch and up the scarp on ladders while the Dutch poured small-arms fire down upon them. When the survivors reached the top of the parapet, the Haarlemmers exploded a mine beneath their feet, killing forty or fifty of them in one horrible fountain of blood, earth, and human tissue.[22] Alba's report to the king deliberately minimized the number of casualties but he could not conceal the magnitude of his losses. Quite simply, he was running short of Spaniards; the ranks of officers, in particular, were disastrously thin.[23]

The duke was seriously worried. For the first time he sent a brief and urgent letter of instruction to his son, insisting that he must at all costs gain the parapet and terreplein. He softened it by saying that "it could be that I speak nonsense because I am not present," but his growing lack of confidence was apparent.[24] On the same day Albornoz wrote to an unnamed person in camp, telling him "for the love of God" to have Fadrique read and reread the duke's letter.[25] The truth of the matter was that for the first time since his arrival in the Netherlands the duke's men were encountering serious, professional opposition. The defenders of Haarlem were not merely townspeople but more than 4,000 Beggars, German mercenaries, and other trained fighting men. On January 17, Alba had grudgingly admitted that they were "very good soldiers,"[26] perhaps the highest compliment in his limited vocabulary of praise, and by February 11 his admiration was giving way to astonishment. "I tell Your Majesty that certainly until now there has never been a place so defended by rebels, nor by others that defend their natural prince. They have within a good engineer who has done things never before heard or seen."[27]

Stung by his father's doubts, Fadrique redoubled his activity. Piling more sandbags around the ravelin, he installed two guns in it facing the parapet, an effort that might well have preceded the last assault but that now seemed rather belated. More mines were dug, but to little effect. Meanwhile the weather was beginning to break, and to their intense discouragement the Spaniards saw that in anticipation of the coming thaw, the defenders were building oared galleys to replace the supply sleds. Alba ordered Bossu to build a fleet of his own in the hope of gaining control of the mere, but worse surprises were in store. Fearing that Fadrique's mining might ultimately succeed, the Dutch began strengthening the fortification of the gate itself. Working feverishly by night, they constructed a demilune that measured more than a hundred yards from horn to horn, making the gate invulnerable to assault. Father or no father, Fadrique was ready to quit.

It is at this point that an exchange took place that is in its own way very revealing. Learning of his son's vacillation, the duke sent

Bernardino de Mendoza with a message that was to become famous. The chronicler was instructed to tell Fadrique that "if he thought to raise the siege without the town surrendering he would not own him for his son, whatever he might have thought previously, and if he died in the siege, the duke would come in his own person to carry it on, and if both of them fell, the duchess, his wife, would come from Spain to do the same."[28] This has a fine adamantine ring to it, a tone reminiscent of the Roman heroics invoked by Alba on other occasions when it suited his purpose. He was not unaware of the parallel so insistently drawn by Dutch propagandists between his *tercios* and the legions of ancient Rome, and if he was too tasteful to indulge directly in humanist rhetoric he was not above camping where Caesar had camped or striking other attitudes familiar to an audience nurtured on the classics.

Great care was taken that these words should be overheard by Fadrique's men, and Mendoza relates that they "showed great contentment" with them, but to Fadrique they held an altogether different and more compelling message. To this dutiful son, cursed from birth with formidable parents and now himself on the threshold of middle age, this was not mere bombast, however it might seem to modern ears. It was instead the invocation of ancient tradition, the tradition in which he, like his father, had been reared, and to which, in theory at least, even the most extravagant ambitions of the house of Toledo were subordinate. It called up images of Fernán Alvarez before the walls of Lisbon, of his great-grandfather and namesake in the endless campaigns of Granada, and of Don García bleeding his life away among the palms of Djerba. Even the reference to his mother was more than mere hyperbole. He knew, of course, that she would never come, but he knew, too, what to expect of a woman who would send her five-year-old son, his elder brother now long deceased, on a campaign against the Moors of Tunis. All his life he had sought to appease these parental furies, usually without success, and he must have felt that if his mother were there she would be doing a better job than he. Against his better judgment the siege continued.

By now a steady stream of supplies, heavy artillery, and fresh troops was crossing the Haarlemmermeer to the beleaguered city. A flurry of Spanish assaults brought on by the duke's admonition was repulsed with terrible losses; among those slain was the irreplaceable engineer Bartolomeo Campi. Then, toward the end of February, the Dutch succeeded in knocking out the ravelin's battery with guns shipped across the water from Leiden. March was no better. Showing themselves to be soldiers indeed, the rebels launched a series of fierce *encamisadas* that ended on March 25 with a massive raid on the German sector of Fadrique's camp. Everything was wrecked, the Germans temporarily driven off, and their cannon taken or spiked.[29]

Alba was nearly beside himself. Not only were these reverses intolerable in themselves but they were making his political situation extremely difficult. For the first time, the true nature of his dilemma and that of Spanish rule in general was beginning to come home to him. As Albornoz put it, "If the Spaniards stay, the provinces revolt; if they leave, religion will be lost."[30]

The problem was Hydra-headed. In Nijmegen and at Brussels, Alba's Netherlandish supporters were beginning to desert him in the face of what they perceived as a new wind blowing from Holland. The Duke of Aerschot was saying things "scandalous enough to have come from the Prince of Orange," and the malice long hidden by his counselors was beginning to show. "You may believe that they hate our nation more than the devil," wrote Albornoz. "The duke is loathed by the heretics. They spit when they hear his name."[31]

Worse yet was the news from beyond the Rhine. Cavalry were being raised in Denmark, Saxony, and the Palatinate, but Alba could raise no more of his own through lack of money. His remaining Germans were on the point of mutiny, his Spaniards "nearly finished," and those who survived were twenty-five pays in arrears.[32] Sailors, too, were a problem. He needed men as well as ships for Bossu and to recover Flushing, but virtually the whole maritime population supported the Beggars and he was forced to recruit seamen in the Baltic ports at great expense.[33]

None of this, however, was as critical as the situation at court, where his enemies had at last come boldly into the open. Playing upon the reverses before Haarlem, they tried to convince Philip that the cause as Alba understood it was lost. Then they revived their old tactic of encouraging support for the Holy League against the Turk, and even tried to block the agreement with the English. This last was ridiculous, and Alba easily countered it by pointing out the absurdity of losing the Netherlands so as not to "dishearten the English Catholics." Still, there was reason for concern. The king might finally agree to send reinforcements and even money, but a "new style" had crept into his letters, and it was causing "very great inconveniences."[34]

Specifically, the undermining of Philip's confidence in his governor-general encouraged Netherlanders of every persuasion, and their recalcitrance was confirmed when they heard that on January 30 Luis de Requesens, a noted exponent of Eboli's views, had been appointed to replace the hated duke.[35] This was in fact meant to signal a change in policy, but for the time being it meant a replay of Medinaceli and the Tenth Penny on bloodier ground. Though Requesens tried to escape his politically hazardous fate Philip insisted, and for the next ten months the prospect of a more lenient successor was to frustrate Alba's attempts to end the revolt on his own terms. The launching of Bossu's fleet on March 29 marked the beginning of the end for the heroic defenders of Haarlem, but for Alba this had come too late. His position was thoroughly undermined and his reputation was compromised; moreover, the denouement at Haarlem was, of course, only that and not an ending.

By April 19 Bossu had gained mastery of the lake, cutting off supplies and making Haarlem untenable, but the garrison still refused to surrender. The mood of the siege had been vicious and desperate from the start. The Haarlemmers believed that surrender meant certain death, and as if to confirm that outcome both sides committed frequent atrocities. Dark tales are told of basketsfull of human heads catapulted over the walls in both directions and of innumerable prisoners executed in sight of the enemy by Spaniards and Netherlanders alike.[36] There is no reason to doubt that such outrages did occur. Now the besieged, driven by desperation, outdid themselves in insult. Loaves of precious bread were thrown into the Spanish camp as a magnificent gesture of defiance. Holy images were removed from the churches and placed in the line of fire while rebel soldiers capered along the parapets in stolen vestments.[37] No more effective pledge to continue until the last man, woman, or child was dead can be imagined, but for all the bravado and despair Orange had not yet exhausted his schemes for relieving the city.

As a diversionary tactic Beggar troops were sent to cut the road from Utrecht to Amsterdam. This was relatively easy to do, as the road ran for much of its length along the top of a dike in otherwise impassable country. Had they succeeded, Amsterdam would have been cut off from its food supply, for the entrance to the Ij was still blockaded by rebel ships. Orange's force was defeated on May 15, but Alba had been forced to take the threat seriously. As if to compensate him for his worry the duke received an unexpected dividend from the affair: the body of Antoine Oliver, betrayer of Mons. Captured on the dike, the painter was killed by a German before he could be taken to Nijmegen. This was a disappointment, for Alba later declared that he would have given the German anything to have kept him alive, but he at least had the grim satisfaction of quartering the remains on four poles.[38]

Meanwhile, at Sassenheim, Orange was outfitting another fleet. The new force, greatly superior to the old, was desperately needed. By the end of April stringent rationing had been introduced at Haarlem, and as May wore on the food situation became increasingly grave. On May 28 Orange's vessels sallied forth and were again defeated by Bossu. Though the prince continued to recruit troops and to devise new and more elaborate schemes of relief it was now obvious that succor was out of the question. The few supplies that reached the city came on the backs of men who used long poles to vault over canals and fortifications. Communication was almost entirely by carrier pigeon, an arrangement that furnished amusement, information, and roast squab to Spanish marksmen but whose failure seemed to have little effect on the morale of the defenders.[39] The siege continued.

Dissatisfaction with this state of affairs and with Alba's leadership in general reached a peak in April and May. Fortunately, the coming of spring had left him in sufficient health to cope with the opposition, though this fact is not always apparent from his own account. Albornoz informed the duchess that he no longer needed his pills and that he was able to walk to daily Mass under his own power. He ate well and even requested that boxes of fresh limes should be sent from Spain,[40] but if the secretary was confident the duke was less so. A prolonged convalescence and the fear that it would end as it usually did with an attack of the flux prompted him to a discourse on the gout, dispatched to his fellow sufferer the Prior Don Antonio.

> He who is not of the profession might be surprised to have a *gotoso* tell him that gout in the foot can affect the hand, but I certainly am not surprised, for when the foot pains me, there is nothing in my entire person that I can put to good use. It oppresses me that it has touched you with more rigor than is its wont; we old men have a good thing, that each day we can expect more misery than we began with. Even though you are not of my age, I put you with so many others in the dance of the old ones, and if it is true, what must I be?[41]

Whatever he may have been, it did not prevent him from striking at his detractors with verve and eloquence.

Most of the complaints against which he had to defend himself came originally from loyal Netherlanders who resented his heavy-handedness and patent distrust of the native officials. They were transmitted to court through Hopperus, the secretary for Flanders and no friend of Alba,[42] or more informally through various members of the Eboli faction. Alba generally learned of criticisms through such allies as Zayas or Don Antonio, though he was occasionally confronted directly by the king. In general they fell into two categories: complaints about the quality of justice meted out by the courts, and protests over his appointments to the councils.

The judicial problems were the more serious in that they involved an area close to the fundamental concerns of the king. It was said that there was no justice in the Netherlands and that all the troubles sprang from this. Alba agreed, but tried to turn the complaint on its head by broadening it to include the judicial system as a whole. His enemies had referred primarily to the Council of Troubles, but Alba responded with a diatribe against the local courts that roundly damned the natives and was a striking admission of his own failure as a reformer:

> There is not a case, civil or criminal, that is not sold as meat is sold in the butcher shop. . . . This is a matter, *señor*, on which so much could be said to Your Majesty about the abominable lack of justice in these estates that it is impossible to put it into writing, and God is witness to the bad days, nights, hours, and moments that this matter has given me.[43]

As for the Council of Troubles, he could see nothing wrong. It was overworked and understaffed, but its only fault was excessive lenience with those who offended the Crown. As he could personally attest, it acted with all possible rigor against those who offended God.[44] To the allegation that its legal authority was dubious and its procedures summary he made no reply.

Alba's continuing belief that the presence of a rebellion gave him almost unlimited powers is evident not only from these remarks but from his admitted interference with the work of the councils. Though claiming innocence in the matter of wrongful appointments, he acknowledged the other charges with pride. He had indeed interfered with the Privy Council whenever it dealt with a case involving the revolt. Similarly, he had no intention of allowing the Council of Finance to handle money. The council might debate policy, but he was horrified by their contention that they should collect the taxes as well.[45]

Clearly he had learned nothing and forgotten nothing. As his regime struggled on toward its inglorious conclusion he remained obsessed by two interrelated ideas. The first was that the rebellion was entirely a matter of religion. This view, so soothing to his conscience, was powerfully reinforced by the blasphemies committed at Haarlem and by an episode that occurred in early April. The government of Amsterdam had attempted to intercede with certain rebel towns and had been told that if the king granted them freedom of conscience they would lay down their arms. As Alba told Granvelle, "This, señor, is the Tenth Penny and the other complaints they have."[46] He had always believed this, but as the pressure increased his crusading instincts grew in proportion. Little else could be expected from one who, upon learning that the Haarlemmers had hanged some Catholics from the city walls, permitted himself to envy their martyrdom.[47]

The second was the old refrain that no Netherlander could be trusted in a position of authority. If anything, his contempt for them had increased. He distrusted their orthodoxy, their fiscal integrity, and even their learning. Later in the summer of 1573 he was to declare that his councillors "know as little of matters of state as of Latin."[48] These opinions remained, as they had always been, the root of his intransigence whenever the Tenth Penny or a general pardon was mentioned.

By this time, Hopperus, the Ebolistas, and Philip himself were pushing for immediate repeal of the tax and issuance of a pardon, but Alba continued to obstruct them as best he could. He insisted that no attempt should be made to negotiate the Tenth Penny until the rebels had been suppressed. Then the issue could be brought into the courts, where the judges would certainly rule that the tax had been legally adopted by the Estates.[49] On the pardon he was more flexible but found grave dangers in the version that had been dispatched with Medinaceli in the preceding year. There should be, he thought, no general exceptions, as this would only cause people to be "scrupulous and fearful." It was far better to make exceptions by name, thus avoiding confusion as to who fell into the excepted categories and who did not. Religion should not be mentioned and he was horrified at the provision that extended clemency to those involved in the troubles of 1566. This could lead only to lawsuits and, by invalidating the work of the Council of Troubles, force the Crown to return the confiscated properties.[50]

None of this was new, nor were his objections wholly unreasonable: they simply ignored the likelihood that concessions would have to be made to end the revolt. His views on this subject had been a major source of the friction between himself and Medinaceli, but now the renewed pressure from his enemies at court forced him to an act of near-disobedience. He flatly refused to publish the pardon in its existing form until separate and specific instructions to that effect were sent from Madrid.[51]

These epistolary blasts seemed to clear the air, for after a long delay occasioned by illness, Philip answered in a conciliatory tone on July 8.[52] In the meantime Alba had launched several treatises on his mistreatment and that of his son,[53] but in spite of these occasional bursts of irritation May and June were relatively tranquil. Haarlem had not yet surrendered but would obviously have to do so in the very near future, and there were a number of other encouraging signs on the horizon. Not only did reinforcements arrive from Germany and Milan but the emperor finally issued an order prohibiting Orange from recruiting in the empire.[54] The duke had time to haggle over the relics of St. Leocadia, collect books for the new Royal Library at Antwerp,[55] and worry about Barbara Blomberg.

This lady, the mother of Don Juan of Austria, had been a problem ever since Alba arrived in the Netherlands. After her celebrated affair with Charles V, she had been settled in Antwerp, where her conduct proved embarrassing to Don Juan, the king, and her neighbors, who complained that she freely entertained men at all hours of the day and night. Alba, whose own sexual restraint has been noted, attempted to solve the problem by introducing two respectable women into the household, but she managed to drive them away and replace them with what the duke called "bawds" and *ruines mujeres*. By 1573 she must have been nearing fifty but had lost none of her capacity to attract men, and her house was, if anything, more disorderly than before. Unlike Brantôme, Alba could not admire this sort of "gallantry," especially in the mother of an international hero. In desperation he offered to kidnap her and have her shut up in a convent.[56]

Such burdens were light indeed after the traumas of winter, and on July 12 they were lightened even further. Deprived of hope and sustenance alike, Haarlem at last surrendered on terms. There was no joy, only relief. The victory had been costly beyond measure in both lives and prestige, and even after seven months of bitter struggle there was legitimate doubt as to what had been accomplished. The Waterland was now isolated by land if not by sea, and Holland was split in two, but no other towns offered to surrender and Orange, indomitable as ever, was still at large.

Alba, seeing the error of his ways, resolved to spare what remained of the city. There would be no sack provided that the inhabitants paid an indemnity of 100,000 fl. This they were almost contemptuously glad to do, for money was the one thing they had in plenty, as it could neither be eaten nor fired from their guns. The duke was belatedly determined to show that those who surrendered could do so in safety,[57] but he could not yet bring himself to show real mercy to rebels or heretics. With scrupulous regard for the laws of war he insisted on executing 2,300 soldiers who had served Orange without the formal consent of their own rulers, and completed his work by summarily convicting the Beggar leaders of treason. The result was precisely what he might have expected. His "mercy" was seen as barbarous cruelty by the Dutch and as unpardonable by his own troops, who felt they had earned the right to a sack. Alkmaar, Enkhuizen, and the rest of the north stood firm for Orange. Alba's Spanish troops, unpaid for twenty-eight months and deprived of what they considered their rightful spoil, mutinied on the spot.[58]

Alba was forced to go to camp in person on August 14 to offer himself as hostage as he had done in 1555, but when he offered the Spaniards thirty *escudos* each from the composition of Haarlem, his personal popularity and obvious sympathy with their plight did the rest. His *magníficos señores hijos*, as he called them, returned to their duties.[59]

This, of course, did nothing to solve the basic problem, which ran far deeper than the men of the *tercios* knew and was rooted partly in court politics and partly in the system itself. Alba's enemies were making every effort to deny him funds, alleging that 12,000,000 ducats had already been spent to no avail and that to send more was absurd. The duke might ask how much they thought the King of France had spent on his rebellion,[60] but this was not a rational argument. Matters came to a head at the time of the mutiny, when the *hacienda* refused to honor an *asiento* of 40,000 ducats. Their excuse was that Albornoz was supposed to have received a kickback on the deal, but this was never proved.[61] The tragedy was that all of Philip's commanders were vulnerable to such tactics and that the chief victims were the Spanish troops, the only segment of his army upon which the king could absolutely rely. Mercenaries had first claim on whatever money was found, because they could leave if they were not paid while such a course was nearly impossible for Spanish sub-

jects. The Spaniards' pay was thus invariably in arrears, and as time
went on they began to mutiny with dismal regularity. The year 1573
was thus a harbinger of things to come, and not all of Alba's successors could credibly address the troops as he had done on July 30:

> You are soldiers of God, of the King of Spain, of the nation, and
> above all of mine, for each one of whom I would shed whatever blood
> I have without leaving a drop in my body. You do not wish that we
> should come, you and I, to be the laughingstock and opprobrium of the
> other nations.[62]

Under these circumstances settlement of the mutiny did not save
the duke from plunging once again into despair. He read its meaning
more clearly than anyone and knew that his enemies were higher
than ever in the counsels of the king. At the same time all attempts
to profit from his "mercy" at Haarlem proved fruitless. On July 28
he distributed a circular to the effect that those who now acknowledged the authority of the Crown would be "gathered under the
royal wing," while those who did not would be utterly destroyed.[63]
When the circular was greeted with derision, Alba fell into another
rage. He advised the king that "the way in which these rebels have
abused the admonitions and pardon that I have published" proved
conclusively that "gentleness" was futile.[64] He was thankful only
that the king had not signed the documents, thus further diminish-
ing his authority; a reference, one may suppose, to the disadvan-
tages of a general pardon. His next target was Alkmaar, and he was
resolved that "if Alkmaar be taken by force, I am resolved not to
leave a creature alive, but to put them all to the knife, as they have
not profited by the example of Haarlem."[65]

Unfortunately for Alba, Alkmaar showed no signs of cooperation
and when his forces marched northward to reduce it, they were in
very poor condition indeed. The troops—now numbering some
16,000—were unenthusiastic. There was inadequate transport, owing to the lack of money, and moving the artillery proved nearly
impossible.[66] To cap his misfortunes, Fadrique, exhausted and de-
spondent, suffered a physical breakdown. His ailment was diagnosed as the ancestral gout, but there may have been something
else, for he was never really well again in the twelve years of life
that remained to him. He went to Alkmaar in a cart.[67]

The one piece of good news that came to the duke during this
period was that his ancient rival Ruy Gómez de Silva, Prince of
Eboli, was dead. Strangely enough, Albornoz reports that he was

"much affected." The secretary was less generous, hoping only that God would pardon his misdeeds,[68] but it may be that the duke's reaction is perfectly understandable. He was at an age when the death of younger men carries with it a hint of one's own mortality; perhaps, too, the loss of a great enemy is nearly as wrenching as the loss of a friend. He had a large emotional investment in the deceased, and though his passing marked the end of an era it was not the end of opposition. In fact, the situation at court was as bad as ever.

The faithful Zayas reassured him that no one doubted his authority,[69] but Alba had been totally eclipsed. Eboli's friends continued to work upon the feelings of the king and, with Requesens expected in the near future, Netherlanders of all sorts felt free to ignore the duke completely. Worst of all, what little prestige he retained was soon obliterated by events at Alkmaar. There a mortally weary Fadrique failed to take the city in two successive assaults, and after absorbing heavy casualties his men had refused to attempt a third. In the meantime it was noticed that several dikes had been broken in the vicinity of the camp and that the fields were becoming soggy. The country around Alkmaar is largely below sea level, and when it was learned that the defenders were awaiting only a favorable conjunction of wind and high tide to open the great sluices and wash the Spaniards away forever Fadrique lifted the siege. It was October 8, 1573, and Alba's war was over.

When he learned of his son's plans Alba wrote as he had done at Haarlem, asking him to "carry the cross" for just a few more days so that the situation could be turned over "live" to Requesens.[70] His major concern was that Fadrique should avoid the appearance of a rout. He had worked long and hard to rehabilitate his son in the eyes of the king and did not wish to see his efforts evaporate just as relief was near at hand, but all was in vain. The situation was untenable and they both knew it. Within two weeks the duke's hopes and plans had been reduced to a single objective. As he told Don Antonio:

> For the love of God, quit me of this government and get me out of it, and when you cannot do it in any other way, [do it] by sending someone to give me an arquebus shot . . . because there is now nothing more to the king's advantage than this, as I have said, and I do not wish to wait upon events, nor to see them, nor to hear them, nor paint them on the wall, as I have more mortified feelings in this regard than by a death of sixty days, and even if there were nothing else, it should be enough to be, after tomorrow, sixty-six years old.[71]

It was not until November 17 that Requesens reached Brussels. He had never really wanted to go,[72] and for some time had flatly refused to do so until he had received absolution from the pope.[73] When he finally arrived, the duke received him with great courtesy in spite of his "gout, fever, and fluxions of the chest,"[74] but differences quickly arose over the inevitable question of who was to command. For obvious reasons Requesens wanted to put as much distance as possible between himself and Alba, and as a result of his long association with Ebolista policies thoroughly distrusted both father and son.[75] He was therefore horrified when Alba insisted that he should assume office immediately, for he feared that the weather or something more sinister might keep the duke in Brussels for months to come and that his own regime would be indelibly blackened by the association.[76]

The duke would not be denied. He began sending petitioners directly to Requesens, telling them that he was no longer the governor. Requesens sent them back. The duke responded by having his secretaries write "that the *Señor Commendador Mayor* orders this" on all important documents, a tactic which, as Requesens put it, "I could well forgive if I thought he was dealing with me honestly and fairly."[77] All this maneuvering was accompanied by the most urgent personal entreaties, but Requesens held fast for several days. His reluctance was due not only to his desire for a clean break with the past but to his inability to understand the reasons for Alba's haste. He knew that Alba would be greeted coldly on his return to Madrid and that Fadrique might well be imprisoned.[78] He himself was not the man to face such things head on, and he could not imagine that Alba might prefer to confront the court openly and without regard for anyone's embarrassment. Still suspecting a plot, he at last permitted himself to take the oath of office when Alba once again grew too ill to work.[79]

There was, of course, no plot. Alba may have found time to complain that the installation ceremonies were more elaborate than those allowed him in 1567,[80] but this was little more than a momentary fit of pique. He had no real desire to make trouble for his successor and many compelling reasons to be gone. On December 19, in the depths of a northern winter and still so sick that he could barely travel, he began the long journey, not to the warm sun and sparkling trout streams of El Abadía, but to an uncertain welcome at Madrid.

XIII

DISGRACE

Alba was delighted to be going home. Requesens thought that he was "in better disposition than I have seen him in many years,"[1] but the trip cannot have been an entirely joyous one. By almost any measure he had failed in the most important undertaking of his life. Orange was still at large and the rebellion was clearly unsuppressed, with most of Holland free and conditions in Walcheren essentially what they had been a year and a half before. The situation had deteriorated since 1567, when the only armed opposition came from disorganized bands of largely discredited Beggars. Well might his enemies say that he had found the country submissive and single-handedly reduced it to civil war, spending 12,000,000 ducats in the process.

From the standpoint of his successor conditions were even worse than this accusation implies. The new year found Requesens with an army of more than 62,000 men, most of whom were unpaid and scattered in garrisons all over the countryside. What little money there was on hand had been committed to various creditors, and the administration was a shambles. He believed nothing the duke or his men told him and even feared that Zayas, who was still responsible for northern affairs, might in some way subvert his communications with the king.[2] "Things are in the worst state there ever was" became a recurring phrase in his correspondence, and he quite literally did not know which way to turn.[3]

Alba could, and did, blame the debacle on the intrigues of his

262

enemies, whose fiscal and administrative obstructions had cost him the loyalty of his troops and who had encouraged rebel hopes in the darkest hours of the war. He could also take some comfort from the fact that he was as yet unbeaten in the field, but though there is much truth in all this it is partial truth and tends to obscure the real reasons for his failure.

To understand what happened it is necessary to dispose of the notion that Eboli was right from the beginning and that had his views prevailed in 1566 the whole ghastly mess would have been avoided. Like all "what if" questions, this thesis can neither be proved nor disproved, but it is at best a dubious proposition. To begin with, Eboli's policy was almost completely passive. If he had a program other than benign neglect it is not apparent from the sources. Given the situation in 1566, this meant that the Netherlands would have drifted further and further from Spain, under the guidance of independent noblemen whose chief allies were the Calvinists of the towns. Orange had shown that the nobles could maintain order but not that they could restrain heresy, reform the government, or provide Philip with revenues. In short, adoption of Eboli's opinions might have avoided war and maintained nominal allegiance, but at a cost that any sixteenth-century monarch would have found literally unconscionable.

Such an answer, as we have seen, was unacceptable to Philip from the moment he began to realize its implications in 1565, and he never really adopted it thereafter. Even the appointment of Requesens and issuance of the pardon to which Alba had so violently objected were tactical retrenchments rather than a reversion to Eboli's views of seven years before. Not only was such a policy immoral, at least from the perspective of the king, it was also dangerous from the standpoint of international *Realpolitik*. A disorganized, virtually independent, and semi-heretical Netherlands would have been constantly at risk to the French and possibly to the English as well. Rather than accept the creation of such a hostage to fortune he would have been better advised to give the region to France outright, as Alba had suggested in 1544.

Practically speaking, then, Philip had little choice but to pursue an active, and by twentieth-century standards intolerant, policy— unless we are to suggest that this sixteenth-century idealist ought somehow to have anticipated the values of the Enlightenment. It has been argued that William the Silent did exactly that, and this may be true, but William's tolerance was unique even among his own partisans. Moreover, he had little choice. It is one thing to be entrusted with the preservation of an empire and a faith and quite another to be faced with building a state out of political and religious elements as diverse as those of the Netherlands.

Alba, therefore, was not necessarily wrong to insist on an active policy of repression. Repellent as it is, it was probably the last and best hope of restoring royal authority in the Netherlands and obedience to the Church as well. Moreover, had the initial plan been followed, it might very well have worked. As we have also seen, it was the king's failure to relieve Alba after he had completed his bloody work that started him on the short road to disaster.

Yet, it is impossible to deny that after defeating Orange in 1568 Alba made things much worse than they needed to have been. His continued presence made the situation difficult but by no means irretrievable. All the active rebels were dead or in exile. Both the central government and that of the towns were in the hands of Catholic loyalists, and the populace as a whole seemed willing to accept the situation. It should have been possible, with a modicum of tact and caution, to stanch the wounds if not heal them completely, but this Alba notoriously failed to do. It is as though his political judgment deserted him entirely.

The key to this lapse is found in the personal crisis that befell him in the winter of 1568/69. Sick, depressed, and furious at what he saw as betrayal, he fell into a pattern of behavior that led to ever more disastrous mistakes. This was not a simple case of disrupted plans bringing catastrophe in their wake, but of adversity blinding him to the remaining possibilities while bringing out defects in his character that might otherwise have been controllable. His instincts had always tended toward rigidity, dogmatism, and xenophobia, but during most of his career they had been subordinated to a tactical flexibility born of intellect. After 1568 this check was gone.

The most immediate consequence was that Alba failed to take the Netherlandish loyalists into his confidence and use them to develop an effective administration. An exclusive reliance on Spaniards and Italians is understandable in the midst of a purge. By 1568, however, the Netherlanders had proved themselves trustworthy if not lovable, and by refusing to use them Alba denied himself their full support and perpetuated a government that was both alien and woefully inefficient. This in turn guaranteed the ultimate failure of his reforms. Moreover, it created opposition to the Council of Troubles that might not have developed had the personnel and procedures of that body been regularized. It is noteworthy that even in 1573 the complaints of Viglius, Tisnacq, and the others were not that the council was wrong or unnecessary but that it was irregular in its workings, and that Philip's first order to Requesens was not to abolish but to reform it.[4]

A similar rigidity and distrust are evident in his mishandling of the Tenth Penny. On this issue he not only failed to confide in his ministers but viewed them from the start as adversaries, forcing them into a defensive posture. Then by demanding far more than he was prepared to accept he convinced even the sycophants that he had to be stopped. Not even hindsight can tell us if a more adroit approach would have succeeded but, as Alba noted in complete bewilderment, the same people who rejected the Tenth Penny were willing to grant Orange a similar tax at far higher rates.[5]

His final and most disturbing error lay in attempting to quell the revolt of 1572 through use of exemplary terrorism. This strategy has always been popular in spite of its consistent failure to achieve the desired results, and generally proceeds from a readily definable state of mind. Those who adopt it are often frustrated to the point of desperation and have long since succeeded in dehumanizing, on ethnic or ideological grounds, their proposed victims. In Alba's case, his frustration and its causes require no further comment, but his progressive dehumanization of the Dutch on the theory that their revolt was purely religious in character is somewhat mystifying. How could such a simplistic idea come to dominate the mind of an astute and experienced politician who in 1567 had obviously known better?

Religion was, of course, the fundamental issue to many of the Beggars and its importance to the struggle as a whole cannot be denied. Nevertheless, there were other motives at work, the grievances of the nobility not least among them. Alba recognized this when he brutally suppressed their leading advocates without attempting in any way to impugn their orthodoxy. He may have believed that Egmont, Hornes, and the others were traitors but he knew perfectly well that they were not Protestants. The problem arose only after the dissident nobility had been crushed. As their cause was now virtually dead, what could justify this continued resistance? He could scarcely admit even to himself that much of the fault lay with his own policies and with the monumental insensitivity of his government. Heresy was the only possible explanation. To one whose piety was rooted directly in the Reconquista it was a congenial answer, and the impression was strengthened by the behavior of the rebels at Haarlem. Surely no one would fight with such persistence for anything less than God or the devil. They might if they thought that surrender meant massacre—but this was one of those night thoughts that generals willingly suppress.

As is usually the case, Alba's rationalizations must have been at least partially conscious. He really believed in the theory of a holy war, for to do otherwise would have imposed too heavy a tax on his self-respect, but he must also have been aware that the religious issue was his one remaining point of contact with the king. Though apparently seduced by the Ebolistas, Philip could never entirely escape from the fear that mercy and compromise might lead to the increase of heresy. Only by hammering incessantly on this point could Alba secure acceptance of his views and, above all, his vindication.

As he retraced the Spanish Road, Alba mulled over the causes of his failure, but he could not wallow in them; too much was at stake. The fortunes of his numerous family and its dependents still rested upon his shoulders. If interest dictated that he work against the policy of lenience, conscience demanded no less. It was imperative that he vindicate himself and restore his son to favor. To these ends Alba devoted the next six years.

The journey was a long one, for his poor health necessitated frequent rests and the weather prevented haste. He reached Barcelona in mid-March and was summoned to Madrid with great cordiality,[6] but in fact his influence was greatly eroded. Though Eboli had died, his place was taken by that formidable intriguer Antonio Pérez. Pérez had become a secretary to the Council of State in 1570, and with his enormous charm and willingness to please had little trouble in succeeding the late prince as royal confidant. His grudge against Alba had not abated, and he soon became the leader of the anti-Toledo faction, which now included two thoroughly dangerous advocates with direct experience in the Low Countries: Medinaceli and Requesens.

Medinaceli, who still smarted from the slights put upon him by Alba in 1572, frequently served as an advocate for the nobles with whom he had established close contact during his stay.[7] There was no personal rancor in the letters of Requesens but they were, if anything, more damaging than the complaints of Medinaceli, for the new governor had found a disastrous state of affairs and in sheer self-protection was not inclined to minimize the difficulties of restoring order. It is not surprising, then, that Alba reached court in a cloud of recriminations. A typical example is the memorandum sub-mitted to Philip three days before he welcomed the duke to Spain. The anonymous author accuses Alba of executing 6,000 people, of tampering with the general pardon, and of creating the Tenth Penny, the last two crimes being primarily responsible for the revolt; he ends by accusing Vargas, Albornoz, and others of corruption.[8]

That this sort of thing did relatively little damage was due partly to Philip's long experience with partisanship and partly to the fact that even at this low point in his career Alba was not without friends. One of them was Arias Montano, who though he had come to welcome the duke's removal wrote from Antwerp to defend him against charges of cruelty and corruption. "He left," said Arias, "with a clear conscience."[9]

Thus Alba remained in the Council of State, but his advice on the Netherlands soon became a monotonous refrain. In December, 1574, Philip set up a special *junta* to deal with the Netherlands. Its mem-bers were the inquisitor-general, Gaspar de Quiroga, Bishop of Cuenca, the Marqués of Aguilar, the Count of Chinchón, and Andrés Ponce. It will be noted that none of these men was of the old factional leadership, though Chinchón often supported Alba's views. The *junta* met regularly from December into February and carefully solicited the comments of both Alba and his opponents. Their recommendations and Alba's response to them indicate that little had changed. Alba was prepared to accept the idea that if the king could not go in person Don Juan of Austria should be sent, but he was cautious about the establishment of a Council of the Nether-lands and opposed to the restoration of privileges currently under litigation. Concessions might be made, but he was determined that they should appear to be granted purely through the king's good-will. In practice, this meant that Requesens should not negotiate with the Netherlanders—and of course nothing could be done that would encourage freedom of conscience.[10]

Alba's advice was ignored and Requesens negotiated, though without conceding religious freedom. He issued a pardon and re-pealed the Tenth Penny. As if to confirm Alba's prediction, the re-sults were negligible. Holland simply ignored the new policy. The rest of the country, including those parts firmly under Spanish con-trol, continued to agitate for the return of their ancient privileges and for the right to worship as they pleased. Requesens was forced to arms and died in the field, leaving behind an unpaid army that promptly mutinied, with horrible results. When at last Don Juan of

Austria went to Brussels to replace Requesens, he was permitted to take the oaths only after he had expelled all Spanish troops from the country.

Throughout all this the aging duke continued to breathe fire and blood, but no one was listening. It was not precisely that he was wrong, for his arguments, however extreme, had the tautological perfection of a geometric theorem. Few doubted that overwhelming force could restore faith and obedience, but the sad fact was that the means to achieve this no longer existed. Philip's "bankruptcy" of 1575 meant that new and imaginative policies were needed, and these Alba could not supply. He had become predictable and something of a bore.

This attachment to past courses would have rendered him virtually useless from the royal point of view had it not been for his continuing role as senior military advisor. No one knew more about the Spanish army than he, but it soon became evident that here, too, he had fallen into one of those special traps reserved for aging generals. Though his advice was always logical and militarily correct, it was increasingly divorced from economic reality.

In the light of Alba's earlier career this was indeed ironic. As Michael Roberts has pointed out, sixteenth-century war led invariably to stalemate,[11] and we have seen that Alba was among the first to recognize this fact and profit from it. He relied upon superior discipline, logistics, and time to drive his opponents from the field, and he had amply demonstrated that God favors not the biggest battalions but those that are best financed and organized. By the 1570s these ideas were the common property of military thinkers everywhere, but they had within them a tragic flaw that not even Alba seems to have perceived. Put in its simplest terms, the form of warfare he represented was enormously expensive. He knew this, of course, and openly relied upon the superior resources of the Spanish empire to triumph over such shaky opponents as the French or William of Orange. What he did not know and perhaps could not have known, given the contemporary level of economic wisdom, was that this style of war was beyond the financial capability of any early modern state. It was not simply a matter of limited resources but of inadequate tax collection and a primitive system of public credit. As a result, many of his projects have about them a curiously futile and even nostalgic air.

A good example is Alba's regularization of the army system of pay and bonuses.[12] By setting a uniform pay-scale for the various

ranks, inequity and opportunities for corruption were drastically reduced. It was a great advance, worthy of Le Tellier or Louvois and
fully a century ahead of its time, but it came when there was no
money to pay the soldiers at all.

His impassioned defense of administrative centralization was of
the same order. Conventional wisdom had long insisted that the
safety of the realm depended upon royal control, not merely of the
forces at hand but of the whole system of provisioning, armament,
and military construction. It was thought that this not only ensured
higher quality but prevented the emergence of over-mighty subjects
upon whom the Crown might one day be forced to depend. Wallen-
stein was not yet born, but the emergence of figures like him was
apparently seen as a predictable consequence of decentralization. It
was with something like this in mind that Alba launched himself
into a spirited battle over issuance of galley contracts to private
individuals.

Spain's Mediterranean coasts were still very much subject to harassment by Muslim pirates operating out of the coastal towns of
North Africa. The massive Spanish invasions of past years had not
substantially reduced the hazard and it was necessary to maintain a
number of galleys on constant patrol. This was costly in the extreme,
and when the Duke of Medina Sidonia offered to create and maintain such a fleet for a set annual fee it was soon determined that his
suggestion would result in major savings. Alba rightly and vigorously opposed this as a threat to royal authority and a terrible precedent for the future,[13] but in the end he lost. Philip seems to have
agreed with him in principle, but in 1575 the Crown had been forced
to default on its loans and economies were essential. This was not
the end of the issue—it continued to raise its head in various forms
throughout the reign and beyond, with Alba appearing more and
more as a prophet without honor in his own time, but in reality
there had been little choice. Under the pressures of finance, military
decentralization continued in Spain and elsewhere until, in the
Thirty Years' War, something very like anarchy was achieved.

One other project should be mentioned, if only to dispel once
and for all the notion that Alba was ignorant of the uses of seapower.
His experience in the Netherlands had convinced him that the provinces could be recovered only if Spain gained control of the North
Sea and its approaches. From 1574 until his death he was Spain's
leading advocate of a northern fleet.[14] Once again his advice, though
militarily unimpeachable, was almost useless. There was no money

to build such a fleet and it would have been the height of folly to divert ships from the protection of the bullion fleet for such a purpose.

There was probably a good deal more of the same, but because the duke was at court and did not have to commit his thoughts to paper, relatively little of it has been preserved. It is obvious, though, that for all his apparent understanding of the economic component of war he had begun to think in purely operational terms. In nearly every case, had his advice been followed the military posture of Spain would have been improved, yet he rarely if ever suggested the means by which these measures could be implemented. Philip, who for all his faults was forced to look at the broader picture, must have heard his counselor's advice with increasing weariness of spirit. For Alba this growing disenchantment, hidden as always behind the royal mask of patient courtesy, was to prove exceedingly dangerous. The debacle in the Netherlands had not been sufficient to disgrace him but it had broken his aura of infallibility. His enemies, who were still legion and whose malice had not diminished with the passing years, were quick to capitalize on his growing weakness. Indeed, with the emergence of Antonio Pérez as Eboli's successor a more purely personal note seems to intrude itself in the endless wranglings of faction.

Much of this was due to the continuing resentment of Pérez over Alba's behavior in 1566. There is no need to say more about Alba's reasons for opposing him: with the passage of time it becomes more and more evident that his judgment was correct. Beneath Pérez's charm, good looks, and quick intellect lay an egotistical cynicism that bordered on the sociopathic. Alba could parse a soul as well as any man, and it may be that he had caught some glimpse of the latent treachery, the love of intrigue for its own sake, and the fundamental lack of judgment that would ultimately result in disaster.

In the beginning Philip must have listened at least with one ear to the duke's warnings. He divided the secretariat of Gonzalo Pérez into two parts, giving half to Antonio and half to Zayas, but with the passage of time it was Antonio who became the indispensable man. This was primarily a tribute not to his very considerable talents but to his personality. Philip, for all his reserve and self-control, needed a confidant. When Eboli died Pérez, who seems to have resembled him in some respects, filled the void. By the time Alba returned from the Netherlands Pérez was on his way to becoming a true *privado*, or favorite, with almost unlimited access to the king.

This provided him with the means to exact vengeance for past injuries.

Alba's other major enemy was Eboli's widow, the formidable Doña Ana de Mendoza. One of the great beauties of the court whose black eye-patch seemed only to enhance her fascination, she was an accomplished intriguer with a ruthless contempt for all obstacles whenever her interests or desires were involved. Her association with Pérez was so close that they were thought, probably wrongly, to be lovers,[15] and her hatred for Alba bordered on the obsessive.

It is a measure of Alba's continuing security that these two accomplished little against him in the years immediately following his return. They and their allies indulged in small plots, but Pérez was chiefly restricted to displays of extreme rudeness, while La Eboli in an ill-advised theatrical gesture had entered a nunnery on the death of her husband, thus severely, if temporarily, restricting her effectiveness. Still, there was one point at which the duke remained vulnerable: the situation of his son Fadrique.

That this should be so requires an explanation, for vindictive as he sometimes appeared to be it is hard to believe that Philip would have persecuted a man so vigorously for a seduction attempted eight years before. Still, it is a measure of the king's wrath that upon returning to Spain Fadrique was once again exiled from court. His letters from this period, at first filled with bravado and questionable remarks about women, soon trail off into despair and a growing concern for his deteriorating health.[16] When in July, 1576, Philip had Fadrique removed to a stricter detention at the royal castle of Tordesillas, the prisoner no longer seemed to mind so long as his new residence proved less conducive to gout and fevers.[17]

This extraordinary severity was due at least in part to Pérez, who lost few opportunities to incite the king against him as a means of harassing Alba, but there were other causes as well. One of them appears to have been nothing more than a deep personal dislike that left Philip more responsive to innuendo than he might otherwise have been. It was a feeling shared by many, though its source is unclear. A great deal of material by and about Fadrique exists, but it leaves behind a curiously vague impression. From his portrait we know that he was shorter and heavier than his father, with staring, almost protruberant eyes and an air that is both dandyish and somehow disquieting. His letters reveal a clear style and a grandiose signature, but little else beyond the fact that he knew so little Latin that he could not read a letter written to him in that language.[18] Examination of his military career is unrewarding. His only independent commands, if they can be called that, were at Haarlem and at Mons for the few weeks before his father's arrival. In neither case can he be charged with incompetence, but it is equally difficult to find evidence of exceptional ability. That he knew the technical side of war seems obvious, and if his men did not love him neither do they appear to have hated or despised him. This is inoffensive enough as far as it goes, but one other fact must be noted: for a man of such prominence and with such powerful connections he seems to have utterly lacked friends or defenders.

After a lifetime under the thumb of his father it is hardly surprising that he failed to impress his contemporaries, but he was not especially pleasant or ingratiating. Alba could afford to be abrupt, condescending, and often difficult because for decades he had been virtually indispensable. Fadrique was far from indispensable, and his counterfeit of the paternal manner must have been intolerable. Even among the papers of his father's allies there are few words of praise or even sympathy for this man who, in retrospect, seems to have deserved at least a modicum of the latter.

This inability to win friends, together with the king's overt dislike, made him a perfect stalking-horse in the effort to undermine Alba. If at first there was no specific reason for persecuting him it was quickly supplied by Don Luis de Requesens. In the months after his arrival in the Netherlands Requesens discovered that his worst fears and misgivings had been unduly optimistic. The situation had deteriorated to the point where even a miracle of biblical proportions could not have saved it, and this meant that he could best use his time and energies to cover himself against the recriminations to come. To achieve this it was essential to paint the blackest possible picture of the ruins on which he was expected to build, and to find a scapegoat for the impending collapse. That scapegoat was Fadrique.

In a long circumstantial letter dated September 19, 1574, Requesens placed most of the blame for the disaster of Alba's reign squarely on the shoulders of his son, who had, he claimed, effectively dominated both the army and the administration from 1568 to 1573.[19] This charge, however preposterous, was made plausible by the fact that Alba in attempting to demonstrate his son's capabilities had given him effective command during the Holland campaign of 1572–1573, where his brutal conduct had greatly strengthened Dutch resistance. He had propelled him into other visible positions for similar reasons, and many Netherlanders believed, or affected to believe, that Fadrique was a sort of *éminence grise* raised to power by a doting and half-senile father. Requesens knew that Alba was anything but doting in either sense of the word, but he also knew that a direct attack on a national hero who was beloved by the soldiers and who embodied in his own person many of the cherished ideals of sixteenth-century Spain was likely to backfire. It was far safer to show the duke as a great captain blinded by paternal affection and to cast the blame on the universally disliked Fadrique.

This theory, reinforced by other communications from Requesens and a variety of Netherlanders, was inevitably a major factor in the continuing harassment of Fadrique, and the mainstay of Pérez's campaign of insinuation. It took the wily secretary a long time to achieve his ends, for he had to solidify his own position and find a suitable occasion for the coup, but in the end, through Fadrique, Pérez succeeded in destroying his rival. It is evidence of the complexity of the process that, like a spider caught in its own web, he managed at the same time to destroy himself.

No plot, of course, can exist in a vacuum. This one was integrally related to all the other schemes and counter-schemes at court. It was not until the summer of 1578 that it finally matured, and when it did so it was as the result of two other matters which, on the surface at least, seem unrelated.

The first of these was the murder of Don Juan of Austria's secretary Juan de Escobedo. After Requesens died in 1576, the hero of Lepanto was dispatched to the Netherlands as his successor. From the standpoint of public relations it seemed a brilliant choice, but in accepting the post Don Juan had purposes of his own that were to create endless difficulties. Handsome, imaginative, and charismatic, he had long chafed under the restrictions imposed by his brother and wanted, above all, a kingdom of his own and the coveted right to be addressed as "Your Highness." Though he knew he could never achieve such grandeur in the Netherlands, he went there in the hope of using his powers as governor-general to conquer England. Steeped, no doubt, in visions of his forthcoming coronation at Westminster Abbey, he began an elaborate series of negotiations with the pope, the French, and, of course, the English Catholics.

This was not treason, as Don Juan had every intention of laying the new realm at the foot of the throne, but it was a harebrained and exceedingly dangerous scheme that could only arouse Philip's suspicions. Pérez, as Eboli's successor, had long favored an invasion of England and actively conspired with Don Juan to that end, but for reasons that remain unclear he presented matters to the king in a very different light, while leaking confidential documents to both sides. When Don Juan finally discovered what was happening he sent Escobedo to Madrid in the hope of clearing himself—and, by so doing, brought Pérez into mortal danger. The secretary, knowing that revelation of his dealings would be fatal, denounced Escobedo to the king as the instigator of Don Juan's plot and, with Philip's approval, had him assassinated on March 31, 1578.

At this point an ordinary man would have wiped the sweat from his brow, breathed a sigh of relief, and resolved to step cautiously for a while, but Pérez was nothing if not unusual. It is a tribute to his capacity for self-delusion that he chose this of all moments to conclude that his position was inviolable. Was he not safe from exposure, and had he not managed to implicate the king in a political murder? Surely Philip would not dare to turn against him now. After twelve years of impatient waiting he at last felt free to settle accounts with the Duke of Alba.

In the midst of all this, another situation was developing that would trigger the prodigious wrath of Ana de Mendoza and spur the two conspirators to direct action. Five years after Eboli's death, his widow was still trying to settle the estates he had left her in Italy. One of her cherished projects was a campaign to exempt them from quartering troops, a burden that fell heavily on much of the kingdom of Naples. In a maneuver that typifies the way in which Philip used the factions to his own advantage he referred the matter to Alba, thus guaranteeing that it would fail.[21] Angry beyond measure and anxious to forestall a negative decision, Doña Ana decided to revive the case against Don Fadrique in a new and more compelling way.

For some years she had been in communication with Juan de Guzmán, the brother of the lady to whom Fadrique had proposed marriage in 1566. The lady herself, Doña Magdalena de Guzmán, had without apparent complaint spent the twelve intervening years in a convent, but on July 22, 1578, she wrote the first of a series of impassioned letters to the king, complaining bitterly of the injustice of her lot.[22] It was not entirely fortuitous. Someone—probably Pérez—had tested the water a month before, and the king had ordered some papers on the subject sent to Pazos, the president of the Council of Castile.[23]

The question remains as to what Pérez and Doña Ana were attempting to accomplish. At the very least they were maliciously creating an embarrassment, but they may also have been using the issue to blackmail Alba into a favorable decision on the Italian estates. They had set a terrible snare at his feet, but whether they knew this or whether they could have foreseen that he would rush headlong into it is doubtful.

Philip reacted to Doña Magdalena's demand that Fadrique be forced to marry her by appointing Pazos head of a commission to investigate the merits of her case. This placed the house of Toledo in a dangerous position, for it was entirely possible that the heir-apparent would be ordered to marry someone who could bring neither wealth nor influence to the family, or he might be prohibited from marrying anyone at all. The only way to forestall such a catastrophe was to present the king with a fait accompli by marrying Fadrique to someone else.

The chosen spouse was his cousin, Doña Maria de Toledo, daughter of the late Don García, Marqués of Villafranca. The idea of a marriage to Doña Maria was not new. Back in 1569, when Fadrique's situation first caused the duke to consider the future of his house, discussions were begun with Don García but quickly foundered on the threat of royal displeasure and on Alba's hectoring demands for an extravagant dowry.[24] In spite of this Doña Maria had been sent to Spain and had remained there ever since, in the hope that the various obstacles to the match could be overcome. Now that all hope of accommodation with Philip had vanished it seemed pointless to worry about his displeasure, and in the face of what he considered a direct threat to the survival of his lineage Alba was even ready to forego the pleasure of haggling over dowries.

Accordingly, on October 2, 1578, Fadrique left Tordesillas without royal permission and made his way to Madrid, where Alba, anticipating the king's wrath, drew up a kind of private *cédula* granting him permission to marry. The document was not intended primarily for Fadrique but for "His Majesty and the rest of the persons with whom it may be necessary to justify this deed."[25] For the moment, though, this justification was not to be made public. The couple were secretly married in Alba's house and Fadrique returned to Tordesillas as quietly as he had come.

Nothing, of course, remains quiet for long at the courts of princes. A few days after the wedding the indefatigable Juan de Guzmán reported the whole affair to Pazos, stating that his information came direct from the Princess of Eboli.[26] How the princess discovered the matter is unknown but it is probable that she had spies among Alba's household staff and used them on this occasion to extraordinary advantage. By October 17 the king knew the whole story and instructed Pazos to find out if it was true, "even though I cannot believe such a thing of the duke."[27]

The next few weeks were, for the president, decidedly trying. He had at least two interviews with Alba, perhaps more, and the duke was on his worst behavior. From the beginning he insisted, as he had in the *cédula*, that the king had authorized Fadrique's marriage as long ago as 1572. This apparently referred to an offhand comment in which Philip said that he ought eventually to get married! Then he wanted to know precisely what Philip had told Pazos. Pazos refused to say, as he had, on royal orders, refused a similar request from Juan de Guzmán.[28] On November 26, Alba came to him late at night "so full of complaints that one would need soft ears to hear them." He wanted to know when the king would finish with all this, reiterated his claim to have been given authorization, and equivocated about Fadrique's visit to Madrid. The old duke had by this time worked himself into a memorable state of dudgeon. Did the king really want his son and the heir to his estates to marry Doña Magdalena de Guzmán? Did he want to cut off all their heads? He ended by saying that the whole question should be remanded to an ecclesiastical court. Failing that, having already imprisoned Fadrique for twelve years, the king should simply behead the lot of them and have done with it.[29]

As subsequent events made clear, Pazos did not take these scenes personally, but he and his committee were now faced with something more serious than the vagaries of Don Fadrique. By arranging the marriage of his son to preempt a royal investigation Alba had committed what was at the very least a gross impertinence. His behavior since then had not been conciliatory and the king was understandably outraged. On December 22 the committee recommended that Alba should be imprisoned, and on January 1 this recommendation was endorsed by the king.

The place chosen for his exile was Uceda, a village some thirty miles northeast of Madrid. There is an air of remoteness about it even today, but it is not an unpleasant place. Perched on the bluffs above the Jarama, it boasted a magnificent view and a castle owned by the Archbishop of Toledo, since totally destroyed. In this castle Alba was to remain for an entire year.

Contemporaries were shocked at this treatment of an old and trusted servant, and speculation as to the reasons for it abounded. Alba's offense was admittedly an attack on Philip's jealously guarded authority, and it is possible that his imprisonment was no more than an expression of the king's righteous anger. On the other hand, broader considerations may have been involved. Cabrera de Córdoba said that the king was tired of Alba's *demasiada suficiencia*,[30] and it is evident that Antonio Pérez did what he could to worsen the situation. At this point many historians have considered the question settled, but it is at least possible that Alba's fall was no more an affair of pique than of factional politics. It certainly marked the beginning of a fundamental change in the inner workings of Philip's government.

It is significant that while Pazos dealt with Alba and Fadrique he was also investigating more serious charges against Pérez. Escobedo's relatives had begun to demand an inquiry into his death, and as Philip learned more about it he began to realize that Pérez had duped him. Philip would not hesitate to have a man stabbed by ruffians in a city street, but that the man should be guiltless and that he, Philip, should have been tricked by his own favorite into committing an unjustifiable homicide was intolerable.

Then there was the matter of Portugal. On August 4, 1578, Dom Sebastian, King of Portugal, was killed, together with much of the Portuguese nobility, on a witless crusade in North Africa.[31] He left no heirs in the direct line, and as Philip was the son of Isabella of Portugal he felt that he had a viable claim to the throne. To ensure the success of his candidacy he embarked on a series of excruciatingly delicate negotiations with the Portuguese only to discover that, once again, Pérez appeared to be undermining him.

The point of these intrigues has been lost. They seem to have had something to do with putting the Duchess of Bragança on the throne and marrying her son to one of Eboli's daughters,[32] a scheme so naive and at the same time so devious as to boggle the imagination. Whatever their purpose, they were brought to the attention of the king by Mateo Vázquez, Pérez's rival in the secretariat and an established conduit for the complaints of the Escobedos. It is therefore unlikely that in ordering Alba's arrest the king was seduced to any noticeable degree by Pérez, for by July, 1578, the secretary's charm had worn very thin. Instead, as he began to uncover the treacheries of Pérez, the ongoing machinations against Alba may have suggested the means by which he could forever rid himself of both factions.

Caution is always advisable in searching out the motives of Philip II, but there is no reason to assume that he was at any time the simple pawn of his courtiers. The factions had served a real purpose for many years. They had ensured the presentation of divergent views and enabled the king to repudiate policies without accepting personal blame for their failures, but by 1578 they had ceased to function. The Ebolistas had apparently intrigued with both the Dutch rebels and the opponents of Philip's claim to the throne of Portugal, while Alba's usefulness as an advisor had been much attenuated by his utter predictability.

In short, it was all but essential to root out the factions, and for the first time in his long reign Philip was in a position to do so without damaging his administration. Since 1573 he had developed a nucleus of officials who, like Mateo Vázquez and Pazos himself, were not aligned with either group; Vázquez in particular had already reached a position of eminence. This is not to say that the demise of the factions resulted from a sudden or even conscious decision; it came about, rather, from an awareness of the necessity for change and the gradual emergence of the means by which that change could be effected. It appears in retrospect that by the summer of 1579 Philip was prepared to govern through his own men, and this goes far toward explaining his conduct.

It should now be possible to weave from this skein of cross-purposes a plausible, if largely conjectural, explanation for Alba's imprisonment. The king's dislike for Don Fadrique, reinforced by accusations that he was responsible for much of the trouble in the Netherlands, opened the door to Pérez, who used it for purposes of his own. Feeling secure as a result of Escobedo's murder, the secretary, together with Ana de Mendoza, raised the ghost of Doña Magdalena and caused Philip to launch an investigation of her charges. Meanwhile the king, suspicious by nature and encouraged by the information supplied by Vázquez, began to unravel the tangled affairs of Pérez himself. Finding nothing but treachery and impertinence on every hand, it dawned upon him that the factional system had outlived its usefulness and he resolved to destroy it—beginning with Fadrique. Pazos, who knew nothing of all this, was inclined toward lenience,[33] but the king would not hear of it. So determined was he to destroy Fadrique that he was even prepared to bring charges arising out of the latter's conduct in Flanders if the less sensitive marriage issue failed to achieve the desired result.[34] Under these circumstances Alba's disobedience, or something like it, may or may not have been foreseen, but it was certainly welcome. It provided Philip with the excuse he needed to rid himself of Alba. Pérez's turn came later. On the night of July 28, 1579, Pérez and

Doña Ana were arrested at their respective homes, never to return to court. The age of faction, if not of intrigue, was over.

Ironically, Pazos and Vázquez, the chief beneficiaries of this shift, seem to have remained unaware of what was happening. Instead, the growing signs that Pérez, too, would be arrested led to their first efforts to secure Alba's release. The duke was disliked by many who knew him personally, but in the country as a whole he was a popular man. On June 9, 1579, Pazos advised the king that the Cortes had requested his pardon. On July 6, at the suggestion of the *junta*, Fadrique, who had been transferred to the Mota of Medina del Campo after his marriage, was released to a private home.[35] At last, on October 15, long after the arrests of Pérez and Doña Ana, Pazos and his commission found the courage to ask for Alba's release under their own names. Philip brusquely replied that he had no time to consider the matter at present.[36]

It is evident that these political "neutrals" believed that with Pérez out of the way they could safely respond to a growing chorus of complaint over the treatment of a man widely regarded as a hero.[37] It is also possible that they saw in the secretary's arrest just another turn of the factional wheel and were protecting themselves against an uncertain future. In any case, their efforts were unavailing until the decision to invade Portugal provided them with a compelling excuse to free the old *caudillo*.

Dom Sebastian had been succeeded on the throne of Portugal by his ancient, infirm, and celibate uncle the Cardinal Henrique. On January 31, 1580, the cardinal, having lived longer than anyone had expected, passed to a better world in which few Spanish ambassadors could be expected to trouble him. Before doing so he had reached an agreement with Philip's emissary, Cristóbal de Moura, on a transfer of power to the king of Spain under conditions that would leave Portuguese institutions virtually intact. The Spaniards had done their work well, and this bequest had the support of the remaining Portuguese nobility. It was, however, extremely unpopular with the lower orders, and a grassroots movement on behalf of Antonio, the Prior of Crato, quickly developed. The prior was a bastard of the royal house, charming but not particularly able, and the revolt on his behalf was a rather disorganized affair. Nevertheless, it meant that the country would have to be pacified if Philip's succession was to be assured.

This was an embarrassment. There was no question this time of staying home. Philip would have to go in person, and he had no one to supervise the administration in his absence. His half-brother

Don Juan had died of the plague after the failure of his scheme to conquer England. His secretaries, though able, lacked the status for the job: the most prominent of them, Mateo Vázquez, was the son of a woman redeemed from Moorish captivity and a father whose identity remains uncertain.[38] In this extremity the king turned once more to a relic of the Golden Age. On the very day that Pérez was imprisoned, Cardinal Granvelle, now sixty-two, arrived in Madrid to take up the reins of government.

The other half of Philip's problem involved the army. At the field-commander level Spain had talent in abundance, but as a result of the withdrawal of the grandees from active participation in military life few of them had sufficient experience to lead an army of occupation. When his decision to invade Portugal became known Philip was inundated with requests that Alba be named to command the royal armies.[39] Not only was his competence unquestioned but he was enormously popular with the soldiers, and the presence of such a renowned commander would, in the words of the Venetian ambassador, assuage the "vanity" of the Portuguese.[40] In less picturesque terms, Philip's emissaries had secured the support of the Portuguese nobility, and the appointment of Alba would give them an excuse to surrender with minimal loss of face.

Granvelle has been widely credited with orchestrating this campaign, but his involvement is open to question.[41] Though he had once been an ally of the duke, their relationship had cooled after Alba opposed the incorporation of the Brabant abbeys into the archdiocese of Mechelen in 1568. If Granvelle supported him—and there is no documentary evidence to verify this—it was only because he wanted a speedy solution to the Portuguese question. In his own way he was worse than Alba, for he saw Portugal as little more than an excuse to divert resources from the Netherlands.[42]

The real burden of the argument was carried by Pazos and Vázquez, but the king resisted as long as he could. If the rest of our hypothesis is correct, he did so primarily because he feared that Alba's release would revive the factions. There was little doubt that the campaign would be successful, and success would inevitably increase the duke's already enormous prestige. Worse yet, the command would increase his patronage, thereby arousing the remaining Ebolistas to further intrigue. After all, the Princess of Eboli had teenaged sons, and her Mendoza relatives were as hungry as ever. Only if the leaderships of both factions were suppressed equally could he expect to be free of them.

Alternative explanations for the king's behavior come to mind, but they are not convincing. He might have been concerned to demonstrate that his authority remained intact, but this had already been accomplished by the arrest, and further persecution could only serve to make him appear petty and vindictive. Perhaps he knew that the imprisonment had become a *cause célèbre* and felt that he could not abandon his stance without some pretext other than political expedience. Pazos evidently thought of this and tried to justify Alba's release by belatedly impugning the testimony of Doña Magdalena. On January 7, 1580, he told the king that she was now claiming to have had sexual relations with Don Fadrique, which was, he said, a manifest lie as she had never made such claims before.[43] It was Pazos who lied, for the lady had from the very beginning hinted at secrets so dark that they had to be concealed even from her confessor.[44]

The king remained adamant. Finally, with time running out and no other candidate available, he summoned Alba to the staging point at Badajoz. He did so tardily and with the worst possible grace, refusing the duke so much as an interview, because he wanted the world to see that though Alba had been recalled he had not been restored to favor. Alba, by contrast, answered the call promptly and with expressions of undiminished loyalty, an exemplary response consistent with his behavior throughout. Though an heroic complainer in ordinary circumstances he had this time issued only a dignified apology and left the king's behavior to speak for itself in the forum of public opinion.[45] Philip's treatment of Alba had indeed been shabby, though not entirely irrational, and Alba's grace when confronted with manifest injustice does much to explain his historical reputation for nobility of character.

Perhaps, too, the year at Uceda had not been entirely unpleasant. The duke was now seventy-two years old. In his conscious mind he had never enjoyed life at court, and in many ways he remained a countryman at heart. He relished the clean air, the sparkling streams, and the slow pace of village life to a degree that baffled most of his contemporaries. His duchess, to his considerable delight, had been permitted to accompany him, and if his communications with the outside world tended to be few and laconic they were not especially despairing. The best index to Alba's state of mind was invariably his physical health, and at Uceda it seems to have been unusually good. His only recorded ailment was an affliction of the chest so minor that he was able to conceal it from the duchess. She was, it seems, as vigorous and inclined to drastic measures in medical questions as on other matters, and the Iron Duke feared her solicitude.[46]

But if he made the best of his exile he was ready to rise and depart by February, 1580. The king's order, however grudging, was an admission of real need and the prospect of one last campaign was too compelling to resist. To be once again indispensable was flattering to a man in his seventies. More important, it invoked the tradition handed down to him by his grandfather and to which he had devoted his life. He might, as he is supposed to have said, have been "sent in chains to subjugate kingdoms,"[47] but he would command, and that, according to his whole conception of himself, was a God-given right and obligation.

XIV

PORTUGAL

The annexation of Portugal was one of Philip II's greatest achievements. The dream of unifying the Peninsula and with it the two great seaborne empires of Spain and Portugal survived its author by only forty-two years, but it was brought into being with a subtlety and precision worthy of a longer life. Unfortunately, the brilliance of Moura's effort to secure the succession without bloodshed has beguiled historians into thinking that the military campaign was unimportant. As Alfonso Danvila puts it: "Portugal was thus gained by letters, and arms were only an accident motivated by the rebellion of the Prior of Crato, a glorious accident to be sure, but one that came to destroy in part the designs of Philip II." For him, Alba's last campaign was thus "a prodigious military parade," the greatness of which lay "in the magisterial organization of the troops and the exactitude with which they complied with the orders of their chief."[1] The first part of this judgment embodies a classic historical fallacy. Like it or not, Don Antonio's rebellion did occur, and had it not been suppressed Philip could never have ascended the throne. As far as the second part is concerned, it is perhaps well that Alba never heard it—he would not have known whether to laugh or cry.

The many misconceptions that surround the Portuguese campaign of 1580 are based on the idea that Don Antonio's revolt was doomed from the start. This is true enough as far as it goes, but the process of securing his doom was remarkably complicated. The de-

283

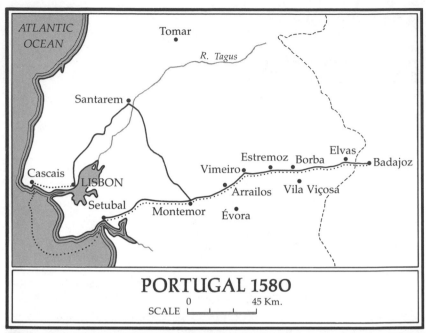

PORTUGAL 1580

SCALE 0   45 Km.

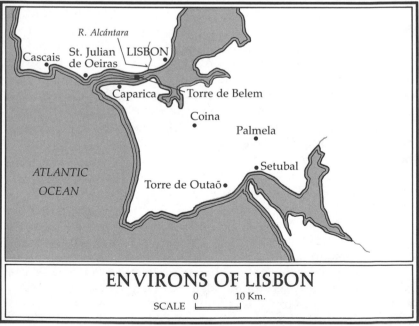

ENVIRONS OF LISBON

SCALE 0   10 Km.

Map 7.

feat of whatever field army he might be able to muster was not the problem nor was the capture of his person, for he escaped in the end without causing Philip more than minor irritation. The heart of the task was to accomplish all this while at the same time establishing a foreign army of occupation that could hold the towns without further alienating the people. Alba had studied this subject in the hard school of the Netherlands, and it is a measure of his flexibility that he did not make the same mistakes again.

His first concern, though, was not the hearts and minds of the Portuguese but the feet and stomachs of the Spanish army. As he rode away from Uceda his mind was occupied with problems of recruitment and provisioning that would have taxed the resources of any kingdom. The army would in the nature of things have to be large. The king was thinking of at least three forces. One, under Alba's command, would cross into Portugal from Extremadura, traverse the Alentejo, and rendezvous at the seacoast with another brought by sea from Seville by Don Alvaro de Bazán, Marqués of Santa Cruz. A third, smaller, army under the Duke of Medina Sidonia would attempt to occupy the Algarve.

Alba's army was intended to comprise about 50,000 men, a necessity if garrisons were to be established en route but the source of virtually insoluble logistic problems. There were probably not 50,000 experienced troops in the whole empire, even if the garrisons in Flanders and Italy were wholly abandoned. This meant that the complement would be made up of new recruits seasoned with a handful of veteran units and supplemented by German and Italian mercenaries. It took little imagination to see that, in a situation that called for total discipline, such a horde would be almost uncontrollable. The king thought to forestall this by mixing veterans of the Army of Flanders into the new units but Alba objected vehemently and won his point. He knew that individually his "sons" were no more controllable than anyone else. Indeed, many of them were the kind of out-and-out cutthroats that can be produced only by fifteen years of bitter warfare in a hostile land. Their famed discipline came not from their character but from the cohesiveness of the old *tercios*. It would be far better to keep them together for use in situations where recruits would fall apart, and otherwise hope for the best.[2]

He need not have worried. The contingent from Flanders failed to arrive in time, and it began to look as though there would not even be enough recruits. Five years earlier Alba had noted that almost 80,000 men had been sent out of the country since 1567, not counting those who had gone to the Indies. This was an example of the duke at his worst, for his private figures showed the actual number to be 42,875,[3] but he was making a valid point. The usable manpower reserves of Castile had been seriously depleted, and last-minute efforts in the great estates along the Portuguese border could be expected to yield little. Extremadura and the old kingdom of León had already done their part and more.

Even if men could be found, the problem of supporting them in the field remained. The final staging point for the invasion was Badajoz, a small city in an uncommonly barren district. Feeding such a multitude was utterly beyond the resources of Extremadura and its adjoining regions; all supplies would have to be brought long distances and at great expense. To make matters worse, there would be no hope of living off the land once the army was in Portugal. Foraging was out of the question for political reasons, but even if it had been permitted the results would have been meager. In terms of its wealth and productivity the Alentejo is an extension of Extremadura. The Spanish army would have to carry with it nearly every morsel of food it expected to consume between Badajoz and the sea.[4] It is perhaps understandable that before turning westward Alba paid a pious visit to the undecomposed remains of San Diego de Alcalá.[5]

His fretful mood came partly from an attack of gout and partly because after his year of exile he felt "like a man that comes from another world, new to this one."[6] Above all he disliked the confusion and lack of direction that seemed to prevail in every aspect of the preparations. By the time he arrived in Extremadura his health had improved and he was "working like a twenty-year-old,"[7] but his concern over provisions never left him.

His old purveyor and commissary-general, Francisco de Ibarra, had retired, and his place was taken by the Marqués de Auñón. Alba thought Auñón incompetent and eventually arranged for the appointment of the *alcalde*, Fernando Pareja de Peralta, to serve as his deputy.[8] This created a divided office, and to make matters worse much of the real responsibility lay far away at Seville in the able but overworked hands of Francisco Duarte. Duarte was factor of the Casa de Contratación and commissary-general of Andalusia and was responsible not only for the bulk of Alba's provisions but for the annual *flota* as well. In these circumstances coordination was inevitably poor. At one point, having received a letter from Duarte that had him "in the greatest confusion and fear in the land,"[9] Alba tried to take control himself. With his normal impatience and encyclopedic grasp of detail he sat down and drafted a long letter to the king in which he described the provisions needed, the districts from which they were to come, and even the tactics to be used in dealing with local officials.[10]

Undeniably, the system was a bad one. Anxious to keep matters in his own hands and avoid corruption, Philip had at first refused to deal with sutlers,[11] but he failed to provide a unified administration of his own. The duke was terrified lest "we . . . wall ourselves in with hunger, and with our disorder, give our enemies the arms to undo us,"[12] but, ironically, the result was the opposite of what he feared. A golden rain descended on Extremadura. Thanks to an enthusiastic but disorganized commissariat food came from every direction: whole districts of Andalusia were depleted, and garrisons as far away as Peñón and Ibiza found themselves on short rations. By the time he left Alba had enough food to carry him until February, 1581, and a considerable surplus had to be sold off at bargain prices to the ecstatic citizens of Llerena and Badajoz.[13]

The difference, perhaps, was that there was now no Ruy Gómez or Eraso to undermine him. Portugal was the king's own project in a way that Italy or the Netherlands had never been, and he was determined to provide whatever was required. Personally, he continued to treat Alba with great coldness, but no one dared to divert resources to other projects or stand in the way of preparations except through stupidity. This could sometimes reach exalted heights, as when Spanish customs officers tried to prevent delivery of provisions to the army in Portugal because no one had paid duty on them,[14] but in general things went well. If Alba needed money it often arrived in three days.[15] If he wanted someone appointed to a particular job it was generally done according to his wish. Typically, he did not abuse the privilege. Though he was troubled by accusations of nepotism he was clearly right to insist on his son Hernando's appointment as master of the mounted arquebusiers,[16] and he was equally wise to block the appointment of Juan de Tejada as auditor-general. He argued that Tejada, as an *alcalde*, was ineligible for the post,[17] but his real concern was the man's utter rigidity and lack of common sense. Tejada remained an *alcalde* and within weeks was threatening to flog the sutlers Alba had gone to such trouble to attract.[18] None of these was a major issue, but there was a time when they might have been. The duke, at seventy-two, had outlived his enemies.

This was fortunate. Supplies were abundant and behind-the-lines intrigue minimal, but the troops were even worse than expected and the road more difficult than anyone had foreseen. As always, Alba attempted to forestall the worst of his difficulties by careful planning, but his success was only relative. To cope with the untrained rustics who comprised most of his army he turned the encampment into a vast military academy[19] and secured the appointment of Juan de Bolea as provost. Bolea, who had served him in Flanders, had a reputation as a harsh disciplinarian. There was much opposition to his appointment, but Alba overrode it, citing the need for absolute control. Looting and disorder could turn the Portuguese into implacable enemies of the Crown.[20] He brought in experts on Portugal and conferred with them far into the night while his engineer, Gian Battista Antonelli, scoured the countryside, sending back ominous reports on the state of the roads.[21]

On June 13, Philip came to review the troops.[22] Two weeks later the vast throng began its laborious march into Portugal. There were in all some 40,000 men, though—as always—the precise number is open to question. The vast majority, some 33,000, were infantry and there were 136 guns, but cavalry were deliberately in short supply as they were thought not to be needed. To supply them an immense baggage train had been gathered, and the endless lines of creeping oxcarts held progress to a crawl. What with the baggage, the carts, and the new recruits, Alba felt that if they were attacked on the road the results would be disastrous.[23]

Fortunately, the march was without incident. Don Antonio remained far away at Santarem, and the defense of the Alentejo was entrusted to the youthful and inexperienced Don Diego de Meneses. Too many of those Portuguese who might have known what to do lay dead under the brazen skies of Africa. Elvas, only a few miles from Badajoz, surrendered without incident. At Estremoz, on July 3, the local *alcalde* tried to resist, but the citizens quite sensibly ignored him and the town was taken without bloodshed.[24]

By this time the Spanish were beginning to understand the nature of their enterprise. Even today there is a faintly ominous character to Portugal's eastern marches. The Alentejo in summer is a vast, silent emptiness dotted only occasionally with poor towns that seem deserted in the noonday heat. Water is scarce and the cork oaks provide little relief from the murderous sun. At the best of times it would have been a grim journey, but in the summer of 1580 a dread presence lurked wherever travelers sought relief from heat and thirst. The plague, like the Spaniards, had come to Portugal.

The exact nature of this *catarra*, as it was called, is unknown. It was probably not a form of the Black Death but of influenza, for many of its victims recovered and those who died did so after a lingering ailment resembling pneumonia. Still, the mortality rate was high among populations weakened by successive bad harvests, and in the months to come its impact was locally devastating.

Like all the soldiers of his time Alba knew that disease was his greatest enemy, and his letters are redolent of concern. "I would not dare to send His Majesty even a thread of cloth from that castle [Vila Viçosa] considering the little health the town has."[25] "Keep His Majesty away from Borba, it is the most infected place on this frontier."[26] "I go with great anxiety because the road that I thought to take to avoid Arraiolos is, they tell me, so closed that in ten days the carts could not go four leagues . . . and thus I come to pass a league from the said Arraiolos and two from Evora, where they tell me that from one end to the other the hills are full of *hombres apestados*."[27] On the day after they passed through this valley of the shadow many fell sick, and Albornoz wrote, "God be with us as we go in fear,"[28] but after the first fright it was seen that no new cases developed.[29] The epidemic would ultimately have its victory, and many of those who marched with Alba died of it before the year was out, but as long as they kept to the open road they were safe if not comfortable.

The greatest problem was morale. Desertions increased as the men marched through this silent wasteland with unseen horrors at every side, and for some days, the heat and the condition of the roads caused almost as much anxiety as the plague. Frustration reached a peak of sorts on the day before Alba's arrival at Montemor. "Yesterday was a terrible day of heat and of bad roads, and very long, and many carts broken."[30] Indeed, "the oxcarts break as if they were made of twigs."[31] "Since I was born I have never seen country so rough; they have ruts so broad and so deep and so hard that they seem to be frozen as at Christmas." Each day as the march ended he had to send back a hundred of the lighter mule-drawn carts to collect the food left behind as the oxcarts broke down, and he was beginning to wonder if they would have enough carrying capacity to take them to the coast.[32]

Alba did not fear the Portuguese themselves. As he approached Montemor he dispatched an inquiry to the king that is almost offensive in its arrogance. "If by any chance Don Diego Meneses is so crazy as to want to try to defend himself in Montemor, I beg Your

Majesty to order me forthwith what I am to do with him, and with those that are found with him therein, so that I will know how to govern myself."[33] This is so typical of Alba that it deserves closer examination. The insult to the Portuguese is real but it veils a far sharper barb directed at the king. From the start Philip had kept him on a short leash, probably fearing that he would repeat the atrocities of the Netherlands if left to his own devices, and Alba resented it. He knew perfectly well that the situation required tact, and was behaving more moderately than anyone could have believed.

His conduct in Portugal, a marked contrast to what he had done in the Netherlands, was the product not of senescence but of policy. From the start he had insisted that Portugal was the king's by right of inheritance and that any resistance to his coming was rebellion. To accept anything less would be to acknowledge the legitimacy of Don Antonio. He was therefore leery of Moura and his plan to have Philip confirmed by the Portuguese Cortes, and was disinclined to accept Portuguese assurances at face value.[34]

In other words, he was as uncompromising as ever in theory, but his actions displayed extreme sensitivity to Portuguese opinion. To the astonishment of those who knew him, he had already spared the fire-eating *alcalde* of Estremoz, saying that "the laws of war would well permit beheading, but this people is so remote from the customs of it that they would think it was the rigor of the laws of Castile."[35] At Evora he refused to confiscate rents, depositing them instead until the courts should determine their legal disposition. Then he released all the prisoners in the jail.[36]

The real touchstone of his policy was security. If the safety of his army was not in question he was prepared to tolerate almost anything. On July 6 he came to the gates of Montemor and found that Don Diego de Meneses had indeed fled. The townspeople surrendered, claiming that their previous allegiance was the fault of "a boy from Arraiolos" about whom no further particulars could be given, but they remained armed. The situation made Alba nervous. He suggested to the king that the populace should be disarmed and a garrison of 300 Spaniards placed in the town.[37] Philip replied that this was too harsh. He had no objection to the garrison, as Montemor was the crossroads of the region and of considerable strategic importance, but he thought that the people should keep their arms and an *alcalde* of their own. If security were a problem Alba could always seek out and punish the chief supporters of Don Antonio. An example was needed.[38] It is a tribute to his newfound clemency that

Alba chose to ignore this. Philip told him to use his own judgment and in the end he not only left them their arms and their *alcalde* but pardoned the lot. He believed that all "the crimes that touch Your Majesty" should be pardoned, unless, of course, they are "ugly or atrocious."[39]

This was certainly a change from his days in the Netherlands but it was not due to any softening of character. Privately, he thought the Portuguese authorities were "highwaymen" and "murderers,"[40] and when his own troops erred they were treated as harshly as ever. Within two days of crossing the border he hanged one soldier for stealing a bundle of wheat and another for mistreating a sutler.[41] This pattern, too, would continue throughout the campaign, for he was still the terrible old man of years past and if he spared civilians it was only because his circumstances were very different from what they had been in 1572. He was not cut off from support or facing the collapse of six years of bitter effort, and the Portuguese were both Iberians like himself and good Catholics. It is also just possible that he had learned his lesson. Some months later he was genuinely hurt when the supporters of Don Antonio called him cruel.

From Montemor he moved on toward his rendezvous with the fleet at Setúbal. This in itself was a matter for concern as he did not know where Santa Cruz was, and feared, correctly, that he was taking "sentry boxes" in the Algarve.[42] Aside from thinking this a waste of time he knew that the pestilence lay heaviest there and that the fleet would inevitably be infected.[43] It was a classic case of interservice misunderstanding. Alba, who had by this time decided to eat the oxen, as they were accomplishing nothing on the road,[44] cared only for his supply lines.[45] The overland route was worse than he had expected and he wanted to open regular communications by sea as soon as possible. Santa Cruz, on the other hand, had nightmares about trying to double Cape St. Vincent in a westerly gale. His fragile galleys and unwieldy supply ships would not last long on a lee shore; he needed places for them to ride out a storm without interference. In this case the sailor was probably right, but it was with growing anxiety that Alba approached the walls of Setúbal.

When he arrived before the town on the evening of July 16 there was no sign of the fleet. A handful of Portuguese warships lay peacefully at anchor amid the remaining merchant vessels, and the city gates were closed. That night, to the accompaniment of sporadic arquebus fire, the Spaniards surrounded the place and on the morning of the seventeenth Don Hernando de Toledo called upon the inhabitants to surrender. After some delay an Englishman, of all people, emerged to ask for a twenty-four-hour delay and to hear from Alba's own lips a response molded in the bloody ditches of Holland. He would, he said, "cut all their throats and not leave stone on stone." With that, he began to place his artillery.

But Setúbal was not to be another Haarlem. Within its walls a lively debate was taking place between the townspeople and the soldiers, most of whom were foreigners. The townspeople had overthrown their pro-Spanish governor and were prepared for an heroic defense, notwithstanding the fact that their town was totally indefensible. Its walls pre-dated the use of gunpowder, but it would scarcely have mattered had they been modern. The city lies along the shore of a spacious bay, with hills rising above it on the landward side. From those hills Alba's guns could fire directly into its crowded streets with little fear of retaliation either from artillery or infantry, who would have had to charge uphill against entrenched positions. The soldiers knew this very well and were doing their best to convert the citizens; hence the delay.

At about 6:00 P.M. the Englishman returned with a civilian named Don Simón Miranda and offered to surrender the city on the following morning. Alba agreed and sat back to await events. They were soon in coming, though the Spaniards, resting armed and quiet in their camps, missed the best of it. At some point in the evening the townspeople tried, unsuccessfully, to lynch Miranda as a collaborator. Shortly after midnight, the foreigners left, some boarding a ship in the harbor, others more foolishly taking the road to Lisbon. Daylight and the defection of the only trained soldiers among them brought even the enthusiasts to their senses. Looking up at the yawning muzzles of the Spanish guns, they surrendered.[46]

It was the signal for Alba's troops, as he put it, "to baptize disorders." They were, after all, untrained recruits who had just endured a wretched march. The previous night had seen sporadic looting among the houses outside the walls, but in the course of pursuing the foreign troops some of them ran completely amok. "They have hanged and are hanging so many that I think they have run out of rope, and I go making all the efforts that are possible to me in the world for the remedy, and look upon the disorders here with great anxiety, for though it be but a grain of wheat, for me it is made into a tower."[47] Fortunately, none of those killed was Portuguese, but Alba was right to worry about what his men might do in the weeks to come.

The campaign had reached its critical phase. He had brought his army through plague and thirst and the wreckage of their oxcarts, but he still had to take Lisbon, and this required mature consideration. The geographic obstacles alone were formidable. For several days he contemplated them while his men subdued the surrounding countryside. It was not an uneventful period, for Prospero Colonna took three days to capture the Torre de Outaō at the mouth of the harbor and would have taken longer had not Santa Cruz arrived at long last with the fleet and pounded the place into submission.[48] Then there were the machinations of a local Portuguese named Martín Gonzales. This Gonzales first tried to defend the bake ovens at Coina by promising freedom to several hundred Negro slaves if they would hold off Hernando de Toledo and Sancho Dávila. Then he attempted germ warfare by having a poor man of Palmela distribute infested clothes to the invading troops. Though Alba was alert to this sort of thing and later accused the Portuguese of poisoning the wine,[49] he was mortally offended by the business with the Negroes. He never explained it in so many words but he apparently felt that their miserable status should not have been exploited to send them to a pointless death. The seventy brave souls who actually stood their ground against the *tercios* were let go, and even the ragpicking angel of death was let off with a warning.[50] As no one else would have cared what happened to these wretched folk, this was not politics but simple decency.

Finally, on July 27, the duke gathered his officers and reached a consensus on what to do next.[51] That he did not simply issue them their orders is a measure of the risk they were about to take. As he described it to the king, there were three possible ways to attack Lisbon. The worst involved marching back toward Montemor and then north to the crossing of the Tagus at Santarem. This was not only a longer march than the one that had brought them from Badajoz but it required boats small enough to navigate upstream, and of these he had none.[52] The second was more direct and outwardly easier, but Alba felt that it might prove more dangerous. He could march straight to the entrance of Lisbon's harbor and be ferried across somewhere in the neighborhood of the Torre de Belem. The crossing might be managed by the fleet, but this meant that Santa Cruz would have to be confined for many hours in a narrow channel covered by shore batteries. As Alba was sure that the pilots would be drunk, the scheme was unthinkable.

In the end the course they adopted was outwardly the most hazardous of all, but in proposing it Alba showed that he could be as daring and imaginative as he was normally pedantic. Leaving his guns and some of the troops behind, he would sail from Setúbal and make a landing on the beach at Cascais. Once he was established there the rest of his train could be brought up at leisure and he would march to Lisbon along the shore, taking the batteries as he went. Unfortunately, the beach at Cascais was small, stony, and open to the Atlantic. It was also under the guns of a citadel located in the town. Ordinarily, such difficulties would have been prohibitive, but the garrison at Cascais was unprepared and the distance from Setúbal was short enough for Santa Cruz to pick his weather, a major advantage in operations off a lee shore.

The very next day, July 28, Santa Cruz judged that conditions were right and the expeditionary force crawled out to sea. The landsmen aboard must have been furious, for it took three miserable days of beating to windward to reach Cascais, but Santa Cruz had chosen wisely. A wind off the land was a blessing not to be ignored.

Dawn on July 30 found them within sight of their goal. Wind and sea had moderated, but though they were not expected their opponents were awake and the Spaniards could hear the warning guns of Cascais answered by those of San Julian at the bar of the Tagus. Seeing that the beach itself was covered by the citadel Alba decided to disembark at the Marina Viejo, just out of range in the direction of Estoril.[53] He himself was on the beach before more than six hundred of his men had landed, and it is said that when someone later reproached him for taking unnecessary risks he answered only that the present enemy was inept "and one ought to give something to fortune when there is no risk."[54]

The enemy in question was none other than Don Diego de Meneses, whose uninspired performance in the Alentejo had caused him to be sidelined to a place of relative safety. Certain that he was doomed, he resolved upon an heroic defense and actually managed to hold out for two days. The thirtieth and thirty-first were largely devoted to the process of landing, but by August 1 all was in place and Alba even had a few of his guns brought up at the last moment from Setúbal. The siege was brief. Cascais was no better fortified than most Portuguese towns and a breach was quickly opened in the walls of the citadel. The engineer Antonelli rolled barrels of sand into the foss to level it, and by 6:00 P.M. the garrison surrendered. They were few in number and had no desire to commit suicide on behalf of Don Diego de Meneses, who was found later hiding in the innermost recesses of the castle.[55]

At this point the greatest single blot on Alba's conduct of the campaign occurred. On the day after the surrender he summarily hanged the wretched Meneses, but this was perhaps forgivable—the young man was a persistent and irreconcilable enemy of the king and even royal mercy cannot be infinite.[56] At the same time, however, Alba seems to have lost control over his troops. Cascais was ransacked to its foundations, and in the words of one of his critics: "The disorder of the soldiers of this army in sacking and robbing without consideration of friends or enemies is so great that I fear some great punishment of God; and it is certain the duke does all he can and is possible in a man of his age, but . . . the duke orders it and desires it, but it is not done."[57]

Alba did not deny it. As he told the king, "indiscipline runs from the colonels on down," making it almost impossible to eradicate.[58] He knew that political necessity demanded savage punishments, and he was quick to hang several Spaniards, imprison others, and send more than fifty to the galleys, but privately he thought the policy unjust. His men were entitled by immemorial custom to the goods of rebels, and though he would never concede it publicly he understood their actions.[59] This internal conflict, coupled with an attack of gout and fever, turned the week after his victory into an agonizing ordeal. Too sick to stand, he tried to restore order and supervise the landing of supplies from a litter, but the process consumed six full days. He was also worried about the future. They were now within striking distance of Lisbon, but he hoped against hope that they would not have to besiege it. The city was too large and too well situated to fall immediately, and his troops were obviously not trustworthy. Would they hold up to a long, bitter siege without deserting, and even if they did what might they do when the place finally surrendered? So appalling was this thought that Alba tried to open talks with Don Antonio on his own initiative, but nothing came of it.[60] On August 8 he marched off to attack the fortress of St. Julian de Oeiras.

St. Julian was the first of the two fortifications that controlled the sea approach to Lisbon. It fell on August 12.[61] The second was that most charming of castles, the wedding-cake Torre de Belem. It, too, fell, but only after a comic-opera scenario that lasted until August 23. Part of the problem was Alba, who spent days in writing to Don Antonio, begging the king to grant a general pardon to the citizens of Lisbon and otherwise trying to avoid bloodshed.[62] The rest was due to the unenviable position of the Portuguese *alcalde*. The poor man wanted to surrender but could not bring himself to do so as he was caught between two fleets, that of Don Antonio immediately upstream and that of Santa Cruz immediately below. His solution to this dilemma was a model of its kind.

Santa Cruz first demanded the *alcalde*'s surrender on August 17, just as he was receiving the commandant of the Pretender's fleet. Thinking quickly, the *alcalde* sent a courteous refusal in his name and, to make sure his position was fully understood, his guest's as well. Then with magnificent defiance he fired a single shot at the Spaniards, being careful to ensure that the cannon was not loaded. Santa Cruz immediately got the point. He dispatched a frigate whose crew returned fire in the form of a few arquebus shots and "many ugly words," and let him alone for six more days.[63]

In the meantime Alba moved forward. On August 21 he camped in the level area between the tower and the monastery of Belem. All attempts at conciliation had failed. It is probable that the officials of Lisbon wanted to surrender but were afraid of the violently anti-Spanish mob. As long as Don Antonio remained adamant they could do little but pray. The prior responded to Alba's offers with sheer insolence. Advised by the papal nuncio Frumenti and speaking through Diego de Cárcamo, a loyal Castilian who had once been in his service, he agreed to a meeting with Alba on a boat in the Tagus and then failed to appear. When he presented a list of conditions ending with a demand for payment of his expenses during the campaign it was enough. "This put mustard in my nostrils," said Alba, "and I consigned him to the devil."[64]

The next two days were spent in reconnaissance, as it was now apparent that Don Antonio had raised an army in the city and was preparing a defense. By this time the Torre de Belem was completely surrounded on its landward side, and it opened its gates after one of the shortest bombardments on record. Alba, who had spent eight hours in the saddle without dismounting, thought that "the *alcalde* merits hanging from a turret," but was so amused by his deceptions that he pardoned him.[65]

A battle was now unavoidable. At the last moment Alba wrote to the king: "I beg Your Majesty to pardon me for tolerating all these indignities [the demands of Don Antonio] as I desire so much to avoid the bloodshed and great harm that would follow upon entering Lisbon by force that without further orders from Your Majesty I will continue and make more obeisances than a French cleric,"[66] but he knew it would do no good. The Portuguese were in position and determined to fight.

Immediately to the west of Lisbon is a deep, rather narrow ravine through which the meager waters of the Alcántara flow to the Tagus. Many of its landmarks have been obliterated by the northern approaches to the great bridge built in 1966, but it is still possible to grasp the outlines of Alba's last battlefield.

On the morning of August 24, 1580, a motley force of 10,000 Portuguese were strung out along the eastern margins of this ravine from a cluster of mills on the bank of the Tagus to a point some 2 km up the almost dry riverbed of the Alcántara. They were for the most part amateurs: artisans, laborers, and ordinary citizens, united only by their hatred of the Spaniards. The strongest part of their position was at its southern end, where they held the mills and the modest bridge over which the Lisbon-Cascais road crossed the little stream. Here too were the ships of Don Gaspar de Brito, a valuable source of covering fire if they could get in close enough and were not driven from their post by Santa Cruz. Further up the ravine the situation was less encouraging. They had fortified a country house and laid out entrenchments, but the latter were no more than parallel ditches left open and undefended at their ends.

Alba's strategy, inspired by slightly superior numbers, was simply to extend his own lines even further. The Italians under Prospero Colonna were set up against the bridge and covered by two artillery batteries. The bulk of the Spanish infantry was then placed in the center, and Sancho Dávila took his arquebusiers almost to Horta Navia on the extreme Portuguese right. Meanwhile Don Hernando, taking full advantage of the rough ground, passed unseen to the headwaters of the creek and crossed over to lie in wait on the enemy's side of the field.[67] By nightfall the Portuguese were flanked without a shot being fired.

Acting on the theory that such rank amateurs would be easy to unnerve, the Spaniards spent most of the night howling and firing random shots into the darkness. At about three Alba himself arose, heard Mass, and had himself carried in a litter to a point overlooking the entire valley. There, with his usual caution, he began to unfold the plan whose results were all but certain but which would nevertheless be carried out with academic precision. The assault was preceded by an artillery barrage that lasted until dawn, the heaviest fire being directed at the positions nearest the bridge. Then, as soon as it was light enough to see, Colonna attacked.

The Portuguese resistance was much fiercer than expected. After an interval of bitter hand-to-hand fighting the Italians were driven back, enabling their enemy to establish a salient on Alba's side of the bridge. Colonna was beside himself. He had either been unaware of or had chosen to ignore the mills, which were now found to be full of arquebusiers. These had to be dislodged by a series of complicated maneuvers while the rest of his men tried to hold their somewhat battered line athwart the road. Alba, who had concealed the overall plan from his commanders, sent a thousand German pikemen to stiffen the line but refused all other assistance and paid for it by having to endure the fretting of his advisors in addition to the agonies of gout. Slowly, Colonna's men drove the Portuguese from their mills while their commander railed against the Spanish fleet for standing idly offshore. A landsman to his fingertips, he did not realize that the same low tide that kept Santa Cruz away was his own protection against the guns of Don Gaspar de Brito. His opinion of Alba at this moment has not been preserved but may be imagined.

Colonna, of course, was in the classic position of all field officers sent to execute orders whose purpose is deliberately hidden from them. Dimly aware that nothing much seemed to be happening elsewhere on the field, he fought as though the entire campaign depended upon him and managed in spite of himself to create the impression desired. Convinced that Alba had staked everything on the taking of the bridge, Don Antonio himself came to what he saw as the thick of the fight and throughout the morning reinforced this position by drawing troops away from his right and center.

Sometime between ten and eleven Colonna completed his arrangements for a second assault. The "sleeve" of arquebusiers that had taken the mills now flanked the Portuguese on their extreme left, as his main column overran the Portuguese salient and threw itself across the bridge. It was the moment for which Alba had been waiting. With the enemy's attention focused securely on the bridge, he ordered Sancho Dávila across the Alcántara with 2,100 arquebusiers who rapidly overwhelmed the trenches on Don Antonio's right, sweeping them with fire from their undefended ends. At the same time, Don Hernando came down from the north, scattering the rearguard, seizing the baggage, and spreading panic almost to the bridge itself. It was over in half an hour. Of the Portuguese defenders nearly 2,000 died; the remainder melted into the suburbs of Lisbon, and Don Antonio, seriously wounded, was carried off in great haste along the road to Santarem. [68]

Alcántara was Alba's last battle. In the classical sense it may also have been the only one he ever fought. Mühlberg, Jemmingen, and the other triumphs of a long career had relied upon surprise or prior demoralization of his enemies. In his final action Alba drew up his troops and took the measure of a foe in the style of Gonsalvo de Córdoba, but of course the scale and substance of the victory were minor. He had defeated 10,000 inexperienced men with perhaps 12,000 who were at least slightly better trained and were reinforced by a cadre of German and Italian mercenaries. Though he was greatly aided by the incompetence of Don Antonio the issue had never been in doubt. He did not rejoice, but then Alba's view of himself and his successes had always been based on the cumulative assessment of the professional. One more action in the course of sixty years meant little; indeed, he was annoyed that he had been forced to fight at all. His son Don Hernando said only that "The dead have been more than we might have wished,"[69] and the father would surely have agreed, yet in its careful planning and perfect execution the little battle of Alcántara was worthy of a more formidable opponent than the Prior of Crato.

The aftermath, and indeed the rest of Alba's life, was an anticlimax, interesting only in that all the troubles of decades past were played out again in yet another foreign town. By Christmas he was weary beyond imagining, but there was to be no relief short of the grave.

Aside from some looting on the outskirts of Lisbon the hours after the battle were undramatic. The city surrendered without incident, and though the population remained sullen Alba had little difficulty in imposing his rule. He intended only to prepare for the arrival of the king, but with what must have seemed terrible predictability the king failed to arrive.

This time the reason was the plague. It reached Lisbon soon after the Spanish army and eventually afflicted nearly everyone, though the mortality rate was not more than ten percent.[70] Alba himself came down with it in the last week of September and recovered only to undergo an especially painful siege of gout that lasted through much of October. His faithful secretary Albornoz was not so lucky. After a long struggle he made an exemplary end on October 1, no doubt providing great encouragement to those whose activities were as suspect as his own had been.[71]

In these circumstances it was thought foolish for the king to enter the city, though in truth the dangers were easily as great at Badajoz. Philip proved this by nearly dying of the pest without leaving Spain, and on October 26 he lost his queen, Anne of Austria. He was probably immune by this time, but in the absence of an adult heir he can hardly be blamed for taking precautions. Aged, ill, and increasingly annoyed at being left in yet another untenable position, Alba found himself the untitled viceroy of the Portuguese empire. At least this time he did not have to harvest the fruits of a repressive policy.

His most immediate problem, aside from maintaining discipline in an army cheated of its customary rewards, was the apprehension of Don Antonio. In this he failed. The redoubtable Dávila was sent north to capture the fugitive but found that this could not be done through military means. The Prior of Crato may have been a quixotic figure but he symbolized the aspirations of many Portuguese who were prepared to risk everything by hiding him and nursing his wounds as he moved about from place to place. Don Sancho could do little but follow the rumors, stirring up new pockets of resistance as he went. Though his military operations were impeccable, he found nothing but hostility or the blank uncomprehending stares of peasants long schooled in the protection of village secrets. Coimbra surrendered, and serious resistance was finally broken for the last time at Oporto, but Don Antonio remained at large. After many weeks he made his way to France, but not before the whole affair had become a serious embarrassment.

The failure to catch Don Antonio inevitably produced criticism at court. It was said that Alba ought to have dispatched a flying squad of light horse to apprehend him before he reached the north, and some modern authorities have been forced to agree.[72] Officially, he failed to do so out of reluctance to divide his forces in an unstable situation,[73] but he may also have been influenced by contempt for his prey. Don Antonio would never be king of Portugal, and Alba was not one to waste time on mere symbols, an attitude much less practical than it sounds. There was, of course, no guarantee that the Prior would have been any easier to find in September than he had been in October or November, but for a textbook general the failure to mount a routine pursuit was certainly odd.

Between this and the rising tide of complaint over the lack of discipline of his troops Alba soon found himself in difficulties. Looting in the suburbs had been minor and incidents within the city itself were negligible, but the duke's age and the extreme sensitivity of the court to Portuguese opinion weighed heavily upon the suspicions of the king. From the standpoint of his servants Philip's tendency to double-check their activities was a sign of ingratitude but it was perhaps his greatest strength as an administrator and was an integral part of the Spanish system. A man like Alba might respond to a request for his accounts by saying, "I can easily draw up a list of the realms gained and the services done for Your Majesty during my long life,"[74] but the *visita* and *residencia* were precedents that could not be ignored. It was only natural that Philip should respond to criticism by sending Dr. Francisco Villafaña of the Council of Castile to investigate, and equally natural for Alba to submit his resignation as soon as he heard about it.

Alba was, in fact, in a marvelous dudgeon and after December 5 his requests for leave came at two-day intervals. His basic argument was that he had nothing to do, unless it was "to cure the *apestados* and disband the army," and that this "is not the office of a general,"[75] but in fact his grievances were legion. As he told Zayas: "I see myself, señor, surrounded here by three or four things, any one of which would be enough to [make me] jump out of the windows."[76] He was worried, as always, about his household and the host of people dependent upon him. Commissioners had been sent to deal with the rebels so he could not handle them as he wished,[77] and people were beginning to think that he was "in exile" and "a joke."[78] Above all, he was old and unwell, and to keep him in the plague-stricken city was, in the words of his new secretary, Arceo, "cruelty."[79]

Philip's response to all this was callous but perfectly suited to the occasion. The duke was indispensable where he was. If he was worried about his health, he should go to Belem or San Benito.[80] His honor stung, Alba replied by return post that he would stay where he was and would "not be the first of my house to have died in the service of his prince over Lisbon."[81] To Zayas he wrote that he was not impeded by fear of death, especially as so much of his life was over, and that in view of what he had to eat he had more fear of dying of hunger than of plague.[82] In a sense his words were prophetic on both counts.

The king was of course correct, though it would be easy to fault him on the usual grounds of cold-heartedness and ingratitude. Even without interference from court Alba would soon have wanted to retire, but to have done so prior to 1582 would have created serious problems. For a long time Philip could not come. When he did, it was not to visit Lisbon but to convene at Tomar the Cortes that would proclaim him king. In the interim someone of the highest rank was needed to manage the business of government, and once again Alba was the appropriate choice. The logic of such things is inexorable. In 1580 Alba was there and possessed the necessary qualifications. By the time Philip arrived in the spring of 1581, Alba was no longer needed to govern but his experience and specialized knowledge made him indispensable as a counselor. There could be no thought of allowing him to go home; only time could free him from the chains of his own competence, and at seventy-four time was running out.

The interval between the fall of Lisbon and the coming of the king was thus far busier than Alba would admit. The *apestados* had to be governed even if they could not be cured, and the army had to be disbanded whatever the precedent. The unruliness of the men coupled with sporadic shortages of money made this otherwise routine task as difficult as Philip had predicted, and at times the duke was driven to the edge of distraction.

All of this, of course, had to be done in conjunction with responsibilities of a more grandiose nature. There was, for example, the problem of the East Indies fleet. Portugal had always lacked the population necessary to man a far-flung empire, and after Alcazar-el-Kebir and Alba's invasion the shortage of troops was acute. For weeks the fleet lay anchored while Alba tried to find men willing to face the long voyage and the exotic tropical diseases at the end of it. Philip suggested that he should send Castilians,[83] but this he refused to do. The higher rate of pay accorded the Portuguese would cause trouble, as would the mingling of Portuguese and Spaniard in places that were theoretically reserved for the former. It would be better to give the Portuguese even higher pay in the hope that generosity would attract recruits and leave the Spaniards at home.[84] In the end the fleet sailed short-handed.

Then there was Sir Francis Drake. On September 26 he landed at Plymouth after a three-year circumnavigation of the globe, his ship ballasted with Spanish silver. Philip had tried to catch him by sending Pedro Sarmiento de Gamboa to lie in wait for him off the tip of South America, but the wily Englishman eluded this trap by striking out across the Pacific. Sarmiento returned to Spain with nothing more than a plan to fortify the Straits of Magellan against future raids. The Council of the Indies turned the question over to a junta of military experts including Alba and Santa Cruz, and on their recommendation Alba was ordered to arrange for the construction of two forts that would control the passage. Almost as an afterthought Philip instructed him to send eight ships to the Azores as an additional precaution.

Nothing more clearly reveals the depth of Spanish confusion in the face of English attacks. Philip II was responsible for an inordinately large part of the earth's surface. It all had to be protected, but the English might strike anywhere and there were unsubstantiated rumors that they were outfitting another expedition. As the Azores were thought to favor the Prior of Crato, the king inferred that they were a likely target, but nothing happened.[85]

The attempt to close the Straits was even more misguided. Though Alba guessed that it might be difficult, it is obvious from his correspondence that neither he nor the king had any idea of what was involved. Thanks in part to the optimism of Sarmiento's report, they knew nothing of the appalling climate, the wild Indians, or the passage around Cape Horn, discovered by Drake, that made use of the Straits unnecessary. On December 9, 1582, after much confusion and a disastrous false start, they dispatched a fleet of twenty-three ships laden with, among other things, a cargo of stones from which the forts were to be built.[86] After many adventures including desertion by his immediate superior, Sarmiento finally managed to establish a colony at the Straits in 1584. Three years later a solitary survivor was found starving and half-mad amid the howling gales of Tierra del Fuego.[87]

In spite of their generally dubious results these ventures in imperial policy must have been a relief from Alba's normal duties. By early spring the plague had moderated, but tensions between Spaniards and Portuguese remained high and resolving them played a large part in his daily routine. The people of Lisbon had not wanted a Spanish regime and even when the occupying forces behaved themselves their presence was a constant irritant. The more respectable elements "think that they have to do His Majesty favors by complaints . . . even though they are lies."[88] The poor created incidents. One of the worst of these occurred at Easter, 1581. Four or five Spanish soldiers, including an *alférez*, were killed by a Portuguese mob. A Spanish captain who tried to break it up was seriously injured. By way of reprisal, several other Spaniards went secretly to the church of Nostra Senhora do Monte and killed several worshipers on their way to Mass. Alba was infuriated. Arceo claimed, "I have never in my life seen him in such a rage or one that lasted so long."[89] In Alba's words, the incident was "so ugly and so atrocious" that he wanted to hang ten of them,[90] but it was not to be. Even his own secretary thought that "if it were not unthinkable, in part it [the reprisal] was well done,"[91] and the rest of the Spaniards agreed. To preserve what was left of Spanish morale, only four men were hanged in the street where the incident took place, but even this moderation drew nothing but complaints.[92]

These conflicts were inevitable, but for an old man in poor health they were a heavy burden. He was also troubled at this time by the health of his wife. She had remained on their estates at Coria, and in March and April fell ill with a serious attack of the tertians. For a while he had no letters from her and thought she was dead, but Philip would not let him abandon his post for any reason. When at last she wrote, his gratitude to Zayas for arranging the post showed a side of his character not ordinarily revealed: "I owe you all the love that I have for you and the tenderness with which I love you, and with it everything I can do in all the things of your pleasure and contentment." Of Philip, he could say only: "And in nothing, señor, have I given such proof of my obedience and desire to serve His Majesty as in this, for I have not taken a litter and gone to visit my wife, but kings do not have sentiment and tenderness in the place that we have ours."[93]

Though Alba continued to work with surprising energy, it was a time of frustration and resentment. In a personal sense its brightest hours were spent in conversation with his new confessor, Fray Luis de Granada. Fray Luis was a year older than the duke and his great devotional writings were well known, but it was not his fame that endeared him to Alba. The serenity of his faith, the limpid purity of his discourse, and the simplicity of his character caused Alba to say of him, "He is the man in the world who is furthest from its things."[94] Fray Luis was the perfect spiritual guide for an old man grown weary of blood, intrigue, and the faithlessness of kings. Alba had always relished the conversation of pious men, and at the end of his life the discovery of Fray Luis was a great consolation.

With the coming of the king on June 29, 1581, Alba largely disappears from the historical record. He remained in Lisbon, presumably as a counselor, but his proximity to the court again made correspondence unnecessary. At some point in the autumn of 1582 he fell ill of a disease whose exact character is unknown. Back in Madrid, Granvelle heard that he had diarrhea and a slow fever and that he had been suckled at a woman's breast to keep him alive,[95] but such measures were ultimately of no avail. Unable to take food, he died on December 12, 1582.

In the Biblioteca Nacional at Madrid there is a beautiful letter of consolation written to the Duchess of Alba by Fray Luis de Granada.

It describes in some detail an ending worthy of a saint. Though his great weakness made it difficult for Alba to pray at his usual length, one of his last confessions was "in the form of a dialogue with our Lord so inspirational that it would have converted a great sinner. Another sign of his predestination was the pleasure and consolation he received in speaking of our Lord, which I have never seen in a person of his quality." One statement stands out almost as an epitaph: "He certified to me in truth that his conscience was not burdened with having in all his life shed a single drop of blood against it."[96]

XV

EPILOGUE

In November, 1619, a full generation after Alba's death, his grandson, the fifth Duke Don Antonio, decided to transfer his grandfather's remains from the convent of San Leonardo in Alba de Tormes to the Dominican convent of San Esteban at Salamanca. It was one of several such moves, for Alba's bones have not been allowed to rest easy. In the course of the move Don Antonio caused the lid of the coffin to be opened, whereupon, to everyone's astonishment, he immediately fell to his knees in a gesture of humility and respect. The duke was still as he had been in life. "The composure of his countenance, the gravity of his white hairs, the authority of a superior person had not been lost." The stunned onlookers agreed that "it was more than human."[1]

In death as in life, this was the impression Alba made on those who knew him. The conscientious biographer, tracking a man through a long life of hard choices, loses himself and perhaps his subject in the byways of detail and second-guessing. Warts and blemishes, temper tantrums and mistakes make it easy to forget that he is dealing with a hero. Alba was a hero to some and very much the archvillain to others, but he was always memorable. The reasons for this are in some ways obvious.

He was, without argument, the greatest soldier of his generation, acknowledged as such even by those who hated him. His notions of war may not have been romantic or inspiring but they were rooted firmly in the realities of the time and they were successful. It would be tempting to say that he was, like Napoleon, the founder of a whole concept of warfare, but such a statement would be unhistorical in both cases. Generals often like to believe that military revolutions spring full-blown from the genius of great captains. Alba, whatever his faults, knew better. Practical of intellect, saturnine in personality, he made no claims or high theoretical pronouncements. On the battlefield he sought only to adapt himself to the conditions at hand, and he did so with intelligence, courage, and a technical mastery that was the wonder of the age. His style as a commander was remarkably unpretentious. He cared nothing for glory, in the ordinary sense, but a great deal for the welfare of his troops. When he died, hardened veterans from Flanders to Portugal said, "The father of the soldiers is dead," and they wept.

As a statesman also he was above the common run. Though he managed a wide variety of diplomatic missions and managed them well, his chief contribution was as an advisor and analyst. In this only Granvelle was his equal, and even then Alba's judgment was sometimes the keener. His success came from a peculiar combination of traits. He saw the purposes of foreign policy with crystal clarity but was at the same time worldly enough to be flexible about the means. If at times he overreacted, as in Elizabeth's seizure of the payships, he was normally patient and cautious. This seems to have come from a soldier's pessimism. He worshiped a god who played no favorites and was unforgiving of carelessness. His master might send out fleets and armies with a pious "God will provide," but Alba had seen fiascoes and catastrophes beyond Philip's home-bred imaginings and was disinclined to leave things to chance. Oddly enough, this sense of limitations sometimes made him seem bold and original, as when he insisted that the Netherlands rather than Milan be ceded at Crépy but, more typically, it caused fools to accuse him of cowardice. It scarcely mattered. He was often right and always worth listening to, and as contempt came easily to him he cared little for the opinions of others unless they appeared to influence the king. Then his formidable talents as an advocate would be brought into play. Forceful, well-informed, and vividly eloquent, he was indeed the "dead shot" that Ruy Gómez had feared.

Yet none of this explains his hold on the popular imagination. Alba is remembered not because he was a great soldier and statesman but because he is a symbol. To one of the "two Spains" he is the epitome of virtue: devout, spartan, courageous, prudent, and, above all, loyal, not only to his Church and king but to the hard values of that land of "saints and stones" which gave birth to the Golden Age. To much of the rest of the world he is therefore the epitome of intolerance, cruelty, and harsh fanaticism, truly Breughel's Herod in the flesh.

It is almost conventional in such cases to sigh that the humanity beneath the symbol has been lost, but this temptation should be avoided. Alba was human, sometimes excessively so, but he wanted to be the symbol he became, and he pursued virtue—as he understood it—with savage determination. His career, by and large, was exemplary—a living demonstration of the sterner virtues, antique as well as Christian. Only in the Netherlands did he fail, but that failure was so catastrophic, its historical implications so vast that it became an ideological touchstone for future generations. The irony is that a less virtuous man might not have failed so badly or at the very least would certainly have shed less blood.

Of course it is quite possible from Alba's point of view that he did not really fail at all. He died believing in the righteousness of his cause and the fundamental soundness of his policies, and perhaps he was right. If there are such things as struggles in which fundamental principles are at stake, then those who have devoted their lives to such principles are morally obligated to defend them even in the face of defeat and death. The only permissible retreats are strategic and temporary, the limits on action virtually none. Belief carries a price, and that price is human suffering, but is it possible to believe and yet be tolerant? Alba did not think so, and he was prepared to accept the consequences of his certainty. It is for this reason that he would, from the grave, deny our judgments. Symbols are Janus-faced, and each of their visages reflects the character of its beholder. Alba must be taken as he was. If there are paradoxes here it is we who must live with them, and it is perhaps this that caused the fifth duke to fall to the ground in surprise and consternation.

A Note on Sources

The starting point for any study of Alba is his *Epistolario*, 3 vols. (Madrid, 1952), a collection that prints or provides locations for 2,714 of his letters. Edited under the direction of the tenth Duke of Berwick y Alba, it includes virtually all the duke's personal letters in the Archivo de los Duques de Alba (Madrid), the British Library, the Bibliothèque Nationale (Paris), the Vatican Archive, and the Archivo General de Simancas. The work has been criticized for minor errors in dating and transcription and for the editor's decision to modernize the orthography, but each letter has been checked against the original and it cannot be said that these faults greatly diminish its value for the historian. It must, however, be used in conjunction with the *Colección de documentos inéditos para la historia de España*, 113 vols. (Madrid, 1842–1895). Many of the duke's letters found their way to the royal archive at Simancas and were published in various sections of this monumental work. Rather than reprint them in the *Epistolario*, volume and page references were provided.

Other Alba letters are found in the Vatican Library and in the Konincklijke Bibliothek at The Hague. The huge collection of Alba materials at the Archives Générales du Royaume in Brussels largely duplicates the holdings at Simancas, as copies were normally retained of all dispatches to Madrid. The exception is a number of routine administrative letters that were thought to be of purely local interest. They are found in the Papiers d'Etat de l'Audience. Alba also produced memoranda on various subjects, most of them military. A few have been printed in the *Documentos inéditos* but the majority remain in the Estado, Estado-Castilla, and Guerra Antigua sections of Simancas and in the manuscripts section of the Biblioteca Nacional, Madrid.

The letters to which Alba was responding are more difficult to locate. Many have been preserved in the Archivo de los Duques de Alba but many others are scattered through the immense holdings at Simancas. The bulk of the latter are in the Estado section, and those that pertain to the Netherlands have been catalogued by M. Van Durme.

Other collections of correspondence that deal with Alba and the events in which he participated are numerous, but their usefulness varies. The papers of Cardinal Granvelle are particularly interesting. Many of them have been collected in two great published series, the *Papiers d'état du Cardinal de Granvelle*, ed. C. Weiss (9 vols., Paris, 1841–1852), and the *Correspondance du Cardinal de Granvelle, 1556–1586*, ed. E. Poullet and C. Piot (12 vols., Brussels, 1877–1896). It is a tribute to the cardinal's energy that these twenty-one volumes record only a portion of his labors. Additional unpublished collections of his letters may be found in the Bibliothéque Municipal, Besançon, and the Biblioteca del Palacio Real, Madrid. Another fine published series is the *Correspondance française de Marguerite d'Autriche, Duchesse de Parme, avec Philippe II*, ed. J. S. Theissen and H. A. Enno van Gelder (3 vols., Utrecht, 1925–1942). Many of the papers of Mateo Vázquez and Luis de Requesens may be found at the Instituto de Valencia de Don Juan in Madrid.

The *Correspondance de Philippe II sur les affaires des Pays-Bas, 1558–1577*, ed. L.-P. Gachard (5 vols., Brussels, 1848–1879) is a series of extracts taken from selected letters. They are well chosen and intelligently summarized but, as in all such cases, there is no substitute for the originals, which are at Simancas and Brussels. Much the same can be said of the monumental Calendars of State Papers produced by the British. The *Foreign, Roman, Spanish,* and *Venetian* series all include material on Alba and the events described in this book, but the documents are either summarized or translated into English, often with considerable license. The reports of the Venetian ambassadors to Spain are found in Eugenio Albèri, ed., *Le relazione degli ambasciatori veneti al Senato*, series 1 (6 vols., Florence, 1839–1863). They are useful, especially for Alba's middle years, but like the ambassador's reports in the Calendars of State Papers, they contain much idle gossip and misinformation.

The secondary literature on this period is surprisingly weak, though there are two excellent general surveys, J. H. Elliott's *Imperial Spain, 1469–1716* (New York, 1963) and John Lynch's *Spain under the Hapsburgs*, vol. 1 (Oxford, 1964). F. Braudel's *La Méditerranée et le monde méditerranéen à l'époque de Philippe II* (2 vols., Paris, 1966) is essential to an understanding of the limits and possibilities of Alba's world and contains valuable insights on sixteenth-century warfare. There are also some useful biographies. Alba's biographers are discussed in the preface. The standard biography of Charles V is by Karl Brandi (Munich, 1937). Translated into English by C. V. Wedgwood in 1939, it concentrates on the emperor's German interests and must be supplemented by M. Fernández Alvarez, *Charles V* (London, 1975). Fernández Alvarez is also responsible for a much larger volume, *La España del Emperador Carlos V*, vol. XVIII in the *Historia de España*, ed. R. Menéndez y Pidal (Madrid, 1966). Unlike the volumes on Philip II in the same series, by L. Fernández y Fernández de Retana, it is quite useful.

Philip II, after long neglect and a series of indifferent and often polemical biographies, has at last begun to receive more serious attention. Peter Pierson's *Philip II of Spain* (London, 1975) is an excellent summary of his political career, while Geoffrey Parker's *Philip II* (Boston, 1978) provides a more personal and anecdotal glimpse of the monarch's complex, sometimes opaque character. A superb contemporary source, Luis Cabrera de Córdoba, *Felipe II, Rey de España (1619)* (4 vols., Madrid, 1876–1877) remains indispensable for the light it sheds on the reign as a whole and especially on the activities of the court, which Cabrera describes in detail. The political ideas of both Philip and his father, essential to an understanding of Alba's role in the Netherlands and elsewhere, are ably described by Fernández Alvarez in his *Política mundial de Carlos V y Felipe II* (Madrid, 1966). For Philip's youth and some interesting glimpses of Alba and his great rival Ruy Gómez de Silva, there is the valuable *Niñez y juventud de Felipe II* (2 vols., Madrid, 1941), by J. M. March, S.J.

Alba's collaborators and enemies at court are less well served. There is no biography of Ruy Gómez de Silva, and owing to the destruction of his papers there may never be one. Granvelle, however, has been studied by M. Van Durme, *El Cardenal Granvela* (Barcelona, 1957, translated from the Flemish edition of 1953 published at Brussels), and by Martin Philippson, *Ein Ministerium unter Philipp II: Kardinal Granvella am spanische Hofe 1579–1586* (Berlin, 1895). The latter is useful for events at court during Alba's exile and subsequent absence in Portugal. Hayward Keniston, *Francisco de los Cobos, Secretary of the Emperor Charles V* (Pittsburgh, 1960) is sound but somewhat disappointing in its failure to place this very important figure in context. His *Garcilaso de la Vega: A Critical Study of His Life and Works*

(New York, 1922) may be criticized on similar grounds, though it should be noted that Keniston was not an historian but a specialist in Spanish literature, and his interest in larger historical questions appears to have been minimal. A. Gonzalez Palencia, *Gonzalo Pérez, secretario de Felipe II* (2 vols., Madrid, 1946), is also a disappointment. It contains much useful information, but there are many errors of fact and interpretation and the relationship between the secretary and Alba is oversimplified. Gregorio Marañón's *Antonio Pérez* (2 vols., Madrid, 1963) is somewhat better. Though not without its mistakes and eccentricities, it is a believable portrait of the man that displays remarkable insight in its description of court life and of the factional disputes so often ignored or misunderstood by other writers. Alba's replacement in the Netherlands, Luis de Requesens, has not found his biographer, but there is a monograph on his years at Milan: J. M. March, *El Comendador Mayor de Castilla, Don Luis de Requesens, en el Gobierno de Milan, 1571–1573* (Madrid, 1946) and two articles by A. W. Lovett: "A New Governor for the Netherlands: The Appointment of Don Luis de Requesens, Comendador Mayor de Castilla," *European Studies Review* I, no. 2 (1971), 89–103, and "The Governorship of Don Luis de Requesens, 1573–1576: A Spanish View," *European Studies Review* II, no. 3 (1972). Lovett is also the author of *Philip II and Mateo Vázquez* (Geneva, 1977), a monograph that does not pretend to be a biography but which contains much information on the secretary's life and career. For the various popes with whom Alba had to deal, Ludwig von Pastor's venerable *The History of the Popes from the Close of the Middle Ages,* 24 vols., remains the standard. I have used the St. Louis edition of 1936.

Alba's family background and early life must be pieced together from a variety of sources whose concern with the house of Alba is tangential at best. One exception to this rule is an article by the Duke of Berwick y Alba, "Biografía de doña Maria Enríquez, mujer del Gran Duque de Alba," *Boletín de la Real Academia de Historia* CXXI (1947), 7–39. Another is A. Salcedo Ruiz, *Un bastardo insigne del Gran Duque de Alba: el prior don Hernando de Toledo* (Madrid, 1903). Unfortunately, the author has him hopelessly confused with someone else of the same name, and the book is thus virtually useless. This is a pity, as Don Hernando was one of the most influential and interesting figures of the later reign of Philip II. Otherwise, the best sources for the family are the chronicles printed in the Biblioteca de Autores Españoles (BAE): Enríquez del Castello, *Crónica del Rey Don Enrique el Cuarto de este nombre* (BAE 70, vol. III, 99–222); Francesillo de

Zúñiga, *Crónica* (BAE 36); Hernando de Pulgar, *Crónica de los Señores Reyes Católicos* (BAE 70, vol. III, 225–565); and Prudencio de Sandoval, *Historia de la vida y hechos del Emperador Carlos V* (BAE 80–82). The latter, with Alonso de Santa Cruz, *Crónica del Emperador Carlos V* (5 vols., Madrid, 1920–1922), is also useful for the first twenty years of the duke's career. For those interested in Alba's genealogy, much information is available, and most of it has been summarized in J. Paz y Espeso, *Arboles genealógicos de las Casas de Berwick, Alba y agregadas* (2nd ed., Madrid, 1948). Those wishing to place the adventures of Alba's immediate ancestors in perspective should consult the fine monograph by Luis Suárez Fernández, *Nobleza y monarquía en la Castilla del siglo XV* (Madrid, 1963).

The sources for Alba's early campaigns and for his activities in Italy are discussed in the notes to chapters II–V. They are a rather piecemeal collection of documents, contemporary accounts, and some of the less-inspired products of late-nineteenth-century French and German scholarship. The exceptions, once again, are von Pastor's volumes on Paul III and Paul IV, which provide reasonably coherent narratives of an extremely difficult period. F. Martín Arrue's *Campañas del Duque de Alba* (2 vols., Toledo, 1880), must be used with caution, but L. de Avila y Zúñiga, *Comentario de la Guerra de Alemania* (BAE 21, 410–49) is an excellent contemporary account of the Schmalkaldic Wars. There is also a shortage of secondary works on Spanish domestic politics and the life of the court, but in 1969 two works appeared that deal with the secretaries of state in the curiously disembodied way characteristic of institutional histories: J. A. Escudero, *Los Secretarios de Estado y del Despacho 1474–1724* (4 vols., Madrid, 1969), and A. Yalí Román Román, "Origen y evolución de la Secretario de Estado y de la Secretario del Despacho," *Jahrbuch für Geschichte von Stadt, Wirtschaft und Gesellschaft Lateinamerikas* VI (1969), 41–142.

The Netherlands has received ample attention. The survey embodying the most recent scholarship is Geoffrey Parker's *The Dutch Revolt* (London, 1977), but Pieter Geyl's *The Revolt of the Netherlands* (2nd ed., London, 1962) is still worth reading even if some of his basic contentions have been roughly handled by later historians. Among his more forceful critics is Charles Wilson, *Queen Elizabeth and the Revolt of the Netherlands* (Berkeley, 1970). The question of the Netherlands is, of course, fraught with emotional and ideological pitfalls, and few authors tumbled into them with greater enthusiasm than J. L. Motley in his magnificent *The Rise of the Dutch Republic* (3 vols., New York, 1855). Though violently anti-Spanish, it is a superbly researched and brilliantly written narrative that provides more information on the revolt than any other source in English. Subsequent reprintings have been too numerous to list here; I have used the London edition of 1886 throughout. On the origins of the revolt, we await the publication of a work by P. D. Lagomarsino that will be based at least in part on his fine Cambridge Ph.D. dissertation, "Court Factions and the Formulation of Spanish Policy toward the Netherlands, 1559–1567" (1973).

There are also a number of monographs on specific aspects of the revolt. On the military side, the starting point is Geoffrey Parker's *The Army of Flanders and the Spanish Road, 1567–1659* (Cambridge, 1972), a work that is essential to an understanding of Spanish military organization and sixteenth-century warfare as a whole. "Spain, Her Enemies and the Revolt of the Netherlands," *Past and Present*, no. 49 (1970), 72–95, by the same author, relates the military problems of the Netherlands to Spain's other concerns with special emphasis on the contemporary Turkish threat in the Mediterranean, while I. A. A. Thompson, *War and Government in Habsburg Spain, 1560–1620* (London, 1976), deals primarily with the effects of war on Spanish administration. For a narrative description of the fighting in 1568 and in 1572–1573 it would be hard to equal the eyewitness account of Bernardino de Mendoza, *Comentario de lo sucedido en las guerras de los Paises Bajos* (BAE 28, 389–570). Mendoza is of course resolutely Spanish in his point of view, but he is, understandably, less vitriolic than the Dutch writers whose work appeared later on. Of these, P. C. Bor, *Oorspronk, begin en vervolgh der Nederlandsche oorlogen* (4 vols., Amsterdam, 1679), P. C. Hooft, *Nederlandsche Histoorien sedert de ooverdraght der heerschappye van Kaiser Karl den Vijfden op Kooning Philips zijnen zoon* (4 vols., Amsterdam, 1642), and E. Van Meteren, *Historie der Nederlandschen ende haerder naburen oorlogen einde geschiedenissen* ('s Gravenhage, 1614) are probably the best, but none is contemporary and all should be used with great care. The changing geography of the region is best described by A. M. Lambert, *The Making of the Dutch Landscape: An Historical Geography of the Netherlands* (London, 1971).

As in the case of Alba's Spanish associates, there is a dearth of good biographies on his friends and adversaries in the Netherlands. Even the redoubtable William of Orange has been denied the treatment he deserves. C. V. Wedgwood's *William the Silent* (London,

1956) is well written but hagiographic and based on only a fraction of the sources available. Felix Rachfahl, *Wilhelm von Oranien und der Nederländische Aufstand* (4 vols., Halle and The Hague, 1906–1924) is far more detailed and accurate but limits itself almost entirely to the 1560s. Viglius is the subject of a curious and weighty compendium, C. P. Hoynck van Papendracht, *Analecta Belgica seu vita Viglii ab Aytta Zwichemi ab ipso Viglio scripta*, 3 vols. (The Hague, 1743), and his *Mémoires* are printed in the *Collection de mémoires relatifs à la histoire de Belgique* II (Brussels, 1858), but he has no true biography. Margaret of Parma, the counts of Egmont and Hornes, Louis of Nassau, and the rest are almost wholly neglected.

Alba's government has also received only the most cursory attention, though certain of his measures have been studied in detail. The exception is a recent controversy over his paymaster, Francisco de Lixalde. A. W. Lovett, in "Francisco de Lixalde: A Spanish Paymaster in the Netherlands, 1567–1577," *Tijdschrift voor Geschiedenis* 84 (1971), 14–23, argues that Lixalde was the victim of inadequate administrative procedures, while Geoffrey Parker, "Corruption and Imperialism in the Spanish Netherlands: The Case of Francisco de Lixalde, 1567–1612," *Spain and the Netherlands, 1559–1659* (London, 1979), answers convincingly that the charges of corruption levied against him were justified. In the process Parker develops a remarkably sinister picture of Alba's little court. The Council of Troubles has also been studied in some detail, notably by A. L. E. Verheyden in his *Le Conseil des Troubles: liste des condamnés* (Brussels, 1961). This stout folio not only lists the victims but prints a number of useful documents. Unfortunately, Verheyden's figures include numerous double listings and are inflated by approximately fifty percent. They have been promptly and emphatically corrected by M. Dierickx, "De lijst der veroordeelden door de Raad van Beroerten," *Revue Belge de Philologie et d'Histoire* 40 (1962), 415–22. Dierickx has also written two indispensable works on the reorganization of the Church in the Low Countries, *De Oprichting der nieuwe bisdommen in der Nederlanden onder Filips II, 1559–1570* (Antwerp, 1950), and a fine collection of sources, *Documents inédits sur l'érection des nouveaux diocèses aux Pays-Bas (1521–1570)* (3 vols., Brussels, 1960–1962).

In general, Belgian historians have been more favorable to Alba and his regime than their Dutch counterparts and have tended to concentrate on the duke's efforts at reform. This faintly revisionist tendency is evident in two articles by Dierickx, "La politique religieuse de Philippe II dans les anciens Pays-Bas," *Hispania* XVI (1956), 131–43, and "Nieuwe gegevens over het Bestuur van de Hertog van Alva in de Nederlanden," *Tijdschrift voor Geschiedenis* (1964), 167–92. It is also found in the work of the economic historians who play so prominent a role in modern Belgian historiography. Three articles by Jan Craeybeckx are particularly helpful in understanding Alba's tax policies: "La portée fiscale et politique du 100ᵉ denier du duc d'Albe," *Recherches sur l'Histoire des Finances Publiques en Belgique* (Brussels, 1967) I, 343–74; "De moeizame definitieve afschaffing van Alva's tiende penning (1572–1574)," *Album Aangeboden aan offert a Charles Verlinden* (Ghent, 1975); and "Alva's tiende penning een Mythe?" *Mededelingen betreffende de geschiedenis der Nederlanden* 76 (1962), 10–42. H. A. Enno Van Gelder, "De Tiende Penning," *Tijdschrift voor Geschiedenis* 48 (1933), 1–35, is now somewhat dated.

It is impossible to understand Alba's government without considering it in relation to other European powers. J. H. Elliott has provided a survey of the period in *Europe Divided, 1559–1598* (New York, 1968), but there is no truly satisfactory account of imperial politics during this era. France is better served. James Westfall Thompson, *The Wars of Religion in France, 1559–1576* (New York, 1909), and Lucien Romier, *Les origines politiques des guerres de religion* (2 vols., Paris, 1913–1914), though old, are good surveys. N. M. Sutherland, *The Massacre of St. Bartholomew and the European Conflict, 1559–1572* (London, 1973), is essential, and there is also a collection of essays edited by Alfred Soman, *The Massacre of St. Bartholomew: Reappraisals and Documents* (The Hague, 1974). The mass of material on Elizabethan England is too great to catalog here, but one book stands out as a particularly useful guide: R. B. Wernham's *Before the Armada: The Growth of English Foreign Policy, 1485–1588* (London, 1966). Though some of Wernham's conclusions may be questioned, he provides a fine survey of a complex subject and gives full weight to French and Spanish sources. Charles Wilson's provocative *Queen Elizabeth and the Revolt of the Netherlands* (Berkeley, 1970) is important, as are two older articles on specific, rather difficult, points: Conyers Read, "Queen Elizabeth's Seizure of the Duke of Alba's Pay-Ships," *Journal of Modern History* V (1933), 433–64, and J. B. Black, "Queen Elizabeth, the Sea Beggars and the Capture of Brille, 1572," *English Historical Review* XLVI (1931), 30–47. For the flavor of the early English expeditions, the memoirs of two Welsh participants are superb: Sir Roger Williams, *The Actions of the Low Countries*, ed. D. W. Davies (Ithaca, 1964), and the account with hand-drawn maps by Walter Morgan in D. Caldecott-Baird, *The Expedition in Holland* (London, 1976).

Aside from Marañón, very little has been written about Alba, Antonio Pérez, and life at court between 1573 and 1580, but there are two valuable works on the annexation of Portugal. Alfonso Danvila, *Felipe II y la sucesión de Portugal* (Madrid, 1956), concentrates primarily on the negotiations that preceded annexation, while J. Suárez Inclán, *Guerra de Anexión en Portugal* (2 vols., Madrid, 1897), is the standard history of the military campaign.

Many other sources that deal with Alba and his times were consulted in the preparation of this work, but the above are most likely to be useful to the general reader.

Abbreviations

AA	Archivo de los Duques de Alba, Madrid
AGRB	Archives Générales du Royaume, Brussels
AGS	Archivo General de Simancas CMC Contaduría Mayor de Cuentas E Estado GA Guerra Antigua
AON	*Archives ou correspondance de la maison d'Orange-Nassau*, ed. G. Groen van Prinsterer (Leiden, 1841)
BAE	Biblioteca de Autores Españoles
BM	British Museum, London
BN	Biblioteca Nacional, Madrid
CDS	*Correspondencia diplomatica entre España y la Santa Sede durante el Pontificado de S. Pio V*, ed. L. Serrano (Madrid, 1940), 4 vols.
CFMP	*Correspondance française de Marguerite d'Autriche, Duchesse de Parme, avec Philippe II*, ed. J. S. Theissen and H. A. Enno van Gelder (Utrecht, 1925–1942), 3 vols.
CG	*Correspondance du Cardinal de Granvelle, 1556–1586*, ed. E. Poullet and C. Piot (Brussels, 1877–1896), 12 vols.
CPh	*Correspondance de Philippe II sur les affaires des Pays-Bas, 1558–1577*, ed. L.-P. Gachard (Brussels, 1848–1879), 5 vols.
CSP-Foreign	*Calendar of State Papers Foreign, 1547–1574* (London, 1861–1876), 12 vols.
CSP-Roman	*Calendar of State Papers Roman 1558–1578* (London, 1916–1926), 2 vols.
CSP-Spanish	*Calendar of State Papers Spanish, 1547–1579* (London, 1912–1954), 6 vols.

319

CSP-Venetian	*Calendar of State Papers Venetian, 1534–1580* (London, 1873–1890), 9 vols.
DEND	*Documents inédits sur l'érection des nouveaux diocèses aux Pays-Bas (1521–1570)*, ed. M. Dierickx (Brussels, 1960–1962), 3 vols.
DIE	*Colección de documentos inéditos para la historia de España*, ed. M. Fernández de Navarrete et al. (Madrid, 1842–1895), 113 vols.
EA	*Epistolario del III Duque de Alba, Don Fernando Alvarez de Toledo*, ed. Duke of Berwick y de Alba (Madrid, 1952), 3 vols.
IVDJ	Instituto de Valencia de Don Juan, Madrid
KKK	*Korrespondenz des Kaisers Karl V*, ed. K. Lanz (Leipzig, 1844–1846), 3 vols.
PEG	*Papiers d'état du Cardinal de Granvelle*, ed. C. Weiss (Paris, 1841–1852), 9 vols.
RAH	Real Academia de Historia, Madrid
RAV	*Le relazione degli ambasciatori veneti al Senato*, ed. E. Albèri, series 1 (Florence, 1839–1863), 6 vols.
TvG	*Tijdschrift voor Geschiedenis*

Notes

CHAPTER I

1. The arguments over Alba's date of birth are summarized in J. Lunas Almeida, *Historia del Señorio de Valdecorneja* (Avila, 1930), 49–53. See also J. M. del P. C. M. S. Fitz James Stewart y Falco, Duke of Berwick y Alba, *Discurso (Contribución al estudio de la persona del III Duque de Alba)* (Madrid, 1919), 6. The date is confirmed by Alba himself, who noted it frequently.

2. This point is stressed by both Berwick y Alba, 17–18, and Antonio Ossorio, *Vida y hazañas de don Fernando Alvarez de Toledo, Duque de Alba,* ed. José López de Toro (Madrid, 1945), 20.

3. Ossorio, 20; Julio de Atienza, *Nobiliario Español* (Madrid, 1954), 125.

4. Luis Suárez Fernández, *Nobleza y monarquía en la Castilla del siglo XV* (Madrid, 1963), 17–18.

5. Ibid., 28.

6. Ibid., 89, 105, 109.

7. Ibid., 86.

8. Mosén Diego de Valera, *Memorial de diversas hazañas* (BAE 70, vol. III), 59.

9. Diego Enríquez del Castillo, *Crónica del Rey Don Enrique el Cuarto de este nombre* (BAE 70, vol. III), 162.

10. Ibid., 166.

11. Valera, 55.

12. Enríquez del Castillo, 194–95.

13. Ibid., 197–98.

14. Berwick y Alba, 40–41.

15. Francesillo de Zúñiga, *Crónica* (BAE 36), 11.

16. His exploits are best described by Pulgar in his treatment of the Granadan wars: Hernando de Pulgar, *Crónica de los Señores Reyes Católicos* (BAE 70, vol. III), 445–64.

17. Ossorio, 20. The quotation is from Townsend Miller, *The Castles and the Crown* (New York, 1964), 302.

18. L. Marineo Sículo, *Obra de las cosas memorables de España* (Alcalá de Henares, 1539), ff. 24–25.

19. J. H. Elliott, *Imperial Spain, 1469–1716* (New York, 1963), 106.

20. For example, his seizure of Miranda in 1487. See Pulgar, 444.

21. Edward Armstrong, *The Emperor Charles V* (London, 1902), I, 175.

22. Prudencio de Sandoval, *Historia de la vida y hechos del Emperador Carlos V* (BAE 80–82), II, 248.

23. Zúñiga, 30.

24. For a genealogy of the Toledos, see Julian Paz y Espeso, *Arboles genealógicos de las Casas de Berwick, Alba y agregadas* (2nd ed., Madrid, 1948).

25. The best accounts of this expedition are in Andrés Bernaldez, *Historia de los Reyes Católicos* (BAE 70, vol. III), 741–44, and in Sandoval, I, 21.

26. Francisco Sánchez (El Brocense), *Obras de Garci Lasso* (Salamanca, 1574), 96 n. 169.

27. Ibid., 21.

28. Ossorio felt that Fadrique raised Fernando to take the place of his dead son, pinning all his hopes upon him (p. 21).

29. Ossorio, 22.

30. Berwick y Alba, 23.

31. Ibid., 22.

32. Ibid., 26.

33. M. Menéndez y Pelayo, *Juan Boscán, estudio crítico* (Madrid, 1908), 47.

34. Ibid., 48. The letter to Erasmus is printed on p. 49. See also A. Salcedo Ruiz, "El ayo y el preceptor del Gran Duque de Alba," *Revista de Archivos, Bibliotecas y Museos*, 3er epoca XVI (1907), 374.

35. Salcedo Ruiz, 376.

36. Alba to Antonio de Lada, August 31, 1573, *EA*, III, 512–14. He also found fault with the grammar of the Portuguese laws: Alba to Philip, August 30, 1580, *DIE*, 32, 489–93.

37. J. A. Fernández-Santamaria, *The State, War and Peace: Spanish Political Thought in the Renaissance, 1516–1559* (Cambridge, 1977), 164–65.

38. Salcedo Ruiz, 377.

39. Menéndez y Pelayo, 1–33.

40. Berwick y Alba, 23.

41. Ossorio, 22.

42. Ibid.

43. Berwick y Alba, 18.

44. "Los duques d'Alva pequeños de cuerpo, antes de su madre de don Fernando prolongase su casta"; Luis Zapata, *Varia Historia* I, ed. G. C. Horsman (Amsterdam, 1935), 67.

45. Ossorio, 38.

46. Ibid., 28.

47. Ibid., 24–26; Sandoval, II, 40; Alonso de Santa Cruz, *Crónica del Emperador Carlos V* (Madrid, 1920–1922), II, 81.

48. El Brocense, 97 n. 177.

49. Berwick y Alba, "Biografía de doña Maria Enríquez, mujer del Gran Duque de Alba," *Boletín de la Real Academia de Historia* CXXI (1947), 10–11.

50. There is a biography of Don Hernando, but unfortunately it confuses him with one of Alba's nephews of the same name: A. Salcedo Ruiz, *Un bastardo insigne del Gran Duque de Alba: el prior don Hernando de Toledo* (Madrid, 1903).

51. Erika Spivakovsky, *Son of the Alhambra: Don Diego Hurtado de Mendoza, 1504–1575* (Austin, Texas, 1970), 35.

52. Ibid., 36.

53. This letter, dated August 15, 1568, is in *Documentos Escogidos del Archivo de la Casa de Alba*, ed. Duchess of Berwick y de Alba (Madrid, 1891), 85–86.

54. For a description of Alba's devotional habits and some insights into his religious life, see the letter of consolation written by Fray Luis de Granada to the Duchess of Alba, December 15, 1582: BN MS 2058, ff. 82–85.

55. Alba was the subject of a remarkable number of portraits and drawings. Among the best are a disquieting but brilliant work by Anthonis Mor (Antonio Moro) dated 1549 (Hispanic Society of America, New York); a later portrait generally attributed to Willem Key (Rijksmuseum, Amsterdam); and an unattributed work dated 1574 that purports to show the duke at seventy-four years of age (Collection of the Dukes of Alba, Madrid). The Alba collection also contains a Titian done probably in the early 1560s, a Sánchez Coello signed and dated 1567, and an unsigned portrait of Alba as a young man, said to be copied from a lost Titian. There is also an idealized portrait bust by Jonghelinck in the Frick Collection, New York.

56. Berwick y Alba, *The Great Duke of Alba as a Public Servant* (Oxford, 1947), 11.

57. Berwick y Alba, "Maria Enríquez," 8–9.

58. Berwick y Alba, "Maria Enríquez," incorporates much material that appears to have been lost, but see also A. Morel-Fatio, "La duchesse d'Alba Dª Maria Enríquez et Catherine des Medicis," *Bulletin hispanique* VII (1905), 360–86, for further information. A number of papers concerning the duchess and her activities may be found in AA caja 26.

59. See M. de Aguillera y de Liques, Marqués de Cerralto, "Los Duques de Alba y Santa Teresa," *Hidalguía*, no. 8 (January-February, 1955), 1–16.

60. Berwick y Alba, "Maria Enríquez," 21. In English, the passage would read: "It has been a long time since I saw thee last. Dost thou prosper? I do not remember thy name. What is it?" In Spanish, this familiar form of address is used only to children, animals, and very close friends, hence the captain's annoyance and his own use of the diminutive "Alfonsito" for Alfonso.

61. For a discussion of the sorts of people supported by her generosity and that of her husband, see Berwick y Alba, *Discurso,* 43–49.

62. Berwick y Alba, "Maria Enríquez," 12. See also the praise accorded her for this by Alonso Enríquez de Guzmán, *Libro de la vida y costumbres de don Alonso Enríquez de Guzmán,* ed. H. Keniston (Madrid, 1960), 283.

63. The legend is discussed by Hayward Keniston, *Garcilaso de la Vega: A Critical Study of His Life and Works* (New York, 1922), 126. That Barcelona was the starting point of the ride may be determined from Pedro Girón, *Crónica del Emperador Carlos V,* ed. Juan Sánchez Montes (Madrid, 1964), 31. See also M. García Cerezeda, *Tratado de las campañas y otros acontecimientos de los ejercitos del emperador Carlos V . . . desde 1521 hasta 1545* (Madrid, 1873–1876), I, 336–38.

64. Alba to Zayas, April 27, 1581, *DIE,* 34, 273–75, is an example.

65. Paz y Espeso, passim.

66. Ossorio, 31.

67. A good example is his support of Juan Ginés de Sepúlveda, the humanist and political thinker. The two probably met at Vienna in 1532. Sepúlveda dedicated his *Democrates Primus* to Alba in 1535 and openly acknowledged his patronage in a letter to Francisco de Toledo on November 10, 1536 (in *Epistolario de Juan Ginés de Sepúlveda,* ed. A. Losada [Madrid, 1966], 60–62). In 1555 he is found holding a benefice at Alba de Tormes: see Angel Losada, *Juan Ginés de Sepúlveda a traves de su "Epistolario" y nuevos documentos* (Madrid, 1973), 69, 155.

68. Alba to Chantonnay, August 21, 1568, *DIE,* 37, 347–50.

69. Alba's view of the Dutch is well known. A famous example is his comment on their governing classes: "It is a mediocre and a little less than mediocre people" (Alba to Philip, May 5, 1570, *EA,* II, 367–71). His opinion of the Italians is revealed in a passing comment about Tomas Fiesco: "Even if he is an Italian, he is an *hombre cuerdo*" (Alba to Zayas, August 21, 1572, *EA,* III, 190–91). The English and the French apparently annoyed him less.

70. Gregorio Marañón, *Antonio Pérez* (Madrid, 1963), I, 154–55.

71. Geoffrey Parker, *The Army of Flanders and the Spanish Road, 1567–1659* (Cambridge, 1972), 42, provides an excellent example.

72. Enríquez de Guzmán, 76.

73. The available documents show only expenses, not income. They are "Gastos de la cámara del Duque, 1544–1559," AA caja 222, f. 15; "Libramientos expendidos, 1551–1556, 1571, 1573," AA caja 73, f. 1; "Cuentas de la cámara y cocina," AA caja 171, f. 1; and "Gastos de la casa," AA caja 166, f. 3. The last two deal mainly with 1557–1558, though there are partial accounts from the seventeenth century mixed in with the others. None appears to be complete.

74. Berwick y Alba, *Discurso,* 17–18.

75. See his comments on music to Bernardino de Mendoza, May 31, 1555, *EA,* I, 136–41.

76. There is as yet no systematic study of clientage among the Castilian nobility; it may well have been more highly developed there than in contem-

porary France or England. Analogous institutions in France have been touched upon by R. Mousnier, *Les institutions de la France sous la monarchie absolue, 1598–1789* (Paris, 1974), and R. R. Harding, *Anatomy of a Power Elite: The Provincial Governors of Early Modern France* (New Haven, 1978). For England, see Lawrence Stone, *The Crisis of the Aristocracy, 1558–1641* (Oxford, 1965).

77. Enríquez de Guzmán, 14–15.

78. Hayward Keniston, *Francisco de los Cobos, Secretary of the Emperor Charles V* (Pittsburgh, 1960), 85.

79. Enríquez de Guzmán, 75.

CHAPTER II

1. Hayward Keniston, *Garcilaso de la Vega: A Critical Study of His Life and Works* (New York, 1922), 104–10.

2. Ibid., 111. Keniston notes, however, that Garcilaso may have been released for the campaign (115–16).

3. M. Fernández Alvarez, *Charles V* (London, 1975), 99.

4. Antonio Ossorio, *Vida y hazañas de don Fernando Alvarez de Toledo, Duque de Alba*, ed. José López de Toro (Madrid, 1945), 29–30; Alfonso de Ulloa, *Vita dell' invittissimo e sacratissimo imperator Carlo V* (Venice, 1589), 125.

5. Ossorio, 30.

6. John Lynch, *Spain under the Habsburgs,* vol. 1 (Oxford, 1964), 86.

7. Prudencio de Sandoval, *Historia de la vida y hechos del Emperador Carlos V* (BAE 80–82), II, 450.

8. Ibid.

9. The negotiations are described in Karl Brandi, *The Emperor Charles V*, trans. C. V. Wedgwood (London, 1939), 349–52.

10. Pedro Girón, *Crónica del Emperador Carlos V*, ed. Juan Sánchez Montes (Madrid, 1964), 42.

11. Ossorio, 31.

12. Sandoval, II, 522.

13. Ibid., II, 531; Alonso de Santa Cruz, *Crónica del Emperador Carlos V* (5 vols., Madrid, 1920–1922), III, 272.

14. Ossorio, 33.

15. Santa Cruz, III, 273.

16. Sandoval, II, 546; see also the *Relación* in *DIE*, I, 192.

17. Sandoval, II, 550.

18. Ibid., II, 551.

19. Conde de Nieva to Duque de Frias, September 6, 1535, *DIE*, 14, 427; Sandoval, II, 564.

20. Santa Cruz, III, 298–301. See also V. Castaldo, "Il viagio di Carlo V in Sicilia (1535)," *Archivo Storico per la Sicilia Orientale* XXV (1929), 85–108.

21. Ossorio, 37; Sandoval, II, 555.

22. Sandoval, II, 10.

23. Ossorio, 38–40.

24. Sandoval, III, 16–17.

25. Santa Cruz, III, 347.

26. Alba to Charles V, September 7, 1536, *EA*, I, 1.

27. V.-L. Bourrilly, "Charles-Quint en Provence," *Revue Historique* 127 (1918), 256–57.

28. Sandoval, III, 16–17.

29. The most thorough account of Alba's part in the campaign is in M. García Cerezeda, *Tratado de las campañas y otros acontecimientos de los ejercitos del emperador Carlos V . . . desde 1521 hasta 1545* (Madrid, 1873–1876); specific reference, II, 173–74.

30. Ibid., II, 175–77.

31. Ibid., II, 178–81.

32. Sandoval, III, 15–16, 19.

33. *Mémoires de Martin et Guillaume du Bellay*, ed. V.-L. Bourrilly and F. Vindry (Paris, 1912), III, 298–303.

34. Sandoval, III, 19; García Cerezeda, II, 195–96.

35. Girón, 105.

36. J. M. del P. C. M. S. Fitz James Stewart y Falco, Duke of Berwick y Alba, *Discurso (Contribución al estudio de la persona del III Duque de Alba)* (Madrid, 1919), 18.

37. Brandi, 387–88.

38. Girón, 278.

39. Sandoval, III, 52; Ossorio, 45–46.

40. Girón, 278. See also Paulo Accame, "Una relazione inedita sul convegna di Acquemorte," *Giornale storico e letterario della Liguria* VI (1905), 407–17.

41. Brandi, 326–27.

42. Ibid., 414.

43. The Cortes is described by F. de Laiglesia, "Una crisis parlamentaria en 1538," *Estudios Historicos* (Madrid, 1918), I, 265–68; by Sandoval, III, 61–70; and in *Actas de las Cortes de los antiguos reinos de Aragon y Castilla* V, 77–78. See also Hayward Keniston, *Francisco de los Cobos, Secretary of the Emperor Charles V* (Pittsburgh, 1960), 218–19.

44. The incident is described by Keniston, *Francisco de los Cobos*, 219–220. See also Sandoval, III, 71; Santa Cruz, IV, 21–23.

45. Keniston, *Cobos*, 220.

46. These negotiations are described in detail by Brandi, *Charles V,* 400–421.

47. The best account of the journey is Santa Cruz, IV, 50–59. See also V. L. Saulnier, "Charles-Quint traversant la France," *Fêtes et cérémonies au temps du Charles-Quint* (Paris, 1960).

48. Pierre Brantôme, *Les vies des grands capitaines*, in *Oeuvres complètes* (Paris, 1858), II, 154–55.

49. Girón, 344.
50. Alba to Cobos, January 23, 1540, *EA,* I, 2–3.
51. Brandi, *Charles V,* 429–30; Fernández Alvarez, 119.

CHAPTER III

1. Antonio Ossorio, *Vida y hazañas de don Fernando Alvarez de Toledo, Duque de Alba,* ed. José López de Toro (Madrid, 1945), 48–49. This view has been accepted by a number of more recent historians, including J. L. Motley, *The Rise of the Dutch Republic* (London, 1886), II, 104.
2. R. B. Merriman, *The Rise of the Spanish Empire* (New York, 1962), III, 335.
3. Full specifics are preserved in AGS GA20.
4. Alba to Charles, September 20, 1541, *EA,* I, 10–11; Ossorio, 49.
5. Ossorio, 49.
6. Alba to Charles, September 2, 1541, *EA,* I, 5.
7. Ossorio, 50.
8. For a full account see Mendoza to Charles, October 15, 1541, AGS E. K1698, f. 68; also Alba to Charles, October 7, 1541, *EA,* I, 11–12, and October 13, *EA,* I, 12–13.
9. Carta del Comendador Vañuelos, November 10, 1541, *DIE,* I, 229; Prudencio de Sandoval, *Historia de la vida y hechos del Emperador Carlos V* (BAE 80–82), III, 109.
10. Carta de Vañuelos, November 10, 1541.
11. Alfonso de Ulloa, *Vita dell' invittissimo e sacratissimo imperator Carlo V* (Venice, 1589), 126.
12. The estimate is Merriman's (III, 339).
13. Sandoval, III, 112.
14. Ibid., III, 125.
15. See AGS E. K1702, ff. 24, 31, 36, 48, 49, 54–56, 60, 69, 79, 85.
16. Ossorio, 52–56.
17. The notion that Prince Philip was present has been dispelled by Erika Spivakovsky, "The Legendary First Campaign of Philip II," *Renaissance Quarterly* XXI, no. 4 (1968), 413–19.
18. See below, n. 20.
19. Printed in F. de Laiglesia, *Estudios Historicos* (Madrid, 1918), I, 41–67.
20. The original of this passage is printed in Laiglesia, I, 84–85.
21. Brandi, *Charles V,* 491. C. V. Wedgwood's translation is not of the original but of Brandi's defective translation into German (see the German original [Munich, 1937], 421). Ironically, Brandi's transcription of the document itself is accurate: *Karl V, Berichte und Studien* (Munich, 1941), 78–81.
22. BN MS 10,300.
23. Hayward Keniston, *Francisco de los Cobos, Secretary of the Emperor Charles V* (Pittsburgh, 1960), 269.

24. M. de Foronda y Aguilera, *Estancias y viajes del Emperador Carlos V* (Madrid, 1914).

25. Keniston, 268.

26. Alba to Juan Vázquez, May 6, 1543, *EA*, I, 28.

27. Alba to Charles, July 29, 1543, AGS E60, f. 230 (English translation in *CSP-Spanish, Henry VIII*, VI, 448–50); Alba to Charles, May 6, 1543, *EA*, I, 25; Alba to Juan Vázquez, May 9, 1543, *EA*, I, 28 and May 16, *EA*, I, 32–33; Alba to Cobos, July 19, 1543, *EA*, I, 43. For his parting shot, see Alba to Cobos, AGS E63, f. 100.

28. *Secret Instruction* of May 6, Laiglesia, I, 83.

29. L. Fernández y Fernández de Retana, *Historia de España*, ed. R. Menéndez Pidal (Madrid, 1966), XIX, part 1, 239.

30. Alba to Mateo Vázquez, May 18, 1580, *EA*, III, 671–72.

31. Geoffrey Parker, *Philip II* (Boston, 1978), 82.

32. The house itself is currently used to store agricultural equipment, but the remains of earlier irrigation works are still to be seen in the surrounding area.

33. RAH Salazar MSS A48, f. 34.

34. Juan de Zúñiga to Charles, September 10, 1543, printed in J. M. March, *Niñez y juventud de Felipe II* (Madrid, 1941), I, 259. See also Alonso Enríquez de Guzmán, *Libro de la vida y costumbres de don Alonso Enríquez de Guzmán*, ed. H. Keniston (Madrid, 1960), 236–37.

35. Mariano Berrueta, *El Gran Duque de Alba* (Madrid, 1944), 38–39.

36. March, II, 89.

37. Magdalena de Bobadilla to Diego Hurtado de Mendoza, RAH Salazar MSS A52, n. f.

38. M. Fernández Alvarez, *Charles V* (London, 1975), 129.

39. The best account of these discussions is in F. Chabod, "Milan o los Paises Bajos?" *Carlos V: Homenaje de la Universidad de Granada* (Granada, 1958), 331–72. The *minuta* of the meeting (AGS E67, ff. 13–16) is printed on pp. 365–72.

40. The ceremonies are described in M. de Foronda y Aguilera, *Fiesta del Toison de Oro celebrada por Carlos V en Utrecht en 1546* (Madrid, 1903).

41. For the former view, see L. de Avila y Zúñiga, *Comentario de la Guerra de Alemania* (BAE 21), 410–19. For the latter, see Brandi, *Charles V*, 550.

42. This was certainly the view of some contemporaries. See J. Janssen, *History of the German People* (St. Louis, 1905–1925), V, 337–38; F. Martín Arrue, *Campañas del Duque de Alba* (Toledo, 1880), I, 151; and M. Fernández Alvarez, *La España del Emperador Carlos V*, Historia de España XVIII, ed. R. Menéndez Pidal (Madrid, 1966), 697–99.

43. Alba was appointed captain-general of the imperial forces at Regensburg on July 22, 1546 (Alonso de Santa Cruz, *Crónica del Emperador Carlos V* [Madrid, 1920–1922], IV, 503). Details of his salary and expenses, which were not paid until 1553, are in AGS E506, ff. 126, 128.

44. The battle is described by C. Oman, *A History of the Art of War in the Sixteenth Century* (New York, 1937), 229–43.

45. Brandi, *Charles V*, 551.

46. Sandoval, III, 243; Santa Cruz, IV, 509.

47. Avila y Zúñiga, 415; Brandi, *Charles V*, 552–53.

48. Avila y Zúñiga, 416.

49. Avila y Zúñiga, 417; Brandi, *Charles V*, 553.

50. Avila y Zúñiga, 418.

51. This account is drawn almost entirely from Avila y Zúñiga, 416–24, the only coherent account of the campaign to have survived.

52. Sandoval, III, 267.

53. Ibid.

54. Avila y Zúñiga, 426–29.

55. See Michael Roberts, "The Military Revolution, 1560–1660" (Belfast, 1956), reprinted with some changes in M. Roberts, *Essays in Swedish History* (London, 1967), 195–225.

56. Pierre Brantôme, *Les vies des grands capitaines*, in *Oeuvres complètes* (Paris, 1858), I, 158.

57. The battle of Mühlberg is described in chapter 36 of Pedro de Salazar, *Crónica de nuestra invictissima Emperador Carlos quinto . . . en la qual se tracta la justissima guerra q su Magestad mouio côtra los luteranos y rebeldes del Imperio* (Seville, 1552), reprinted as "La batalla de Mühlberg," *Revista de Archivos, Bibliotecas y Museos* XXV (1911), 432–50; specific reference to the surrender at p. 444. See also Brandi, *Charles V*, 566–68, and M. Lenz, *Die Schlacht bei Mühlberg* (Gotha, 1879).

58. Charles V, *Mémoires*, in A. Morel-Fatio, *Historiographie de Charles-Quint* (Paris, 1913), 173.

59. Charles to Mary of Hungary, April 25, 1547, *KKK*, II, 561–63.

60. Salazar, 448. This, apparently Alba's idea, was greatly resented by the Saxons: G. Mentz, *Johann Friedrich der Grossmütige, 1503–1554* (Jena, 1903–1908), III, 314.

61. M. Van Durme, *El Cardenal Granvela* (Barcelona, 1957), 87.

62. The incident is described by Van Durme, 80–83; Avila y Zúñiga, 448; Sandoval, III, 305; and Brandi, *Charles V*, 572–73.

CHAPTER IV

1. Karl Brandi, *The Emperor Charles V*, trans. C. V. Wedgwood (London, 1939), 590.

2. There are perceptive discussions of the nature and purpose of Burgundian court ritual in O. Cartellieri, *The Court of Burgundy* (London, 1929), and L. Pfandl, *Philipp II* (Munich, 1951), 120–57. For the ritual as applied in Spain see Jean Sigonney, "Relación de la forma de servir que se tenia en la casa del Emperador Don Carlos," BN MS 1080.

3. Antonio Ossorio, *Vida y hazañas de don Fernando Alvarez de Toledo, Duque de Alba*, ed. José López de Toro (Madrid, 1945), 22.

4. This, at least, is the view of L. Fernández y Fernández de Retana, *Historia de España*, ed. R. Menéndez Pidal (Madrid, 1966), XIX, part 1, 246, who also claims that Philip was displeased by the innovations.

5. A full description of the responsibilities involved is in A. Ballesteros y Beretta, *Historia de España* (Barcelona, 1927), II, part 2, 519.

6. J. Calvete de Estrella, *El felicísimo viaje del muy alto y muy poderoso príncipe Don Felipe* (Madrid, 1930), I, 3; Alonso de Santa Cruz, *Crónica del Emperador Carlos V* (Madrid, 1920–1922), V, 178.

7. Ossorio, 165. For another account see Prudencio de Sandoval, *Historia de la vida y hechos del Emperador Carlos V* (BAE 80–82), III, 337.

8. Luis Zapata, *Varia Historia*, I, ed. G. C. Horsman (Amsterdam, 1935), 32–33.

9. Santa Cruz, V, 227.

10. This was a common reaction among Spaniards; hence the expression *"Estamos en Flandes?"* (Are we in Flanders?) as a reproach for gross behavior. See M. Herrero García, *Ideas de los Españoles del siglo XVII* (2nd ed., Madrid, 1966), 432–33, for the stereotype of the drunken Dutch.

11. A. W. Lovett, "A New Governor for the Netherlands: The Appointment of Don Luis de Requesens, Comendador Mayor de Castilla," *European Studies Review* I, no. 2 (1971), 102, notes its use by Requesens.

12. See the incident quoted in Cobos's supposed letter to Charles V: Hayward Keniston, *Francisco de los Cobos, Secretary of the Emperor Charles V* (Pittsburgh, 1960), 270.

13. Printed in Santa Cruz, V, 178.

14. The relevant papers are in *DIE*, 35, 225–27, 243–44, 261–63.

15. Ballesteros y Beretta, II, part 2, 519.

16. See the comment of Tiepolo and Soranzo in *RAV*, V, 68–69.

17. Ruy Gómez remains as elusive in death as he was in life. There are no biographies, and his papers, with few exceptions, seem to have been destroyed. Some information on him may be found in L. Salazar y Castro, *Historia Geneálogica de la Casa de Silva* (Madrid, 1685), II, 456–531, and in Gregorio Marañón, *Antonio Pérez* (Madrid, 1963). There is a brief but classic sketch of him by the Venetian ambassador Badoero in *RAV*, III, 241.

18. Erika Spivakovsky, "La Princesa de Eboli," *Chronica Nova* IX (1977), 9.

19. He is described by Badoero as good and likable but not very bright (*RAV*, III, 246).

20. See Alba's minute instructions on everything to be done for the defense of La Goleta in 1566 (*EA*, II, 628–31). See also the unseemly bullying that accompanied negotiations for the marriage of Don Fadrique, Alba's son, and Doña Maria, the daughter of Don García (Alba to the Cardinal of Burgos, April 5, 1569, *EA*, II, 196–97, and Don García to Alba, April 20, 1569, AA caja 52, f. 209).

21. For Mendoza, see DeLamar Jensen, *Diplomacy and Dogmatism: Bernardino de Mendoza and the French Catholic League* (Cambridge, Mass., 1964).

22. J. H. Elliott, *Imperial Spain, 1469–1716* (New York, 1963), 255–57; Marañón, I, 154–55.

23. Marañón, I, 127.

24. Helen Nader, *The Mendoza Family in the Spanish Renaissance, 1350–1550* (New Brunswick, N.J., 1979), 168–73.

25. Erika Spivakovsky, *Son of the Alhambra: Don Diego Hurtado de Mendoza, 1504–1575* (Austin, Texas, 1970), 17.

26. The Spanish administration is described in J. M. Batista i Roca's foreword to H. G. Koenigsberger, *The Practice of Empire* (Ithaca, 1969), 9–35, and in J. Gounon-Loubens, *Essais sur l'administration de la Castille au XVIe siècle* (Paris, 1860).

27. Keniston, 314.

28. The standard source on Gonzalo Pérez is A. Gonzalez Palencia, *Gonzalo Pérez, secretario de Felipe II* (Madrid, 1946). See also J. A. Escudero, *Los Secretarios de Estado y del Despacho 1474–1724* (Madrid, 1969), I, 110.

29. A. Yalí Román Román, "Origen y evolución de la Secretario de Estado y de la Secretario del Despacho," *Jahrbuch für Geschichte von Stadt, Wirtschaft und Gesellschaft Lateinamerikas* VI (1969), 60–62.

30. Ibid., 75.

31. Badoero, in *RAV*, III, 248.

32. It was he, for example, who first informed Alba of Champagny's appointment to Antwerp and that of Don Hernando, Alba's son, to the viceroyalty of Cataluña. See AA caja 56, ff. 85, 89.

33. Zayas to Alba, April 23, 1571, AA caja 56, f. 89.

34. Yalí Román Román, 62.

35. For information on both of these men see A. W. Lovett, *Philip II and Mateo Vázquez de Leca* (Geneva, 1977).

36. *CSP-Venetian (1555–1556)*, 637–38.

37. G. de Leva, "La elezione di Papa Giulio III," *Rivista Storica Italiana* I (1884), 21–36.

38. Spivakovsky, *Son of the Alhambra*, 35–36, 160, 236.

39. Ibid., 245.

40. Philip's tour of the Netherlands is described in Vincente Alvarez, *Relación del camino y buen viaje que hizo el principe de España Don Felipe* (Brussels, 1551). There is a critical edition in French translation by M. T. Dovillée (Brussels, 1964).

41. Brandi, 602–3.

42. Ibid., 608–11.

43. Alba's response, dated May 11, 1552, is in AGS E89, f. 310.

44. Ossorio, 168.

45. Ruy Gómez to Eraso, April 5, 1552, AGS E89, f. 129.

46. Philip to Charles, June 30, 1552, AGS E504, f. 115.

47. Brandi, 612–14.

48. M. Van Durme, *El Cardenal Granvela* (Barcelona, 1957), 140.

49. Brandi, 619; Van Durme, 140; Ossorio, 173; F. Martín Arrue, *Campañas del Duque de Alba* (Toledo, 1880), I, 229–30.

50. Alba to Arras, October 15, 1552, *KKK*, III, 449–500.

51. For an eloquent, if scandalized, portrait see J. Janssen, *History of the German People* (St. Louis, 1905–1925), VI, 450.

52. Alba to Mary of Hungary, October 8, 1552, *KKK*, III, 494–95; Alba to Charles, October 8, 1552, ibid., III, 495–96.

53. Brandi, 619.

54. Alba to Charles, October 15, 1552, *KKK*, III, 497–98.

55. B. de Salignac, "Siége de Metz par l'empereur Charles-Quint en 1552," *Nouvelle collection des mémoires relatifs à l'histoire de France*, ed. Michaud (Paris, 1857), VIII, 524–25.

56. There is a substantial literature on the siege of Metz, though from the standpoint of understanding the military problems involved, all of it leaves something to be desired. In addition to Salignac, see Karl Brandi, "Karl V vor Metz," *Elsass-Lothringisches Jahrbuch* XVI (1937), 1-30; J. Griessdorf, "Der Zug Kaiser Karls V gegen Metz," *Hallische Abhandlung zur neuren Geschichte* XXVI (1891); and "Brief discours du siége de Metz en Lorraine," *Archives Curieuses de l'Histoire de France*, ed. M. L. Cimber and F. Danjou, Iʳᵉ série, III (1834–1840) 117–38. Neither Alba nor any of the other participants on the imperial side describes it at any length, but the Duke of Guise, as the victor, is less reticent in his *Mémoires-Journeaux*, printed in Michaud, ed., *Nouvelle collection des mémoires pour servir à l'histoire de France*, Iʳᵉ série (Paris, 1851), VI, 1-539.

57. *Venetianische Depeschen vom Kaiserhof: Dispacci de Germania*, ed. G. Turba (Vienna, 1889–1896), II, 587.

58. Printed in Guise, 86–89n.

59. See Guise's correspondence in *Mémoires-Journeaux*, 112–59. The views of Montluc and Montmorency are cited elsewhere.

60. Charles to Ferdinand, January 12, 1553, *KKK*, III, 530–34.

61. Griessdorf, 54.

62. Ossorio, 183.

63. Alba to Eraso, November 2, 1553, *EA*, I, 57–59.

64. Brandi, 626.

65. *CSP-Spanish*, XIII, 185.

66. M. A. S. Hume, "The Visit of Philip II," *English Historical Review* VII (1892), 264.

67. Ibid., 256.

68. The incident is described in J. de Figueroa to Charles V, July 26, 1554, *CSP-Spanish*, XII, 361.

69. Simon Renard to Charles V, September 3, 1554, *CSP-Spanish*, XIII, 45–46. See also *Acts of the Privy Council*, V, 61–62.

70. See the account in *CSP-Spanish*, XIII, 31. Hume believes this to have

been written by one Pedro Enríquez, a kinsman of the Duchess of Alba (p. 256).

71. *CSP-Spanish*, XIII, 11–12.

72. Ibid., XIII, 33.

73. She had been offended in this way by the Earl of Derby almost at the start of her visit (see Hume, 274).

74. *EA*, I, 64–65.

75. E. H. Harbison, *Rival Ambassadors at the Court of Queen Mary* (Princeton, 1940), 209.

CHAPTER V

1. Ruy Gómez to Eraso, April 15, 1554, *CSP-Spanish*, XIII, 162–64. (The editor was unsure of the recipient, but references to Eraso's wife, Doña Mariana, and to other personal matters make the attribution secure.)

2. Ibid.

3. Ibid.

4. Alba to Francisco de Toledo, April 15, 1555, *EA*, I, 68–69.

5. *CSP-Spanish*, XIII, 213.

6. Alba to Bernardino de Mendoza, April 7, 1555, *EA*, I, 66; Alba to Philip, April 20, 1555, *EA*, I, 71–73; Ramón Carande, *Carlos V y sus banqueros* (Madrid, 1967), III, 43–448, describes Alba's financial problems at length, but without reference to the politics involved.

7. Alba to Bernardino de Mendoza, June 14, 1555, *EA*, I, 170–74.

8. *CSP-Spanish*, XIII, 213.

9. *CSP-Venetian (1555–1556)*, 49.

10. Alba to Philip, May 18, 1555, *EA*, I, 118–20.

11. Alba to Philip, May 28, 1555, *EA*, I, 125–26.

12. Alba to Ruy Gómez, June 29, 1555, *EA*, I, 234–37.

13. Alba to Ruy Gómez, May 11, 1555, *EA*, I, 102–5.

14. *CSP-Venetian (1555–1556)*, 74–76.

15. Alba to Francisco de Toledo, June 14, 1555, *EA*, I, 178–80.

16. Alba to Bernardino de Mendoza, June 21, 1555, *EA*, I, 202–3.

17. Alba to Cristóbal de Mendoza (his own majordomo), *EA*, I, 263–65.

18. *CSP-Spanish*, XIII, 243.

19. Alba to Cosimo de'Medici, September 8, 1555, *EA*, I, 301–3.

20. Alba to Francisco de Toledo, June 9, 1555, *EA*, I, 253–56; Alba to Cosimo de' Medici, June 14, 1555, *EA*, I, 168.

21. Alba to Charles V, June, *EA*, I, 237–41.

22. Alba to Francisco de Toledo, July 5, 1555, *EA*, I, 248–49.

23. Alba's letters on the progress of the fleet are in *EA*, I, 190–92, 257, 284–86, and 289–90.

24. Alba to Charles V, August 5, 1555, *EA*, I, 284–86.

25. Ibid. The first warnings came much earlier: see Alba to Philip, June 8, 1555, *EA*, I, 159–64.

26. Alba's official report, dated June 28, 1555, is in *EA*, I, 231–33. The quote is at p. 232.

27. Alba to Charles V, July 24, 1555, *EA*, I, 272–76. See also *CSP-Foreign (1555–1556)*, 180.

28. Alba to Cosimo de' Medici, September 4, 1555, *EA*, I, 299–301.

29. Ibid.

30. Alba to Charles V, September 23, 1555, *EA*, I, 310–11; Alba to Cosimo de' Medici, September 23, 1555 (incorrectly dated September 13), *EA*, I, 304–5.

31. Alba to Charles V, September 10, 1555, *EA*, I, 303–4.

32. Pierre Brantôme, *Les vies des grands capitaines*, in *Oeuvres complètes* (Paris, 1858), II, 159–60.

33. F. Martín Arrue, *Campañas del Duque de Alba* (Toledo, 1880), I, 237.

34. Prudencio de Sandoval, *Historia de la vida y hechos del Emperador Carlos V* (BAE 80–82), III, 452–53.

35. Alba to Brissac, August 10, 1555, *EA*, I, 286–87.

36. Alba to Antonio de Toledo, August 3, 1555, *EA*, I, 277–79.

37. Gregorio Marañón, *Antonio Pérez* (Madrid, 1963), I, 154–55; J. H. Elliott, *Imperial Spain, 1469–1716* (New York, 1963), 254. The original document, dated Portofino, January 11, 1556, is in *EA*, I, 352–56.

38. Alba to Bernardino de Mendoza, May 31, 1555, *EA*, I, 135–36.

39. These letters, to Ruy Gómez and Antonio de Toledo, are in *EA*, I, 340–41, 341–45, 364–65, and 365–67.

40. Alba to Philip, February 14, 1556, *EA*, I, 362–63.

41. Alba to the Princess of Portugal, March 29, 1556, *EA*, I, 390–91.

42. Alba to Philip, June 18, 1556, *EA*, I, 412–17.

43. See Alba's letters to Philip and the Princess of Portugal, *EA*, I, 381–91.

44. Alba to Philip, June 18, 1556, *EA*, I, 408.

45. Alba to Philip, June 18, 1556, *EA*, I, 412–17.

46. Alba to Philip, March 28, 1556, *EA*, I, 383–85.

47. Alba to the Marqués de Sarria, May 1, 1556, *EA*, I, 394–95.

48. Giuseppe Coniglio, *I vicère spagnoli di Napoli* (Naples, 1967), 94–95.

49. Alba to Philip, March 28, 1556, *EA*, I, 387.

50. Alba to Philip, March 28, 1556, *EA*, I, 383–85.

51. The best analysis of this situation, and of the character of Paul IV, remains Ludwig von Pastor, *The History of the Popes from the Close of the Middle Ages* (St. Louis, 1936), XIV, 56–137.

52. *CSP-Venetian*, VI, part 2, 850–57.

53. Ibid., 800–802.

54. Ibid., 850–57.

55. Pastor, XIV, 148.

56. Ibid., 92.

57. Alba to Cosimo de' Medici, September 4, 1556, *EA*, I, 299–301.

58. Pastor, XIV, 93.

59. Alba to Philip, June 18, 1556, *EA*, I, 409–12.

60. The entire text is printed in *DIE*, 2, 437–46.

61. *CSP-Venetian (1555–1558)*, part 1, 592–94.

62. Alba to Juan Vázquez de Molina, August 21, 1556, *EA*, I, 430.

63. Alejandro Andrea, *De la guerra de campaña de Roma y del reyno de Nápoles en el pontificado de Paulo IV* (Madrid, 1589), 39–45.

64. Pastor, XIV, 140.

65. Ibid., 144.

66. Alba to the Cardinal of Paris, September 16, 1556, *EA*, I, 432–33.

67. Alba to Cosimo de' Medici, September 29, 1556, *EA*, I, 433–34.

68. The best and indeed the only coherent account of this campaign is provided by Andrea, 46–85.

69. Andrea, 86–87.

70. *CSP-Venetian*, VI, part 2, 815–18.

71. Though he was a cousin of Diego Hurtado de Mendoza, his actions appear to have been inspired by greed rather than faction.

72. Andrea, 147; *CSP-Venetian*, VI, part 2, 925–30; *CSP-Foreign (1553–1558)*, 286.

73. Andrea, 114–16, 155. Alba's instructions are in *EA*, I, 450–61.

74. Pastor, XIV, 152–58.

75. Duke of Guise, *Mémoires-Journeaux*, in Michaud, ed., *Nouvelle collection des mémoires pour servir à l'histoire de France*, 1ʳᵉ série (Paris, 1851), 347–51.

76. Andrea, 235–48.

77. Ibid., 260–72.

78. Ibid., 306–8.

79. *CSP-Venetian* VI, part 2, 1268–69.

80. Ibid., 1272–74.

81. Ibid., 1274–76.

82. Ibid., 1298–99.

83. Ibid., 1304–06; Pastor, XIV, 167.

84. The original grant of the tithes is found in AA caja 29, f. 67, together with a document dated Rome, June 18, 1554, verifying that the grant had been confirmed by Pope Alexander VI.

85. *CSP-Venetian (1555–1558)*, part 1, 457–58. The decision was appealed in 1564, but Alba's rights were again upheld. See AA caja 27, ff. 68–77, for a series of reports on the progress of the suit.

86. Brantôme, II, 159–60.

87. *CSP-Venetian*, VI, 1152–54.

88. Ibid., 1456–57.

89. Ibid., 1436–37.

90. *CSP-Venetian (1557–1558)*, part 3, 1438–39.

91. Licenciado Espinosa to Alba, April 3, 1567, AA caja 34, f. 136.

CHAPTER VI

1. F. Braudel's contention (*La Méditerranée et le monde méditerranéen à l'époque de Philippe II* [Paris, 1966], II, 265–66) that the treaty completed an evolution toward a policy based on the Mediterranean must be taken with a grain of salt. True, much attention was devoted to Spain, Italy, and the problem of the Turk, but an immense effort was also expended on the Netherlands and in the American kingdoms.

2. Much of the enormous correspondence between these two men can be found in the *Papiers d'état du Cardinal de Granvelle,* ed. C. Weiss (Paris, 1841–1852), and the *Correspondance du Cardinal de Granvelle, 1565–1586,* ed. E. Poullet and C. Piot (Brussels, 1877–1896), but there remain large unpublished collections in the Biblioteca de Palacio, Madrid, and in the Bibliothéque Municipale, Besançon.

3. C. V. Wedgwood, *William the Silent* (London, 1956), 28.

4. Much information on Viglius may be found in C. P. Hoynck van Papendracht, *Analecta Belgica seu vita Viglii ab Aytta Zwichemi ab ipso Viglio scripta* (The Hague, 1743). His *Mémoires* may be found in the *Collection de mémoires relatifs à la histoire de Belgique* (Brussels, 1858), II.

5. James Westfall Thompson, *The Wars of Religion in France, 1559–1576* (New York, 1909), 21.

6. Lucien Romier, *Les origines politiques des guerres de religion* (Paris, 1913–1914), I, 299.

7. M. Van Durme, *El Cardenal Granvela* (Barcelona, 1957), 213.

8. *CSP-Venetian (1558–1580),* 29–39.

9. *PEG,* V, 338–45.

10. The funerals are described in *CSP-Foreign (1558–1559),* I, 66–71.

11. The reports of the Commissioners are in *CSP-Foreign (1558–1559),* I, 122–23, 137–39, and 155–58.

12. *CSP-Venetian (1558–1580),* 33–35.

13. Ibid., 49.

14. *CSP-Foreign (1558–1559),* 137–39.

15. Ibid., I, 155–58.

16. *CSP-Venetian (1558–1580),* 44–45.

17. A. de Amézua y Mayo, *Isabel de Valois: Reina de España* (Madrid, 1949), I, 57–62.

18. *CSP-Foreign (1558–1559),* I, 324–29.

19. An excellent description of the whole affair is in Thompson, 1–4.

20. H. G. Koenigsberger, *Estates and Revolutions* (Ithaca, N.Y., 1971), 135–36.

21. For a full discussion of this issue see M. Dierickx, *De Oprichting der nieuwe bisdommen in der Nederlanden onder Filips II, 1559–1570* (Antwerp, 1950). See also Pieter Geyl, *The Revolt of the Netherlands* (London, 1962), 71.

22. Philip's idea of governance, derived ultimately from his father, is discussed in M. Fernández Alvarez, *Política mundial de Carlos V y Felipe II* (Madrid, 1966), and by Peter Pierson, *Philip II of Spain* (London, 1975). For a new

psychological portrait of Philip and the influence of personality on his methods of governance, see Geoffrey Parker, *Philip II* (Boston, 1978).

23. Granvelle's relations with the nobility, and in particular the origins of his quarrel with Orange, are discussed in Van Durme, 240–44.

24. There is a massive literature on the problems leading to the revolt of the Netherlands. Among the best summaries are Geoffrey Parker, *The Dutch Revolt* (London, 1977), 41–67, and Geyl, 69–79, though Geyl's ideas on the development of Netherlandish nationalism have been much criticized. An older and far more detailed work is Felix Rachfahl, *Wilhelm von Oranien und der Nederländische Aufstand* (Halle and The Hague, 1906–1924), II, part 1, 3–288. See also the superb dissertation of P. D. Lagomarsino, "Court Factions and the Formulation of Spanish Policy toward the Netherlands, 1559–1567" (Diss., Cambridge University, 1973).

25. The problem is examined by Dierickx, 177–88.

26. Ibid., 115–27.

27. Granvelle to Philip, May 12, 1576, IVDJ 47, f. 49; noted by Parker, *Dutch Revolt*, 283 n. 24.

28. Geyl, 74.

29. Van Durme, 232.

30. This campaign of defamation is described at length by M. Tridon, *Simon Renard* (Besançon, 1882), and in L. Febvre, *Philippe II et la Franche-Comté* (Paris, 1911), 411–18.

31. For this and his counterattack against Renard, see *PEG*, VII, 11, 44, 151, 208.

32. *CSP-Venetian (1558–1580)*, 88–89.

33. Ibid., 256.

34. Granvelle to Mary of Hungary, November 17, 1551, in A. von Druffel, *Beiträge zur Reichsgeschichte*, I, 805–6. See also *PEG*, IV, 298–300, and V, 683–86.

35. Their letters, to be found in AGS E523, ff. 52–53; E526, ff. 96, 100, 125, 133; and E529, f. 38, are analyzed in depth by Lagomarsino, 49–57.

36. His instructions are in *CPh*, I, 265.

37. Alba to the Bishop of Osma, March 11, 1564, *EA*, I, 574–75.

38. Alba to Cardinal Pacheco, March 13, 1564, *EA*, I, 573–74.

39. Amézua y Mayo, II, 44–45.

40. Alba to García de Toledo, October 4, 1563, *EA*, I, 562–63.

41. Alba to García de Toledo, October 1, 1563, *EA*, I, 566.

42. See the virtually undecipherable letters of Don Antonio de Toledo to Alba in AA caja 52, ff. 105–10.

43. Alba to Philip, October 21, 1563, *EA*, I, 557.

44. His attitude seems to parallel that expressed in his recommendations on Milan in 1555–1556 (see Chapter V).

45. Lagomarsino, 89, 129–31.

46. Egmont's requests with Philip's marginalia are in AGS E527, f. 51.

47. Pierre Brantôme, *Les vies des grands capitaines*, in *Oeuvres complètes*

(Paris, 1858), II, 78. This view was accepted by Kervyn de Lettenhove, *Les Huguenots et les Gueux* (Bruges, 1883), I, 217–20, but is inherently improbable. The nobles had earlier opposed the wars with France and a reversal would have cost them much of their newfound popularity.

48. A draft of this reply with notes is in AGS E527, ff. 4–5. The draft alone is printed in *CPh*, I, 346.

49. Philip's letters are in *CFMP*, I, 40–49.

50. Many of the documents on Eraso's *visita* are contained in AGS E147.

51. Alba's reports on the conference are in *EA*, I, 582–607. See also Amézua y Mayo, II, 191–332, for a detailed description of the ceremonies and personalities involved.

52. AGS E527, f. 14. This document is analyzed at length by Lagomarsino, 176–79.

53. See the letters of July 22 (a series of five), *CFMP*, I, 53–77.

54. A memo summarizing Villavicencio's investigation of Viglius is found in AGS E526, f. 97.

55. Pérez's report on the meeting is in *CPh*, II, 564.

56. AGS E527, f. 16 (to Egmont), and ff. 6 and 94 (to Granvelle).

57. For a portrait of Don Diego himself, see M. Fernández Alvarez, *Tres embajadores de Felipe II en Inglaterra* (Madrid, 1951), 137–90. His reports to Philip on the Low Countries are in *DIE*, 89, 239, 246, and in *CPh*, I, 385. For his report to Eboli, see *CPh*, I, 383.

58. For a discussion of this meeting see L. van der Essen, *Alexandre Farnèse, Prince de Parme* (Brussels, 1933–1934), I, 139.

59. For the exodus, see Assonleville to Granvelle, January 15, 1566, *CPh*, I, 342. Much of the propaganda was produced on Brederode's estate at Vianen. For a discussion of this literature see H. de la Fontaine Verwey, "Hendrik van Brederode en de Drukkerij van Vianen," *Het Boek* 30 (1949–1951), 3–42.

60. Philip to Margaret of Parma, July 17, 1562, *DIE*, 4, 278–84.

61. Lagomarsino, 219–20.

62. Ibid., 214.

63. As usual, the most vivid account in English is J. L. Motley, *The Rise of the Dutch Republic* (London, 1886), I, 478–81. An eyewitness account may be found in L.-P. Gachard, ed., *Correspondance de Marguerite d'Autriche, Duchesse de Parme, avec Philippe II* (Brussels, 1867–1881), III, xii–xiii. The requests themselves are printed in *AON*, 1st ser., II, 80–89.

64. The controversy over this is discussed in L.-P. Gachard, "Sur l'origine du nom de Gueux," *Etudes et Notices Historiques Concernant l'Histoire des Pays-Bas* (Brussels, 1890), I, 130–41.

65. *CFMP*, II, 269, 274.

66. *CPh*, I, 445.

67. See W. S. Maltby, "Iconoclasm and Politics in the Netherlands, 1566," *The Image and the Word*, ed. J. Gutmann (Missoula, Mont., 1977), 149–64.

68. For a discussion of these illnesses see Luis Cabrera de Córdoba, *Felipe II, Rey de España (1919)* (Madrid, 1876–1877), I, 487; *Dépeches de M. de Fourquevaux*, ed. E. Douais (Paris, 1896–1904) I, 124, and Dr. Man's report in *CSP-Foreign*, VIII, 129. The psychosomatic theory was first advanced in Nuncio to Alessandrino, September 25, 1566, *CDS*, I, 352.

69. This letter was quoted in part by Arteaga in "Breve noticia de Gonzalo Pérez," *DIE*, 7, 541. The original is in the Bibliothèque Municipale, Besançon, tome 13, f. 224. I am indebted to P. D. Lagomarsino for providing me with a photocopy of the original.

70. A. Gonzalez Palencia, *Gonzalo Pérez, secretario de Felipe II* (Madrid, 1946), I, 9, 323–25. This whole question has been fraught with confusion. As we have seen, Marañón believed, wrongly, that Alba and Pérez had always been enemies. Gonzalez Palencia, on the other hand, was so convinced of their friendship that he regarded the letter to Granvelle as a malicious forgery (p. 324).

71. For evidence that Antonio's defection was recent, see Cabrera de Córdoba, I, 491.

72. The term is from Cabrera de Córdoba, I, 491.

73. Their patents are printed in J. A. Escudero, *Los Secretarios de Estado y del Despacho 1474–1724* (Madrid, 1969), III, 645–46.

74. See Cavalli's report in *RAV*, series I, V, 180.

75. Antonio Ossorio, *Vida y hazañas de don Fernando Alvarez de Toledo, Duque de Alba*, ed. José López de Toro (Madrid, 1945), 331–32.

76. Lagomarsino, 234.

77. *Dépeches de M. de Fourquevaux*, I, 133.

78. An extract of this letter is in *CPh*, I, 465 (noted by Lagomarsino, 249).

79. Ossorio, 336–41; see also Cabrera de Córdoba, I, 490–97.

80. The problems of Don Carlos were widely known. For a modern study, see C. D. O'Malley, *Don Carlos of Spain: A Medical Portrait* (Los Angeles, 1969).

81. *CSP-Foreign*, IX, no. 1225.

82. These deliberations are described in Fourquevaux, I, 133, 139, 148, and by Morillon, *CG*, II, 105, 114; Granvelle to Alba, May 16, 1567, *CG*, II, 442.

83. See, for example, Licenciado Espinosa to Alba, April 3, 1567, AA caja 34, f. 136.

84. Alba's reluctance was widely known. See Morillon to Granvelle, March 29, 1567, *CG*, II, 327; Granvelle to Alba, May 16, 1567, *CG*, II, 442.

85. Cabrera de Córdoba, I, 495.

86. Fourquevaux, I, 164; *CDS*, I, 419.

CHAPTER VII

1. AA caja 165, f. 27. AA caja 159 contains full details on the planning.

2. P. D. Lagomarsino, "Court Factions and the Formulation of Spanish

Policy toward the Netherlands, 1559–1567" (Diss., Cambridge, 1973), 271.

3. Nuncio to Allesandrino, December 19, 1566, *CDS*, II, 29.

4. Alba, however, seems to have believed that it was a real possibility: see AA caja 160, f. 18.

5. This document, entitled "Los agravios hechos a 43 despues salio nombrado aviendo acceptado El cargo de venir a Flandes," is found in AA caja 160, f. 18. ("43" was Alba's code name.)

6. *Dépeches de M. de Fourquevaux*, ed. E. Douais (Paris, 1896–1904) I, 178 (February 13–15, 1567).

7. Alba to Philip, April 27, 1567, *DIE*, 4, 354–57.

8. Philip's refusal to grant the additional amount is in AGS E149, f. 185; the warrant is in AGS CMC2a, f. 49. An account of the whole transaction is in Geoffrey Parker, *The Army of Flanders and the Spanish Road, 1567–1659* (Cambridge, 1972), 108.

9. Alba to Eraso, April 26, 1567, *DIE*, 4, 349–50.

10. Luis Cabrera de Córdoba, *Felipe II, Rey de España (1619)* (Madrid, 1876–1877), I, 525–26; Antonio Ossorio, *Vida y hazañas de don Fernando Alvarez de Toledo, Duque de Alba*, ed. José López de Toro (Madrid, 1945), 343-44.

11. Parker, 87; Bernardino de Mendoza, *Commentario de lo sucedido en las guerras de los Paises Bajos* (BAE 28), 405, gives the number as 8,780 Spanish infantry, 5 companies of Spanish light horse, 3 of Italians, 2 of Albanians, and 2 of Spanish mounted arquebusiers.

12. Parker, 81.

13. Alba to Diego de Espinosa, May 6, 1567, *DIE*, 4, 360–62.

14. Alba to Philip, May 24, 1567, *DIE*, 39, 8–13.

15. Mendoza, 406.

16. Pierre Brantôme, *Les vies des grands capitaines*, in *Oeuvres complètes* (Paris, 1858), II, 162, 164–65.

17. Alba to Diego de Espinosa, June 1, 1567, *EA*, I, 646–47.

18. Alba to Margaret of Parma, June 6, 1567, *CFMP*, III, 285–86.

19. Alba to Espinosa, June 1, 1567, *EA*, II, 646–47.

20. Zayas to Alba, June 30, 1567, AA caja 56, f. 61.

21. This story was widely circulated. Its earliest mention appears to be in Khevenhüller, *Historia de mi vida*, BN MS 2751. See also P. C. Bor, *Oorspronk, begin en vervolgh der Nederlandsche oorlogen* (Amsterdam, 1679), IV, 182, and P. C. Hooft, *Neederlandsche Histoorien sedert de ooverdraght der heerschappye van Kaiser Karl den Vijfden op Kooning Philips zijnen zoon* (Amsterdam, 1642), IV, 150.

22. Margaret to Philip, July 19, 1566, *CFMP*, II, 258.

23. There were two original patents: the first, dated December 1, 1566, is in *CPh*, II, 600. The second, dated January 31, 1567, is in *CPh*, II, 619, with the Spanish version in *DIE*, 4, 388. A third document, granting him extraordinary powers to be used if necessary, is dated March 1, 1567, *CPh*, II, 626.

24. Margaret to Philip, April 10, 1567, *CFMP*, I, 334–35.

25. Alba to Espinosa, July 11, 1567, *EA*, I, 656–57.
26. Margaret to Philip, August 29, 1567, *CFMP*, I, 409–11.
27. Though Geoffrey Parker is undoubtedly correct in saying that death warrants had not been signed in advance (*The Dutch Revolt* [London, 1977], 293 n. 30), the destruction of Egmont and Hornes was clearly premeditated.
28. *DIE*, 4, 416–21.
29. Alba to Philip, September 18, 1567, *DIE*, 4, 444–48.
30. Alba's letters to the emperor and the Duke of Cleves are in *EA*, I, 673–75, and 681–83, respectively. The results of his long inquiry into their appeal to the Order are in Alba to Philip, January 19, 1568, *EA*, II, 12–16.
31. Alba to Espinosa, September 10, 1567, *EA*, I, 669.
32. See the numerous letters in which Alba personally authorizes passage of individual items of cargo after imposing his embargo of English goods: AGRB, Audience, Liasse, 1697².
33. Geoffrey Parker, "Corruption and Imperialism in the Spanish Netherlands: The Case of Francisco de Lixalde, 1567–1612," *Spain and the Netherlands, 1559–1659* (London, 1979), 160.
34. For a discussion of this larger issue, which was obviously complicated by religion, see A. W. Lovett, "Some Spanish Attitudes toward the Netherlands (1572–1578)," *TvG* LXXXV (1972), 17–30, and A. Th. van Deursen, "Holland's Experience of War during the Revolt of the Netherlands," *Britain and the Netherlands* VI. *War and Society*, ed. A. C. Duke and C. A. Tamse (The Hague, 1977), 21–23.
35. As late as May, 1573, Alba was still arguing that more Spaniards and Italians were needed and that it was necessary to get rid of "this ancient sect of dogmatizers, the *cabrón* of which is Viglius" (Alba to Philip, May 15, 1573, *EA*, III, 399–401).
36. A. W. Lovett, "Francisco de Lixalde: A Spanish Paymaster in the Netherlands (1567–1577)," *TvG* 84 (1971), 14–23.
37. Parker, "Corruption," 256 n. 21.
38. The case was finally closed in 1612 with the payment of 13,000 ducats by Lixalde's heirs. The scandal is discussed in detail by Parker in "Corruption," 152–61.
39. There are some interesting examples in AA caja 41, f. 128.
40. Zayas to Alba, September 2, 1569, AA caja 56, f. 71. However, L. van der Essen suggests that he may have been a kind of secret agent for Margaret of Parma. See his "Rapport secret de Géronimo de Curiel, facteur du roi d'Espagne à Anvers sur les marchands hérétiques," *Bulletin de la Comission Royale d'Histoire* 80 (1911), 336.
41. BM add. 28.702, ff. 261–62.
42. Parker, "Corruption," 155–57.
43. Lixalde to Albornoz, August 31, 1573, AA caja 41, f. 174.
44. AA caja 41, ff. 179, 184.
45. Lovett, "Lixalde," 17.
46. Requesens to Philip, December 29, 1573, AGS E554, f. 166.

47. Alba to Antonio de Toledo, January 23, 1571, *EA*, II, 503.
48. These reports are in AA caja 41, ff. 113–37.
49. Albornoz to Zayas, October 22, 1569, AGS E541, f. 158.
50. See, for example, *CSP-Roman*, I, 450–51.
51. Parker, *Army of Flanders*, 114.
52. Albornoz to the Duchess of Alba, December 23, 1569, *EA*, II, 299–300.
53. Hernando de Toledo to Zayas, February 12, 1570, AGS E544, ff. 111–12.
54. Albornoz to Zayas, October 31, 1569, AGS E541, f. 161.
55. Parker, "Corruption," 153.
56. AGS E544, f. 112.
57. Parker, *Army of Flanders*, 107.
58. See the "Secret Instructions" printed in A. L. E. Verheyden, *Le Conseil des Troubles: liste des condamnés* (Brussels, 1961), 508.
59. Alba to Philip, January 6, 1567, *DIE*, 37, 82–85.
60. J. L. Motley, *The Rise of the Dutch Republic* (London, 1886) II, 147–48, makes much of this, but it is possible that they were named by the troops rather than by Alba himself, in much the same way that artillery pieces came to acquire names.
61. For illustrations of the citadel, see the Plan of Antwerp engraved by Pauwels van Overbeke, 1568 (Antwerp: Stedelijk Prentenkabinet), and the engraving by Frans Hogenburg in the Bibliothèque Royale, Brussels. There is also a drawing in some copies of *CPh*, II.
62. Alba to Philip, June 3, *DIE*, 38, 120–22.
63. Alba's vitriolic comments on this area in *EA*, II, 17–20, and *DIE*, 37, 378–83.
64. Alba to Philip, September 12, 1569, *DIE*, 38, 182–86.
65. *CSP-Foreign*, VIII, 395.
66. Alba's report on this affair is in *DIE*, 39, 186–87.
67. Margaret of Parma estimated that over 100,000 had fled, but surely this is an exaggeration (*CFMP* I, 411–14). Parker estimates the total population of the major Dutch exile communities in England and Germany in 1570 as 28,200 (*Dutch Revolt*, 119).
68. Alba to Philip, April 13, 1568, *DIE*, 4, 487–96.
69. L. van der Essen, "Croisade contre les hérétiques ou guerre contre des rebelles," *Revue d'Histoire Ecclésiastique* LI, no. 1 (1956), 42–78.
70. Alba to Diego de Espinosa, March 10, 1569, *EA*, II, 180–81.
71. Brantôme, II, 173.
72. See, for example, Alba to Philip, September 13, 1567, *DIE*, 4, 425–27: "I understand that the quietude of these states does not consist in beheading men moved by the persuasion of others."
73. Alba to Philip, October 2, 1567, *DIE*, IV, 451–60.
74. Lagomarsino (p. 285 n. 68) points out that Hopperus and Villavicencio both took credit for the idea, but Alba also had by a very early date a clear idea of what was to be done.

75. Alba to Philip, September 9, 1567, *DIE*, 4, 416–18. The translation is Motley's (II, 134).

76. Alba to Philip, October 24, 1567, *EA*, I, 693–98.

77. Alba to Philip, April 13, 1568, *DIE*, 4, 487–96.

78. *CPh*, II, 5, 11–12.

79. Alba to Philip, October 4, 1567, *DIE*, 4, 466–70.

80. He claimed that the parties involved "were not without prejudice" (Alba to Philip, January 6, 1568, *DIE*, 37, 80–81). See also Alba to Philip, June 23, 1568, *DIE*, 37, 285–90.

81. Alba to Philip, September 1, 1568, *DIE*, 37, 378–83.

82. These figures are from Verheyden, 3–13.

83. Alba to Philip, April 13, 1568, *DIE*, 4, 487–96.

84. Verheyden, 16.

85. Alba to Stalpaert (the receiver of confiscated goods at Amsterdam), December 6, 1568; Verheyden, 538–39.

86. Stalpaert to Alba, 1569 (with marginalia by Alba); in Verheyden, 540–42.

87. See the estimate of Albornoz (Albornoz to Zayas, January 23, 1571, *EA*, II, 498–503).

88. See W. S. Maltby, *The Black Legend in England* (Durham, N.C., 1971), 48.

89. Verheyden, xi, gives the totals as 12,203, 1,085, and 20, respectively. These figures were corrected by M. Dierickx, "De lijst der veroordeelden door de Raad van Beroerten," *Revue Belge de Philologie et d'Histoire* 40 (1962), 415–22.

90. Alba to Philip, April 13, 1568, *DIE*, 4, 487–96.

91. Motley, II, 138.

92. There were, for example, more than 600 executed for complicity in the Northern Rebellion of 1569–1570 (J. E. Neale, *Queen Elizabeth I* [London, 1934], 189).

93. The painting is in the Palais des Beaux Arts, Brussels. It is not to be confused with an earlier work by Breughel the Elder that exists in two versions, one at the Kunsthistorisches Museum, Vienna, the other at Hampton Court. Following an old tradition, S. Ferber, "Pieter Breugel and the Duke of Alba," *Renaissance News* XIX (1966), 205–19, argues that the latter also depicts Alba, but does not adequately respond to the objections of Ch. Terlinden, "Pierre Breugel le Vieux et l'histoire," *Revue Belge d'Archéologie et d'Histoire de l'Art* III (1942), 250–51. Moreover, the central figure in this painting does not, save for his beard, resemble Alba. The son's copy changed the basic composition and many of the details. The central figure is an excellent likeness of Alba as he was represented by Titian and Mor, and it is likely that Breughel the Younger was using the earlier artistic conception to make a very different political point.

CHAPTER VIII

1. C. V. Wedgwood, *William the Silent* (London, 1956), 103. Orange's efforts to gain support are described in detail by F. Rachfahl, *Wilhelm von Oranien und der Nederländische Aufstand*, III, 451–88.

2. Alba to Philip, November 6, 1567, *EA*, I, 703–4.

3. Alba to Philip, February 10, 1568, *EA*, II, 23–24.

4. Alba to Philip, March 11, 1568, *DIE*, 37, 183–84.

5. The Spaniards were well aware of this. As Mendoza put it: "All that is needed [to raise an army] is money for the first pay" (Bernardino de Mendoza, *Commentario de lo sucedido en las guerras de las Paises Bajos* [BAE 28], 428).

6. Londoño's report to Alba, and Alba's to the king are in *DIE*, 37, 235–43. See also Mendoza, 411–14.

7. *CSP-Foreign*, IX, 590; Mendoza, 410.

8. J. L. Motley, *The Rise of the Dutch Republic* (London, 1886), II, 188.

9. Alba's report to the king, dated June 9, 1568, is in *DIE*, 37, 273–80. Most of the correspondence for the campaign is printed in L.-P. Gachard, *Correspondance du Duc d'Albe sur l'invasion du Comte Louis de Nassau en Frise, en 1568* (Brussels, 1850). Mendoza's account is at pp. 411–14.

10. Alba to Philip, June 9, 1568, *DIE*, 37, 273–80.

11. Even Granvelle issued a mild protest: Granvelle to Philip, November 2, 1567, *CG*, III, 67–68.

12. Alba to Philip, September 18, 1567, *DIE*, 4, 444–48.

13. Ibid.

14. The papers of the Council of Troubles are in AGRB Raad van Beroerten. There is a printed inventory by A. Jamées. Egmont's interrogation may be found in Raad van Beroerten, 156. That of Hornes was published in *Supplément à l'histoire des guerres civiles de Flandre sous Philippe II du père Famian Strada* (Amsterdam, 1729), I, 103–210.

15. Dated March 24, 1567, in IVDJ, envio 6, carpeta 1, no. 4.

16. Alba to Philip, January 19, 1568, *EA*, II, 12–16.

17. Alba to Philip, April 13, 1568, *DIE*, 4, 487–96.

18. This story apparently originated with Morillon: *AON*, series I, supplement, 81.

19. Years later, Antonio Pérez recalled that Alba had once told him: "Kings use men like an orange, squeezing out the juice and throwing it away" (Gregorio Marañón, *Antonio Pérez* [Madrid, 1963], I, 159).

20. Motley, II, 203. The incident is described by Hooft and Bor, among others.

21. Alba to Philip, June 9, 1568, *DIE*, 37, 273–80.

22. Without wishing to become embroiled in the controversy over Geyl's "river defense" theory and the attack on it by Charles Wilson, I must point out that this indicates that the rivers themselves were not an insuperable barrier, at least when they were undefended. See Pieter Geyl, *The Revolt of*

the Netherlands (London, 1962), and Charles Wilson, *Queen Elizabeth and the Revolt of the Netherlands* (Berkeley, 1970), 8–11.

23. Alba to Philip, July 18, 1568, *DIE*, 37, 298–305.

24. *DIE*, 30, 445, quoted by Motley, II, 214.

25. Alba's reports on the campaign are in *DIE*, 37, 295–305; on Jemmingen, in *DIE*, 30, 445. See also Mendoza, 418–27; F. Martín Arrue, *Campañas del Duque de Alba* (Toledo, 1880), II, 77–82, 88–111; Motley, II, 208–19; and Rachfahl, III, 501–55. All these accounts are substantially in agreement.

26. Mendoza, 427. The order to Chiappino Vitelli is in AA caja 165, f. 9.

27. Philip to Alba, June 27, 1568, *DIE*, 37, 290–95.

28. The correspondence is in *DIE*, 37, 347–50, 358–63, 412–24, 432–37, 441–50, 465–73, and in *EA*, II, 74–78, 80–83. There was also a request for English aid from the Count of Emden on August 12, 1568, *CSP-Foreign*, VIII, 520–21.

29. Alba to Philip, July 6, 1568, *DIE*, 37, 295–98.

30. Mendoza, 428.

31. Philip to Alba, September 15, 1568, *DIE*, 37, 402–9.

32. Philip to Alba, September 15, 1568, AGS E540, f. 131.

33. Espinosa informed Alba of the king's displeasure. Alba's vehement defense is in Alba to Espinosa, November 6, 1568, *EA*, II, 108–9. See also Alba to García de Toledo, November 23, 1568, *EA*, II, 118–20.

34. Alba to Philip, September 11, 1568, *DIE*, 37, 394–400.

35. Mendoza, 428.

36. Ibid., 432.

37. Ibid., 430. Mendoza, like many other Spaniards, was fond of likening their situation to that of the ancient Romans.

38. See Mendoza's discourse on the impropriety of treating with rebels (p. 429).

39. Alba outlined his strategy for the campaign in Alba to Philip, September 11, 1568, *DIE*, 37, 394–400, and in the letter of October 22, *DIE*, 37, 477–78. He reiterated it by way of justification after the fact on November 23, *DIE*, 4, 506–14. See also his remarks to Don García de Toledo, November 23, 1568, *EA*, II, 117–20.

40. Mendoza, 431.

41. Wedgwood, 109.

42. Albornoz to Zayas, October 30, 1568, *DIE*, 37, 490–93.

43. Wedgwood, 108.

44. Alba's report is in *DIE*, 37, 474–76. He originally estimated the casualties as 3,000, but later revised it downward (Alba to Philip, November 22, 1568, *EA*, II, 112–14).

45. Improbably enough, a similar incident is said to have prevented him from meeting Alba on his arrival in 1567 (Motley, II, 250).

46. The dispatches on this campaign other than those previously noted are in *DIE*, 37, 394–400, 418–21, 426–53, 474–78, 496–99, and 502–4. The account in Martín Arrue, II, 116–35, is based on Mendoza, 431–35. The route

followed by Orange was established by H. Hettema, "De route van Prins Willem in 1568," *Bijdragen voor Vaderlandsche Geschiedenis*, 6th series, III (1926), 1–35.

47. *DIE*, 4, 506–14.

48. James Westfall Thompson, *The Wars of Religion in France, 1559–1576* (New York, 1909), 370. The duke had already been authorized by Philip to aid Charles, should Orange join forces with Condé (Philip to Alba, October 14, 1568, *DIE*, 37, 463–64).

49. Alba to the Count of Anguisola, December 6, 1568, *EA*, II, 124–25.

50. Alba to Zayas, December 18, 1568, *DIE*, 37, 505–6.

51. Alba to Philip, November 23, 1568, *DIE*, 4, 506–14.

52. Alba to García de Toledo, November 23, 1568, *EA*, II, 117–20.

53. Alba to Philip, November 22, 1568, *EA*, II, 112–14.

54. Alba to García de Toledo, November 23, 1568, *EA*, II, 117–20; Alba to Antonio de Ulloa, January 20, 1569, *EA*, II, 154–55.

55. H. Schubart, *Arias Montano y el Duque de Alba en los Paises Bajos* (Santiago de Chile, 1962), 50.

56. Ibid., 32.

57. J. A. de Vera Zúñiga y Figueroa, Conde de la Roca, *Resultas de la vida de don Fernando Alvarez de Toledo, tercero duque de Alva* (Milan, 1643), 121–23.

58. There is a full discussion of the issue in J. M. del P. C. M. S. Fitz James Stewart y Falco, Duke of Berwick y Alba, *Discurso (Contribución al estudio de la persona del III Duque de Alba)* (Madrid, 1919), 86–90.

59. Geoffrey Parker, *The Dutch Revolt* (London, 1977), 112.

60. Alba to the Bishop of Orihuela, October 31, 1569, *EA*, II, 279–80.

61. See Zayas's description of the choices in Zayas to Alba, April 6, 1569, *DIE*, 38, 61–65.

62. There is a fine engraving of the statue in P. C. Bor, *Oorspronk, begin en vervolgh der Nederlandsche oorlogen* (Amsterdam, 1679), I.

CHAPTER IX

1. R. B. Wernham, *Before the Armada: The Growth of English Foreign Policy, 1485–1588* (London, 1966), 290.

2. Ibid., 291–96. There has been a recent attempt to rehabilitate Dr. Man, but it ignores the Spanish sources. See G. M. Bell, "John Man, the Last Elizabethan Resident Ambassador in Spain," *Sixteenth Century Journal* XII, 2, (1976), 75–93.

3. Ibid., 299.

4. James Westfall Thompson, *The Wars of Religion in France, 1559–1576* (New York, 1909), 318.

5. Alba to Francés de Alava, October 2, 1567, *EA*, I, 683–84.

6. Alba to Francés de Alava, October 4, 1567, *EA*, I, 684.

7. Alba to Francés de Alava, October 10, 1567, *EA*, I, 686–87.

8. Alba to Philip, November 1, 1567, *EA*, I, 699–702; J. L. Motley, *The*

Rise of the Dutch Republic (London, 1886), II, 146, incorrectly attributes the remark about the Salic law to Alba.

9. Ibarra's reports are in AGS E544, ff. 67, 72.

10. AGS E544, f. 71.

11. Alba to Philip, November 1, 1567, *EA*, I, 699–702.

12. Alba to Francés de Alava, October 4, 1567, *EA*, I, 685.

13. Alba to Francés de Alava, July 21, 1569, *EA*, II, 231–33.

14. Alba to Philip, December 17, 1568, *EA*, II, 127.

15. Alba's response, dated August 20, is in *EA*, II, 74–78. There is an English translation in Salisbury MSS part 1, 359.

16. Alba to Philip, September 18, 1568, *DIE*, 37, 412–18.

17. Chantonnay to Alba, September 12, 1568, *DIE*, 37, 432–37. For the full extent of the emperor's activities, see *DIE*, 37, 432–63.

18. Alba to Philip, September 18, 1568, *DIE*, 37, 412–18.

19. J. H. Elliott, *Europe Divided, 1559–1598* (New York, 1968), 245.

20. Philip to Alba, January 12, 1569, *DIE*, 37, 529–31. Alba's reports on these negotiations are in *DIE*, 38, 77–82, 100–108, and *EA*, II, 254–56. They ultimately broke down in 1570, due to obstruction by the emperor (Alba to Philip, December 14, 1570, *EA*, II, 470–71).

21. Conyers Read, "Queen Elizabeth's Seizure of the Duke of Alba's Pay-Ships," *Journal of Modern History* V (1933), 443–44.

22. Ibid., 448.

23. *CSP-Foreign*, VIII, 541–42.

24. Charles Wilson dismisses the whole incident as a "pointless act of piracy" expressing little more than the queen's basic instincts: *Queen Elizabeth and the Revolt of the Netherlands* (Berkeley, 1970), 25.

25. Alba to Philip, January 4, *DIE*, 37, 517–19.

26. Read, "Pay-Ships," 449.

27. Ibid., 450–52.

28. It is not true, as R. B. Wernham suggests, that Alba requested the new taxes of 1569 to compensate for the loss of the payships (p. 301). The sum involved was almost trifling in terms of Alba's needs: see below, Chapter X.

29. Wernham, 299.

30. Ibid., 301.

31. Alba to de Spes, July 2, 1569, and July 14, 1569, *DIE*, 38, 150–52, 159–61.

32. Alba to Philip, July 19, 1569, *DIE*, 38, 161–68.

33. See Alba to Philip, April 4, 1569, and June 1, 1569, *DIE*, 38, 51–57, 113–20.

34. Salisbury MSS (no. 1458) I, 450–51, dated December 8, 1569, describes Alba's supposed invasion plan in some detail.

35. Alba to Philip, March 18, 1570, *EA*, II, 347–49. To avoid repetition, all quotes from the same document appearing consecutively in the same paragraph have been footnoted together.

36. Alba to Philip, August 8, 1569, *DIE*, 38, 172–77.

37. Thompson, 412.

38. A copy of the brief is in *DIE*, 4, 514–16.

39. *CSP-Roman*, I, 320–21.

40. Alba to Zúñiga, December 4, 1569, *DIE*, 4, 516–19. (Alba is of course referring to the treaty of Granada of November, 1500, and its aftermath.)

41. A. O. Meyer, *England and the Catholic Church under Elizabeth*, trans. J. R. McKee (London, 1916), 78–83.

42. Alba to Juan de Zúñiga, May 3, 1570, *EA*, II, 380–84.

43. Wernham, 307.

44. A number of English reports on this nonexistent invasion are in *CSP-Foreign*, IX, 174–75, 200, 205, 219–20, 335, 347, 379.

45. Wernham, 308.

46. Alba to Philip, June 1, 1569, *DIE*, 38, 113–20.

47. Alba to Philip, January 4, 1569, *DIE*, 37, 517–19.

48. Alba to Philip, April 2, 1569, *DIE*, 38, 44–50.

49. Alba to Philip, December 11, 1569, *DIE*, 38, 248–54.

50. Alba to Fiesco, October 25, 1569, *EA*, II, 269–70, and Alba to Vitelli, October 25, 1569, *EA*, II, 271–72.

51. Alba to Philip, March 11, 1569, *DIE*, 38, 5–11.

52. See Philip to Alba, November 18, 1569, *DIE*, 38, 228–47, and January 22, 1570, AGS E544, f. 136.

53. An example is Alba to Philip, October 31, 1569, *DIE*, 38, 208–12: "It is a work worthy of Your Majesty's greatness to succor this poor and meritorious people."

54. Alba to Francés de Alava, October 14, 1569, *EA*, II, 267–68.

55. Alba to Francés de Alava, October 20, 1569, *EA*, II, 269.

56. See Curiel to an unknown correspondent, April 6, 1569, *DIE*, 38, 59–61. Guerau de Spes's correspondence is found in *CSP-Spanish*, II, 68–364. For a sample of the arguments advanced by Eboli's supporters at court, see Feria to Zayas, May 10, 1571, *CSP-Spanish*, II, 308–10.

57. Wernham, 312.

58. Philip to Alba, August 30, 1571, AGS E547, f. 5.

59. Alba to Philip, July 7, 1571, *EA*, II, 659–65. Ridolfi, on the other hand, claimed that Alba simply wanted to return to Spain and leave the problem for his successor: Ridolfi to the Archbishop of Rossano, October 8, 1571, *CSP-Roman*, I, 463–66.

60. Philip to Alba, January 22, 1571, AGS E544, f. 119.

61. In *EA*, II, 523–28.

62. Alba to Philip, December 14, 1570, *EA*, II, 470–71.

63. Philip to Alba, July 14, 1571, AA caja 7, f. 58.

64. Alba to Juan de Zúñiga, April 8, 1571, *EA*, II, 559–60.

65. *CSP-Spanish*, II, 264.

66. Ibid., II, 329, 333.

67. Ibid., II, 308–10.

68. Ibid., II, 323.
69. Alba to Philip, August 3, 1571, *EA*, II, 681–85.
70. Philip to Alba, August 30, 1571, AGS E547, f. 5.
71. Philip to Alba, September 14, 1571, AGS E547, f. 3 (extract in *CPh*, II, 198–202).
72. Philip's marginalia on Alba to Philip, October 19, 1571, *EA*, II, 760.
73. Wernham, 315–16.
74. Ibid., 317.

CHAPTER X

1. "Secret Instructions," A. L. E. Verheyden, *Le Conseil des Troubles: liste des condamnés* (Brussels, 1961), 508.
2. E.g., M. Dierickx, *De Oprichting der nieuwe bisdommen in der Nederlanden onder Filips II, 1559–1570* (Antwerp, 1950), 255, and Max Horn, "Nos innovations fiscales depuis la guerre. Un grand précurseur: le duc d'Albe," *Revue Belge* 5ᵉ (February 1, 1928), 191–216.
3. Alba to Philip, January 6, 1568, *DIE*, 38, 82–85.
4. See *Algemene Geschiedenis der Nederlanden*, V, 20, VI, 81; Pieter Geyl, *The Revolt of the Netherlands* (London, 1962), 74. A full discussion of this reform is in E. Poullet, *Histoire du droit pénal dans le duché de Brabant*, in *Mémoires couronnés et . . . des Savants Étrangers* 35 (1870), 178–212. Alba also attempted, with little success, to codify customary law on a regional basis. See J. Gilissen, "Les phases de la codification et de homologation des coutumes des XVII provinces des Pays-Bas," *Tijdschrift voor Rechtsgeschiedenis* 18 (1950), 255–68.
5. Dierickx, 168; Geyl, 74.
6. Alba to Philip, February 29, 1568, *EA*, II, 32–36; *DEND*, III, 340–48.
7. The description of the dioceses in 1567–68 is drawn from a memo dated Madrid, March 23, 1568, and published in *DEND*, III, 352–61.
8. Alba to Philip, January 20, 1568, *EA*, II, 17–20.
9. Alba to Philip, February 29, 1568, *EA*, II, 32–36.
10. *DEND*, III, 361–82, 461–65.
11. Alba to Philip, March 1, 1568, *EA*, II, 40–42; *DEND*, III, 348–52.
12. Dierickx, 255.
13. Alba to Philip, June 3, 1569, *EA*, II, 206–8; *DEND*, III, 587–90.
14. Alba to Philip, January 15, 1570, *EA*, II, 310; *DEND*, III, 672–73.
15. Philip to Alba, March 31, 1568; *DEND*, III, 361–82.
16. M. Van Durme, *El Cardenal Granvela* (Barcelona, 1957), 280.
17. Morillon to Granvelle, February 15, 1565, *DEND*, III, 113–14.
18. Morillon to Granvelle, October 17, 1569, *DEND*, III, 658–59.
19. Alba to Philip, June 21, 1568, *EA*, II, 63–66; *DEND*, III, 393–99.
20. Granvelle to Alba, November 26, 1568, *DEND*, III, 486–95.
21. Van Durme, 284.

22. Alba to Granvelle, December 31, 1568, *EA*, II, 132–33; *DEND*, III, 509–11.

23. Alba to Philip, April 13, 1568, *DIE*, 4, 487–96.

24. Alba to Philip, June 9, 1568, *EA*, II, 59.

25. Alba to Philip, June 23, 1568, *DIE*, 37, 285–90.

26. Dierickx, 267–68.

27. Philip to Juan de Zúñiga, May 26, 1569, *DEND*, III, 576–77.

28. Dierickx, 264; Van Durme, 285.

29. Alba to Philip, April 4, 1569, *DIE*, 38, 51–52; *DEND*, III, 563–64.

30. Alba to Philip, May 31, 1569, *EA*, II, 202–5; *DEND*, III, 579–85. For Deventer, see Alba to Philip, January 31, 1569, *EA*, II, 175–76; *DEND*, III, 522–24.

31. Alba to Philip, January 19, 1568, *EA*, II, 8–9.

32. Alba to Philip, February 29, 1568, *EA*, II, 30.

33. Alba to Antonio de Toledo, October 9, 1570, *EA*, II, 443–46.

34. Alba to Philip, October 31, 1569, *DIE*, 38, 217–19.

35. Philip to Alba, December 24, 1569, AGS E542, f. 4 (extract in *CPh*, II, 118).

36. Alba to Philip, January 15, 1570, *EA*, II, 310–13.

37. Alba himself remarked on this fact: Alba to Philip, February 11, 1573, *EA*, III, 285–89. For a discussion of Orange's finances, see Geoffrey Parker, *The Dutch Revolt* (London, 1977), 150.

38. Between 1567 and 1570/71, revenues from the royal domain increased from 75,485 fl. to 242,957 fl.: Jan Craeybeckx, "La portée fiscale et politique du 100e denier du duc d'Albe," *Recherches sur l'Histoire des Finances Publiques en Belgique* (Brussels, 1967), I, 372.

39. Alba to Philip, January 15, 1570, *EA*, II, 310–13.

40. Alba believed it necessary owing to "the hundred thousand robberies they make there": Alba to Philip, January 15, *EA*, II, 310–13. For a discussion of this order see J. Riemersma, *Religious Factors in Early Dutch Capitalism* (The Hague, 1967), 50.

41. Alba to Philip, April 13, 1568, *DIE*, 4, 487–96.

42. J. Cuvelier, "Un projet d'impôt au temps du duc d'Albe," *Académie Royale de Belgique: Bulletin de la Classe des Lettres* 5e série, XI (1925), 74. The egalitarianism of his placard on the Hundredth Penny is noted by Horn, 201.

43. Alba to Philip, April 13, 1568, *DIE*, 4, 487–96.

44. Alba to Philip, June 9, 1568, *EA*, II, 59.

45. Alba to Philip, November 4, 1568, *DIE*, 37, 500–502.

46. Alba to Philip, October 12, 1568, *DIE*, 37, 430.

47. Alba to Philip, August 22, 1568, *DIE*, 37, 356–58.

48. Philip to Alba, January 10, 1569, *DIE*, 37, 519–26.

49. Alba to Philip, March 11, 1569, *DIE*, 38, 5–11.

50. Alba to Philip, April 4, 1569, *DIE*, 38, 57–59.

51. Alba to Philip, June 29, 1569, *DIE*, 38, 141–42.

52. Alba to Philip, September 12, 1569, *DIE,* 38, 182–86, and January 15, 1570, *EA,* II, 304–9.

53. Alba to Philip, October 31, 1569, *DIE,* 38, 208–12.

54. Philip to Alba, December 24, 1569, *DIE,* 38, 273–85.

55. Alba to Philip, January 15, 1570, *EA,* II, 304–9.

56. J. H. Elliott, *Imperial Spain, 1469–1716* (New York, 1963), 194.

57. Alba to Philip, August 10, 1570, *EA,* II, 395–99. Contrary to Craeybeckx, 348, Alba never made specific claims for the amount to be realized. In his letter to the *contador* Garnica, October 19, 1571, *EA,* II, 761–62, Alba provides estimates of the population and the total annual value of manufactures in the states and leaves Garnica to draw his own conclusions. He notes that an estimate of 13,000,000 fl. could be derived from these figures, but is obviously referring to the amount that could be realized from the full collection of the tax if such a thing were possible. As we have seen, in October, 1571, he had no intention of collecting the full tax or anything like it.

58. Total receipts rose from 2,178,594 fl. in 1569 to 8,809,793 fl. in 1570/71: Craeybeckx, 372.

59. Albornoz to Zayas, January 23, 1571, *EA,* II, 498–503.

60. Alba to Antonio de Toledo, October, 1570, *EA,* II, 447–52.

61. Alba to Philip, February 21, 1571, *EA,* II, 516–20.

62. Viglius, *Commentarius rerum actarum super impositione decimi denarii,* in C. P. Hoynck van Papendracht, *Analecta Belgica seu vita Viglii ab Aytta Zwichermi ab ipso Viglio scripta* (The Hague, 1743), I, part 1, 297.

63. Alba to Antonio de Lada, June 7, 1571, *EA,* II, 619–21.

64. Craeybeckx, 357–58.

65. Alba to Philip, February 21, 1571, *EA,* II, 516–20.

66. Viglius, 297.

67. Ibid., 299.

68. Ibid., 303.

69. Found in BM MS 757695.

70. Alba to the Estates of the Netherlands, June 31, 1571, *EA,* II, 674–77.

71. The earliest source of this story seems to be a pamphlet, *Placcaet van den Thienden ende Twentichsten Penninck* (Brussels, 1581). See also Parker, *Dutch Revolt,* 127.

72. Hopperus to Philip, November 8, 1571, AGS E546, f. 157 (extract in *CPh,* II, 210).

73. Ibid. Also Noircarmes to Philip, September 5, 1571, AGS E547, f. 111 (extract in *CPh,* II, 210).

74. Alba to Philip, July 5, 1571, *EA,* II, 652–54.

75. Alba to Philip, August 3, 1571, *EA,* II, 677–79.

76. Arias Montano to Zayas, August 25, 1571, *DIE,* 41, 253–54.

77. Alba to Philip, September 23, 1571, *EA,* II, 738–40.

78. H. A. Enno Van Gelder, "De Tiende Penning," *TvG* 48 (1933), 1–36.

79. Alba to Philip, September 23, 1571, *EA,* II, 738–40.

80. Alava's reports are in AGS E549, ff. 125–27 (extract in *CPh*, II, 215–17).

81. Alba's report, dated July 6, 1571, is in *EA*, II, 654–55.

82. H. Van der Wee, *The Growth of the Antwerp Market and the European Economy* (The Hague, 1963), II, 240.

83. An English translation of the text, drawn from Motley, is printed in Parker, 127.

84. The suspicion that this was actually an attempt to stir up trouble for the Spaniards was laid to rest by J. B. Black, "Queen Elizabeth, the Sea Beggars and the Capture of Brille, 1572," *English Historical Review* XLVI (1931), 42–43. Wernham still has doubts (p. 318), but Charles Wilson, *Queen Elizabeth and the Revolt of the Netherlands* (Berkeley, 1970), 27, agrees with Black.

85. P. C. Bor, *Oorspronk, begin en vervolgh der Nederlandsche oorlogen* (Amsterdam, 1642), VI, 366–67.

CHAPTER XI

1. C. V. Wedgwood, *William the Silent* (London, 1956), 120–21.

2. Zweveghem, Alba's agent in London, had warned him on March 25 that Brill was their objective, but how he came to know this is unclear (see Geoffrey Parker, *The Dutch Revolt* [London, 1977], 126). The original letter is in AGRB, Audience, 404, f. 139.

3. Alba to Philip, April 26, 1572, *EA*, III, 91–94.

4. Pieter Geyl, *The Revolt of the Netherlands* (London, 1962), 127.

5. Ibid., 131.

6. Ibid., 124.

7. *CSP-Spanish (1568–1579)*, 397. N. M. Sutherland, *The Massacre of St. Bartholomew and the European Conflict, 1559–1572* (London, 1973), discusses the scheme in some detail (p. 272), but Elizabeth's motives remain unclear.

8. Parker, 125.

9. The account of this action in J. L. Motley, *The Rise of the Dutch Republic* (London, 1886), II, 359–63, is excellent.

10. Sutherland, 265.

11. Morillon to Granvelle, March 16, 1572, *CG*, IV, 142. According to Morillon, the author of this demand was Espinosa. For similar problems over the accounts for the citadel of Antwerp, the alleged depredations of Albornoz, etc., see *CG*, IV, 152–65.

12. Morillon to Granvelle, August 26, 1572, *CG*, IV, 398–402.

13. Morillon to Granvelle, July 13, 1572, *CG*, IV, 300–307.

14. Alba to Philip, July 2, 1572 (with sarcastic marginalia by Philip), *EA*, III, 153–56. For Alba's response to his critics see Alba to Zayas, August 21, 1572, *EA*, III, 190–91.

15. *CPh*, II, 267–71, contains summaries of much of the correspondence on this question. See also Sutherland, 242–46, 289–93. For evidence that all

this worry was not in vain see Charles IX to Louis of Nassau, April 27, 1572, AGS E551, f. 107.

16. Bernardino de Mendoza, *Commentario de lo sucedido en las guerras de los Paises Bajos* (BAE 28), 458. Morillon characteristically claims that the skirts were cut off above the navel, and thought it a "dishonest" thing to do to His Majesty's subjects (*CG*, IV, 324–28).

17. The best account of this affair and its aftermath is Mendoza, 459–61.

18. Sutherland, 293–94.

19. Alba to Don Antonio de Toledo, July 19, 1572, *EA*, III, 169–70.

20. Alba to Espinosa, June 14, 1572, *EA*, III, 143–44.

21. Morillon to Granvelle, June 17, 1572, *CG*, IV, 255–61.

22. *CPh*, II, 290.

23. Alba's views are set forth in *EA*, III, 107–10, 150–51, 181–85.

24. Philip to Alba, June 29, 1572, AGS E553, f. 45 (extract in *CPh*, II, 264–65).

25. Alba to Philip, August 21, 1572, *EA*, III, 181–85.

26. Mendoza, 464–65; Alba to Philip, September 6, 1572, *EA*, III, 195–98. Orange's march is described in H. Hettema, "De route van Prins Willem I in 1572," *Bijdragen voor Vaderlandsche Geschiedenis*, series 6, V (1927), 193–214, and VI (1928), 17–60.

27. This view is taken by H. G. Koenigsberger in his introduction to Alfred Soman, ed., *The Massacre of St. Bartholomew: Reappraisals and Documents* (The Hague, 1974), 8–9.

28. Mendoza, 464.

29. Alba to Diego de Zúñiga, September 9, 1572, *EA*, III, 203–6.

30. Alba to Philip, September 9, 1572, *EA*, III, 201–3. See also Alba's letters to Espinosa and to Don Antonio de Toledo of September 16, 1572, *EA*, III, 214–15.

31. The best account of the siege of Mons remains Mendoza, 464–71. See also Alba's reports to the king of September 9 and September 13 in *EA*, III, 201–3, 206–8.

32. See Alba's instructions to his nephew Don Hernando, whom he was sending to the king as an envoy (AGS E552, f. 61; extract in *CPh*, II, 280).

33. M. H. Keen, *The Laws of War in the Late Middle Ages* (London, 1965), 195.

34. Alba remained convinced of this until the end. When Amsterdam interceded with certain rebel towns in April, 1573, they answered that they would return to obedience if freedom of conscience were granted. "This," said Alba, "is the Tenth Penny and the other complaints they have" (Alba to Granvelle, April 9, 1573, *EA*, III, 318–19).

35. See, for example, his description of the atrocities committed by the Protestants at Zutphen in Alba to Philip, July 18, 1572, *EA*, III, 160–63; or Morillon on the subject as a whole, *CG*, IV, 283–96.

36. Alba to Diego de Zúñiga, October, 1572, *EA*, III, 238–39.

37. Alba to Philip, October 2, 1572, *EA*, III, 219–21.

38. Alba to Philip, September 6, 1572, *EA*, III, 195–98.
39. Alba to Diego de Zúñiga, October, 1572, *EA*, III, 238–39.
40. Ibid.
41. *AON*, IV, 4.
42. Alba to Philip, November 19, 1572, *EA*, III, 245–50.
43. Mendoza, 476–77.
44. Alba to Philip, November 19, 1572, *EA*, III, 245–50.
45. Alba to Philip, November 19, 1572, *EA*, III, 244–45.
46. Alba to Philip, November 28, 1572, *EA*, III, 250–53.

CHAPTER XII

1. P. C. Bor, *Oorspronk, begin en vervolgh der Nederlandsche oorlogen* (Amsterdam, 1679), I, 417–19; P. C. Hooft, *Nederlandsche Histoorien sedert de ooverdraght der heerschappye van Kaiser Karl den Vijfden op Kooning Philips zijnen zoon* (Amsterdam, 1642), 276–79. The account in J. L. Motley, *The Rise of the Dutch Republic* (London, 1886), II, 407–11, is drawn largely from these two sources.
2. Bernardino de Mendoza, *Commentario de lo sucedido en las guerras de los Paises Bajos* (BAE 28), 497.
3. Alba to Philip, August 19, 1572, *EA*, III, 259–64. The anonymous account in *DIE*, 75, 130–55, holds that terms were refused by the rebels after a parley (specific reference, p. 135).
4. Hooft, 279.
5. Alba to Philip, August 19, 1572, *EA*, III, 259–64.
6. Mendoza, 478.
7. An account of this engagement is in *DIE*, 75, 155–58.
8. The preceding account is taken from Mendoza, 477–82; Alba's reports to the king in *EA*, III, 259–64, 273–76, 278–79, 285–89; and the anonymous *Relación* in *DIE*, 75, 130–55.
9. See, for example, his letters of November 12 and November 27 in AGS E552, ff. 154 and 156 (extracts in *CPh*, II, 293–96).
10. Alba to Philip, November 28, 1572, *EA*, III, 250–53.
11. Alba to Diego de Zúñiga, December 23, 1572, *EA*, III, 270.
12. Alba to Antonio de Toledo, November 5, 1572, *EA*, III, 241–43.
13. *CSP-Spanish (1568–1579)*, 397.
14. Ibid., 392.
15. Charles Wilson, *Queen Elizabeth and the Revolt of the Netherlands* (Berkeley, 1970), 29.
16. Alba to Philip, November 28, 1572, *EA*, III, 250–53.
17. *CSP-Spanish (1568–1579)*, 397.
18. For a firsthand account of this expedition and of the two attempts on Goes see Sir Roger Williams, *The Actions of the Low Countries*, ed. D. W. Davies (Ithaca, 1964), 66–80. Another Welsh soldier, Walter Morgan, wrote a brief account of the entire series of campaigns from Brill to Alkmaar that has been

published together with Morgan's excellent maps in D. Caldecott-Baird, *The Expedition in Holland* (London, 1976).

19. The words are attributed to Williams, xxii.
20. Alba to Philip, January 17, 1573, *EA*, III, 279–81.
21. A resumé of the articles is in *CPh*, II, 518–19.
22. Mendoza, 428–83.
23. Alba to Philip, February 11, 1573, *EA*, III, 285–89.
24. Alba to Fadrique, February 5, 1573, *EA*, III, 282–83.
25. Albornoz to unknown recipient, February 5, 1573, *EA*, III, 283.
26. Alba to Philip, January 17, 1573, *EA*, III, 278–79.
27. Alba to Philip, February 11, 1573, *EA*, III, 285–89.
28. Mendoza, 486.
29. Ibid., 487–88.
30. Albornoz to Zayas, March 8, 1573, AGS E556, f. 119 (extract in *CPh*, II, 316–18).
31. Ibid.
32. Alba to Zayas, March 7, 1573, *EA*, III, 300–301.
33. Alba to Philip, January 8, 1573, *EA*, III, 273–76.
34. Alba to Philip, March 18, 1573, *EA*, III, 302–5.
35. The letter of appointment is printed in *CPh*, II, 308–9.
36. Predictably, the best collection of these tales is in Motley, 429–31.
37. Mendoza, 488.
38. Alba to Diego de Zúñiga, May 15, 1573, *EA*, III, 398–99.
39. Mendoza, 488.
40. Albornoz to the Duchess of Alba, April 7, 1573, *EA*, III, 314–15.
41. Alba to Antonio de Toledo, April 16, 1573, *EA*, III, 353–55.
42. Alba's supporters questioned his loyalty, because he had friends among the rebels. See Albornoz to Zayas, April 16, 1573, AGS E556, f. 103 (extract in *CPh*, II, 351).
43. Alba to Philip, April 16, 1573, *EA*, III, 331–38.
44. Ibid.
45. Ibid.
46. Alba to Granvelle, April 9, 1573, *EA*, III, 318–19.
47. Alba to Philip, June 7, 1573, *EA*, III, 418–23.
48. Alba to Antonio de Lada, August 31, 1573, *EA*, III, 512–14.
49. *Minuta* of Alba to Philip, April 16, 1573, *DIE*, 102, 97–98.
50. Alba to Philip, April 16, 1573, *DIE*, 102, 97–98.
51. Ibid. See also Alba to Antonio de Toledo, April 16, 1573, *EA*, III, 353–55.
52. Philip to Alba, July 8, 1573, AGS E554, f. 73 (extract in *CPh*, II, 384).
53. See especially Alba to Zayas, June 7, 1573, *EA*, III, 415–17.
54. Alba to Monteagudo, June, 1573, *EA*, III, 450.
55. Alba to Philip, May 8, 1573, *EA*, III, 389–90; Alba to Philip, May 16, 1573, *EA*, III, 403–4.

56. Alba to Zayas, June 7, 1573, *EA*, III, 415. Earlier correspondence on the subject dating back to 1569 is found in *DIE*, 38, 146–47, and *EA*, II, 289, 373–74, 437. A good example of the complaints against her is Catherine de Bosbeque to Albornoz, August 16, 1573, AGS E556, ff. 204–5.

57. Alba to Philip, July 14, *EA*, III, 458–59.

58. Alba to Philip, July 28, 1573, *EA*, III, 471–74. For a full account of the mutiny see Alba to Philip, August 2, 1573, *EA*, III, 485–87.

59. Alba to Philip, August 30, 1573, *EA*, III, 491–96. Alba's letters to the troops are in *EA*, III, 489, and *DIE*, 102, 200, 203. See *EA*, III, 488–89, for related correspondence.

60. Alba to Zayas, August 31, 1573, *EA*, III, 504–5.

61. The correspondence on this affair is in *EA*, III, 504–10, 516–18.

62. *DIE*, 102, 200–203.

63. Bor, I, 445–46, purports to print this document in its entirety. The wording may not be accurate but its overall message corresponds with Alba's later comments to the king.

64. Alba to Philip, August 31, 1573, *EA*, III, 502–4.

65. Alba to Philip, August 30, 1573, *EA*, III, 491–96.

66. Ibid.

67. Alba to Diego de Córdoba, August 31, 1573, *EA*, III, 491–96.

68. Albornoz to Dr. Milio, September 2, 1573, *EA*, III, 518–19.

69. Zayas to Alba, August 28, 1573, AA caja 56, f. 120.

70. Alba to Fadrique, October 8, 1573, *EA*, III, 530–31.

71. Alba to Antonio de Toledo, October 23, 1573, *EA*, III, 545–46.

72. Requesens's letters on the subject are in *DIE*, 102, 35–42, 45–46, 64–65, 74–76, 103–6.

73. Alba to Antonio de Toledo, October 23, 1573, *EA*, III, 545–46.

74. Albornoz to the Duchess of Alba, December 7, 1573, *EA*, III, 565. For an account of the meeting, see Alba to Philip, December 2, 1573, *EA*, III, 561–63, and Requesens to Philip, December 4, 1573, AGS E554, f. 151 (extract in *CPh*, II, 432–36).

75. See, for example, Requesens to Juan de Zúñiga, November 22, 1573, *DIE*, 102, 373–75.

76. Requesens to Juan de Zúñiga, November 15, 1573, *DIE*, 102, 353–55.

77. Requesens to Juan de Zúñiga, November 22, 1573, *DIE*, 102, 378–81.

78. Ibid.

79. Requesens to Pedro Manuel, December 4, 1573, *DIE*, 102, 420–22.

80. Alba to Philip, December 2, 1573, *EA*, III, 561–63.

CHAPTER XIII

1. Requesens to Hernando de Toledo, December, 1573, *DIE*, 102, 455–56.

2. Requesens to Philip, November 22, 1573, *DIE*, 102, 378–81.

3. Requesens to Pedro Manuel, December 4, 1573, *DIE*, 102, 420–22.

4. Philip's instructions to Requesens are in *DIE,* 102, 299–306.

5. Alba to Philip, February 11, 1573, *EA,* III, 285–89.

6. Philip to Alba, March 20, 1574, *CPh,* III, 40–41.

7. A. W. Lovett, "Some Spanish Attitudes to the Netherlands," *TvG* 85 (1972), 20.

8. *CPh,* III, 39–40.

9. Arias Montano to Zayas, April 18, 1574, *DIE,* 41, 302–8.

10. Summaries of the arguments on both sides of this question from December 30, 1574, to February 10, 1575, are in *CPH,* III, 220–53.

11. Roberts, "The Military Revolution, 1560–1660" (Belfast, 1956), 6–7.

12. Duque de Alba, "Discurso sobre reforma de la milicia," BN MS 12179, no. 11, f. 43. This document provides a good summary of Alba's views on discipline, training, and morals: he is, of course, in favor of all three.

13. AGS GA78, ff. 59, 91, 97; AGS GA80, f. 323. For a detailed discussion of the entire issue, see I. A. A. Thompson, *War and Government in Habsburg Spain, 1560–1620* (London, 1976), 163–84.

14. A typical memo on the subject is found at AGS GA81, f. 219. The document is analyzed by I. A. A. Thompson, 187.

15. Gregorio Marañón, *Antonio Pérez* (Madrid, 1963), I, 189–213, provides a full discussion of this question and concludes in favor of innocence.

16. These letters, most of them addressed to Albornoz, are found in AA caja 52, ff. 151–60. Reports from Fadrique's secretary, Esteban de Ibarra, who remained with him, are in AA caja 38, ff. 123–24, 129–34, 137–39.

17. Fadrique to Albornoz, August 1, 1576, AA caja 52, f. 162.

18. Fadrique to Albornoz, April 24, 1574, AA caja 52, f. 153.

19. Requesens to Philip, September 19, 1574, AA caja 48, f. 72. It is a tribute to the effectiveness of Alba's private intelligence system that a copy of this confidential document is found among his papers.

20. The evidence concerning Escobedo's murder is examined at length in Marañón, I, 345–72.

21. The relevant documents are in *DIE,* 56, 71–78.

22. *DIE,* 7, 469–71.

23. Billete of Vázquez to Pazos, May 29, 1578, *DIE,* 7, 466–67.

24. García de Toledo to Alba, April 20, 1569, AA caja 52, f. 209; Alba to the Cardinal of Burgos, April 5, 1569, *EA,* II, 196–97.

25. The *cédula* is printed in *DIE,* 8, 487–88.

26. Billete of Pazos to Philip, October 17, 1578, *DIE,* 7, 483–84.

27. Billete of Pazos to Philip, undated, *DIE,* 8, 489.

28. Billete of Pazos to Philip, October 20, 1578, *DIE,* 7, 485–87.

29. Billete of Pazos to Philip, November 26, 1578, *DIE,* 7, 502–5.

30. Luis Cabrera de Córdoba, *Felipe II, Rey de España* (1619) (Madrid, 1876–1877), II, 528–29.

31. The story that Alba advised Sebastian against the campaign is probably apocryphal. It appears to have originated with Cabrera de Córdoba, II,

471. For a letter dated June 20, 1578 (almost certainly false), and a discussion of the evidence, see *EA*, III, 640.

32. J. H. Elliott, *Imperial Spain, 1469–1716* (New York, 1963), 260; Marañón, I, 275–87.

33. Billete of Pazos, June 25, 1578, *DIE*, 7, 471–73.

34. Billete of Pazos, marginalia by Philip, 1578, *DIE*, 8, 485.

35. *DIE*, 8, 508–11.

36. Ibid., 8, 511–13.

37. Cabrera de Córdoba, II, 528–29. For specific examples see the letters of Bernardino de Mendoza to Zayas, *CSP-Spanish*, II, 648, 678, 687.

38. The question of Vázquez's parentage is dealt with by A. W. Lovett, *Philip II and Mateo Vázquez* (Geneva, 1977), 3–9.

39. Summarized by Pazos in *DIE*, 8, 516–19. See also the comments of Moura and Delgado, among others, in BN MS E71.

40. "Relazione de Morosini, 1581," *RAV*, V, 303–4.

41. Martin Philippson, *Ein Ministerium unter Philipp II: Kardinal Granvella am Spanischen Hofe 1579–1586* (Berlin, 1895), 128; M. Van Durme, *El Cardenal Granvela* (Barcelona, 1957), 351; Elliott, 265. The only documentary evidence appears to be the letter of Morosini cited by Philippson.

42. Granvelle to Morillon, July 6, 1580, *CG*, VIII, 96.

43. *DIE*, 8, 513–16.

44. See Pazo's *billete* to the king, 1578, *DIE*, 8, 484.

45. His apology, dated March 23, 1579, is in *DIE*, 8, 504.

46. Alba to Mateo Vázquez, November 15, 1579, *EA*, III, 649–50.

47. Cabrera de Córdoba, II, 576.

CHAPTER XIV

1. Alfonso Danvila, *Felipe II y la sucesión de Portugal* (Madrid, 1956), 5–6.

2. Alba to Delgado, February 23, 1580, *DIE*, 32, 17–20.

3. Geoffrey Parker, *The Army of Flanders and the Spanish Road, 1567–1659* (Cambridge, 1972), 42.

4. See Alba's comment, dated April 2, 1580, in AGS GA99, f. 45.

5. Alba to Delgado, February 22, 1580, *DIE*, 32, 15–17.

6. Alba to Delgado, February 20, 1580, *DIE*, 32, 9–14.

7. Albornoz to Zayas, April 11, 1580, *DIE*, 34, 365–66.

8. Philip to Alba, June 14, 1580, *DIE*, 34, 507–13.

9. Alba to Delgado, April 18, 1580, *DIE*, 32, 82–83.

10. Alba to Philip, April 18, 1580, *DIE*, 32, 84–89.

11. Alba claimed to be scandalized by this: Alba to Delgado, April 2, 1580, *DIE*, 32, 33–37.

12. Ibid.

13. I. A. A. Thompson, *War and Government in Habsburg Spain, 1560–1620* (London, 1976), 210–11.

14. Alba to Delgado, June 30, 1580, *DIE*, 32, 188.
15. See, for example, *DIE*, 34, 472–75, 489.
16. Alba to Delgado, May 1, 1580, *DIE*, 34, 435–42.
17. *DIE*, 34, 423, 437, 458–59.
18. Alba to Philip, July 5, 1580, AGS GA99, f. 146.
19. The term is used by J. Suárez Inclán, *Guerra de Anexión en Portugal* (Madrid, 1897), I, 226. This is still the best military history of the annexation.
20. *DIE*, 34, 437–38.
21. Suárez Inclán, I, 214, 218–20.
22. Ibid.
23. Alba to Philip, June 30, 1580, *DIE*, 32, 183–84.
24. Alba to Philip, July 3, 1580, *DIE*, 32, 195–98.
25. Alba to Philip, July 1, 1580, *DIE*, 34, 529–30.
26. Alba to Delgado, July 1, 1580, *DIE*, 34, 531.
27. Alba to Philip, July 5, 1580, *DIE*, 34, 549–51.
28. Albornoz to Zayas, July 6, 1580, *DIE*, 34, 568–69.
29. Albornoz to Zayas, July 8, 1580, *DIE*, 32, 211–12.
30. Alba to Philip, July 9, 1580, *DIE*, 34, 216–19.
31. Albornoz to Zayas, July 9, 1580, *DIE*, 32, 212–13.
32. Alba to Philip, July 10, 1580, *DIE*, 32, 222–25.
33. Alba to Philip, July 5, 1580, *DIE*, 34, 547–49.
34. Alba to Zayas, May 16, 1580, *DIE*, 32, 144–45. See also his worries about Philip's safety: Alba to Delgado, February 20, 1580, *DIE*, 32, 9–14, and Alba to Zayas, April 3, 1580, *DIE*, 32, 38–39. There is some evidence that his attitude was influenced by Zayas, who opposed Moura and his schemes for other reasons: see Danvila, 24.
35. Alba to Philip, July 3, 1580, *DIE*, 32, 195–98.
36. Albornoz to Zayas, July 5, 1580, *DIE*, 32, 199–201; Philip to Alba, July 7, 1580, *DIE*, 34, 571–74, for the royal approval.
37. Alba to Philip, July 6, 1580, *DIE*, 32, 202–5.
38. Philip to Alba, July 9, 1580, *DIE*, 34, 576–79.
39. Alba to Philip, July 10, 1580, *DIE*, 32, 226–27.
40. Alba to Philip, July 5, 1580, *DIE*, 34, 547–49.
41. Alba to Delgado, June 29, 1580, *DIE*, 34, 516.
42. From his later complaint to Delgado, July 19, 1580, *DIE*, 32, 283.
43. Alba to Delgado, July 12, 1580, *DIE*, 32, 236–38.
44. Alba to Delgado, July 15, 1580, *DIE*, 32, 253–54. In the end, the oxen were spared to haul the artillery.
45. Suárez Inclán, I, 210–11.
46. Alba's reports to the king on the taking of Setúbal are in *DIE*, 32, 267–70, 276–81.
47. Alba to Philip, July 18, 1580, *DIE*, 32, 276–81.
48. See the *Relación* in *DIE*, 40, 358–61.
49. Alba to Philip, August 5, 1580, *DIE*, 32, 362–64.

50. Both these incidents are described in Alba to Philip, July 25, 1580, *DIE*, 32, 316–19.

51. Their deliberations are recorded in Alba to Philip, July 27, 1580, *DIE*, 32, 319–24.

52. He had seriously considered this option as long ago as July, but his request for boats had not been answered: Alba to Philip, July 9, 1580, *DIE*, 32, 219–21.

53. Alba's account of the landing is at *DIE*, 32, 337–41.

54. Suárez Inclán, I, 362.

55. The taking of Cascais is described by Alonso Zimbrón Velarde, a participant, in *DIE*, 40, 364–70; see also Suárez Inclán, I, 365–66.

56. There is a lengthy discussion of the legal and moral issues in Suárez Inclán, I, 364–74.

57. Pedro Bermudez to Delgado, August 2, 1580, *DIE*, 32, 352–54.

58. Alba to Philip, August 6, 1580, *DIE*, 32, 368–69.

59. Alba to Philip, August 11, 1580, *DIE*, 32, 378–82.

60. Alba to Philip, August 5, 1580, *DIE*, 32, 365–68.

61. The siege is described in *DIE*, 32, 378–82, 386–87, 389–91.

62. These letters are in *DIE*, 32, 395–96, 407–10, 414–16.

63. Alba to Philip, August 17, 1580, *DIE*, 32, 417–21.

64. Alba to Philip, August 20, 1580, *DIE*, 32, 426–30. There is a full account of these dealings in Alba to Philip, August 17, 1580, *DIE*, 35, 91–96.

65. Alba to Philip, August 23, 1580, *DIE*, 32, 443–44.

66. Alba to Philip, August 23, 1580, *DIE*, 32, 447–48.

67. Alba's written dispositions are in *DIE*, 7, 327–33.

68. Alba's account of these events is in his letter to Philip, August 25, 1580, *DIE*, 32, 455–59. See also Suárez Inclán, II, 1–35. For Don Hernando's activities see his letter to Diego de Córdoba, August 25, *DIE*, 40, 373–76.

69. Hernando to Diego de Córdoba, August 25, *DIE*, 40, 373–76.

70. "Relación de la junta de breadores y médicos," November 29, 1580, *DIE*, 33, 260–63.

71. Arceo to Zayas, October 12, 1580, *DIE*, 33, 139–41.

72. Suárez Inclán, II, 76–79.

73. See Don Hernando's defense of his father in *DIE*, 31, 228–30.

74. Berwick y Alba, *The Great Duke of Alba as a Public Servant* (London, 1947), 24.

75. Alba to Zayas, December 5, 1580, *DIE*, 33, 294–95; December 15, 1580, *DIE*, 33, 335–40.

76. Alba to Zayas, December 12, 1580, *DIE*, 33, 330–31.

77. Alba to Zayas, December 15, 1580, *DIE*, 33, 335–40.

78. Alba to Zayas, December 5, 1580, *DIE*, 33, 294–95.

79. Arceo to Zayas, December 11, 1580, *DIE*, 33, 324–25.

80. Philip to Alba, December 15, 1580, *DIE*, 33, 341–43.

81. Alba to Philip, December 18, 1580, *DIE*, 33, 347–48. The reference is to the death of Fernán Alvarez in the time of Enrique II.

82. Alba to Zayas, December 18, 1580, *DIE*, 33, 345–46.

83. Philip to Alba, February 15, 1581, *DIE*, 34, 40–41.

84. Alba to Philip, February 23, 1581, *DIE*, 34, 53–55.

85. Philip to Alba, February 10, 1581, *DIE*, 34, 11–12, and March 1, *DIE*, 34, 75–76.

86. The correspondence on this is in *DIE*, 34, 59–60, 71–74, 76–77, 116–17.

87. There is an account of this episode in C. Fernández Duro, *Armada Española* (Madrid, 1896), II, 353–74. See also Richard Hakluyt, *The Principle Voyages, Traffiques & Discoveries of the English Nation* (Glasgow, 1904), VIII, 284.

88. Alba to Zayas, February 17, 1581, *DIE*, 34, 14–16.

89. Arceo to Zayas, March 31, 1581, *DIE*, 34, 185–87.

90. Alba to Philip, April 5, 1581, *DIE*, 34, 203–6.

91. Arceo to Zayas, March 31, 1581, *DIE*, 34, 185–87.

92. See, for example, Arceo to Zayas, April 5, 1581, *DIE*, 34, 207–8.

93. Alba to Zayas, April 27, 1581, *DIE*, 34, 273–75.

94. Alba to Zayas, March 5, 1581, *DIE*, 34, 89–93.

95. Granvelle to Cristóbal de Salazar, December 10, 1582, *DIE*, 35, 354–56.

96. BN MS 2058, ff. 82–85.

EPILOGUE

1. The episode is described in *DIE*, 35, 361–80 (specific reference at p. 363).

General Index

Abruzzi (region of Italy), 101, 104–6
Acuña Vela, Juan de, 141
Aerschot, Philippe de Croy (1526–95), Duke of, 128, 252
Afflighem, abbey of, 211
Aguilar, Juan Fernández Manrique, Marquis of, 267
Aigues Mortes, peace conference at (1538), 39, 40, 42, 43, 47
Alava, Francés de (1519–83), Spanish ambassador to France, 140, 196, 223
Alba, Antonio Alvarez de Toledo, 5th Duke of, 20, 306, 308
Alba, García Alvarez de Toledo (d.1488), 1st Duke of, 3–5, 11
Alba, Fadrique Alvarez de Toledo (d.1531), 2nd Duke of, 1, 5–13, 21, 23, 123, 251
Alba, Fadrique Alvarez de Toledo (1537–85), 4th Duke of, 20, 38, 89; in The Netherlands, 172–3, 230–1, 233, 236–7, 241, 243–52, 259–60, 261, 272–3; marriage scandal of, 139, 271–8
Alba, Fernando Alvarez de Toledo (1507–1582), 3rd Duke of: early life and education, 10–14, 27; character and appearance, vii, ix, 13, 21, 26, 27, 43, 67–9, 308; biographers of, vii–viii; marriage and sexual attitudes of, 14–20, 97, 132, 257; religious views of, 16, 21, 98, 100, 153, 181, 256–66, 304–5; intellectual interests, 12, 20, 251; agricultural interests, 90; political ideas of, 40–2, 53–4, 95–6, 98, 157, 189–90, 238–9; as faction leader, 22–4,

26, 34, 66–7, 69–77, 85, 87–8, 132; military doctrine of, 27, 35, 37–8, 48, 55–6, 59, 60–1, 268–70; use of terror by, 94, 157, 238–40, 242, 258, 265, 267; military reputation of, 38, 48, 49, 63, 81, 108–9, 306–7; statue of, 179–81; relations with Charles V, 33–4, 38, 49–51, 64, 81; with Philip II, 68–9, 121, 123–4, 126–7, 276–7, 281, 287, 300–1, 304; with Cardinal Granvelle, 112, 121–2, 124, 210–11, 280; attitude toward royal authority, 40–2, 51, 78, 82, 121, 304; toward England, 83–4, 85, 114, 197; toward the English Catholics, 201, 252; toward the Netherlands and its people, 43, 53–4, 124, 127–9, 147, 154, 206, 255, 263–6; and the Vienna campaign of 1532, 27–8; at Tunis (1535), 29–32; at Algiers (1541), 45–7; and the Schmalkaldic wars, 55–63; reorganization of the Spanish court by, 66–7, 70; at Metz (1552), 79–81; in England (1554), 82–5; in Piedmont and Milan (1555), 90–6; as Viceroy of Naples, 97–8; and the Papal War of 1556–7, 99–109; at Cateau Cambrésis, 110–4; his appointment as Governor-General of the Netherlands, 133–7; character of his regime, 146–51, 223, 264–5; regulation of insurance by, 215; his reformation of the Penal Code, 206; and the reorganization of the Church in the Netherlands, 206–14; and the Council of Troubles, 153–8, 255–6,

363

Modern Authorities Mentioned in Text

Designer: Eric Jungerman
Compositor: Imperial Litho/Graphics
Printer: Vail-Ballou, Inc.
Binder: Vail-Ballou, Inc.
Text: 10/12 Palatino
Display: Palatino and Sistina